With His Face to the Foe

Reviews

'... possesses all the merits of meticulous research, historical empathy and detailed contextualisation. If asked where Anglo-Zulu War studies should be going, I would answer: in this direction.'

Professor John Laband,
Journal of the Anglo-Zulu War Historical Society

'... a most enjoyable read ... Knight paints an alluring picture of the country ... He is equally understanding at depicting personalities.'

Elizabeth Talbot Rice
Journal of the Society for Army Historical Research

'Knight tells this ... fascinating story in close detail ...'

John Spurling
Times Literary Supplment

'This book is extremely well written and, while offering a meticulously researched analysis, it still finds time for moments of humour too.'

Ian Castle
Military Illustrated

'The Victorian ethos of death, mourning and heroism is superbly evoked and the characters vividly drawn ... Anyone with an interest in this period will not want to miss this fascinating book.'

The Armourer

'Ian Knight gives a most revealing portrait of a frustrated young man seeking a role in life to match his upbringing ... This book is highly recommended.'

The Society of Friends of the National Army Museum

WITH HIS FACE TO THE FOE

Ian Knight

SPELLMOUNT

British Library Cataloguing in Publication Data:
A catalogue record for this book is available
from the British Library

Copyright © Ian Knight 2001, 2007
Maps © Ian Castle 2001, 2007

ISBN 978-1-86227-367-2

First published in the UK in 2001 by
Spellmount Limited
Cirencester Road, Chalford,
Stroud, Gloucestershire, GL6 8PE

Tel: 01453 883300
Fax: 01453 883233
E-mail: enquiries@spellmount.com
Website: www.spellmount.com

1 3 5 7 9 8 6 4 2

Printed in Great Britain by
Oaklands Book Services
Chalford, Stroud, Gloucestershire, GL6 8PE

Contents

List of Maps

Foreword

On the afternoon of 1 June 1879 the exiled heir to the French Imperial throne was killed in an obscure skirmish in a remote part of Zululand, in southern Africa.

His death provoked an extraordinary degree of interest among the media of the day, despite the fact that the incident itself would hardly have been newsworthy under other circumstances. It took place against the background of a brutal conflict between the British Empire and the Zulu kingdom which was then drawing to a close, and which had already cost many thousands of lives; by that stage of the campaign, minor clashes between parties of scouts were almost commonplace.

What made the story remarkable was not the scale of the blood-letting, but the identity of one of those killed, and the controversial behaviour of his companions. Prince Napoleon Eugene Louis Jean Joseph was a Bonaparte, heir to arguably the greatest military name in the history of nineteenth-century Europe. How he, a quintessential Frenchman if ever there was one, came to be in Zululand, fighting in a quarrel which, by rights, was none of his business, and how he came to be wearing the uniform of a British officer, are not the only extraordinary aspects of his curious life. Moreover, the sequence of events which led to his death seemed to call into question many of the assumptions and values which underpinned the British Army of the Victorian era. The spotlight of press and public attention shone unflinchingly on a few moments of brutal fighting, and in doing so illuminated the full range of human reaction to combat, in all its ambiguity – of honour, courage, terror and moral frailty. Though the repercussions of that incident are forgotten today, they were deeply disturbing at the time.

The story of the Prince Imperial touches on two hugely complex strands of history. While the present work does not attempt to be a history of either the Bonaparte family or of post-Napoleonic France, it seemed to me essential to place Louis' life within the context of

Bonaparte tradition. He lived entirely in the shadow of his family name, which defined his sense of self, and shaped all of his hopes and aspirations. It is impossible to understand what led him to Zululand without exploring something of the Bonaparte myth which drove him. For the Zulu people, of course, his death was no more than a footnote in a particularly tragic period of their history, a period which saw the destruction of their political and economic independence, and paved the way for a century of exploitation and oppression. Yet the skirmish of 1 June also falls within a very particular context of the events of the Anglo-Zulu War, and since the Sussex destinies of a great European family and of an African kingdom crossed in that remote *donga* by the Tshotshosi, I have tried to tell something of both.

So sensitive was the story at the time that for a century afterwards researchers were forbidden access to many of the official documents – and in particular the records of the court martial of Lieutenant J.B. Carey – and I have been fortunate in the help I have received in allowing me access to them. These have included not only the court martial papers, but the extensive correspondence regarding Louis' death, and in particular the Empress Eugénie's pilgrimage to Zululand in 1880, to be found in Queen Victoria's private papers. I have, where possible, tried to let contemporary observers speak in their own voices through such material, though I acknowledge the limitations of my schoolboy French, which has forced me to work largely from English translations. Where contemporary grammar or spellings – particularly of Zulu names – varies from current practice, I have retained the original in passages of direct quotation.

Many people have, as usual, been extraordinarily generous with their time and the fruits of their own researches. Professor John Laband, of the University of Natal, whose masterful *Rope of Sand* is undoubtedly the most thorough and perceptive history of the destruction of the nineteenth-century Zulu kingdom, made freely available his own work on Zulu interpretations of the Prince's death, and on Eugénie's 1880 visit. Keith Reeves and Ian Castle offered support and advice, and Ian drew the maps. Adrian Greaves of the Anglo-Zulu War Historical Society brought a perceptive eye to bear on the rough draft. Colonel Digby Hague-Holmes selflessly discussed with me many aspects of the events of 1 June, though he was writing his own book on the subject at the time. Ron Sheeley made available his remarkable collection of original photographs of the Prince; many of the unique images published here are reproduced with his kind permission. Similarly, Rai England allowed me – as ever! – free access to his collection of contemporary newspapers, while Ian Woodason and Tim Day were especially helpful on the subject of Carey's background and career. I am particularly grateful to Lady Sheila de Bellaigue, Registrar of the Royal Collection at Windsor Castle, for permission to use material from the Queen's archives.

Other thanks are of a more personal nature. This book took far longer to write than I had expected, and Jamie Wilson, my publisher, coped with the delays and my excuses with remarkable good humour. My wife Carolyn and son Alexander suffered my distraction and frequent frustration with understanding and patience.

Ian Knight
Sussex, England

I

'... the most melancholy mission'

At about 3.45 pm on Friday, 23 April 1880, the Union Steamship Company's vessel *German* was spotted off the port of Durban, South Africa. Despite being eagerly awaited by a crowd onshore she 'was close up before being seen', commented one observer, approaching from the south, 'and, coming along gallantly with a fair wind and smooth sea, she anchored in the roadstead about 4.10 pm'.[1]

In 1880 Durban was the only viable port along nearly a thousand miles of the south-east African seaboard.[2] Although European navigators had tacked carefully up this coast for three hundred years, circumnavigating the Cape on their way to the rich trading grounds of the Indies, few had been inclined to chance a landfall. The coast was famously treacherous, the alluring green hills of the distant shore cut off by relentless surf, reefs, and a deep offshore trench which made currents unpredictable. Dozens of rivers emptied into the Indian Ocean along this coast, but wide sandbars, which sealed their mouths in all but the wet season, made them impractical for navigation. The Portuguese explorer Vasco da Gama had first logged the existence of this land for the European world on Christmas Day 1497, and named it *Terra Natalis*, in honour of Christ's birth. But da Gama sailed on, and although circumstances sometimes conspired to drive the careless or the adventurous onshore over the succeeding centuries, it was not until 1824 that the first attempt was made to establish a permanent European settlement in the region. The most likely landfall was a deep inlet among the hills, known as the Bay of Natal, but the narrow entrance was cut off by a dangerous sandbar, and it took a powerful lure to prompt travellers to risk the crossing. That lure finally came when tales of the rise of the neighbouring Zulu kingdom filtered through to the Cape Colony, and persuaded a handful of predominantly British adventurers to try to establish commercial contacts with the Zulu.

In those days the Bay of Natal had been a shimmering lagoon of aching beauty, a sheet of sluggish water broken here and there by sand-dunes, and fringed with mangroves. Huge flocks of flamingos cast a smear of pink reflection across a world of green bush and glittering brown water, and hippos splashed and grunted in the shallows. Beyond the sandy beaches, a tangle of bush gave way to rolling open grassland, teeming with the full array of African wildlife. Man's hold on such an environment was tenuous; on their very first night ashore, that little group of traders, hunters and sailors had been attacked by jackals, and could only drive them off with burning branches from their camp fire. It would be a further twenty years before the last elephants were driven from the Berea bush beyond, and for a few short years, Port Natal offered a Robinson Crusoe lifestyle to those who settled there, a precarious world of adventure, freedom and anarchy. It attracted tough, free-spirited men, rogues and dreamers alike, who made their living by hunting for hides and ivory, and trading with the Zulus.

But even by 1880 so much of this had changed. Within a generation the wildlife had gone, driven out or exterminated by the flint-lock muskets the settlers brought with them, which for all their crudeness were so much more efficient than the spears of the African population. The first ramshackle huts of wattle and daub had given way, too, to more imposing structures of stone, wood and thatch. The growing settlement had assumed the name Durban, in honour of a British Governor at the Cape, and the British had tentatively assumed control of the hinterland. Even at the beginning there was bloodshed, for circumstances contrived to force two very different groups of white interlopers – the British and the Boers – into conflict, and they had fought it out on the very shores of the bay. The British had won, and in 1843 da Gama's *Terra Natalis* had become the Crown colony of Natal.

The fledgling port was the key to Natal's colonial success. It linked the colony to all the great network of maritime trade which the British Empire commanded, and with commerce had come immigration, prosperity and respectability. The African wives and mixed-race offspring of the first settlers were discreetly pushed aside by a society which pretended a more ideological form of paternalism. On the ridges beyond the bay, cooler in the stifling humidity of the summer months, the new white middle class built fine colonial homes, and looked down on the seething activity at the harbour – distancing themselves from their origins, but never quite escaping them.

Much had changed, too, in the relationship with the Zulu kingdom, which lay to the north of Natal. The first settlers had owed both their survival and their prosperity to the protection of the Zulu kings. They brought exotic goods – beads, blankets and brass work – into the kingdom, and extracted cattle, hides and ivory in exchange. The Zulu kings had recognised the value in this, and had established the whites as a client chiefdom. The traders were allowed to live on the land, and to accumulate retainers from among neighbouring African communities, many of whom had only recently been disrupted by Zulu expansionism. Yet therein lay the settlement's insidious danger; as it grew, it came to pose an alternative source of security to groups who opposed the authority of the Zulu kings, and a focus for political and economic rivalry. Eventually, in the manner of some terrible Greek tragedy, the child had swallowed up the father; in 1879 Britain had provoked a war with the Zulu kingdom, and destroyed it. Durban had become the conduit of invasion, and thousands of British redcoats had landed there on their way north to the Zulu borders. Supported, often, by the same African groups in Natal who, a generation before, had clung to the British settlement for survival, the British Army had broken the Zulu kingdom in six months of brutal and bitter fighting. The Zulu king, Cetshwayo kaMpande, had been captured, deposed, and lodged in genteel imprisonment – but imprisonment nonetheless – at the Cape.

The arrival of the steamship German in 1880 was so eagerly anticipated in Durban because she harkened back to one dramatic aspect of that recent history. She carried a particularly distinguished group of passengers, and Durban's white community, hopelessly isolated as it was from the currents of British and European society and fashion, was agog. Yet for all the traffic that now passed regularly through the port, the passengers of the German were in for an uncomfortable time in landing. Nature had so far defeated the best efforts of Durban's engineers, and it was not possible for ocean-going ships beyond a certain draught to enter the bay. The lagoon was almost entirely encircled by two jutting jaws of land; the high, wooded Bluff to the south, and a long sandy spit, known as the Point, to the north. Between the two, across the mouth of the bay, lay the inevitable submerged sandbar. Ships drawing too much water risked running aground – or worse, being dashed to pieces in high weather – if they tried to cross. Between 1845 and 1885, no fewer than sixty-six ships came to ruin on the bar, so that in 1880, ocean-going ships still anchored sensibly offshore. Shallow steam tugs would set out from the rickety wharfs and jetties which had sprung up along the sheltered side of the Point to cross into the deep water to meet them. Once alongside, passengers and cargo had to be transferred from ship to tug by the ignominious means of a basket lowered over the side.

As soon as word spread that the German was offshore, a crowd began to assemble at the Point, arriving in 'carriages, traps of all sorts, on horseback, in the 'busses, by train, and on foot.'[3] The mood among them was one of suppressed excitement, which deepened when a line of carriages arrived to park in anticipation next to the landing stages. The Town Council was taking no chances, and in case anyone became over-exuberant, 'this was kept clear of intruders by Superintendent Alexander and his borough police, Inspector Nolan of the Water police being in attendance.'[4]

Once the *German* was seen to be anchored, the tug *Union* set out to cross the bar to meet her. The *Union* reached the ship safely enough, and could clearly be seen alongside. Yet, to the crowd's disappointment, the *Union* did not return immediately. It had been expected that the ship's important passengers would be taken ashore first, but it transpired that they did not wish to inconvenience their travelling companions. And so the *Union* – and the crowd – waited patiently while the *German* unloaded *all* of its passengers – and their baggage. By about six o'clock it was beginning to get dark, and many of those ashore were becoming disillusioned. 'The sun had long sunk', observed a correspondent from a local newspaper, 'and the moon had risen ere there was any sign of the *Union*'s return, and the gathering grew thinner and thinner.'[5] When at last the *Union* did return, the same correspondent nevertheless found the experience worth the wait:

> The evening had now fully set in, and it was bright moonlight. A lovelier evening has not been experienced in Natal for some time, the atmosphere being clear and beautifully cool, scarcely a breeze stirring within the shelter of the Bluff, and the day being as smooth and as quiet as a sheet of glass. There had been a fresh breeze blowing during the afternoon, but it had entirely subsided. The *Union* came along quickly as soon as she was clear of the *German*, and within twenty minutes her nose showed round the spit. Speedily she was alongside the wharf, and the landing gangway was at once run aboard. Captain Bigge was the first to step ashore to see that all was right and in readiness. Immediately after Her Majesty landed. She was clad in deep mourning, and accompanied by Sir Garnet Wolseley, Sir Evelyn and Lady Wood, the Marquis de Bassano, the Hon. Mrs Campbell, Dr. Scott, Lieut. Slade, and the rest of her suite. As Her Majesty passed down the gangway to her carriage the spectators observed a solemn silence, the men standing all uncovered. Her Majesty bowed frequently from side to side, and soon after taking her seat in the carriage, was driven away to the residence of Capt. Baynton.

> This ended the ceremony of landing. Everything had passed off just as it should have done. Lovely weather, a clear sky, bright moonlight, the hush of a calm evening, the sympathy of the silent

assembly, arrangements without a hitch, no jarring occurrence of any kind – these were the features which characterised the landing in Natal of a lady who comes upon the most sacred, the most holy, the most melancholy mission which could fall to an earthly mother.[6]

It was, perhaps, a moment of characteristic Victorian sensibility, fraught with the ambiguity of unresolved, bitter-sweet emotion – grief, melancholy, romance – and all the more effective because of its exotic backdrop. The woman that the crowd had gathered to see was travelling incognito, under the title Comtesse de Pierrefonds, but none of those who still lined the dock-side in the hope of glimpsing her were fooled. The crowd knew her true identity, and the strange, romantic and ultimately tragic history which had brought her from the inner circle of European power and privilege to an obscure jetty in South Africa. She was Eugénie, exiled Empress of the French, widow of the last of the great Bonapartes, Napoleon III, and she had come to mourn her son, killed by Zulu warriors in an obscure skirmish the previous year.

The story of that death had aroused strong public emotions at the time. Officially no more than an observer, Eugénie's son had nonetheless been attached to the staff of the Commander-in-Chief of the Zululand expedition, Lieutenant-General Lord Chelmsford. Moreover, the young French Prince had worn a British uniform throughout his time in the field, and it had therefore been all the more shocking that, when he found himself under attack while out on patrol, he had apparently been deserted in his hour of need by a British officer. The incident had caused a furore in the European press – far more so than the heavy blood-letting of the rest of the war – and it had left those involved with a heavy burden of shame and remorse.

For Eugénie her son's death had been a crowning bitterness in a life characterised by extremes of fortune. For a year she had been a martyr to sorrow, and only the sudden impulse to travel to Zululand, and spend the anniversary of his death on the remote spot where he had been killed, had restored a sense of purpose. 'I feel myself drawn to this pilgrimage,' she wrote,

> ... as strongly as the disciples of Christ must have felt drawn to the Holy Places. The thought of seeing, of retracing the stages of my beloved son's last journey, of seeing with my own eyes the scene upon which his dying gaze had rested, of passing the anniversary of the night of 1st of June watching and praying alone with his memory, is one for me of spiritual necessity and an aim in life. Since

the end of the war has allowed me to regard this possibility more hopefully, it has become my dominant thought … This thought sustains me and gives me fresh courage; without it I should never have sufficient strength to endure my life, and I should allow myself to be submerged in my sorrow …[7]

The Empress and her entourage had left England on 28 March 1880, and had weathered a trying three-week journey by steamship. Now she was at last upon African soil, retracing with every step the last experiences of her son's life, and her pilgrimage was about to begin in earnest.

The Durban public – at least, the white part – had been secretly delighted at the news of the Empress' visit, confirming, as it did, recognition that, for a brief while at least, they had been at the centre of world events. The Town Council had struggled to find the most appropriate way to express their collective sympathy, until the Empress' aide, Captain Bigge, dampened their enthusiasm. Sent on ahead from Cape Town to finalise the arrangements, Bigge had assured them that what the Empress dreaded above all was fuss. What she most longed for was the chance to grieve in private.

In private – and, moreover, in the absolute middle of nowhere, for the site of the Prince's death was as remote as any which had featured in the recent campaign. He had fallen on the banks of an obscure river called the Tshotshosi, and more than 150 miles of rugged country, of steep ridges and formidable rivers, much of it without tracks of any kind, separated the spot from Durban. The Empress' determination had left unresolved a number of interesting practicalities.

Moreover, the arrival of the Empress' party was something of an embarrassment to the senior British official in Natal. General Sir Garnet Wolseley had arrived in South Africa ten months before, despatched by a home government provoked by the escalating cost of the Anglo-Zulu War, and with authorisation to replace Lord Chelmsford and impose a peace settlement on the Zulu. It was not a position Wolseley enjoyed, the more so because, to his intense frustration, he had arrived too late to take a decisive role in the fighting, and had been merely left with the thankless task of mopping up. He had supervised the destruction of Zulu political power, and had promptly turned his energies to browbeating neighbouring African and Boer groups. Indeed, on the very eve of Eugénie's arrival he had been on a fact-finding mission to the British Transvaal, which was simmering with republican discontent. Preoccupied as he was with matters of geo-politics, Wolseley regarded the Empress' arrival as a distraction and a bore, but etiquette – and the Empress' powerful connections in the British Royal Family – demanded that he be in Durban to greet her. A week earlier, when he had received a telegram confirming the Empress' safe arrival in Cape Town, he had confided to his journal that 'old mother Frere[8] will be in seventh heaven at having an Empress – all alive – as her guest. I wish to heaven she could keep her, and that I was not to be bored by having such a white elephant for a guest in my house.'[9]

Once in Durban, Wolseley

> ... put up with Captain and Mrs Baynton; he is agent for the Union Steamers. They rent the House which was purchased for the steamers, and which is certainly the best in Durban ... The poor Prince Imperial stayed here when he was in Durban, and the Empress is coming here now. Dear Mrs Baynton who must weigh about 18 stone is most kind: I found her in an exhausting melting mood: she was worn out making preparations for this the great event of her life, and my only dread is that the excitement maybe too great for her, & that apoplexy may carry the good woman off, before the Empress can get away ...[10]

In the event, however, Sir Garnet found more to the Empress than he had expected. He and his staff had been aboard the tug *Union*, and he had officially welcomed the Imperial entourage before they disembarked from the *German*. Wolseley was impressed by what he found; clearly, maternal grief was not entirely inappropriate to Eugénie's mournful Spanish eyes, and the charm and vivacity which had once captivated Europe had not completely deserted her in her sorrow. Wolseley was smitten, though he could not quite free himself from the sense of smug superiority which, as a British gentleman, he entertained for all foreigners, royalty or no:

> What a charming woman & so lovely even now: she is made up, Her eyebrows are painted, but Her manner is perfect. Those with Her say she never thinks of herself, but is always studying the wants and comforts of others – very unlike our own Royalties in this respect ... I sat on deck with the poor woman & talked upon all sorts of subjects connected with the war &c. &c. She was constantly recurring to her poor son's death ... The Empress has a horrible trick of making a very disgusting noise in her throat as if she were about to spit in an extremely nasty manner: I never knew anyone in a respectable rank of life capable of such an atrocious habit before ...[11]

From the landing stage on the Point Eugénie and her party were driven away to the privacy of the Baynton home, where 'dear old mother Baynton received her, and they both retired to cry'.[12] The Empress had no desire to appear before the public gaze, and her aides deftly diverted those whose enquiries threatened to intrude. It was all rather frustrating for Durban society, which, while clearly sympathetic, still felt a little cheated at their exclusion. Starved of any real news, a local journalist was reduced to describing the suite in which the Empress had made her passage out in terms of longing which highlighted the deep sense of isolation felt by Durban's white community:

> At the aft end of the magnificent saloon on the port side of the vessel three first-class cabins had been specially prepared. They were those first abutting on the saloon, and had been converted into a drawing room, bed-room and bath-room. As a mark of distinction, showing that royalty occupied the rooms, a crown was painted on the drawing room door. They were furnished (by the Company) with great taste; no expense had been spared; every little detail had been attended to and everything done which in any way add to the comfort of the voyage. The drawing room was about eleven feet square. It was fitted with a rich Brussels carpet of a quiet pattern. A lounge, arm-chair, and occasional chairs *en suite*, upholstered in a rich brown cloth were arranged around. There was an exquisite writing table, in black and gold, with drawers and every convenience for writing, whilst in the corners were shelves, &c, for holding small fancy articles. A very handsome occasional table made the furniture complete. The walls of the room were hung with silver grey silk crepe, which gave the place a very elegant appearance. A bell communicated with the steward's room and other offices. Special screens had been made to fit the top of the compartment, in the case of too much ventilation being obtained ...[13]

Whatever the effect this description of high society opulence might have had on his readers, in fact Eugénie had not been impressed by the journey to South Africa. 'I can well understand the tedium which my poor boy must have endured,' she wrote, 'as the voyage is most monotonous.'[14] The Empress remained at the Bayntons' house for three days, during which the mood of despair, which had weighed her down for almost a year, occasionally lifted. She did not join her entourage for dinner on her first night, but on the second Wolseley found her 'a very intelligent woman [who] talks in the most interesting manner about European politics'.[15] Captain Bigge, reporting carefully on the expedition for the benefit of Queen Victoria, noted the effect that her arrival in Africa had upon Eugénie's state of mind:

> We saw at once a marked improvement in the Empress' health and the Marquis de Bassano assures me that he could not have believed it possible for such a change to have been wrought especially in spirits – at times of course she is sad, for instance on arriving in Cape Town and again at Durban, but often during the voyage the cheerfulness and brightness of former days seemed to revive ...[16]

On 26 April the party left Durban for Pietermaritzburg, the colonial capital, sixty miles inland. When Wolseley had first discussed the Empress' plans with Bigge, he had thought 'his views for the Empress' journey very vague',[17] and certainly much of the practical planning had been left to their arrival in Pietermaritzburg. It was here that transport, equipment, horses, servants and provisions would be assembled, and it was from here that the party would begin its journey into the wilds in earnest. Indeed, as Bigge himself recalled, the trappings of Victorian progress and civilisation in southern Africa soon ran out beyond the confines of metropolitan Durban. The party left ...

> ... by special train and are to pass along five miles of the line not yet open to the general public – a halt will be made at the only clean or in any way English inn, where luncheon is prepared. The train then takes them a few miles further and carriages will meet it at a certain point where the road crosses the line – 27 miles of hilly road have then to be performed with one change of horses ...[18]

Once lodged in Government House in Pietermaritzburg, however, the expedition began to take on the character of an unusually well-run military campaign. Indeed, the expedition leader, Colonel Henry Evelyn Wood, had only agreed to accept command of the party on the rather daunting stipulation that 'the Empress would follow my instructions as if she were a soldier in my command.'[19] It was perhaps wise that she agreed, for Wood was ideally suited for the task in hand. A dapper, confident man with a heavy beard and twinkling eyes, Wood had an experience of campaigning in southern Africa which was largely unequalled. He had commanded a column throughout the war in Zululand; he knew much of the area through which the party was to travel, and he knew, too, many of the influential individuals they were likely to encounter along the way. Such was his reputation that he was known to the Zulus as *Lakuni*, after a hard wood from which they made their knobkerries – a pun which referred as much to his ability to act decisively and ruthlessly as it did to his name. Moreover, Wood held strong views on the incident in which the Prince had been killed, and it was these, expressed at a public banquet in London after the war was over, which had first attracted Eugénie's notice:

> In remembering these spirits, and that gallant youth, the son of England's ally, whose widowed mother is now our honoured guest, and whose body gave a noble answer to the query, 'Had he his wounds in front?' I may say, as Rosse says to Siward in 'Macbeth'
> Your son, my Lord, has paid a soldier's debt.
> He only liv'd but till he was a man.
> The which no sooner had his prowess confirm'd
> In the unshrinking station where he fought,
> But like a man he died
> 'Why, then,' was the response, 'God's soldier be he!' And I will add with him who say that,
> Had I as many sons as I have hairs,
> I would not wish them to a fairer death.[20]

It was a fulsome tribute, couched in terms which encapsulated the popular mood. To the British public in 1879, the French Prince was a heroic and romantic figure, who had taken up arms in the cause of his adopted country and been sadly betrayed. This was a view which ignored the more uncomfortable truths about the Prince's real motives, but it was inevitably and passionately held by Eugénie herself. After reading reports of this speech, she had written to Wood to beg him to accompany her pilgrimage.

It was a curious undertaking to be offered to a serving soldier, but Wood was an ambitious man, and Queen Victoria's conspicuous support for the project had persuaded him to accept it. Nevertheless, there were obvious risks involved, and any accident or illness which might befall the Empress would undoubtedly upset the Queen, and rebound on Wood. To ensure that the expedition was as secure and comfortable as possible, the Queen sent Wood a cheque for £6,000 to defray his expenses. Wood was later to recall rather smugly that 'I handed back on our return to the Empress' secretary £3600.'[21]

Although the Empress had selected a small group to accompany her from among her own most trusted aides, it was left to Wood to choose the rest of the party. In this, he was influenced by his own recent experiences in Zululand, and the group he assembled – and the reasons for his choices – were to profoundly affect the nature of the journey.

Wood had come to the Anglo-Zulu War with a good deal of campaign experience already behind him. He had begun his career as a Midshipman in the Royal Navy, and had seen action in the Crimea, that crucible of Victorian military endeavour. Transferring to the army, he had served in the closing stages of the Indian Mutiny, and then in Asante,[22] in the rain forests of West Africa. When war broke out on the Eastern Cape Frontier in 1877, he had been sent to South Africa, and arrived in time to take part in the most gruelling part of the campaign – the suppression of the last roving bands of Xhosa warriors in their inaccessible mountain strongholds. It was here that he enjoyed his first real independent command, and he had earned a reputation as a dynamic and resourceful colonial fighter, which was on the whole fully justified. At the end of that campaign, most of the British troops who had fought there were marched north to the Zululand borders, in readiness for a fresh outbreak of fighting.

The British invasion was under the command of Lieutenant-General Lord Chelmsford, who had seen Wood at work on the Cape frontier, and recognised his capabilities by offering him the command of one of three invading columns. Wood's theatre was to be the remote northern sector, where no less than three international boundaries converged – the borders of Natal, the Transvaal, and the Zulu kingdom. This was difficult country, a long way from the centres of both colonial and Zulu administration, and fighting there would require from Wood a good deal of independent initiative. This had much to do with the complex web of political allegiances and rivalries in the area; on the Zulu side of the border, particularly, most local chieftains had long since trodden a thin line between fierce loyalty to the Zulu king and a pragmatic acceptance of frontier realities.

From the beginning, Wood's war had therefore taken on a unique character of raid and counter-raid, accomplished with a rare degree of success, which distinguished it from the campaign as a whole. Wood – whose military skills were matched only by his instinct as a political survivor – had soon realised the advantage of this, and had adroitly distanced himself from a series of disasters which had befallen the unlucky Lord Chelmsford elsewhere in the country. Only once did his self-assurance slip; on 28 March 1879 he launched an attack on a Zulu stronghold known as Hlobane mountain. The attack was poorly conceived and badly co-ordinated, and the unexpected arrival of a large Zulu army from the distant royal homesteads at oNdini turned it into a rout. Before Wood could be called to account for the Hlobane debacle, however, he recovered his poise with the defeat of the same Zulu army the following day at Khambula hill. The battle of Khambula was to prove a turning point in the war, and Wood found himself lionised in the British press. Indeed, by the end of the campaign it was widely whispered among the troops in Zululand that the men under Wood's command were pagans – 'because they made an idol of Wood and did not believe in the Lord'. Wood emerged from the war with the local rank of Brigadier-General – to his chagrin the Duke of Cambridge refused to confirm it as a substantive rank – and found that no less a person than the Queen herself had taken an interest in his progress. He was invited to Balmoral to talk over his victories, and noted without any undue modesty that

> I was most graciously received by Her Majesty the Queen, who honoured me with her conversation throughout dinner, and again the next night, in addition to an hour's interview each forenoon and afternoon … My original invitation was for one night only …[23]

Wood was ambitious, intuitively political, and rather vain. He never expressed any public doubts about his handling of the Hlobane affair, but it clearly weighed on his mind. Although he remained vague about his personal involvement in the battle, there was no doubt that the ultimate responsibility for the failure of the expedition lay with him. But what bothered him more than wounded professional pride was the fact that a number of officers with whom he had been on particularly friendly terms had been killed in the battle. Two of his personal staff had been shot dead before his eyes, and another friend had been killed in the rout. The fact that in some cases it had not been possible to recover or bury their remains added to Wood's sense of guilt.

Eugénie had no very firm requirements of the trip, beyond a desire to follow as much in her son's footprints as possible, and to be present at the spot where he fell on the anniversary of his death. The exact details of the itinerary were left to Wood. The young Prince had arrived in Zululand shortly before the final British advance, in June 1879, and he had spent a few days acquainting himself with the prevailing situation. During that time, he had visited friends who were serving under Wood's command at Khambula camp. Wood therefore proposed that the party should include Khambula in its itinerary, despite the fact that it was by no means on the most direct route to the Tshotshosi river. In retrospect, it is clear from the first that Wood's need to make a pilgrimage was almost as great as Eugénie's, and that his private objectives had nothing to do with the Prince's misfortunes; by visiting Khambula, he placed himself within reach of his own ghosts, which haunted the nearby slopes of Hlobane mountain.

The staff selected by Wood to assist him confirm this. As ADCs he appointed two young Royal Artillery officers, Captain Arthur Bigge and

Lieutenant Frederick Slade. Both were ideal for the post. Both had known the Prince; they had served with a peace-time battery to which, for a spell, he was attached. Moreover, both had served under Wood's command during the war, and had 'distinguished themselves by the courage with which they had fought their guns in the open at Khambula twelve months before'.[24] Indeed, it had been Bigge and Slade whom the Prince had once come to Khambula to visit. Capable, loyal, experienced and well connected, Wood could rely on them utterly, not only to take good care of Eugénie, but to support his own agenda without question. Even in his choice of orderley, Wood reflected his earlier experience in Zululand; he selected Private Walkinshaw of the 90th Regiment, who had been his orderly bugler throughout his time in South Africa. Walkinshaw, too, knew Wood's methods and preoccupations intimately; he had served beside him throughout that harrowing day at Hlobane. Only one member of the expedition had served through the war under a command other than Wood's; Surgeon Major Frederick Scott of the Army Medical Department had been part of the Headquarters Staff in 1879, and had been appointed to that post with the Prince's well-being in mind. As such, it had been his unpleasant duty to formally examine the Prince's body after his death, and it was for this reason – and to ensure that the Empress remained healthy – that he had been attached to the party now.

The Empress' own party was small. She had selected just one personal aide from among the trusted circle who had surrounded her during the dark days of her exile, the Marquis de Bassano, the son of the Duc de Bassano, her chamberlain. Significantly, Wood proposed that she should add another lady-in-waiting to her entourage. He had just the person in mind; as a personal acquaintance of the Queen and a widow herself, the Hon. Mrs Katherine Campbell was ideal for the post. More to the point, her husband, Captain Ronald Campbell of the Coldstream Guards, had been Wood's principal staff officer, and closest friend, in Zululand. Campbell had been shot dead at the battle of Hlobane, in circumstances which owed much to Wood's erratic behaviour on the day. Eugénie accepted the proposal, and the inclusion of Mrs Campbell in the party effectively legitimised Wood's decision to include the northern battlefields on the expedition's itinerary. Lest the two widowed ladies find the undiluted company of soldiers difficult, Wood had brought his wife, Paulina, along. According to Wolseley – who was a snob – the Woods' breezy confidence in their dealings with the French party had its comical side – 'dear Evelyn and Lady Wood speak what they believe to be French to the Empress to the Bassons [sic] & the effect is amusing'.[25]

Despite the concise make up of the party, it was impossible that they should venture off into the bush without 'a complete establishment of servants'.[26] The Empress had brought two maids with her – one English and one French – but in Pietermaritzburg, Wood and Bigge set about arranging all the necessary equipment and personnel – tents, wagons, mules, drivers, and cooks – who would make life in the veld tolerable. By the time it left Pietermaritzburg, the party consisted of 'ourselves, an escort of the Natal Police, 22 men, 15 wagons, each drawn by ten mules – in all, 78 people (out of this 33 are natives) and 200 animals'.[27] Among the servants was a French cook called Theodore, appointed especially for the Empress' convenience, and who was presumably expected to add some Gallic flair to a diet which must inevitably consist of preserved vegetables and game meat.

In Pietermaritzburg, too, the party collected two further items of baggage. A local stone-mason had been commissioned to construct two memorials to officers who had died under Wood's command. One – to the memory of Lieutenants Arthur Bright and Frederick Nicholson – was for erection at Khambula, and the other, to the memory of Ronald Campbell, was destined for Hlobane. Both memorials took the form of heavy stone crosses, and the need to transport them by wagon across many miles of open country added greatly to the expedition's responsibilities. When it came to acts of devotion, however, Wood and Mrs Campbell were to prove themselves no more daunted by the practicalities than Eugénie herself.

The party left Pietermaritzburg on Thursday 29 April 1880. As it did so, it became lost to public scrutiny, for despite the intense local interest, no journalists were allowed to intrude upon the Empress' grief. This strange little caravan, the grief-stricken and the guilt-ridden, set out on a journey which none of them seemed to consider in the least bizarre. Ahead of them lay Africa, bruised by recent contact with the European world, but as yet still undefeated and untamed. If the party might reasonably hope to escape the attentions of wild animals – most had retreated to unpopulated areas by 1880, even in Zululand, though the rivers were still full of crocodiles – they could still expect long, hard journeys over very rough country, extremes of weather, uncertain food, suspect water, and, for the ladies, an inevitable and unenviable dependence on the chamber-pot. Despite the presence of Dr Scott, the party would remain vulnerable to accident, sickness or snake-bite, and any mishap in the wilds would have a greater chance of proving fatal. Moreover, the party would be travelling through a country which had only recently been at war. Much of Zululand remained unsettled; most of the Zulus they would meet had probably last encountered white people in battle, and the loss of loved ones, homes and stock inflicted by the last British to pass through was likely to be all too apparent. Escort or no, the party would remain acutely vulnerable to both attack and misfortune, but if they were at all nervous, none of them betrayed it; 'we anticipate no danger', wrote Arthur Bigge, 'tho' the roads might prove troublesome'.[28]

The route which Wood had selected was known in the colony as the Old Border Road. From Pietermaritzburg it struck north-east to Greytown, then plunged into the spectacular country astride the Thukela and Mooi river valleys, winding northwards parallel to the Zulu border. During the war, this road had been acutely vulnerable to Zulu raids, and for much of the time civilian traffic had refused to use it, despite the profits to be made carrying supplies for the military. This had been the route of supply for one of the invading British columns, which had assembled at the hamlet of Helpmekaar, before turning eastwards and descending into the valley of the Mzinyathi river, which formed the boundary with Zululand. There had been a good deal of activity in this sector; within days of the opening shots, this column had been effectively destroyed at the foot of a distinctive hill called Isandlwana, just a few miles into Zululand.

Peace had returned to the border as the tide of war turned, but a year later signs of the conflict were still to be seen in the chain of abandoned supply depots that marked the way. The road from Greytown to Helpmekaar was a test of endurance in its own right, for it clung precariously to the sides of steep, stony hills, which dropped off abruptly into a succession of wild, bush-choked valleys. It is still a fiercely beautiful spot, dry, desolate, an impossible corrugation which stretches off to the distant confusion of the blue horizon. The travellers were impressed; 'They greatly enjoyed the scenery of the Tugela Valley', wrote Wood,

> ... The camp was pitched one day on a slope overlooking a ravine, 150 feet below the tents. Up to Helpmakaar, the track is carried through beautiful, rugged country, and on the 5 May we mounted 650 feet in 5 miles, and descended 1800 feet in the next 5, travelling on an unfenced road, scarped out of the mountainside.[29]

The Empress had at first hoped to ride throughout the journey, but it soon became clear that this was impractical. Instead, she rode in a 'Spider' carriage, with the usual pair of horses doubled up to four, and Wood himself driving. From the start the party established a punishing routine. The transport wagons got underway at 6 am, leaving the Empress' servants to strike her tent at 8, and prepare for the carriages to depart at 8.15. At about 10 am they made a halt for breakfast, and reached their evening camp site at about 3 pm. Dinner was served at 6 pm with as much comfort as could be arranged. Bigge noted with some satisfaction that for the first part of the journey, until they reached Zululand, progress averaged twenty miles a day.[30]

The Empress' moods, too, rose and fell across those first few days. For much of the time she seemed withdrawn and depressed, and kept largely to her carriage and tent, mixed only with those who attended her, and did not join the others for dinner. Now and then, however, some reference to a passing landmark or incident connected with the Prince would draw her out, and she became animated and charming. Suffering herself, she enjoyed the opportunity to sympathise with the occasional sufferings of those around her, an attitude which soon won her the affection of her escort and servants. When Dr Scott attended one of the African servants who had broken his arm, Eugénie visited the patient, and left instructions for his future care. Later the Sergeant in charge of the Mounted Police escort became ill with fever, and Eugénie offered the services of her maids to tend him, leading Bigge to comment ruefully 'I fully expect other patients (for the Dr.) with such nurses!!'[31]

Nevertheless, Wood remained concerned that the associations triggered by the people and places she was sure to encounter along the way would inevitably distress the Empress. In particular, he feared the effect her first sight of Zulus would have upon her. It had preyed upon Eugénie's mind that her son had met his end at the hands of a people whose appearance and customs were so utterly alien and incomprehensible to her, and whom she could only characterise as savages. She was no stranger to war – she had lived most of her life in its shadow, one way or another – but to her warfare had been a romantic mix of nobility and tragedy, a struggle of honour and gallantry among equals, and in the squalor and brutality of her son's death she saw only inhumanity, and for that she blamed not the true face of war, but the Zulus. For nearly a year they had inhabited the darker corners of her imagination, and she had found her mind returning time and again to the ferocity of their attack, haunted by lurid images of the terrible weapons that had drawn his blood. Even her exposure to the African population of Durban and Pietermaritzburg had not suggested to her the limitations of this view; to Eugénie the true Zulu remained a thing to be dreaded, not a human being but an abstract savagery, a darkness of the very soul.

In the event, her first encounter with a party under arms came sooner than expected. On the Mooi river, just beyond Greytown, the Empress saw her first *impi*;

... not being hungry, the Empress sat under a tree outside the small roadside inn while the others breakfasted – Suddenly, the well-known cry of respectful greeting 'Inkose' was heard and a body of about 50 natives, carrying assegais and sticks appeared – Poor Empress, as we who know her best anticipated, the first sight of the assegai caused her great emotion and it was truly a sad scene, she overwhelmed with grief with these almost naked natives sitting in a semicircle before her ignorant of the sorrow caused by their presence – yet we agreed that perhaps it were well that this inevitable trial should be got over; and in due course of time the Empress was able to hear these good people questioned – they were the inhabitants of the neighbouring kraals and had, at the order of the landlord of the inn, been out hunting in search of game for the Empress ...[32]

As the party neared Helpmekaar the debris of the recent war became more apparent. Beside the road stood the dry-stone walls of an abandoned British fort,[33] and Eugénie insisted on walking three miles off the route to visit it. Helpmekaar itself was nothing more than a hamlet, but nearby lay a small cluster of graves on the bare hillside, lasting evidence of the outbreak of disease among the garrison there. The mother of one of the dead, a trooper of the Natal Mounted Police, had written to the Empress before she left England, begging her to pay her respects at the spot. It was an unnecessary entreaty, for as Eugénie drew nearer the old front, she hungered for the sights and sounds which called to her of her son's experiences. Touched by the loneliness of the mournful little cemetery at Helpmekaar, she planted wild shrubs and flowers around the graves. It was as if she was rehearsing for her own act of homage to come.

The party reached the village of Dundee on 7 May. Dundee's location had placed it at the centre of the disputes which had led to the Zulu War, since it lay at the heart of a long spit of Natal territory which jutted north, along the foothills of the Drakensberg mountains. It was bordered on one side by the Transvaal, and on the other by Zululand. This was the so-called 'disputed territory', whose ownership was contested by British settlers, Boers and Zulus alike, and as a result Dundee had seen a great deal of activity during the war. The Empress was becoming daily more interested in the people and places around her, and the sense of being on a frontier, and of the looming presence of Zululand – that strange, wild, savage place which had shadowed her dreams for a year – became ever more tangible.

Yet Evelyn Wood was not keen to enter Zululand by the most direct route – eastwards from Dundee, across the Mzinyathi river – and instead he pressed north, crossing into the Transvaal before turning towards the border. From Dundee the party travelled north-east to Conference

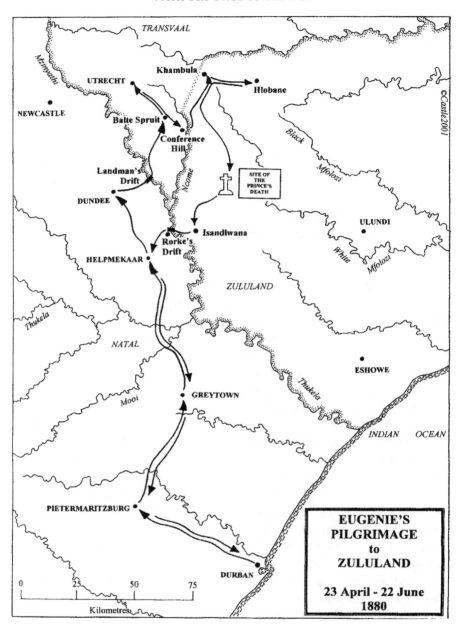

Hill, which had been a depot for the British offensive of June 1879. Here Wood had now arranged a rendezvous with a thirty-day stockpile of supplies. The reason for this roundabout route was obvious enough; it lay astride the most direct route to Wood's old battlefields at Hlobane and Khambula.

Now that she was almost on Zulu soil, however, Eugénie for the first time showed signs of impatience. To travel via Khambula would inevitably delay progress to the Tshotshosi, and Eugénie suggested pointedly that she might go on, accompanied by just a light escort, leaving Wood to complete his own travels without her. 'As the moment approaches when we shall reach our journey's end,' she wrote, 'I am torn between impatience to arrive there, and dread.'[34] It took all of Wood's charm to dissuade her and, clearly playing up his hand, he made the most of the tenuous links with the Prince's progress a year before. Without any apparent sense of absurdity he took her at Conference Hill to a stone upon which the Prince had once sat, while at nearby Balte Spruit he pointed out the very spot on which his tent had stood. From Conference Hill he suggested a visit to the town of Utrecht, twenty miles away, where the Prince had lodged for a few days, almost exactly a year before. If Wood's assurances that Eugénie was delighted at these landmarks remain unconvincing, she was undoubtedly enthusiastic about the trip to Utrecht, although in the event Wood could only count it a partial success. The inhabitants of the town were mostly Boers, who were scarcely used to visiting foreign royalty, and were naturally curious to see an Empress. Despite his best efforts to protect her privacy, Wood could not prevent her from being 'surrounded by a family circle, all bent on making small talk'.[35]

On 13 May the party finally crossed the Ncome river near Conference Hill, and entered Zulu territory. A year before the Prince had ridden out from here to take part in a number of reconnaissances into enemy territory. Here, at last, was Zululand, an open vista of rolling grassland, going brown with the onset of winter, and in its emptiness Eugénie felt her son's spirit close to her. All his life the Prince had yearned to be accounted a soldier, and this was the place where he had fulfilled his destiny, riding into enemy country alongside other soldiers in an army at war. And though it did not occur to her in such terms, just out of sight, beyond the farthest hills, lay the spot where he had been called to pay the price of an extraordinary tangle of imperial and military follies.

Hitherto, the party had been absorbed in its own preoccupations, a small inward-looking circle, consumed by its own sense of loss. Once they crossed into Zululand, however, the wider repercussions of the recent war became immediately apparent. Not only had the British invasion devastated Zululand, but many issues arising out of the conflict had yet to be resolved. The hasty withdrawal of British troops at the end of the fighting had left many local groups who had supported them in a vacuum, uncertain of the extent to which their allegiance would be recognised or rewarded, and not always reconciled to the post-war administration. As Wood put it, 'when we reached Utrecht the whole of the population turned out to see me, and from the moment we crossed the Blood River, I had a succession of Black visitors ...'[36]

Many of these men were motivated by more than social niceties. Some came to press claims on Wood, to ask him to redress specific grievances, others in the hope of securing political advantage. Wood was clearly expecting them, and it is clear he had been given powers to deal officially with them – yet a third strand in the expedition's complex motivation. Among the supplicants were members of the Uys family, bastions of the Boer border community, whose patriarch, Petras Lefras Uys, had been killed at Hlobane. The Uys family were important landowners in the old disputed territory, and 'Piet' Uys had been the only Boer leader of note to support the British invasion. Wood had promised that farms would be given to his dependants in compensation, and the family had come to see whether he was as good as his word; they were afraid that in the uncertain political future of both Zululand and the Transvaal, the British might renege on their obligations. Wood had indeed brought with him official ratification of his promises, but the family was disappointed in the acreage on offer, and to find no compensation for the livestock they had lost to Zulu raids during the war.

In this they were probably not alone. Local African groups had high expectations which were likely to be disappointed, too. Many had been recruited for service in an auxiliary unit raised by Wood himself – Wood's Irregulars – and had also suffered from Zulu reprisal attacks as a result. Wood found himself deciding their claims for the loss of family members, cattle and property. The best he could offer was limited compensation in cattle, a small recompense for the risks, hardships, and the lasting alienation of their Zulu neighbours, which they had endured in the Queen's name.

The most significant of Wood's visitors, however, were two members of the Zulu Royal House, the Princes Mthonga kaMpande and Hamu kaNzibe. The respective positions and aspirations of these men reflected the dramatic changes in fortune to which the old Zulu establishment had been subjected by the war. Although the British had removed the king, Cetshwayo, and had tried to abolish the institution of the monarchy, much of the old Zulu hierarchy remained undisturbed, and many important individuals naturally still harboured deep loyalties to the

Royal House. The British had recognised this, and had tried to turn it to their advantage. They had deliberately encouraged the aspirations of powerful individuals whose ambitions could not be contained by the old system, hoping that they would provide a counter-balance to the influence of the remaining members of the Royal House. In particular, chiefs who were believed to be pro-British, or who had ties with the trading community in Natal, were confirmed in a position of power. Members of the Royal House who were prepared to abandon their allegiance to the king were particularly valuable, and both Mthonga and Hamu in their time had gambled their political future on British support. The results, however, could hardly have been more different.

Prince Mthonga was a brother of the deposed king, Cetshwayo, and had held ambitions on the throne for many years. He had fled Zululand in 1861 when still a young man, and had spent some time in the care of John William Colenso, the Bishop of Natal. From this position he had tried to win support as a candidate for the Zulu throne, and he had not scrupled to play the ambitions of the Natal authorities and the Transvaal off against one another. In 1879 he had realised that armed intervention could only help his cause, and he had openly sided with the British. He had fought alongside Wood's command, and had been present with Wood's personal escort during the battle of Hlobane; and it was Mthonga's retainers who had dug Ronald Campbell's grave under fire with their spears. Yet he had not been rewarded with power in the post-war settlement, largely because the British had realised that his prolonged absence from Zululand had left him isolated within the country. Wood's visit in 1880 allowed him one last opportunity to appeal to the British sense of gratitude, but he was to be disappointed; as many leading Zulu would discover over the next decade, British policy in post-war Zululand was not dictated by sentiment.

Mthonga's position was in stark contrast to that of his half-brother, Hamu. He, too, was a biological son of King Mpande, although by the complex laws of Zulu genealogy he was actually considered the heir to Mpande's brother, Nzibe. As such he was technically debarred as a candidate for the succession, but he was ambitious, and his relationship with Cetshwayo had been strained long before the war. Hamu lived in the northern districts, a long way from the seat of royal authority at oNdini, and such was his power and influence locally that he was able to ignore royal directives almost with impunity. In 1879 the British, well aware of Hamu's disaffection, had made particular efforts to persuade him to defect, and just two weeks before the battle of Hlobane he had abandoned the Zulu cause and fled to the security of Wood's base at Khambula. His surrender was undoubtedly a great political coup for the British, but it did not precipitate a further break-up in the Zulu hierarchy, as they had hoped; Hamu remained the only member of the inner circle to go over to the enemy while the war was still in progress. Many Zulu loyalists regarded him as a traitor, and the deep feelings his defection aroused were already beginning to bear bitter fruit.

Nevertheless, Hamu had received his reward, and was confirmed as an independent chief in his own districts. By liberating his long-standing ambitions, the British hoped he would keep royalist sympathies in check. And so he did. While Hamu exchanged pleasantries with Lady Wood at their camp, joking ponderously about the different Zulu and Christian attitudes towards marriage, his warriors were already acting to eradicate the influence of the former regime in his areas. In particular, Hamu was keen to limit the influence of the abaQulusi, a staunchly pro-royalist group whom the British had deliberately placed under his control. Hamu harassed Qulusi *izinduna*,[37] and confiscated their cattle. Wood himself was not oblivious to the fact. 'He naturally did not tell me,' Wood recalled, 'but I learned from others that both he and Mnyamane, who were the most powerful chiefs, were oppressing their lesser brethren'.[38] Wood could hardly object, however; it was, after all, the logical result of the policy he had come to confirm.

Indeed, the tension in northern Zululand was almost palpable. The abaQulusi complained bitterly of their treatment, and were secretly arming to resist. This raised a very pertinent security issue for Wood, since his itinerary took him through the heart of the disaffected area. The abaQulusi had been among his principal enemies in 1879, and he had campaigned extensively in their area; Hlobane mountain was a Qulusi stronghold. Now he was preparing to visit Hlobane, at a time when the Qulusi might fairly have resented him as the architect of their misfortunes. At the very least, it must have occurred to him that if violence broke out between Hamu and the Qulusi, the expedition would find itself stranded in the cross-fire.

Moreover, the situation was not markedly better in the country beyond. To reach the Tshotshosi the party would have to travel through territory ruled before the war by chief Sihayo kaXongo. Sihayo's followers, too, had little reason to welcome Wood's return. Sihayo had been singled out for particular retribution during the war; his followers had been defeated, his homesteads burnt, and he himself deposed. Everywhere in Zululand supporters of the old regime found themselves impoverished, dispossessed and humiliated, and were increasingly directing their frustration towards the obvious source of their woes – the chiefs appointed by the British. Indeed, so serious was the situation that even as the Imperial party was hovering on the borders of northern

Zululand, significant events were occurring in the south. A deputation of important Royalist chiefs, including several brothers of King Cetshwayo, was making its way to Natal. Their objective was to walk to the colonial capital at Pietermaritzburg, to protest that the British settlement was not working, and to appeal for colonial intervention. They went first to the home of John Colenso, the Bishop of Natal, whose liberal views had made him a champion of justice in Zululand. They arrived on 24 May – the day before the Empress' party finally arrived at the Tshotshosi. In the event, they were to be entirely rebuffed by an unsympathetic Natal government, which had every reason to enjoy the spectacle of the Zulu kingdom shaking itself apart. The disconsolate return of this deputation is seen by many as a decisive moment in the drift towards full-blown civil war.

In fact, however, the Imperial party remained curiously untouched by the events unfolding around them. Wood and his officers masked whatever doubts they might have had behind a show of Imperial self-confidence, never wavering from the official line that British intervention had been entirely beneficial, and that as a result their per-sonal safety was never in doubt. Eugénie, of course, did not care about the Zulus; she was concerned only with her own grief. The expedition pressed on; on 14 May they reached Khambula.

Here Wood was on home ground at least. His column had occupied this site for more than three months in 1879; camp debris still littered the area. The position itself had been well chosen for its defensive capabili-ties, and lay along the top of a bare, narrow ridge, falling away steeply to the south into the marshy beds of streams which formed the headwaters of the White Mfolozi river. Wood had crowned a low peak with a small earthwork redoubt, which served to anchor his defences, and which remained largely intact a year on. The positions occupied by his troops during the battle could still be traced by the spent cartridge cases, which had been trodden into the long grass at the time, and were now exposed again by the elements. For the following few days, the real purpose of the expedition was ignored as Wood enjoyed the satisfaction of walking the party over the site of the greatest victory of his career. 'Indeed to everyone of us,' Bigge wrote with unconscious irony, 'the place is full of interest and no doubt especially to Lady Wood and Mrs Campbell.'[39] Wood pointed out to Mrs Campbell the place where her husband's tent had stood, and her own was promptly erected on the spot. The Prince had visited the camp after the battle, and Wood pointed out to Eugénie, too, where his tent had stood; curiously, perhaps at Wood's suggestion, she preferred to place her own tent elsewhere, and it was erected on ground covered by one of the decisive sorties during the battle.[40]

While at Khambula, the deposed Chief Sihayo and his eldest son, Mehlokazulu, visited Wood to pay their respects. Since the war, Sihayo and his family had been living in poverty, stripped of their cattle, and harried by the chiefs placed over them. If Sihayo entertained any hope that Wood was about to alleviate his suffering, however, he received short shrift, since Wood considered his punishment entirely appropriate. Nevertheless, the meeting was amicable enough, and Wood persuaded the two Zulus to tell the story of the battle from their perspective. Sihayo had been in command of a party of scouts during the battle, and had watched the assault from a distance, but Mehlokazulu, 'an active, wiry youth'[41] a famous warrior who had held a command in the iNgobama-khosi regiment, impressed the party by his graphic description of how he had braved a storm of fire to charge to within 200 yards of the British position before being driven back.

Wood was intrigued to discover that Mehlokazulu had also been present in the action at Hlobane, the day before Khambula, and he questioned him closely about events there. In particular, Wood was keen to discover the fate of one of his friends, Captain Robert Barton of the Coldstream Guards, who had disappeared during the retreat, and whose body had never been found. Mehlokazulu knew little about the incident himself, but recalled that a young officer of the uKhandempemvu regiment, named Sitshitshili kaMnqandi, was widely spoken of among the Zulu army for having killed two British officers during the retreat. Wood was intrigued, and asked that Sitshitshili – who lived many miles away, at iNhlazatshe mountain – be sent for. It was a further distraction from the course of Eugénie's pilgrimage, but many of the feelings of guilt and remorse Wood entertained about the Hlobane debacle had come to focus upon his dead friends, and he clearly needed the release afforded by proper funeral rites to expiate them. If anything, finding Barton's body, and giving it a proper burial, had become more important to Wood even than placing a monument on Campell's grave, and he needed to achieve both to set his mind at rest. Given the lengths he went to, it is clear that he regarded this as more of a priority than the real purpose of the expedition; he carried no sense of personal responsibility, after all, for the death of the Prince.

At Khambula the party erected their first monument. During the battle, Lieutenant Frederick Nicholson RA, had been killed commanding the guns in Wood's redoubt, while Lieutenant Arthur Bright, 90th Regiment, had been mortally wounded during one of the British sorties. Together with the other British casualties they lay buried in a small walled cemetery on the bare slope below the British camp. On 15 May Bigge placed one of the stone crosses they had carried from Pietermaritzburg over their graves. It was a particularly desolate moment; alone in the empty veld, with a cold wind promising a change in the weather, the party clustered around Wood as he led them in prayers for the dead.

This accomplished their objective at Khambula, and the party was due to leave the following day, but the Zululand winter suddenly descended with a vengeance. Snow fell on the Drakensberg mountains inland, and a bitter westerly wind carried it as far as Utrecht; Hamu later complained to Wood that the frost had been severe enough to destroy his crops. The Khambula ridge is exposed to the elements at the best of times, and the sudden gale forced the party to take refuge inside their tents, tying down the canvas, and huddling together in greatcoats and blankets for warmth.

The Empress in particular detested the cold. She retired to her tent, wrapped in furs, and waited out the storm in solitary misery. She had made no complaint to Wood, and had always behaved graciously towards Mrs Campbell, but the delay in reaching the Tshotshosi was preying on her nerves. To avoid the worst of the weather, the party moved off the top of the ridge to the more sheltered slopes below, but it was not until the 18th that they could think of resuming their journey.

From Khambula they travelled eastwards to establish a new camp below the Hlobane complex.

Seen for the first time, Hlobane mountain remains a striking sight, especially from close below the steep slopes and crowning cliffs, and the effect it had on Eugénie's lady-in-waiting, Katherine Campbell, was profound. It was here that her husband had died, the spot 'where my life's happiness had perished,'[42] and no less than Eugénie, she had lived for a year in the shadow of the killing grounds. She, too, had created in her mind an imaginary landscape which suited the dark drama played out there. Hlobane did not disappoint her; 'I cannot tell you', she wrote to her father-in-law, Lord Cawdor, 'what I felt on first seeing it quite close to me – such thankfulness and such wonder that anyone should have dreamt of attacking it'.[43]

Wonder, indeed, remains a common reaction, even to the modern historian. The action at Hlobane on 28 March 1879 remains one of the least understood battles of the war. The mountain itself is a plateau, some four miles long, with the summit almost entirely cut off by a line of steep cliffs. The surface is an undulating crazy-paving of boulders worn almost flat by aeons of wind and rain, and exposed in the hot summer months to electrical storms of terrifying ferocity. For this reason the abaQulusi built their homesteads on the lower slopes rather than the summit, and only retired onto the plateau in times of danger. There were few enough ways up through the cliffs – narrow cattle-tracks which wound up through accumulations of fallen boulders and scree, and which the Qulusi had sealed off with stone walls. It was from Hlobane that the Qulusi had orchestrated Zulu resistance to Wood's operations in 1879. They were assisted by Prince Mbilini waMswati, a Swazi who had abandoned his own country and given his allegiance instead to Cetshwayo, and who had emerged as a ruthless and daring guerrilla leader. Mbilini had close ties with the abaQulusi, and had established one of his own homesteads on the southern slopes of Hlobane.

A year before, Wood's plan had been to deprive the Qulusi of their refuge by mounting a surprise attack with his irregular cavalry at either end of the complex. This in itself displayed a fatal misunderstanding of the terrain, for what had seemed to Wood and his scouts, examining the mountain from a distance through field glasses, to be grassy slopes were actually overgrown staircases of rock. From the first, the plan had miscarried. Wood had left the assault to his irregular cavalry, who had tried to ride onto the mountain at either end. One party had got safely up, but came under Zulu pressure on the summit; the other had abandoned the attempt before it began. The British discomfort was completed by the unexpected arrival of a large Zulu army – 25,000 men – en route from oNdini to attack Khambula, and which caused the horsemen on the summit to scatter in confusion. More than seventy British troops were killed, many of them during the retreat. So widely spread were their bodies that many were never found by their colleagues, and the remains still lay unburied a year later.

Although Wood had left command of the assault parties to his subordinates, the debacle had been largely his responsibility, and his personal actions during the battle were questionable. If his success at Khambula the following day had allowed him to gloss over his general culpability, however, it had not been enough to allay his sense of remorse. In particular, he felt a responsibility for the death of Campbell. Accompanied by just his staff, his personal escort and Prince Mthonga's retainers, Wood had followed in the wake of the assault parties, intending to remain no more than an observer. As they rode across the southern face of the mountain, Wood's party came across a party of irregulars, who were pinned down under a heavy sniper fire from the cliffs above them.

According to his own account – which is not entirely reliable – Wood rode forward in an attempt to encourage these men to advance. Almost immediately, his civilian interpreter, Llwellyn Lloyd, was shot and wounded by his side. Captain Campbell offered to carry Lloyd a few yards down the slope to the protection of a dry-stone cattle enclosure, and as he did so, Wood's horse was also hit, and collapsed under him. Wood scrambled back to join Campbell, only to find that Lloyd had died a few seconds before. Wood was clearly shocked by his death, and for a moment his judgement seemed to desert him. The Zulus were firing from a jumble of huge boulders at the foot of the cliffs, less than a hundred yards away, and Wood angrily called on the irregulars to break cover and charge. They hung back, reluctant to risk a desperate scramble over broken ground under fire, at ranges so close that even the Zulus – notoriously bad marksmen – could hardly miss. Loudly denouncing them, Campbell offered to go forward with Wood's own escort. It was a brave gesture, but not entirely appropriate for a staff officer – but Wood let him go. A handful of men scrambled forwards, but as they reached a deep cleft between two boulders, Campbell was shot at point-blank range. There was no time to tend to him, and the escort stepped over his body to fire into the cleft, driving the Zulus out through a passage farther back. With the immediate threat over, the escort returned to tend Campbell. They had expected to find him wounded, but on turning his face were horrified to find that a musket ball had blown off the top of his head.[44] The escort carried his body down to the cattle enclosure, while behind them the Zulus returned to re-occupy their positions and to open fire once more.

All the evidence suggests that at this point Wood was so upset by Campbell's and Lloyd's deaths that he lost interest in the events unfolding around him. He refused to abandon their bodies to the Zulus, and instead insisted that the escort carry them to the shelter of a hollow farther down the hill. Here he set Mthonga's men to work, scraping out a grave with their spears, while the irregulars, whom he had left behind, tried to contain the Zulus, who, encouraged by the sight of British casualties, were pressing forward down the slope. Indeed, by this time a running fight was in progress across much of the top of the mountain as well, and the splutter of gun-shots which heralded the developing battle must have been clearly audible to Wood. Nevertheless, he seems to have been unable to exercise any further command, and he left the field shortly afterwards, leaving his men to their own devices.

Wood had tried several times to return to Hlobane in the month after the battle, but at that time the abaQulusi still occupied the summit, and no serious attempt was made to recover the dead. In the year since, the family of Llwellyn Lloyd had placed a small wooden cross over the grave he shared with Campbell, but even so the spot remained a difficult one to find, and after such an absence Wood was not entirely sure that he could do so. On the 18th he had set out with his bugler, Walkinshaw, to scout the area. At the time of the battle the grass had been short, cropped by hundreds of Qulusi cattle, which had been herded close by, en route to the summit. A year later, however, the Qulusi herds had long since been devastated, and the grass now grew undisturbed to a height of eight feet, rising above the heads of their horses, and making it impossible to recognise tracks and landmarks. Wood himself had become disorientated, but Walkinshaw retained a better impression of the terrain, and led Wood straight to the grave.

The following day, leaving Eugénie in camp, the rest of the party made the ascent. The ride was a difficult one for Katherine Campbell, but the view from the grave was everything she had expected. Above them, the upper slopes of Hlobane rose steeply to a line of rocky cliffs, which jutted upwards for two or three hundred feet above a jumble of fallen boulders, many of them thirty or forty feet high. A thick tangle of bush and aloes grew among the boulders, and in the long grass below the remains of stone cattle kraals testified to the Zulu occupation of the mountain, which had largely been abandoned after the war. Behind them, away from the mountain, the ground fell away into a wide, pleasant valley, hemmed in on the far side by the wall of the iNyathi ridge rising up beyond. As the sun rises and the temperature soars, the only sounds which normally break the natural quiet on the mountain side are the rhythmic whirring of insects, and the occasional monotonous cry of a bird. Even today, the landscape seems empty, mournful and mysterious.

The impact of this environment on the widow Campbell in that moment was overwhelming. The mid-Victorian era was, after all, an age which projected an intensely romantic sensibility onto the natural world, and invested it with subtle and powerful reflected moods. Artists, poets, writers and intellectuals alike had popularised the view that landscape was a mirror for the human soul. The Pre-Raphaelite school, once young and rebellious, had by the 1870s passed into the comfort of establishment acceptance, and their meticulous, literal representations of the natural world had had a huge impact on the visual arts. Walter Scott's tales of adventure and high drama, set against the backdrop of the Scottish Highlands, were hugely popular. Queen Victoria herself had set the tone with her protracted visits to Balmoral. With the spread of Empire, explorers, travellers and soldiers had brought fresh tales of strange worlds beyond Europe, and the subjugation of landscape – taming it – had become an integral part of the Imperial mind-set. It seemed entirely appropriate that actions of the British military, no longer played out in a familiar European setting, should take place instead against strange and fierce peoples in an alien and incomprehensible landscape. With conquest came knowledge, mapping, delineation, control, and the gradual reduction of the air of mystery which surrounded the unknown. The growth of Empire, and the psychological satisfaction that it conveyed, that very British sense of a pre-eminence within an ever-expanding world, needed to be fed constantly by the exotic. And in 1880, despite the ravages of Imperial conquest, there were few places that seemed to the mind of metropolitan Britain more wild and savage than Zululand. Katherine Campbell's awe at finding herself in such a spot, in such poignant circumstances, placed her very much within the framework of British attitudes to Africa which started in the nineteenth century, but has continued into modern times.

Moreover, it remained entirely possible in the 1870s to romanticise death in battle on the Imperial frontiers. In an age before mass media, before photographs could be reproduced in newspapers, and when in any case only the elite could read, it was still easy for the British public to entertain illusions about the reality of combat. The illustrated papers, which had become a mainstay of British journalism from the 1840s, might be full of stirring engravings of battles waged with monotonous regularity around the world, but the images remained idealised and carefully sanitised, with no hint of the blood, horror and indignity of the real thing. They reinforced the preconceptions of the literate middle and upper classes, many of whom, nostalgic for an age of chivalry which never was, still regarded the experience of battle as a personal test of courage and honour. Paradoxically, the fact that for much of the population of Britain in the nineteenth century, even among the ordered lives of the well-to-do, death was a very real presence, frequently encountered in childbirth or inner-city epidemics, served merely to add distance to the reality of death in battle. The elaborate funeral practices, complex codes of mourning and ostentatious tombstones adopted by the middle classes made death a familiar and more manageable experience at home, and very different from the reality of violent death on the far-flung boundaries of Empire. Poor communications and physical separation meant that families at home sometimes did not hear for months on end that a loved one had died in action, often fighting against an enemy they could not understand in a place of which they had never heard. Only the sense of loss was real; with no means of knowing the actuality, death itself took place in a landscape of the mind, confined to stereotypical images by the inexperience of the bereaved.

In many ways, it was a need to break down this feeling of alienation that had brought both Katherine Campbell and Eugénie to Africa. That they were unique among the many women widowed by the Anglo-Zulu War, being able to make the journey, was due, of course, to their privileged position, and in particular to the resources at Eugénie's command. At first glance, they might seem part of that small but vociferous band of women travellers who braved the wilds of Africa

– including Zululand – in the nineteenth century, but this is misleading. Their motivation marked them out as being very different from explorers like Mary Kingsley or May French-Sheldon, who were driven to discover new anthropological or geographical truths, often as a form of rebellion against the constraints imposed by male-dominated society at home.

Neither Eugénie nor Katherine Campbell had any interest in exploration, nor were they interested in the Zulu people, except where they touched upon the central experience of their bereavement. Indeed, for Katherine Campbell the pilgrimage was very much a part of an image of herself which was clearly defined by her relationship with her husband – what had drawn her to Zululand at all was a feeling that with his death, her own sense of self and happiness had ended. While Eugénie had never fully allowed herself to be defined by her relationships with men, the death of first her husband, and later her son, were clearly crucial moments in her life. Moreover, for all that the idea to visit Africa had been her own, she had been content to let her male escort make all practical arrangements for the journey – a decision which effectively allowed control of it to pass to Wood. But if Eugénie and Mrs Campbell had nothing to prove beyond the expiation of their grief, their attitude towards the deaths of their loved ones in battle was ambivalent. While they sought to understand something of the true nature of individual experience in the Zulu War, they sought, too, to have their romantic illusions confirmed rather than dispelled. It was important to both of them that their men had lived up to the ideal of the noble Christian warrior; the more so, in the Prince's case, because he carried the burden of one of the most illustrious martial names of the age. That being so, for both of them, so distant and otherwise meaningless a death needed a theatre appropriate to the nobility and self-sacrifice with which they had invested the deed.

Katherine, at least, was in luck; Hlobane was everything she had dreaded, and hoped. 'I knelt down by it and they left me alone for some time', she wrote. 'The wish of my soul was at last accomplished and God will surely hear my prayers offered there for strength to bear my great sorrow'.[45] After allowing Katherine time to pray in private, Wood offered to show her the exact spot where Campbell had fallen, and the entire party set off to scramble through the rocks and scree to the foot of the cliffs. 'I felt seized with a sort of wild longing', she wrote, 'and I felt so triumphant to think of Ronald's bravery and daring that I scarcely wept … I never felt so proud in all my life'.[46]

Presumably none of the soldiers who had been present during the battle thought it appropriate to tell her that there was very little of the romantic about a gaping exit wound in the top of the head.

When they descended again to the grave, they found that Bigge, following on behind with a wagon, had brought the memorial stone to the foot of the mountain. It was impossible to drive a vehicle farther, but Wood had anticipated this, and had taken the precaution of sending to a local chief, Msebe kaMadaka, to ask him to provide porters. Some forty or fifty Zulu had arrived to meet the wagon, and they manhandled the cross painfully up to the grave. Katherine found the sight 'most curious and touching',[47] wondering whether the same men might have fought against the British that day. Almost certainly, they had; a year before, Msebe had been one of the Qulusi's senior military commanders. What his men made of the present occasion no one thought to ask them.

There was no time to secure the cross that night, and instead Wood led the party on a sightseeing trip up to the summit. They rode right across the plateau to a steep rocky descent at the western end, known as the Devil's Pass, where much of the slaughter had taken place. It was late by the time they returned to camp, but Eugénie immediately sent to ask how Katherine had coped with her ordeal; she might perhaps have found some comfort in Katherine's sense of release.

The following day the entire party – including Eugénie – returned to the grave to secure the new stone, and to lay wreaths. Already, however, Wood clearly felt he had paid his debt to Campbell, and now Barton's fate was nagging at him. Leaving the party to complete their respects, he rode off with an orderly, Trooper Robert Brown of the Frontier Light Horse, to try to find Barton's body. It retrospect, this seems an impossible task. All Mehlokazulu had been able to tell him was that an officer had been killed several miles from the mountain, during the retreat. Even if it were Barton, his body – whatever was left of it – was lying somewhere in a vast, open and largely unpopulated tract of country. The fact that Wood was prepared to search for it under such circumstances, given the limited time at his disposal, suggests something of the power Barton's death held over him. Wood and Brown followed Barton's probable line of flight, crossing to the eastern end of Hlobane, and descending across a rugged shoulder of land known as Ityenka Nek, which consisted of a series of rocky terraces broken by steep cliffs. Many British troops had been trapped against the precipices and killed, and the survivors had scattered in the open country beyond. A year on, and the remains of some of the dead were still visible; scattered bones, picked over by scavengers and insects, and only sometimes held together by the rotting remains of uniforms. How Wood hoped to trace Barton's body he did not say, and by late afternoon it was obvious even to him that time had run out, and he reluctantly returned to camp. There was no sign of the Zulu *induna*, Sitshitshili, and clearly little chance of finding the body without him.

The party left the Hlobane area on 22 May. Katherine Campbell had certainly found the experience cathartic. 'I am grateful,' she wrote, 'to the Empress for coming so far out of Her way for my sake.'[48] Indeed, Eugénie had borne the enforced delay well, but Katherine noticed that her spirits improved as soon as they began to travel again. The Tshotshosi loomed heavily in her mind; it was only a few days' journey away, and with it the anniversary of her son's death. Wood was reluctant to leave without finding Barton's body, but the resourceful Trooper Brown offered to stay on alone for a few days longer in the hope of meeting Sitshitshili. Not withstanding that the real business of the expedition was now about to begin in earnest, Wood agreed.

Yet there was to be one last distraction before the party reached their goal, not entirely out of keeping with the surreal air which surrounded the entire enterprise. As the convoy trundled slowly towards the Tshotshosi, news arrived that an interloper was trying desperately to intercept them. 'We were troubled by the intrusive action of a lady correspondent of an American newspaper,' said Wood scathingly, 'who endeavoured with much persistence to obtain "copy" for her newspaper.'[49] Showing no less resolve than Eugénie, a woman calling herself Lady Avonmore had persuaded the authorities in Greytown, across the border in Natal, to lend her an escort of two troopers of the Natal Mounted Police, and had set off into the wilds to meet the Imperial party. Given that she had not the advantages of Sir Evelyn Wood's name to protect her, this was nothing if not intrepid. Handsome, persuasive and resourceful, Lady Avonmore had responded to colonial curiosity about her purpose by scattering sensational hints in her wake. On one occasion she explained that she was a personal friend of Eugénie, and wished to join her in her pilgrimage; on another, she suggested she was writing the Prince's biography. Most exciting of all, she had hinted darkly that – despite being closer in age to his mother – she was actually the Prince's secret wife, whom he had married in defiance of Eugénie, and she had now come to engineer a family reconciliation on the very spot where he had died.

In fact, Wood's guess was probably nearer the mark, for very little about Lady Avonmore was what it seemed.[50] Born Theresa Longworth in Chetworth, Lancashire, the daughter of a successful silk merchant of startling non-conformist views – he had raised six children without recourse to marriage, an act of no small courage for a middle-class man of that time – she had already achieved notoriety in a series of sensational law cases in the 1860s. These revolved around a dubious marriage ceremony she had undertaken with Captain the Hon. William Yelverton RA, the second son of Viscount Avonmore. Yelverton – handsome, dissolute and in debt – had encouraged her into a secret wedding, which was necessary – he said – to avoid a family rift. Within a year, however, Yelverton had realised that passion did not pay the bills, had thrown Theresa off, and undergone a very public marriage ceremony with a wealthy heiress. Theresa was not one to accept such treatment, however, and had promptly sued him in a case which had provided a delighted public with all the elements of a real-life melodrama.

Spineless wastrel though he undoubtedly was, Yelverton had eventually won his case on the grounds that the secret marriage was technically illegal, a verdict which effectively damned Theresa Longworth to a future as a fallen woman. Showing far more strength of character than her husband, however, she had refused to accept her lot, and promptly re-invented herself. When Yelverton's elder brother died unexpectedly, and he inherited the title Lord Avonmore, Theresa took shamelessly to styling herself Lady Avonmore. She could never, of course, move freely in British society, but her bold use of a title opened doors for her in the colonies, and she carved out an unusual career – for a Victorian lady – as a writer of adventurous travelogues. Long before she reached Zululand, she had brazened her way through the court of the Rajah of Sarawak, and into the home of the American Mormon leader Brigham Young. Quite what prompted her to try to intercept Eugénie remains obscure. She had tried unsuccessfully to meet the Empress once before, when both were in Turkey during the Crimean War; Eugénie had been visiting the sick, while Theresa was chasing the elusive Yelverton. Perhaps she hoped that the extraordinary circumstances of such a meeting might provoke a gesture of kindness from Eugénie, and thereby satisfy her yearning for social recognition. Perhaps she just hoped the adventure would be material for another book. In either case, she had reckoned without the equally resourceful Evelyn Wood.

News of Theresa's approach had first reached the Imperial party at Khambula. Theresa was entering Zululand by the more direct Rorke's Drift route, and there was a distinct possibility that she might cut across country and reach the Tshotshosi ahead of them. Reassured by the Empress that she did not know the woman, Wood took steps to keep her at bay. Bigge was despatched to head Theresa off, while Wood sent a flat denial of Theresa's claims to the Natal press; when this was published, all the sympathy and support she had worked so hard to build up promptly collapsed. Nevertheless, when Bigge reached her camp at Rorke's Drift, he found 'Lady Avonmore' unrepentant:

She affected to be greatly astonished at the request made that she would refrain from coming to the place during the Empress' stay assuring me that she had travelled 10,000 miles in order to testify her sympathy and affection for Her Majesty and at the same time visiting places where he had been to collect material for writing a biography of the Prince. My only answer was that in my humble opinion the best means of showing her sympathy and affection was by complying with the Empress' request ...[51]

Not entirely convinced that this appeal would work, Wood took more practical steps once the party reached the Tshotshosi. Wood was an officer and a gentleman, and Theresa no doubt counted on the fact that he would not want to risk a scene in front of Eugénie, much less offer violence. Wood, however, had other plans:

I sent for the headman ... and after an explanation of the case, he signed a witnessed deed or lease of all his hand on a radius of 2 miles from the spot where the Prince fell. We explained the law of trespass, and after giving the Zulus some blankets they formed a long line, and clasping hands danced away, showing how they would resist passively the approach of anyone who endeavoured to go onto the property ...[52]

Even without this added complication, Eugénie had found the final approach on the Tshotshosi a strain. 'We shall arrive on the 25th,' she wrote, 'I shall like that better than this long waiting, which terribly unnerves me.'[53] Her attendants, however, were equally in dread of her reaction on reaching the spot.

The final approach to the river was made through undulating country, with nothing of the grandeur of Hlobane about it. For the most part, the track led through open grassland, turned tawny in the Zululand winter, and devoid of trees or bush. Hills stood out here and there like islands, their sides scarred by dongas – erosion gulleys – which carried away the summer rains, but were now dry, empty, and scattered with boulders. Moreover, once the party had crested a final rise and began to descend into the gentle valley of the Tshotshosi, the spot where the Prince fell would be all too apparent while still many miles off. It was marked by a memorial cross which had been erected six months before, and was surrounded by a circle of freshly planted trees. It was the only sign of European impact on an otherwise empty landscape, and Wood dreaded the effect of that final, prolonged approach.

His solution reflected the quick thinking which had characterised much of his time as a serving soldier. Taking control of the Empress' carriage himself, he led the party off the road, descending the heights by a different path which left the cross obscured behind an intervening rise. Eugénie was not aware that she was so close to the spot where her son had died until Wood crossed a donga below the rise, turned to the right, and the memorial came suddenly into view, just a few hundred yards away. Even so, the effect on Eugénie was predictable; she collapsed, and could only descend from the wagon with the help of her aides.

For some time, Eugénie had rehearsed in her mind her reaction to this spot. She had imagined it a thousand times, conjuring it up with the aid of contemporary newspaper illustrations and descriptions. It had come to represent to her all the fierce savagery of Africa, and of war itself, a personal heart of darkness into which her son had ventured, and been consumed. The reality, now that she had arrived at her destination, was crushing. It was a landscape entirely unworthy of his death, a gentle slope, cut by a common donga, a spot significant only for its ordinariness. Furthermore, the efforts of the memorial party had effectively obliterated all trace of the conflict:

> All vestige of the grass trodden by her son and watered with his blood in his last fight had disappeared beneath a layer of white cement, surrounded by an iron railing. The soil of the donga had been carefully raked as far as the top of the banks which bordered it. The two soldiers and the Basuto guide who were killed in the skirmish of June 1 at the same time as the Prince were buried a few paces away, with the result that the spot presented the peaceful and orderly appearance of an English cemetery instead of that wild ravine which had witnessed a scene of death and carnage. The Empress thus experienced a bitter disappointment, if one can rightly apply this commonplace word to this particular instance.[54]

It was a sight which offered Eugénie none of the consolation which had eased Katherine Campbell's pain. With the anniversary of the Prince's death just days away, the Empress retired to her tent, and her private world of grief, drawn time and again to the unremarkable landscape around her:

> The Empress can see from her tent the road taken by the Prince from the kraal to the donga; and as it is exactly the same season, the maize and the grasses are the same height as they were this time last year. As she goes from her tent to the donga she can picture the poor Prince, running by the side of his horse, vainly frying to mount him, and prevented from doing so by tall grass (taller than myself by 30 or 40 centimetres), crossing a first branch of the donga, climbing a

bank, and then stopping to meet his foes ... The Empress is continually going over this tragic road, and passes most of her time in what
we may now call the cemetery.[55]

Wood, meanwhile, had plenty to occupy himself. Trooper Brown returned
from Hlobane, to report that the long awaited Zulu *induna*, Sitshitshili
kaMnqandi, had at last arrived. With unerring accuracy, he had taken
Brown to the spot where he had killed Robert Barton during the rout.
There was little left of the body but a skeleton, but Brown recognised it
by traces of clothing which remained, and by personal effects, including
a troop pay book, completed in Barton's handwriting. Brown had buried
the remains; Wood's ghosts, at least, were at last laid to rest.

Brown's news came as a welcome relief to Wood, for whom only
one last duty now remained. A year on, despite exhaustive official and
press interest in the incident, the exact details of the French Prince's last
moments remained obscure. This was simply because none of the British
survivors who were with him at the time had seen him fall; the only
witnesses to his death were the Zulus who had killed him. Among the
last of his commissions, Wood was charged with tracking down surviving members of the attacking party, and assembling evidence from their
descriptions. Finding them was surprisingly easy – several lived in the
Tshotshosi valley – but at first they were not unnaturally reluctant to talk.
'There are at present ten men at the neighbouring kraal,' wrote Bigge,

> who have been prevailed to come in to us who were in the attack-
> ing party – every effort is being made to inspire them with confi-
> dence in us, and presents of blankets, beads and money have been
> made to them in the hopes of hearing the truth as to what actually
> occurred on 1st June ... Of course, the Empress does not see any of
> these people, indeed, I have not seen her since we came here. There
> are some men residing not in this district who are very much afraid
> of coming to us, but friendly messages have been sent to them.[56]

The Zulus slowly gathered near Wood's camp, but Eugénie could
not bear to face them, and their presence weighed on her mind. In
Britain, the image of the Zulu people had undergone an inevitable
change; now that they were no longer perceived as a military threat,
the British press steadily recast them from bloodthirsty barbarians of
contemporary reports to noble children of nature. It was a shift of
emphasis which made the early defeats endured at their hands more
bearable, but Eugénie could not share it. To her, the Zulu remained
inexpressibly alien, fierce, terrible and scarcely human. They had robbed

her of her son, and she could regard them as no more than 'savages one degree removed from the brute'.[57]

Yet Eugénie still needed to know what that small, quiet, respectful and curious group of Zulu men had to say. Her son's last moments were of desperate importance to her. All his life she had raised him in the shadow of the greatest European military leader of the age, and he had been nothing if he had not been a Bonaparte. In his last few seconds, when all the glamour and cosseting of his upbringing had fallen away, when all the pomp of Imperial grandeur and folly was laid bare, and nothing was left of the nobility of war but the stark horror of killing itself, it was important, then, above all, that the Prince had not betrayed her. Eugénie had to face the future without him; without his honour, however, she would lose the one faith which had sustained her throughout the extraordinary tribulations of her own life.

What, Eugénie demanded of Wood, had the Zulus to say about the Prince's sword? Like most European officers, the Prince had carried a sword into action with him. By the 1870s, the sword was largely an anachronistic weapon, of limited value on the battlefield for personal protection, yet it still carried with it the associations of chivalry and nobility from an earlier age. To fight with a sword at close quarters required courage and skill, and for that reason it remained a highly personal symbol of unflinching devotion to duty. This was all the more true because the Prince's sword was heavy with the full weight of his family tradition.[58] Had he lived up to it? Wood understood her concern, but could not give her the answer she wanted:

> She is much disturbed at the accounts of the Zulus, who all declare that the Prince dropped his sword soon after leaving the kraal. Indeed, one of the men states that he himself picked it up. What of course she would like to believe is that the Prince fought with his sword, but this from all accounts did not take place and Sir Evelyn who really spends the whole day trying to elicit the truth, cannot discredit the account by which it would seem the sword was dropped some 200 yards from where the Prince was killed ...[59]

It was into this emotionally charged atmosphere that Lady Avonmore made her final attempt at intrusion. A day or two before the anniversary of the Prince's death, she moved her camp to within five miles of the monument. It was quite impossible that she should force herself on the Empress in such circumstances, and Wood decided to take the matter in hand himself. Taking Bassano, to speak in the Empress' name, and the ubiquitous Bigge, he rode out to confront her himself:

She proved herself quite equal to so formidable an attack, though, when it suited her purpose, displaying an extraordinary forgetfulness of facts. On being assured that it was impossible that Madame de Bassano could have presented her to the Empress, she replied 'Well it must have been Mdme. Bazaine!' ... Everyone was very civil but at last she asked what were the Empress' wishes as to where she should betake herself. Sir Evelyn then replied that he was not authorised to express any wish on the part of Her Majesty but so far as he personally was concerned he wished her anywhere out of Zululand ...[60]

Faced with such implacable opposition, Lady Avonmore at last backed down. Nothing further was left to her but to allow the anniversary to pass, and make her own way back to Natal.

As the day loomed, Eugénie's torment increased. 'My soul is full of bitterness, regrets, and sorrow', she wrote on 30 May,

It is a curious thing but I can only find peace near these stones which mark the spot where he fell, fighting, with his last breath, 'like a lion' the Zulus say ...

... It fills my heart with bitterness to think that this precious life has been so wantonly sacrificed, and that this child, left alone, fell fighting like a brave soldier with no witnesses for his courage except a handful of savages ...

But I cannot speak of him any more; my heart overflows, and the wound bleeds anew and is powerless to heal. Even though I summon all my pride as a mother, yet I feel that my love is the stronger ...[61]

The anniversary dawned on 1 June, and Eugénie could not bring herself to mix with the rest of the party. Arthur Bigge had brought with him a wreath given by Queen Victoria herself, and early in the morning Eugénie sent to ask him to lay it on the monument. Throughout the expedition, Bigge had been preoccupied with practical duties, but he had been a friend of the Prince, and now his gratitude for this simple gesture dented his self-control. 'I cannot describe the feelings of pride, tho' mingled with sorrow, with which I complied with her request'[62]. At about 10 am Eugénie emerged from her tent, and walked again to the donga, following her son's last journey. She sat beside the monument, lost in private thoughts, until about noon, when she returned to her tent. She ate and drank nothing during the day, and late in the afternoon she returned to the donga, holding her vigil into the night by candle light. An atmosphere of tense silence hung over the camp, and in the still of the African night, Eugénie achieved the communion she had so longed for. 'More than once,' she recalled,

> I noticed black forms on the top of the banks, which moved silently about and watched me through the tall grasses. This scrutiny was full of curiosity, but it was not hostile. I believe these savages wished rather to express their sympathy and their pity! ... And doubtless these were the very men who had killed my son on the same spot. ...
>
> Towards morning a strange thing happened. Although there was not a breath of air, the flames of the candles were suddenly deflected, as if someone wished to extinguish them, and I said to him, 'Is it indeed you beside me? Do you wish me to go away ... ?[63]

NOTES

1. The *Natal Witness*, 27 April 1880.
2. Between Port Elizabeth in the south and Delagoa Bay (Maputo) in the north.
3. *Natal Witness*, 27 April 1880.
4. Ibid.
5. Ibid.
6. Ibid
7. Eugénie, letter to M. Franceschini Pietri, 3 January 1880, reproduced in Augustin Filon, *Memoirs of the Prince Imperial 1856–1879*, 1913.
8. Wife of the British High Commissioner to the Cape, the architect of the Anglo-Zulu War, Sir Henry Bartle Edward Frere.
9. Entry of 16 April 1880. Adrian Preston, *Sir Garnet Wolseley's South African Journal, 1879–1880*, Cape Town, 1973.
10. Entry of 23 April 1880, ibid.
11. Ibid.
12. Ibid.
13. *Natal Witness*, 29 April 1880.
14. Eugénie, letter to M. Pietri, 18 April 1880, quoted in Augustin Filon, *Recollections of the Empress Eugénie*, 1920.
15. Wolseley, Journal, entry of 24 April, 1880.
16. Arthur Bigge, letter to Queen Victoria, 26 April 1880. Royal Archives, RA VIC/R 10/2
17. Entry of 12 April 1880, Ibid.
18. Royal Archives, RA VIC/R 10/2
19. Evelyn Wood, *From Midshipman to Field Marshal*, London, 1906.

20. Speech at the Fishmonger's Company banquet, 30 September 1879. Report in *The Illustrated London News*, 4 October 1879.

21. Wood, *From Midshipman to Field Marshal*.

22. 'Ashanti'.

23. Wood, *From Midshipman to Field Marshal*.

24. Ibid.

25. Wolseley, Journal, entry of 23 April 1880.

26. Wood, *From Midshipman to Field Marshal*.

27. Arthur Bigge, letter to Queen Victoria, 26 April 1880. Royal Archives, RA VIC/R 10/2.

28. Letter, Bigge to Queen Victoria, 9 May 1880, Royal Archives, RA VIC/R 10/8.

29. Wood, *From Midshipman to Field Marshal*.

30. Bigge, letter to Queen Victoria, 9 May 1880. Royal Archives RA VIC/R 10/8.

31. Ibid.

32. Ibid.

33. Bigge's account suggests that this was Fort Bengough, in the Msinga district. This was begun as a temporary entrenchment by a detachment of the 4th Foot on 24 January, in the aftermath of Isandlwana; within days, however, the 4th had been replaced by the 2nd Battalion, 1st Regiment, Natal Native Contingent, under Major Harcourt Bengough. Bengough's battalion greatly strengthened the position, and occupied it for several months.

34. Eugénie, letter to M. Pietri, 11 May 1880, quoted in Augustin Filon, *Recollections of the Empress Eugénie*, London, 1920.

35. Wood, letter to Queen Victoria, 23 May 1880. Royal Archives, RA VIC/R 10/19.

36. Wood, *From Midshipman to Field Marshal*.

37. An *induna* (pl. *izinduna*) was a man of appointed rank, a state or local functionary or military officer.

38. Wood, *From Midshipman to Field Marshal*.

39. Bigge, letter to Queen Victoria, 16 May 1880, Royal Archives, RA VIC/R 10/13.

40. It was placed on the ground covered by Major Hackett's sortie with two companies of the 90th (Bigge, ibid.); Wood considered this sortie decisive.

41. Wood, letter to Queen Victoria, 23 May 1880, Royal Archives, RA VIC/R 10/19.

42. Katherine Campbell, letter to Queen Victoria, 23 May 1880, Royal Archives, RA VIC/R 10/18.

43. Katherine Campbell, letter to Lord Cawdor, 21 May 1880,

Carmarthenshire Record Office.

44. Private Fowler of the 90th confirms the extent of Campbell's injuries; letter published in *The Wigan Observer and District Advertiser*, 28 April 1879.

45. Katherine Campbell, letter to Lord Cawdor, ibid.

46. Ibid.

47. Ibid.

48. Katherine Campbell, letter to Queen Victoria, Royal Archives, RA VIC/R 10/18.

49. Wood, *From Midshipman to Field Marshal.*

50. For an account of the Lady Avonmore episode, see Brian Roberts, *Ladies in the Veld*, London, 1965.

51. Bigge, letter to Queen Victoria, 27 May 1880, RA VIC/R 10/22.

52. Wood, *From Midshipman to Field Marsha*l.

53. Eugénie, letter to M. Pietri, 23 May 1880, Filon, *Recollections*.

54. Filon, quoting Eugénie's description to him, *Recollections of the Empress Eugénie*.

55. Maquis de Bassano, letter of 29 May 1880, quoted in Filon, ibid.

56. Bigge, letter to Queen Victoria, 27 May 1880, Royal Archives, RA VIC/R 10/22.

57. Eugénie, letter to M. Pietri, 'Ityotyozi Kraal, May 30 1879'. Reproduced in Filon, *Recollections*.

58. The sword was a Bonaparte family weapon, though there is some confusion as to its exact origin. According to Filon (*Memoirs*) it was 'an historic sword the Duc d'Elchingen had presented to him'. Archibald Forbes thought it 'the veritable sword worn by the first Napoleon from Arcola to Waterloo' (Forbes, *Memories and Stories of War and Peace*), an impression the Prince probably liked to encourage, since Major Grenfell agreed it was 'one worn by the great Napoleon in all his campaigns' (Grenfell, *Memoirs*).

59. Bigge, letter to Queen Victoria, 27 May 1880, RA VIC/R 10/22.

60. Bigge, letter to Queen Victoria, 7 June 1880, RA VIC/R 10/32.

61. Eugénie, letter to M. Pietri, 30 May 1880, quoted in Filon, *Recollections*.

62. Bigge, letter to Queen Victoria, 7 June 1880, RA VIC/R 10/32.

63. Filon, *Recollections*.

II

'... thirsting to smell powder'

It had been a long road from the palace of the Tuileries to the valley of the Tshotshosi river, and the journey had started many years before.

Perhaps it had begun as long ago as 1795, when the great Napoleon had dispelled the Paris mob with a 'whiff of grapeshot', and might, for the first time, have caught a glimpse of the path his own destiny would smash through the tumbling glass-houses of the old world order. If ever there was a man who harnessed the rushing tide of history and turned it to his own ends, it was Napoleon Bonaparte. Historians still debate the full extent of his legacy to the continent of Europe, though none deny his impact; in the rather more intimate realm of his family, the long shadow cast after his death by this extraordinary personality led, two generations later, to a lonely and violent death in the wilds of Zululand.

Napoleon's rise from the provincial obscurity of his birth had been meteoric. It is said that even as a child he had a military frame of mind, and he had entered the army on the eve of one of the great tumults that periodically convulse European history. An original and instinctive soldier, he had realised, too, the role an army might play in a country shaking itself apart. A heady combination of drive, talent and luck had won him the rank of Brigadier General by the age of twenty-four. From the early days of the Revolution to the escape from Elba, his extraordinary successes on the battlefield, against France's external enemies, would be matched only by his audacity and adroit political manoeuvring at home. His career might have been finished a thousand times; as early as 1799 his Egyptian adventure ended in fiasco when Nelson destroyed his fleet in Aboukir Bay, stranding his army. Undaunted, Napoleon had turned this reverse to his advantage; he had slipped away, and had not scrupled to abandon his troops. Back in France he mounted a *coup d'etat*; ousted the rump of the Revolutionary regime, and established a new government, the Consulate – with himself as First Consul. By 1802 he had made himself consul for life, and in 1804, with deliberate symbolism, he crowned himself Emperor. By 1810 his conquests had surrounded France with a ring of satellite and allied states, and made her mistress of Europe. Beyond that, she stood alone, hated and feared by a powerful combination of unlikely allies who dreaded the export of the Revolution, and resented France's new economic empire. And at the centre of it all stood the figure of the Emperor himself, a mass of contradictions; as much Italian as French, small, balding, yet larger than life, both a visionary and an arch pragmatist, unshakeable in his ego, bending the world to his will on the battlefield at the expense of hundreds of thousands dead.

Only in 1812 did the extraordinary edifice of the First Empire begin to crack under the strain. The *Grande Armée* followed Napoleon in high spirits to Moscow, but even his star was not proof against the desolation of the Russian winter. There followed the long and demoralising withdrawal, and the army gave up to frostbite and avenging Cossacks what it had seldom surrendered in open battle. Quite suddenly, the basis of Napoleon's power disintegrated, and there remained only acceptance, abdication and Elba. But the brief restoration of Royalist fortunes which followed was short-lived, for in 1815 the Great Beast escaped, and the army rallied to him once more. For the 'hundred days' *La Gloire* paraded naked again in the streets of Paris, and the rest of Europe shivered in terrified anticipation. Yet perhaps his day was already done, for the old flair was not quite equal to the unholy alliance of Britain and Prussia, and on 18 June the Imperial eagle fell heavily to earth in the mud near the small Belgian town of Waterloo. Within a fortnight Napoleon had fled the country, only to be intercepted and captured by a British warship, HMS *Bellerophon*.

A vengeful European establishment would take no chances a second time. Napoleon was exiled to St Helena, a bleak rock in the south Atlantic, which was to become a favourite prison for generations of political enemies of the British Empire. Ironically, sixty years later, the island would play host to a banished Zulu king; not the first time the destinies of the Napoleonic dynasty and the Zulu kingdom overlapped.[1]

Napoleon Bonaparte died in May 1821, officially of stomach cancer – though there is a good case to make out that he was poisoned; whether deliberately or accidentally, by supporters or enemies, is open to debate.[2] His passing, if anything, merely enhanced the extraordinary myth which had grown up around him. Napoleon had always been a natural self-publicist – as early as the Italian campaign of 1796 he had commissioned the best French writers and artists of the day to celebrate his victories. In his later years he had deliberately created an elaborate ritual of Empire, centred upon the brilliance of his own person. His charismatic belief in himself as a 'man of destiny', that the fortunes of France were inextricably entwined with his own, had been unshakeable; in a country struggling to throw off the self-laceration of revolution, and find confidence in a new identity and international stature, it had been hugely infectious. Certainly, his legacy to the world was deeply ambiguous. He had given shape and direction to the raw, brutal power for change which the Revolution had unleashed, and the Old World would never be the same again. His military victories, his huge political and economic reforms – the effects of which were felt far beyond the borders of France – had given birth to a new age, and to modern Europe. Yet all this had been achieved by a carnage unparalleled even in Europe's brutal history.

Inevitably of such a man, Napoleon's bequest to those around him was similarly tortured. War and Revolution are equally said to consume their own children, and the Napoleonic myth, born of both, would devour many of those who tried to live in the shadow of his name. In her time, the Empress Eugénie would be one of them; it was a lesson which would come to her many times, and never more forcibly than with the grim news from Zululand.

Napoleon was born to a large family. His parents, Carlo Buonaparte and Letizia Ramolino, were Corsican minor gentry of Italian descent. They had married in 1764, when he was eighteen and she just fourteen; their first two children died in infancy, but over the next twenty years they produced eight offspring who survived. Napoleon – christened Napolione – was born in Ajaccio in August 1769. It was an exciting time, for Corsica was under threat of French invasion, and Carlo had joined the forces of the Corsican patriot, Paoli. In the event, however, though the French conquest was successful, it brought unexpected advantages to the Buonaparte family. Carlo, a trained lawyer, became part of the new French legal establishment, and in time received from the French the title of Count. Napolione was educated at the Ecole Militaire in Paris, and the family began to abandon the outward signs of its Italian ancestry. In 1796, a decade after the death of the patriarch, the family changed the spelling of its name to the overtly French 'Bonaparte'. Napolione had long since signed himself *Napoleon*.

Throughout his career Napoleon had remained fiercely loyal to his family. As his own fortunes had risen, so he had dragged his siblings with him, trusting his brothers with key political positions, scattering royal appointments among them, and arranging powerful strategic marriages for his sisters. In truth, however, none of his brothers matched him in strength of character and vision, and Napoleon was forced to recognise that the future of the dynasty rested with him. Never one to constrain his passions within the narrow confines of marriage – a family trait – he had, by 1809, fathered a number of illegitimate children, but as yet no legal heir. This he blamed squarely on his wife, the Empress Josephine. He had married Josephine de Beauharnais, a widow whose aristocratic husband, the Vicomte de Beauharnais, had gone to the guillotine during the Terror, in the thrall of passion in 1796. By 1809, however, as she was sliding into a rather vain and self-centred middle age, she had yet to produce for him a son. Napoleon's reaction was typically ruthless; he divorced Josephine with scarcely a second thought, and married Archduchess Marie Louise, the young daughter of Francis I, Emperor of Austria. Within a year Marie Louise had fulfilled her duty, and produced an heir, christened Napoleon, whom his father honoured with the title King of Rome.

In the meantime, the Emperor had found time amidst his work reshaping the political geography of Europe to take an interest in the romantic affairs of his younger brother, Louis Bonaparte. Louis, too, had trained as a soldier, a fact which had given an added dimension to fraternal affection. During the Italian campaign of 1796 – which had established Napoleon's reputation – Louis had served as his brother's ADC, and a heady mixture of youth and adventures shared, of military success, of careers spectacularly on the rise, had made Louis Napoleon's favourite. Yet the circumstances which drew them so close together would in time drive them apart, for in Italy Louis contracted rheumatic gout, and with discomfort and disability came an increasingly querulous personality. Napoleon, at first sympathetic, became steadily more exasperated. Nevertheless, he refused to accept that the change was a permanent one, and for years continued to guide Louis' career. In 1806 he set him up as King of Holland. In the event, Louis proved a sad disappointment, not only as a king – he was unable or unwilling to curb the violations by Dutch smugglers of Napoleon's economic sanctions against Britain – but also as a French patriot, since he took up the cause of Dutch nationalism. Napoleon was in the end forced to depose his own brother and send the French army into Holland.

In 1802, before their relationship had so deteriorated, however, Napoleon had arranged a marriage for Louis, selecting as his bride Josephine's daughter by her previous marriage, Hortense de Beauharnais. Hortense, if not quite beautiful, was a striking woman with a lively and strong personality, and it soon became evident that she did not take to her new husband. Their relationship was volatile, and over the next few years she seldom spent more than a few months at a time with him. Instead, she often stayed with her mother and the Emperor. Nevertheless, she produced for Louis an heir – Napoleon Charles – in 1802, and another son, Napoleon Louis, in 1804.

The relationship between Louis Bonaparte and his wife is of considerable interest, for it was upon their off-spring that fate conspired to throw the future mantle of Bonapartism. In 1807 tragedy struck. Hortense's eldest son, Napoleon Charles, fell ill with croup and died, and grief drove a final wedge between the parents. Over the next two years Louis and Hortense were to spend little time together, and in 1809 Louis asked his brother for permission to divorce her.

It is all the more curious, then, that on 20 April 1808 Hortense gave birth to another son, christened – with a fine sense of family loyalty, if not originality – Louis Napoleon. The child was born a month premature, and was so weak that physicians ordered him to be bathed in wine and wrapped in cotton-wool. By now, it was widely rumoured that both Louis and Hortense had sought consolation elsewhere, and there was a good deal of speculation about the identity of the father. The Bonapartes, however, shrugged off any such scandal, and pointed out that Louis and Hortense had spent one of their rare periods together nine months before the birth. So, indeed, they had; but the child was premature, and eight months before, Hortense had been at the palace at St Cloud with the Emperor. It is perhaps no coincidence that Louis applied for a divorce soon afterwards; and that Napoleon seemed to enjoy the company of Hortense's third child over that of all his other nephews.

Whatever hopes Napoleon may have entertained for the next generation of Bonapartes, however, they were to fall victim to the collapse of his own Imperial ambitions. The young Louis Napoleon had not turned six when the Empire disintegrated. While Napoleon departed for Elba, and a Bourbon king returned to Paris, those closest to the passing regime went into hiding. Napoleon's wife, Marie Louise, returned to her father in Austria, taking her son with her; Napoleon would never see him again. His first wife, Josephine, was so distraught at the ruin of her fortunes that she died. Hortense, grieving for her mother and fearful for the fate of her sons, placed herself under the protection of Tsar Alexander I of Russia. Alexander was clearly impressed; he made her a duchess and granted her an impressive allowance.

Nevertheless, when Hortense heard of Napoleon's escape, she threw up her chance of a life of peace and security, and hurried to Paris to greet him. While the great man brooded over the calamities of the past two years, and planned his resurrection, it was she who comforted him. The night before he left for Belgium she hosted a dinner party at the Elysée; when he returned just a few days later, broken by Waterloo, she was there to meet him. They shared a last few days together at her mother's old palace at Malmaison, and her sons were brought to say their farewells. It was the last they saw of him; within days their uncle had gone from France, and from their lives, forever.

After the Hundred Days, the Bonapartes knew they were living on borrowed time, and went to ground. Hortense found herself unwelcome in Paris, and for two years she was harried round Europe from one unsuccessful refuge to another. To add to her woes, her estranged husband – now living in Florence – successfully secured legal custody of her eldest son, Napoleon Louis. In 1817 she finally came to rest at the Château of Arenenburg, near the town of Constance, in Baden. Here, at least, Napoleon's careful web of family alliances offered her some protection, for both the Bonapartes and the de Beauharnais were well connected in the region. At Arenenburg Hortense cultivated a distinctly Empire style, and surrounded herself with mementos of the great man. But if the past gave her life meaning, her exile only served to point up the emptiness of her future – even as her remaining son grew up in the shadow of the Bonaparte legend, he learned to speak French with a German accent and mannerisms.

Nevertheless, this Louis Napoleon was every short inch a Bonaparte. Physically, he bore all the family marks – he had a long body and short legs, but his rather lugubrious expression served only to emphasise the contrasting brightness of his dazzling smile. In later life he grew moustaches and a goatee beard which emphasised the impassiveness of his features, but most who met him found that his taciturn manner hid, not churlishness, but a relaxed good nature. He would always be popular with women, and like his uncle placed no great importance on constancy – though like the great Napoleon, he, too, would remain steadfastly loyal to his family. Indeed, for him, to be a Bonaparte was all, and beneath that unlikely exterior the fires of ambition – that fierce belief that fate had welded his own destiny to that of France – burned just as intensely as in his uncle. As a child, he had been sickly, the result of his premature arrival, but Hortense had nurtured both his body and mind, giving him a broad and cosmopolitan education. When he was sixteen he followed family tradition by attending the Military Academy at Thun, in Switzerland, where he was taught gunnery and field engineering by two former officers of Napoleon. His reaction, in his teens, on hearing the news of the death of his uncle on St Helena was typical:

When I do wrong I think of this great man, and I seem to feel his shade within me telling me to keep myself worthy of the name of Napoleon.[3]

Louis took a keen interest in political events in France, and it was in
the aftermath of the July Revolution in 1830 that he first learned the
ambiguous legacy which was his inheritance. Charles X, the Bourbon
king, fell, and Louis Napoleon moved to Geneva, closer to the French
border, hoping that his cousin – Napoleon II, the Emperor's legitimate
heir – might be called home to save France. But the call did not come,
and instead the succession passed to Louis Philippe and the Orléanists.
Disappointed that the hour of destiny was not to be achieved so readily, Louis Napoleon allowed himself to be drawn into the whirlpool
of Italian politics instead. Here, revolutionaries, encouraged by liberal
successes in France, hoped to throw off the oppressive influence of the
Austrian empire and the Papacy, and create a free and united Italy. The
insurgents, searching for figureheads for their cause, secretly invited
Louis and his older brother, Napoleon Louis, to support them. Hooked
by the appeal to their family name, buoyed up by a heady mixture of
youth and the struggle for liberty, Hortense's sons made their way to
join their first uprising. For the Bonapartes, it seemed, each generation
had to prove itself in revolution; but despite some initial successes – the
fruits of Louis' military training – the adventure proved a disaster. The
full weight of the Austrian army descended on the rebels, who promptly
recognised the dangers of associating themselves so openly with the
Napoleonic tradition. Then tragedy struck; the older brother, Napoleon
Louis, contracted fever while in hiding, and with no medical support
to hand, he died. Hortense – who was already on the road to Italy to
rescue her sons from themselves – was devastated. Worse was to follow; when she finally caught up with Louis, she found him not only a
wanted man, but in the first stages of the same illness. There followed
a wild carriage ride across Italy, in which Hortense spirited her ailing
son away from under the nose of Austrian troops, disguised as her
footman. Determined to place him as far away from danger as possible,
Hortense crossed France – Louis Philippe allowed her safe passage, so
long as she had no intention of staying – and made a stormy crossing to
England.

Hortense and Louis spent three months in England, and the stay completed his political education. Despite the historical antipathy between
the British establishment and the Bonapartes, Louis enjoyed life there,
and came to regard England not only as a place of refuge, but as an ally
to his ambitions. While his mother worked to improve family influence
in English society, Louis discovered that his adventures had made him
notorious, and he enjoyed the sensation. Plotters and schemers from
half the troubled states in Europe made their way to his door, while
the French government looked on in concern, and the British became

embarrassed. For the first time since 1815, it seemed to the world that another Bonaparte waited in the wings. It was all Louis could have hoped for.

At last, they slipped back to Arenenburg, and less than a year later the news came that Napoleon II was dead. Marie Louise's son was just twenty-two, and had never emerged from the fearsome shadow of his Austrian grandparents. With the Great Man's son gone – without issue – and so, too, his own older brothers, Louis Napoleon suddenly found himself the heir to the Bonaparte legacy. True, many of Napoleon's own brothers were still alive, but Louis rightly regarded them as a spent force politically. Of the younger generation, only Napoleon Josef – the son of Napoleon's brother Jérôme – survived to make claims upon the family estate. But 'Plon-Plon', as he was familiarly known, was younger than Louis, and for all that he grew up in a remarkable physical likeness of the Emperor, his personality – brilliant but abrasive – seemed chronically unsuited to the political subtlety which was so essential to the survival of the dynasty.

All that remained was for Louis to claim his birthright in France itself. By the mid-1830s, he judged his time had come. The Orléanist regime, while liberal, had lost support amongst the French people, and disillusion had made them receptive to Napoleonic nostalgia. If Louis could harness to himself the full power of the Bonaparte legend, he might yet sweep into Paris on the shoulders of adoring crowds. At least, so he hoped; and thus the stage was set for the first of his curiously farcical attempts to seize power by *coup d'etat*. Inspired by Napoleon's progress from Elba, Louis and his supporters chose the town of Strasbourg to make their attempt. Here the French garrison included at least one regiment with a tradition of Bonapartist loyalty. Louis canvassed support among the officers, judged them sympathetic, and at the end of October 1836 raised the Imperial eagle among them. For a few hours it looked as if he might succeed, but he lacked his uncle's powers as a rabble-rouser; troops from an infantry barracks at first heckled him, then, on the urging of their officers, arrested him. Unwilling to shed French blood, Louis called upon his own supporters to surrender without a fight, and his revolution spluttered to a halt in scarcely more than a scuffle.

Louis Philippe took the incident remarkably well, under the circumstances; perhaps he was worried about creating martyrs to the Bonaparte cause. He forgave the conspirators, and his troops escorted Louis to the docks and put him on a ship to America, with money in his pocket, to start a new life elsewhere. And for a while Louis indeed seemed content to abandon his destiny, and settle instead for the quiet and prosperous life of a farmer in the New World. Until, just months later, a letter arrived from his mother, telling him that she was gravely ill. Louis hurried back to Arenenburg, passing through Britain and Europe one step ahead of a host of spies and secret policemen who watched his every move, and got home just in time. On 5 October 1837 Hortense de Beauharnais died. With her passing one of the great flames of Bonapartism went out; but in her demise Louis found his own ambition reborn.

Louis was now alone with only his star for comfort, and two years later it led him to the greatest embarrassment of his career. In that time he had established himself in London. His mother's legacy had made him wealthy, he had just turned thirty, and was in his charming prime. Enjoying the amusements London society had to offer – chiefly women and gambling – he carefully established his reputation as his uncle's successor. Even the Duke of Wellington, whose own career had been built on his defeat of Napoleon, was impressed by his audacity. 'Would you believe it,' he said, 'this young man Louis Napoleon will not have it said that he is not going to be Emperor of the French!'[4]

Indeed he would not. In August 1840 he set off in a pleasure cruiser down the Thames with fifty paid recruits, mostly expatriot Frenchmen, a crate of French uniforms, some weapons and a rather bedraggled vulture from a zoo, which someone brought along in optimistic representation of the Imperial eagle. This unlikely party landed on the beach near Boulogne at dawn, much to the surprise of the local coast-guard, and marched to the nearest infantry barracks. Here the soldiery seemed undecided whether to salute them or shoot them, until at last their officers arrived and sent the conspirators angrily away. Undaunted, Louis proceeded to the town, and tried to raise the locals with his oratory. They regarded him with amused indifference until the National Guard arrived to arrest him, whereupon most of Louis' recruits promptly fled to the beach. Reluctantly led away by his entourage, Louis was just clambering into a long-boat when the Guard arrived and opened fire. One of the would-be revolutionaries was shot and killed, and another drowned in the surf. Louis himself was arrested, along with his principal co-conspirators. It was a grim end to an absurd charade; and not the last blood which would be shed in Louis' name.

This time King Louis Philippe was not so lenient. Louis was tried before a High Court of Justice in Paris, and sentenced to life imprisonment.

His prison was to be the medieval fortress of Ham, overlooking the Somme valley, south of Amiens. It was grim and forbidding, and Louis was to spend more than five years there. In that time, he lost many of his romantic illusions, but his belief in himself endured. Indeed, his status afforded him some relief, since he was allowed a suite to himself, and passed the time reading, writing letters and dreaming. When his enthusiasm for life recovered from the shock of his arrest, he cultivated an eccentric range of interests – in chemistry, in agriculture, and in the plan to build a canal across the Panama isthmus. Although all visits of a political nature were carefully controlled, he contrived to establish a friendship with one of the female servants who entered the fortress every day, Alexandrine Vergeot – a very French liason which was connived at by an indulgent Governor. In due course, he fathered two children by her, and when his fortunes later rose again, he would buy her a retirement apartment in the Champs Elysées, and ennoble both her sons.

Then, suddenly, with that same audacity which characterised his entire political career, Louis Napoleon escaped from the prison at Ham. He had been, by and large, a model prisoner, and the garrison no longer watched him as they once had, while his aides – who continued to attend him though their own sentences were long since over – were allowed to come and go as they pleased. On 25 May 1846 Louis Napoleon put on a set of smuggled workman's clothes, and while the daily work-gang went about their duties, he simply walked out the main gate under the nose of the sentries. Once out of sight he met a carriage at a pre-arranged rendezvous, hastened to the nearest station, and within hours he and his companions had crossed the border into Belgium. By the following evening they were in London.

There followed another pleasant spell in the more congenial exile of London, with one eye ever across the Channel. His chance came again in 1848, the Year of Revolutions, when the Orléanist regime fell. The barricades went up in the streets of Paris, and Louis Philippe and his family fled – ironically to Britain. For several tempestuous months a Provisional Government struggled with increasing desperation to retain control. Louis Napoleon strained like a dog on a leash. In June he put himself forward as a candidate for election, only to be forced to withdraw after the Government threatened to arrest him. This time, however, there would be no more mad adventures, for Louis saw that the way forward lay through the plebiscite. In August, after more bloodshed, there were further elections, and this time Louis was successfully elected to the Constituent Assembly of the Republic.

It was an oddly democratic way for a Bonaparte to return to France in triumph, yet the great Emperor had always known how to play a crowd. So too, now, did Louis; when Presidential elections took place at the end of the year, he shamelessly traded upon the Napoleonic legend. To everyone's surprise, he won a landslide victory.

Yet he had not entirely turned his back on old ways, for once he was in power the limitations of democracy soon became apparent. The constitution limited his term to four years in office, and even as he took his seat the Royalists were working to build up popular support against him. Yet the opposition had made the fatal mistake of under-estimating him, for Louis had learned how to beat the rabble-rousers at their own game. By 1851 his term of office was nearing its end, and rumour had it that it was now Louis Philippe who was poised at the dock-side in England to make his come-back. Instead, to everyone's surprise, Louis Napoleon struck, and with a new ruthlessness. At dawn on 2 December 1851 troops under his command quietly and efficiently rounded up leading members of the opposition, before barring the doors of the Constituent Assembly to its members. Louis himself, wearing a general's uniform and accompanied by a glittering military staff, made a triumphal procession through the streets of Paris, en route to the Tuileries. The coup had been so swift and decisive that the first protests did not manifest themselves on the streets of Paris until two days later, and when they did they were suppressed with unexpected ferocity. The harshness of Louis' reaction caught Parisians by surprise; for bitter crit-ics like Victor Hugo, it marked the re-emergence of the true spirit of the Bonapartes:

> The carnage of the Boulevard Montmartre constitutes the original-ity of the *Coup d'Etat* ... Owing to the massacre Louis Bonaparte escapes the charge of plagiarism.
>
> Up to that time he had only been an imitator. The little hat at Boulogne, the grey overcoat, the tame eagle appeared grotesque. What did this parody mean? People asked. He made them laugh; suddenly, he made them tremble.
>
> He who becomes detestable ceases to be ridiculous.[5]

Perhaps a show of force was what Louis had needed all along; now indeed he seemed a true Bonaparte. When he followed the coup with an appeal to the people, over seven million Frenchmen supported the extension of his authority.

Louis Napoleon Bonaparte was now in his early forties, and it seemed that his destiny had been fulfilled. He had confounded those critics who had dismissed him as a ridiculous buffoon, and within a year he con-verted the Second Republic to the Second Empire. Now, at last, a second Bonaparte was Emperor of the French. Lest anyone remain in doubt in whose footsteps he expected to tread, he took the title Napoleon III.

With the sudden and swift ascent to power came the usual Bonaparte preoccupation with dynasty. Like Napoleon I, Napoleon III had fathered illegitimate sons before he became Emperor, but there could be no talk of an heir until he was married. Not everyone wanted him so, even within the family; if he stayed single, the line would pass to his cousin, 'Plon-Plon', who firmly held that it was his right. But while Louis could always be diverted by a pretty face, he never for one moment allowed his dalliances to cloud his sense of destiny, and the old ruthless Bonaparte streak emerged; with echoes of Napoleon's treatment of Josephine, Louis suddenly put aside his mistresses, and in January 1853 he married.

His bride was Marie Eugénie Ignace Augustine de Montijo, whose antecedents – ostensibly, at least – were an exotic blend of the Spanish and Scottish. Eugénie's family background was scarcely less tempestuous than that of the Bonapartes, and indeed she shared much in common with her future husband. She, too, was born to questionable parentage, to a strong-willed mother and absent father, and her early life was clouded by emotional and political insecurity. Eugénie's maternal grandfather was a Scot, one William Kirkpatrick, whose family hailed from Dumfries, traced their descent to Robert the Bruce, and were noted for their Jacobite sympathies. A generation after Culloden life could still be uncomfortable for the Scottish gentry who followed 'the King over the Water', and like many who shared his sympathies, William Kirkpatrick left Scotland to find his fortune elsewhere. He established himself in Malaga, where he prospered in the wine trade, and married the daughter of an expatriot Belgian baron in the same line of business. In 1794 they had the first of three daughters, Manuela, who proved to be spirited, beautiful and, once she reached adulthood, sexually adventurous. Because of his Jacobite leanings and French connections – his sister-in-law married into the de Lesseps family, later of Suez Canal fame – William Kirkpatrick gave his allegiance to the French Emperor rather than to the British King, and sent his daughters to be educated in Paris. The first Empire was then at its height, and Paris teemed with foreign adventurers with colourful uniforms, exotic names and chequered pasts, all of them infected by the romance and charisma of the Imperial court. It was here that Manuela met Don Cipriano Guzman de Palafox y Porto Carrero, Comte de Teba. Cipriano was a Spanish soldier of fortune, an idealist and a fervent admirer of Bonaparte, in whose service he had lost the use of a comprehensive selection of his anatomy – an eye, a leg, an arm. Nevertheless, he captivated Manuela with his charm – or perhaps his prospects (he was the younger son of the Comte de Montijo) – and in 1817 they married.

Yet the post-Napoleonic world was a dangerous one for the great families of Europe. Cipriano had stayed loyal to the Emperor during the Hundred Days, but found it necessary to return to Spain after Waterloo. Here he was to pay a high price for his very public allegiances, and for his supposedly liberal ideals. King Ferdinand of Spain held onto his throne only with the support of the restored monarchy in France, and was suspicious of liberals in general and distrustful of the Comte de Teba in particular. Following a failed liberal insurrection in 1823, Ferdinand rounded up, imprisoned and tortured many leading liberals, among them Don Cipriano. Manuela's husband was destined to remain under one form of arrest or another for more than a decade.

Although, in the early days of his captivity, it is said that Manuela bribed or charmed her husband's guards to allow him visits, in truth the enforced separation destroyed an already shaky marriage. Don Cipriano – older, increasingly misanthropic, despite his ideals, and mean with his considerable fortune – had become impatient with his extrovert, headstrong and extravagant wife, who had grown up in the heady atmosphere of the café behind the wine-trader's shop. During her husband's captivity Manuela gave birth to two daughters, Maria Francisca de Sales – known as Paca, for short – in January 1825, and Eugénie, on 5 May 1826. Cynics observed that nine months before Eugénie's birth, Manuela had been able to spend little time with her husband, but had been in Paris instead, enjoying the company of the British Foreign Secretary, George Villiers, later Lord Clarendon. Indeed, it is true to say that Villiers and Manuela enjoyed an occasional but close friendship which lasted for many years, despite his subsequent marriage, and that he always took a particular interest in Eugénie's progress.[6]

In 1833 the tensions in Spanish politics erupted into violence. Don Cipriano had by then been released from his prison, and by luck succeeded to the title of Comte de Montijo, when his elder brother died without an heir. With it came a comfortable house in Madrid. The family – together for once – had not long been in the capital when civil war broke out. King Ferdinand had died with no son to succeed him, and by a typically sly but deeply destructive sleight of hand had contrived to pass the throne – not to his surviving male relative, his brother, Don Carlos – but to his daughter, Isabella. Don Carlos was outraged, and promptly contested the succession by force. A particularly brutal internecine struggle, dignified with the name of the Carlist Wars, broke out. There were killings in the streets of Madrid, and Manuela promptly decided to take her children to the safety of Paris. The Governor of the French border town of Perpignan recalled their passage, and hinted at their experiences:

Many Spaniards are passing through Perpignan; most of them come from Madrid, and are on their way to Toulouse. The Countess of Teba, a woman of thirty-five – extremely intelligent – is going to

Toulouse. She has a very considerable fortune. Her husband has remained at Madrid for the session of the Cortes. Madame de Teba did not leave Madrid till the 18th; she saw dreadful things done there. The City Guard maimed and assassinated the monks and the Jesuits, even in their churches. The troops of the line were under arms, but looked on without interfering.[7]

Quite what effect these horrors had on the minds of Manuela's impressionable daughters can only be guessed at. Quite probably they gave rise to a strain of morbidity which emerged in Eugénie in later life. Even at the height of her success, she was plagued by a sense of foreboding, which manifested itself in an interest in spiritualism, and by an identification with Marie Antoinette. Eugénie could never quite free herself of a nagging feeling that tragedy was her lot, too; and no doubt those images of horror from the streets of Madrid returned with particular intensity, more than forty years later, when her life was indeed touched by violence and horror.

In Paris Manuela herself took full advantage of the delights of the cosmopolitan society available to her, but she remained protective of her daughters. Paca and Eugénie were at first educated by the nuns at the Sacre Coeur, then at a mixed school which stressed the importance of physical as well as intellectual education – here Eugénie developed a boisterous streak and a love of pranks which would never entirely leave her – and finally at a boarding school in England. Then, in 1839, as the Carlist Wars spluttered to a close, came the news that Don Cipriano was dying, and Manuela swept up her family and returned to Spain.

With the death of her husband, Manuela found herself comfortably placed to enjoy life in the capital. Her husband's liberal reputation had earned her the respect of Queen Isabella, and she was free to indulge her appetite for handsome young men without disapproval or financial constraint. As one observer put it simply at the time, 'the Comtesse de Montijo possessed lovers galore'.[8] But if Spanish society was mercifully free of that cold hand of sexual repression which Prince Albert brought to British society, Manuela's behaviour nonetheless had its effect on her youngest daughter. Poised on the brink of adolescence, and no longer physically separated from her mother's excesses, Eugénie took refuge from the robust earthiness of her mother's court in a fantasy world of romance and adventure. Against such a background, her father's old stories of his youth, of his wild days pursuing the soaring eagle of liberty and Bonapartism, held a particular resonance. When she grew older, Eugénie would be only too aware of the effect her striking looks and charm had on male admirers, but sex would never be her goal, and indeed she came to despise it, and the men who needed it. Instead, she searched for an emotional intensity which few men – least of all a Bonaparte – could ever hope to fulfil. Against such a background, her relationship with her son – the one man whose nature she could shape and control, upon whom she could lavish love according to her needs, not his – became essential.

Certainly, Eugénie was attractive from an early age, with a round face, long, straight nose, soulful, rather hooded eyes, and a shock of red hair which earned her – to her mortification – the nickname 'Carrots' among her English school-friends. While seldom able to challenge her mother's authority directly, she found an outlet for her rebellious streak in her own unconventional and boisterous behaviour. One eye-witness recalled her typically striking appearance at a bullfight:

> Her slender figure is set off by a costly bodice, which enhances her beauty and elegance. Her hand is armed with a riding-whip instead of a fan, for she generally arrives at the circus on a wild Andalusian horse, and in her belt she carries a sharp-pointed dagger. Her little feet are encased in red satin boots. Her head is crowned with her broad golden plaits, interwoven with pearls and rich flowers; her clear brow shines with youth and beauty, and her gentle blue eyes sparkle from beneath long lashes which almost conceal them. Her exquisitely formed nose, her mouth, fresher than a rose-bud, the perfect oval of her face, the loveliness of which is only equalled by her graceful bearing, arouse the admiration of all. She is the recognised queen of beauty. It is she who crowns the victorious toreador, and her white hands present him with the prize due to his courage or agility, while she accompanies her gift with the most captivating smile.'[9]

Manuela's reaction was predictable. The more her daughter attempted to step out from her shadow, the more she reined her in, criticising and belittling her, even in public. 'I am treated like a donkey,' wrote Eugénie with all the hallmarks of teenage angst, 'and beaten before people [and] it is more than I can bear.'[10]

Inevitably under the circumstances, Eugénie's early attempts at romance proved disastrous. In Paris both Eugénie and Paca had befriended the young Duke of Alba, whose rich ancestry connected him to both Jacobite and Spanish aristocracy. They met him again, later, in Madrid, and Eugénie formed a deep attachment to him. Manuela, however, had other ideas, and bullied him instead to propose to Paca; a double betrayal which left Eugénie distraught. Then, on a trip to Paris, Eugénie was courted by the son of the American Minister to Paris, but his parents insisted Eugénie should renounce Catholicism, and bring her future children up as Protestants – and to that she could not agree. When she fell for the Marquess Pepe de Alcanizes she discovered he, too, was in love with Paca, and had merely used her to get close to her sister. Even before she met Louis Napoleon, Eugénie had become disillusioned with men, and her disappointment had emerged in a wilfulness and temper which had made her the terror of Madrid society.

Against such a background, Eugénie was ripe to fall victim to the Bonaparte legend. She apparently met Louis Napoleon for the first time in London in 1847, but, as one biographer wryly observed, 'both had been tossed about the world in a life of change and adventure [and] there may have been an earlier interview at some continental watering-place'[11]. Certainly, by 1848 Eugénie was writing to Louis to encourage his political ambitions, and in October 1852 she had been present in Paris to see Louis, appealing for public support, ride unescorted through the streets. In that moment, both were held in thrall by the power of the Bonaparte legend; Louis, sublimely confident of his own role as Napoleon's deserving successor, and Eugénie lost in wonder. A month later, Louis invited Manuela and her unmarried daughter to the hunt at Fontainebleau. His interest was clearly aroused; when Eugénie's horsemanship caught his attention, he made her a present of the horse she rode. One afternoon, as Eugénie and several other women were gathered on a balcony to watch Louis' party return from hunting, Louis called up to them 'How can I reach you, *mesdames*?' In the witty replies that followed, Eugénie's was pointed; 'As for me, Prince,' she said, 'the only way I perceive is through the chapel'.[12]

But if Louis was genuinely captivated by the pretty Spaniard, nearly twenty years his junior, he was still prepared to set matters of state before personal fulfilment. Indeed, his own record in the marriage stakes was as chequered as every other aspect of his life, for the needs of the Bonaparte dynasty were paramount. Since he looked to his mistresses for affection and sex, such needs held no priority in his search for a wife. As a young man, he had hoped once to marry his cousin, Princess Mathilde – Jérome Bonaparte's daughter. But Jérome was embarrassed by the fiasco of the Strasbourg affair, and broke off the connection, to Louis' disappointment. Through the years of his struggle he considered himself too busy to take a wife, but once ensconced in the Tuileries he began to cast about for a suitable alliance. An early candidate was Princess Caroline of Sweden, a match which would have brought Louis immense political influence because of Sweden's Russian and Austrian connections. But these countries had both suffered too heavily under the great Napoleon to ally themselves with his upstart nephew, and

Caroline was quickly married elsewhere. Nothing daunted, Louis cast a glance across the Channel, and made approaches instead to Princess Adeleide, the seventeen-year-old niece of Queen Victoria.

This move sent a thrill of horror through the British establishment. Although the Queen herself had mixed feelings towards Louis, Prince Albert was firmly set against him. Albert's family, the Coburgs, had risen steadily in power and influence in Europe in the post-Napoleonic years, and were deeply distrustful of the resurgence of Bonapartist fortunes. Although Louis had shown no inclination to renew the traditional French hostilities with Britain, a wave of Francophobia, encouraged by Prince Albert, had swept through England on Louis' accession, and fear of invasion prompted a flurry of fort-building along the south coast. Moreover, Albert, with his narrow views on sexual morality and firm belief in the sanctity of family life, conceived a strong personal antipathy towards Louis, whose philosophy of life seemed to him licentious and corrupt. Like those of Princess Catherine before her, Adeleide's personal ambitions were sacrificed to the need to keep Louis in his place. Queen Victoria herself was relieved. 'I feel', she wrote to Adeleide's mother,

> That your dear child is *saved* from *ruin* of every possible *sort*. You know what *he* is, what his moral character is (without thinking him devoid of good qualities, and even valuable ones) ...
> ... I ask you if you can imagine anything worse than the fate of that sweet, innocent child ...[13]

Louis received a formal rejection of his proposal at the beginning of January 1853. He took it philosophically; two weeks later he asked Manuela, Comtesse de Montijo, for her daughter's hand in marriage.

There were, of course, objections – from his political enemies, from his family, from Eugénie's rivals, and from Louis' mistress – but Louis had proved himself to be a man who was not easily thwarted. The pair were married in a civil ceremony on 29 January 1853, and the following day, amidst much pomp, at Notre Dame. Queen Victoria sent a lady-in-waiting to report on the minutest details of Eugénie's appearance. The Empress had looked stunning, she recalled, but added with some relief 'that a sort of national prejudice made me attribute the grace and dignity of the scene, for what there was of either came from her, to the blood of Kirkpatrick!!!'[14]

In the honeymoon period which followed, the couple seemed genuinely happy. Napoleon managed to stay faithful to his wife for at least six months, while Eugénie relished her role as Empress. The Court of the Second Empire was characterised by an informality which shocked diplomats from stuffier climes. It was not unknown for Napoleon to receive official visitors with Eugénie sitting coyly on his knee, while Eugénie's parties became famous for an almost childish boisterousness. Yet, over all, there was the destiny of France – and that of the Bonapartes – to consider, and scarcely a year after his marriage Napoleon became embroiled in the first of his great foreign adventures. It was to be his most successful, and it had unexpected consequences for his family.

In March 1854 France, Britain and the Italian kingdom of Sardinia went to war with Tsarist Russia. The immediate cause was an obscure quarrel between the Orthodox and Catholic churches over the right to protect the Christian Holy places in Jerusalem. Jerusalem was part of the Moslem Turkish empire, and Russian support for the Orthodox position led to Russian troops being assembled on the borders of the Turkish Balkans. Britain and France rallied to the aid of the rival Catholics, and, quite suddenly, the European powers were on the brink of armed confrontation. After some mutual indecision, the Allies decided to send an expeditionary force to threaten the Russian Black Sea fleet at its base at Sebastopol, in the Crimean Peninsula. The experience would be a challenging and harrowing one for all concerned.

For most of the participants, it was the first major war since the time of the Great Bonaparte, and the Allies proved singularly ill-prepared for the task. Two years of bungling, logistical inefficiency and mutual suspicion followed, leaving the troops in the field to struggle with the consequences of tactical ineptitude and the harsh Crimean winter. Moreover, such was the novelty of British and French troops working together that neither army quite got over it; the senior British commander, Lord Raglan, who had learned his trade under Wellington and lost an arm at Waterloo, referred to the enemy as 'the French' throughout the campaign.

Nevertheless the war afforded Louis Napoleon two great prizes; the chance to associate new French military successes with the name of Bonaparte, and the opportunity to grow closer to Britain.

Napoleon had an affection for Britain born of his days in exile, and was aware that closer ties across the Channel could only enhance his international standing. His first attempts to strike up a friendship with the British Royal Family had been rebuffed, however. Prince Albert had been so shocked at the suggestion that they should meet in person that he had sent his brother – a notorious rake – to act as family ambassador, on the basis that he, at least, could not be contaminated by Napoleon's morals. But as the war progressed, it became difficult to avoid the issue without offence and threat to the alliance, and in the middle of April 1855 Napoleon and Eugénie paid their first state visit to England.

In the battle of wills that followed, the French won hands down. Napoleon – the oldest of the group – was by far the most worldly, sophisticated, charming and politically adroit. In the stuffy Germanic atmosphere of the English court, he and Eugénie sparkled. Accustomed as we are now to the dour, drab image of Victoria in later life, it is easy to forget that, before the strain of motherhood and grief pinched the zest for life out of her, she was actually quite pretty. And Napoleon knew how to deal with pretty women; he flirted shamelessly, listened earnestly to her views on politics, and was wise enough never to cross the line into impropriety. Victoria, to whom charm must have been something of a novelty, was won over. Even Albert, deeply suspicious as ever, thawed when he realised that the Emperor spoke French with a German accent. Moreover, Albert's resolve wilted, too, in the sunshine of Eugénie's smile. When the Imperial party returned home, Napoleon took with him the Order of the Garter. It was tacit recognition that the rifts of the earlier generations had been healed, and that he, the *parvenu*, the upstart Emperor, had been accepted by one of the most conservative royal houses of Europe. '*Enfin*', he told the Queen triumphantly, '*je suis gentilhomme!*'[15]

Four months later Victoria and Albert made a tentative visit to Paris, and returned unscathed. A genuine affection had grown up which would survive the uneven politics of the next twenty years, and ultimately provide the Bonapartes with a sanctuary they would one day sorely need. Moreover, when Victoria learned that Eugénie was pregnant, she felt an immediate sisterly bond with her, and the Queen – who had already endured the risks of the maternal bed eight times – poured forth a stream of sound practical advice.

Eugénie needed it. For Napoleon, of course, an heir was of the greatest importance, and he had set too on his duties with gusto. But Eugénie had already suffered two miscarriages in succession, and although Napoleon – to his credit – showed only concern for her safety, he cannot have been immune to doubts about her suitability as a mother. He was all the more delighted, therefore, at the news of a successful conception. The doctors pronounced that the child was due in the last week of March 1856, an omen of mixed fortunes, since the King of Rome, whose brief life had embodied so many Bonapartists hopes and disappointments, had been born on 20 March. As the date approached, the Emperor and Empress personally selected their suite to care for the child; a grand governess, and two under-governesses – widows of officers killed in the Crimea – an English nurse, Miss Shaw, and a Burgundian peasant woman as wet-nurse. Eugénie's mother hurried to Paris to be at her side, while the Bonapartes gathered to witness the event which would shape their future. Among them was King Jérome's son, Prince 'Plon-Plon', in a foul temper because, if the child were to prove a boy, he would effectively be disinherited.

Against such a strained atmosphere Eugénie's labour began on Friday 14 March, and lasted throughout the weekend. The birth was a difficult one – despite the fact that the Emperor had authorised the doctors to use whatever pain-killing drugs they felt necessary – and at one point Louis was asked to choose between the life of his wife and his child. He chose his wife. Yet in the event, the baby arrived safely at 3.15 am on Sunday 16 March. He was a large and healthy boy. Napoleon was overjoyed; he rushed from the room, and kissed the first five people he met. The only moment of contention came when the Bonapartes signed the *acte de naissance*. 'Plon-Plon' refused to sign, and his sister, Princess Mathilde, rounded on him; she had waited long enough, she muttered, and did he think by not signing he could put the baby back? He signed in such bad grace that he left a large blot to posterity.

Within hours the peace of the Paris night was disturbed as the guns at Les Invalides announced the birth with a salute of a full one hundred and one guns. The boy was baptised with the full gamut of Bonaparte family names – Napoleon Eugene Louis Jean Joseph. For a while Napoleon toyed with settling upon him the title King of Algiers, but chose instead the honour Prince Imperial. And thus he was to be known throughout his life, for the title Napoleon IV was destined to elude him.

For the most part, France and her allies were delighted with the new arrival. However farcical Napoleon III's early career had been, however unlikely he had been to step in the footsteps of his great predecessor, he had undoubtedly arrived, and now it seemed that the Second Empire might surpass the First, by surviving into the span of a second generation. Moreover, the birth coincided with the last spluttering shots of the war in the Crimea, from which French arms had emerged with what few honours there were. There was much to celebrate, and Paris celebrated in style.

Yet the birth had left its mark on Eugénie. She was exhausted by it, and it was two months before she could walk without support. One of her physicians, Dr Barthez, found her

> ... greatly changed. The first time I saw her in 1854 I should have
> said she was twenty-four to twenty-five years old; today she looked
> a good thirty-five. Her painful confinement and the long recovery
> therefrom have faded, coarsened and yellowed the skin of her face,
> which I had thought so fine, transparent, and youthful.[16]

The baby Prince, by contrast, looked well:

> The Prince was sleeping very quietly, his little dimpled hands pret-
> tily resting in the manner peculiar to very young children … [he]
> has a fat, strongly marked face, full cheeks, rather pale, and perhaps
> a trifle flabby. He is like all milk-fed children: his colour is of a dull
> white; he is fat, and a little flatulent, not excessively so.[17]

The change in Eugénie was to have a marked effect on her relationship
with her husband. The doctors pronounced that the birth had been such
a shock to her system that to have further children would be highly
dangerous. Effectively, this meant an end to an active sex life, and it
underlined an unstated truth in their relationship. For all her flirty
nature, Eugénie seems never to have really enjoyed sex, and this experience merely confirmed her growing cynicism with her husband's needs.
Napoleon, on the other hand, had never equated sex exclusively with
love. The result was that he continued to seek his pleasures elsewhere,
while she took strength from her new independence. Ironically, the
lack of physical intimacy created other dependencies, for as he came to
recognise Eugénie's growing strength of character, Louis came to lean
increasingly on her political opinions.

Both, however, remained devoted to their son, but in different ways.
The Emperor, ever good natured, fell into the role of the doting father,
openly affectionate and over-protective. Eugénie, on the other hand,
maintained an emotional distance, opting instead to control and manip-
ulate his emotional development. The child of a domineering mother
herself, and with a history of unfulfilling personal relationships, she
shied away from over-familiarity, yet remained almost obsessive about
her son's well-being.

And there was no doubt that this new arrival was a true Bonaparte,
for military honours and badges of glory were showered upon him
from birth. At just two hours old he was draped in the ribbon of the
Légion d'honneur, 'and seemed to understand, without any surprise, the
honours that were paid to him'[18]. At six months he was introduced to
riding, and strapped to the saddle of a tiny pony, selected to suit his
size. Scarcely before he could walk, he rode beside his father at military
reviews. Before his first year was out, he was enrolled in the 1st Regiment
of the Grenadiers of the Guard, and photographed in a miniature uniform. Indeed, almost every aspect of his childhood took place before the
camera, and he was photographed in and out of uniform, on horseback,
with one or other parent, or both. He was the subject of regular press
releases from the Tuileries. In his way, the Prince was among the first of

a generation to experience that very modern phenomenon – a life lived in public by virtue of almost constant media attention. For the most part he seemed untroubled by the experience, although his round, slightly chubby little face looks out from these early images with a blank, serious expression. Indeed, from birth he seemed to accept everything that took place around him with an air of detachment, born of boredom and resignation, and Dr Barthez, for one, feared that his carefully controlled environment was not sufficiently stimulating:

When all is said, I am not at all surprised at this quiet and serious manner. It may be a result of the Prince's temperament, but it must be increased by his habitual environment. There is never any familiarity in his presence; all those he sees are in full dress, all are quiet in their manner, and notice no-one but himself. He is the point of departure and the goal; the prime centre of a calm, regular, monotonous movement. He lives in spacious apartments, and is carried, for his airings, under lofty trees, or along a wide terrace with a distant view. He knows nothing of the laughter, the jumping, the change of expression, the tears, the angers, the delights, which vary life when a number of children are together; all matters that the very youngest babies regard with interest and curiosity, and through which they become animated and develop themselves; which they understand and remember, from which they form conceptions and begin to learn sooner than is thought.[19]

In his infancy, Louis' education was erratic, administered by the ladies of his household in an indulgent manner, and overseen by the Emperor himself. When he was seven, he was given into the care of male tutors, and a soldier – General Frossard, one of his father's ADCs – was appointed head of his household. Thereafter his education became more structured, but he was never subjected to the extremes of discipline and isolation with which Queen Victoria and Prince Albert tormented their offspring. He could not, of course, attend a normal school, for fears about his security. Instead, teachers were brought to him, and his world was bounded by the confines of the royal palaces. His routine remained largely the same from the time he first began school work. He was awakened at 6.30 by his aides, was offered a light breakfast, then studied for two hours. Then he was allowed to walk in the Tuileries gardens, if the weather permitted, for half an hour, before being taken in to greet his father. The morning passed in school work, the afternoon in a ride on horseback, or in a carriage. Two more hours of lessons followed in the early evening, until he joined his parents for dinner. Much of his time he spent with adults, and his friends of his own age were limited to the children of the inner circle and staff. His main childhood friend and companion was Louis Conneau, the son of his father's physician, Dr Conneau. It was an isolated life, in which the progress of the wider world could only be discerned at a distance, through the palace gates. On the whole, Louis was bright enough, but intellectually lazy; he saw no reason to exert himself over matters which held no interest to him. Perhaps he had already grasped the obvious truth; that his life was predestined to a path which only a sudden and unexpected calamity could derail. It was possibly to alleviate this sense of stifling certainty that Louis developed a reckless streak; or perhaps it was simply a trait he inherited from his mother. As Augustin Filon, who tutored him through adolescence, recalled:

> ... this restlessness became a matter for uneasiness ... when he was playing with his comrades. Then we could not control him, and he would not control himself. Once started off, he would soon have gone through a glass partition, a closed door, or jumped out of a window; he lost every notion of the real or the possible. Even in cold blood, danger courted willingly and deliberately was the greatest pleasure he knew, and there was hardly a day that he did not submit his poor tutor to the most grievous trials by this taste for the most difficult and perilous games. One day as I was going into his study at Saint Cloud, I caught sight of him walking above the void outside the balustrade of the balcony, going from one window to the other along the narrow ledge of the surbase. I drew back swiftly, that he might not see me; if he had no fear of killing himself, he was very much afraid of being scolded, and I feared lest this dread might make him lose his balance ...[20]

Always in his life there was the presence of his grand-uncle, the Great Emperor. Napoleon III had quite deliberately and shrewdly given his son's symbolic care into the joint hands of the army and navy, then set about investing him with all the dreams of glory that still attached to the name Bonaparte. It was a move which struck a chord among the French people, for whom two generations had passed since the calamities of 1815, and who looked back with ready nostalgia on the days of *La Gloire*. Louis was never allowed to forget the giant footsteps in which he trod, even as a child, and the hopes which he embodied. As the Abbé Deguerry once gently explained to him, when he was old enough to understand,

... do you know that I paid you my first visit with many grown up gentlemen, when you were still not quite forty-eight hours old? ... You had the red ribbon already. Now what had you done at two days old to deserve the Legion of Honour? ...

... You had been given the cross, not for the services you had rendered, but for those you will one day have to give. The cross is the symbol of sacrifice. The one that was placed in your cradle meant that you had been marked out from your birth to devote yourself to the people.[21]

Louis grew up fascinated by war. Not by its reality, of course – not by the human face, the rich crop of corpses reaped in the field by industrialised weapons of mass destruction, nor by the horrors of the casualty clearing station, nor the pain of bereavement and the degradation of insecurity and hardship that went with it. Nor even by the unglamorous but essential and increasingly fashionable work of planning, of mobilisation and logistics. To Louis, war was ever a romantic and noble affair, an issue of individual courage, honour and self-sacrifice, in which the image of the first Napoleon, young, dashing in his glittering uniform, leading his troops to victory in the Italian campaign, was always at the forefront of his mind. As a boy, he showed a natural artistic flair, but the subjects of his sketches were invariably military, and telling in their style and content; he sculpted the noble Grenadier of the Old Guard, and sketched dashing German cavalrymen from an age gone by. He grew to manhood in a dream-world of military distinction, lost in the romantic imagery of conquest and glory, of Gros' study of Napoleon at the bridge at Arcole, or David's vision of the First Consul as a latter-day Hannibal, crossing the Alps – and no less unreal.[22] Like his father before him, Louis drew inspiration from the past, and found meaning for the future within it – and all without the faintest idea of what war really meant. His was, perhaps, the last generation for whom such illusions were possible.

In that he was lucky, for he was spared the insecurities which had plagued the early lives of both his parents. He was the first head of the Bonaparte family from the time of the Revolution to grow up in a protected environment, confident of his inheritance. If the first Napoleon had seized his chances as thrones toppled around him, and the third had braved ridicule and imprisonment to win his by sheer tenacity, all his son was required to do was wait. And in the time of his gilded youth, only the most perspicacious saw the clouds that were gathering on the distant horizon.

It was through the medium of Napoleon's foreign policy that the sun first began to set on the Second Empire. In April 1859 Napoleon committed France to the cause of Italian liberation, and went to war with Austria. The Emperor had stayed in Paris throughout the Crimean War, but on this occasion he was determined to command his army in person, and set out for the front, leaving Eugénie to act as regent. At Magenta on 4 June he drove a superior Austrian force out of the town in a battle which suggested, for the first time, just how destructive modern weapons could be. Despite middle age and the onset of ill-health – years later, when it was too late, he was diagnosed as having a stone in his bladder – he had remained doggedly on the field, his face deliberately impassive, enthusing his subordinates with the power of his name, if not his tactical flair. Before the month was out, he was in action again, at Solferino, when the French and Italians again triumphed, at the cost of 17,000 of their own dead, and 22,000 Austrians.

Napoleon III was sickened by the slaughter. In that, he was very different to his uncle, who was inured to the human cost of victory. After the battle of Eylau, Napoleon I had turned over bodies lying in the bloody snow with his foot, muttering 'Small change! Small change! A night in Paris will soon adjust these losses.'[23] In the aftermath of Solferino, the wounded of both sides lay out in the sweltering heat for days with no one to tend them, while local peasants stripped them of their clothes and possessions. So dreadful was the sight that a young Swiss stretcher bearer and later philanthropist, Henri Dunant, was moved in 1864 to set up an organisation of recognised neutrality to tend the wounded of both sides – the Red Cross.

When news of the victories reached Paris, the young Prince Imperial's reaction was typical. When told that his father had won a great victory, Louis replied, 'Only one? My great-uncle won a great many more than that!'[24] Indeed, he was already turning into a chip off the old block. On one occasion a few years later, Louis and his mother were on a yacht which missed the entrance to the harbour on its return at night, and grated against the harbour wall. Eugénie, fearing they might be wrecked, called out 'Louis, don't be afraid'. Her son replied calmly 'A Napoleon is never afraid'.[25]

In the event, Napoleon III had missed his chance to be the saviour of Europe. His successes against Austria brought only limited liberation for Italy, and it would be Garibaldi and Victor Emanuel, not he, who would win the laurels for unification. Neither did he foresee that the emergence of a united Italy would merely create one more political rival in Europe. Moreover, Austria's embarrassment played into the hands of another rising star, more sinister by far. Count Otto von Bismarck of Prussia, stern, authoritarian, matched Napoleon in patriotic fervour, and excelled him in drive and ruthlessness. Bismarck's dream was to bring unity to the patchwork quilt of independent Princedoms which constituted Germany, with Prussia at the centre. Bismarck, afraid at first of French military might, began to sense that Napoleon's vision had faltered, and over the next decade he strove to outmanoeuvre and marginalise France. Napoleon failed to see the danger, and pursued instead a flawed programme clouded by his romantic vision of the world, and of the Bonaparte legacy. In 1863 he backed the Austrian Archduke Maximilian in his attempt to establish an Empire in Mexico. The Prince Imperial, when told of the adventure, reacted typically; 'I congratulate you on the taking of Mexico,' he wrote to his father,

> I am delighted at it. Yesterday I went and told the soldiers in the guardroom that Mexico had surrendered, and everybody was delighted.
>> Your devoted son,
>> Louis Napoleon
> PS. This morning my horse had a fit of kicking, but I sat tight and did not fall.[26]

But in the end Maximilian was so ill-suited to his self-styled role that his regime collapsed, and Maximilian himself was shot by a republican firing squad. Napoleon's intervention had secured nothing beyond the ire of the United States – which was determined to allow no European influence in its back yard – and humiliation at home. The extent to which France had lost its way in Europe became brutally apparent in 1866, when the two newly emergent nations, Prussia and Italy, conspired to attack Austria. Napoleon hoped that his greatest rivals would destroy themselves in a long and costly war of attrition, and refused to ally himself to either side. In the event Prussian troops quickly and efficiently crushed the Austrians. Bismarck's prestige soared, Austrian influence declined – and France lost its claim as the arbiter of Europe.

Yet there was to be a last blossoming of French culture in that Imperial sunset. Napoleon hosted a Grand Exhibition in Paris in 1867, proudly displaying the best of French engineering, art and manufacture. The wealthy and powerful from all over Europe attended, and the Tsar of Russia even braved assassins' bombs to be there; only Queen Victoria, a widow now, grown Francophobe and suspicious of frivolity, stayed away. In 1869 French money and technical expertise were responsible for the opening of the Suez Canal, an engineering marvel which cut weeks off the travelling time to the east, and seemed to threaten British strategic domination of India – upon which so much of the influence of the British Empire was based.

Then, in 1870, quite suddenly, and with awful finality, it all collapsed. The ostensible cause was a quarrel with Prussia over the question of the Spanish succession. The Spanish throne was vacant, and Prince Leopold Hohenzollern had offered himself as a candidate. France, with her Spanish connections at the highest level, was outraged at the thought that the kingdom might pass to a German Princeling. The Prince withdrew, but Bismarck had judged that his moment had come, and deliberately provoked a diplomatic crisis. In Paris, crowds gathered singing the Marseillaise and shouting '*A Berlin!*', and Napoleon was pushed to the brink by a wave of patriotic fervour. On 19 July 1870 France went to war with the kingdom of Prussia. From the first, the Emperor was pessimistic, and told a stunned Assembly 'We are about to commence a long and arduous war'[27]. It was hardly an encouraging start to a campaign, but it was everything Bismarck had hoped for.

Again, Napoleon felt it his duty to command his army in person. On 28 July he took leave of Eugénie at the station at St Cloud. With him went the Prince Imperial, fourteen years old, and desperate for his first great adventure. Eugénie was to remain in Paris as Regent. As she waved her husband and son goodbye, she felt

> ... like a wild animal longing to take my little one far away into the desert and rend anyone who tried to seize him there. Then I reflect, and say to myself that I would rather see him dead than dishonoured ...[28]

According to Filon, her parting words were 'I trust, Louis, that you will do your duty'[29].

It soon became clear that the French troops were woefully ill-prepared. Napoleon's plan was to assemble eight army Corps, a total of 385,000 men, on the narrow Franco-Prussian border in the east. Dubbed the 'Army of the Rhine', this force would be under his personal command, and he hoped to make a quick strike into Prussian territory. In the event, French mobilisation was a shambles, and fewer than 220,000 men mustered at their appointed depots. Artillery, rifles, horses, equipment and even uniforms were in short supply, transport and logistical services were chaotic, and a general sense of bewilderment pervaded the ranks. Moreover, Napoleon himself was clearly no longer fit for the job. He was in almost constant pain now, and it exhausted him, clouding his judgement and corroding his spirit. Though he bore the long hours in the saddle with fortitude, he was incapable of the resolve and determination his role required of him, and from the moment he reached the front he slid into an ill-disguised pessimism.

Nevertheless, realising the importance to public morale of a successful demonstration, on 2 August he attacked the neat little town of Saarbrücken, just across the border. It was held by just one battalion of Prussian infantry, and two squadrons of Uhlans. The French force consisted of almost an entire corps – some 35,000 men. The Prussians made a brief stand, then retired in good order. Young Louis had been at his father's side watching the battle, and was exhilarated at what he saw:

> The Prussian batteries had withdrawn behind the wood that commanded the town; but only two shells reached us. They had still two or three companies in ambulscade behind a bridge, and they fired on all the mounted men that showed themselves. Papa wished to see nonetheless, and we heard some bullets. A splinter of a bomb was picked up quite near the Emperor; I had heard a noise as of old iron, but I didn't know what it was until later ...[30]

Indeed, once the battle was over and Napoleon rode forward to congratulate his troops, one of the staff dismounted and picked up a spent bullet, which he handed to Louis as a souvenir. Louis was delighted, but this simple gesture would earn him the scorn and ridicule of his enemies for years to come. For the moment, however, there was only elation; 'Louis has just received his baptism of fire,' Napoleon cabled to Eugénie,

> His coolness was admirable. He was as unconcerned as if he had been strolling along the Bois de Boulogne.[31]

The French occupied Saarbrücken for just four days. The British war correspondent, Archibald Forbes, who was present with the German forces, thought the whole exercise absurd:

> During their short stay in and about Saarbrück the French behaved with great moderation ... there was little cause for complaint; the French soldiers paid their way honestly. They did, to be sure, drink a brewery dry, but the brewer refrained from reporting them. A corporal attempted to kiss pretty Fraulein Sophie ... but a captain caught him in the act, ran him off the premises, and himself kissed the winsome lass. On the morning of the 6th the Prussian troops were back in Saarbrück ...[32]

It was the only French incursion into Prussian territory during the entire war. Even as the Paris newspapers announced Napoleon's great victory, three German armies – long since fully mobilised and prepared – had crossed the border between the main French concentrations. In a series of brisk engagements, they drove wedges between Napoleon's corps, and within days the French line began to crack. Napoleon himself grasped the seriousness of the situation, and offered to hand command to an experienced professional. His generals were relieved, but when the Emperor announced his intention to return to Paris, he was promptly over-ruled by Eugénie. The Empress had thrown herself into the role of Regent with typical determination, galvanising the government, dismissing the civilian administration and appointing a military government of National Defence. To her, Napoleon's suggestion smacked of defeatism, and she would not countenance the humiliation to the great name of Bonaparte. And so Napoleon stayed, trailing round in the wake of his armies with his retinue, doing what he could to encourage morale, yet painfully aware that his presence embarrassed his officers. The situation was deteriorating daily. The French attempted to rally on Metz, but found that the Prussians were already outflanking them. Part of the army tried to retire towards Verdun, but again the Prussians outmanoeuvred them, and they regrouped around the town of Sedan. The young Prince Imperial was bewildered by the sudden turn of events, and exposed at last to the brutality and chaos of modern war. At Loungueville the Imperial party sheltered in the château, where French troops were camping in the grounds:

> A crash awoke [Louis] with a start and he was sitting up in bed, bewildered, when his father entered with the exclamation 'Up, Louis! Up and dress! The German shells are crashing through the roofs.' As the Prince looked out of the window while he was hurriedly dressing, he saw a shell fall and burst in a group of officers seated in the garden at breakfast, and when the smoke lifted three of them lay dead ...[33]

By this time, Napoleon was full of foreboding. Everywhere the French forces seemed to be crumbling, and the Prussians were closing in. Worried for the safety of his son, Napoleon gave him into the care of three of his aides on 28 August, and set off with the army towards Sedan. For four days the Prince's party moved from village to village, keeping just ahead of the advancing Prussian troops. The countryside was alive with panicking civilians, French deserters, and rumours of catastrophe; on 1 September the party heard guns firing heavily in the direction of Sedan. Louis himself was reluctant to join what seemed to him flight. 'The Prussians are coming?' he said, 'well, we'll fight them.' Only the admonition 'what a coup for the Prussians if they took the heir to the Empire like a mouse in a trap!' persuaded him to keep moving.[34] Messages from the Emperor became erratic as he was swallowed by the fog of war, and instead Louis' aides appealed to Paris for instructions. Eugénie's response was revealing; in a despatch – never, in the end, sent – she outlined her stern disapproval of

> ... these wanderings from town to town. You must remain where you are. If the town were taken it would be time to hide him; you guard him and take him out secretly ... You have a duty more pressing than that of security; it is that of honour, and I feel that this retreat ... is unworthy of him and of us. Each one of us must carry out to the limit of his power the hard duties which are imposed on us. My heart is torn but resolute. I have had no news of my husband or you since yesterday. I am in terrible anxiety, but I wish above all things that each of you should do his duty. Always remember one thing: I can weep for my son dead or wounded, but to think of him fleeing! I could never forgive you if you allowed such a thing to happen ...[35]

Then, suddenly, there came a chilling change, and a telegram which read simply 'Start at once for Belgium'.[36]

It was all over for the Second Empire. Sedan had been a trap, and the French were systematically destroyed by German troops who outclassed them in every respect. Napoleon himself had risen to the occasion, riding fearlessly among his men to encourage them, heedless of his personal safety – perhaps even courting an honourable death – but it was hopeless. After an entire day of slaughter, he offered his surrender. The Prussians had not even realised he was present with the French forces, and were delighted. Bismarck himself dictated the surrender terms, and the Emperor was taken into captivity. Within days he was escorted across the Belgian frontier and lodged in the castle at Wilhelmshohe; ironically, it had once belonged to his uncle, Jérome. Where once the great Napoleon had set his brothers to be Princes over the Germans, now his successor was a German prisoner; the cycle had run its course.

Paris was aghast at the surrender. Eugénie, sustaining herself with coffee and chloral, worked desperately to keep the government together, but the support of the people collapsed, and all the simmering resentments against 'the Spaniard', the outsider, the perfect scapegoat, burst to the surface. On 4 September crowds invaded the Chamber, while Republican representatives announced the end of the Empire from the steps of the Hôtel de Ville. A boisterous crowd marched on the Tuileries, tearing down Imperial insignia. For a while it seemed that Eugénie would fulfil her destiny as a contemporary Marie Antoinette; then, at the last moment, she allowed herself to be led away, through a back-door and into the Louvre, and then to a carriage. Not quite knowing where to turn, she hurried to the house of an American friend, a dentist, Dr Evans. Evans realised the gravity of the situation, and at once took steps to smuggle her out of Paris. At Trouville he persuaded a rather startled English aristocrat, Sir John Burgoyne, whose yacht was anchored in the harbour, to take them across the Channel. Despite appalling weather, Burgoyne eventually agreed:

> At midnight I met by appointment two ladies, closely veiled, one of whom introduced herself to me as the Empress. I took her on board the yacht, and her only remark was 'I know I am safe now, under the protection of an Englishman.' She said, 'Pauvre France!', and became very hysterical for a time. Lady Burgoyne endeavoured to make the Empress as comfortable as possible, and as, not withstanding it was blowing a strong head wind, with a very heavy sea, it was so necessary that I should leave France, I went out of harbour and happily crossed the Channel, and landed the Empress safe at 6 a.m.[37]

Burgoyne had put his charges ashore at Ryde, on the Isle of Wight. Accompanied by Evans, Eugénie then took the ferry to the mainland, where Evans first heard the rumour that the Prince Imperial had also arrived in England.

Louis, too, had been forced to set aside his dignity in his escape from France. No sooner was the order received to flee than he and his aides put aside their uniforms, disguised themselves in civilian clothes, slipped out the back door, and caught an omnibus to Mons. By that same evening they had left French soil – Louis would never return. As they passed through Belgium, avoiding Brussels and heading for Ostende, the news of Louis' identity spread, and

> ... everywhere announced and everywhere recognised, he could not be wholly sheltered from the curiosity, sometimes a little vulgar and indiscreet, of the crowds that flocked to see him pass. At length, on the morning of 6th September, he crossed on the packet Comte de Flandres, which landed him at Dover in the early afternoon ...[38]

The tearful reunion took place in the Marine Hotel, in Hastings. There, in a modest suite in a rather dingy and run-down seaside hostelry, the Imperial family took stock of their spectacular fall from grace.

Their first priority was to find somewhere to live. When the news broke on 9 September that Eugénie and her son were in town, a curious crowd gathered outside the hotel to catch a glimpse of her. No fewer than twelve male admirers promptly offered to put their houses at her disposal, including the Dukes of Hamilton and Sutherland, while the Prince of Wales – who had fond memories of his trip to Paris in 1855 – offered Chiswick House. This gallantry earned him a rebuke from both the Foreign Secretary and his mother, who were appalled at the political implications, and were wary of too obviously embracing the refugees. Indeed, Eugénie herself was not insensitive to the delicacy of her position. She was technically still Regent of France, and a head of state in exile; quite how long either situation would prevail, she could not say. Rather than embarrass her hosts further, she instructed Dr Evans to find a property to rent as quickly as possible. He selected Camden Place, in the village of Chislehurst, Kent, and within days the Imperial party took up residence. There was little about Camden that was physically inspiring; it was an uninteresting Jacobean block with a Georgian facade, with no distinctive features apart from a great clock above the entrance. The grounds consisted mostly of lawns, with long rows of conifers which the French party found rather gloomy. Nevertheless, it was convenient. It belonged to a Mr Nathanial Strode, who out of gallantry offered it at a nominal rent. Under the impression that it was his duty to entertain his guests, Mr Strode remained in residence at first, until a discreet hint alerted him to the fact that Eugénie was uncomfortable living with her landlord on the premises. Thereafter Mr Strode contented himself with visiting his guests on Sundays. Ironically, the place was not without its Bonaparte associations; Louis Napoleon had once courted an English lady there, and more recently it had belonged to Elizabeth Howard – one of his more enduring mistresses. It is just possible that there was more than coincidence in this; the Emperor may have spoken of Camden Place in the past as a possible place of refuge.

The move to Chislehurst inevitably evoked mixed feelings. Here, over the next few weeks, surviving Bonaparte loyalists were to gather, and Eugénie formed a new court. It had little in common with the glamour and glitter of the Tuileries, as the tutor, Filon, recalled:

I recollect with what indifferent eyes we looked for the first time upon that featureless house, that front where there was nothing for the eye to dwell upon, except the Strode motto, engraved above the clock; *Malo mori quam foedari*. And yet that house was to play a historic part, to take a prominent part in the lives that were dearest to us. In that long gallery on the ground floor where we were setting foot for the first time, what an intense life was to be concentrated, how many hopes were to be born and die! ... The Prince entered there a pale and melancholy boy; he went out eight years later a bold and spirited young man, radiant with intelligence, overflowing with energy, glad to be alive, eager for action ...[39]

The Strode motto translates as *death rather than desertion*; in the light of subsequent events, it could hardly have been more appropriate to the new tenants.

The strain of those brief months had taken a conspicuous physical toll on the family. Visitors found Eugénie haggard and depressed, while Louis had withdrawn into his shell:

I could see the depth of the emotions he had passed through from the silence, the apparent oblivion in which he buried them. As a rule, when he came back from a journey he had a thousand and one things to tell. This time he seemed to remember nothing. He hardly spoke. His face, in which his impressions were generally reflected with so much animation, had grown pale and impassive like the Emperor's. One might decipher in it an immense and grievous fatigue in which his spirit shared, the fatigue of a child who had undergone a physical and mental trial beyond his years ...[40]

The general sense of anxiety was not helped by the news from France. The Prussian advance had continued, scattering the remaining French armies into pockets, and threatening Paris. Bismarck at first tried to negotiate with Eugénie, but soon realised she did not hold the confidence of the Republicans, and dismissed her as a spent force. In January 1871, after a dismal Christmas in which Parisians queued for food under desultory bombardment from the Prussian guns, the Republican government agreed to a truce. But the sight of Prussian troops in the streets of Paris was too much for the radical left of the city, who promptly disowned the Republic, and declared themselves a Commune. While Prussian troops looked on, the Republicans laid siege once more to the capital, and Frenchman killed Frenchman with all the bitterness only a civil war can unleash. France, it seemed, was to be spared nothing.

The armistice with Prussia brought one happy development, however, for Napoleon III was released from captivity, and he sailed immediately for England. His reception astonished him. Not only were Louis and Eugénie on hand to greet him as he landed at Dover, but enthusiastic crowds had gathered on the dockside. He was met by the same Mayor of Dover who had entertained him on his official visit in 1855 – when the world had been young. This reception was the product of a wave of noisy sympathy towards the exiles which had swept through Britain in the wake of news of the Prussian victories. Crowds jostled and cheered, there were shouts of '*Vive L'Empereur!*', and Eugénie and Napoleon were pelted with flowers.

Queen Victoria herself took the cue from her subjects, and the political establishment from her. At first, she had been wary of the French presence. Although she recalled their former closeness, she had been persuaded by Albert that French ambition posed the greatest threat to European stability. Since Albert had died, Victoria enshrined his views as if they held a religious truth. Yet the events of 1870 had confused her, for it had soon become apparent that Prussia, not Napoleon, had been the aggressor, and the British public had become deeply suspicious of wider German aims. For a Queen with so many links to Germany – her daughter was married to the Crown Prince of Prussia – this was problematic; nor had Albert's set views on European politics prepared her for this. She was sympathetic towards Eugénie, but it was difficult, too, to know how the unexpected turn of events would impact on Anglo-French relations in the long run. With her government advising caution, the Queen had therefore been slow to react, and it was not until 30 November that she visited Camden Place to pay her respects. She was clearly troubled by the changes which had come over her friend:

> There is an expression of deep sadness on her face, and she frequently had tears in her eyes. She was dressed in the plainest possible way, without any jewels or ornaments, and her hair simply done, in a net, at the back. She showed the greatest tact in avoiding anything that might be awkward ... The Prince Imperial is a nice boy, but rather short and stumpy. His eyes are rather like those of his mother, but otherwise I think him more like the Emperor ...[41]

Yet the public reacted positively to the move, and only a week after Napoleon himself arrived in Britain, Victoria received him at Windsor:

> At a little before three, went down with our children and Ladies and Gentlemen to receive the Emperor Napoleon. I went to the door with Louise and embraced the Emperor '*comme de rigeur*'. It was a moving moment, when I thought of the last time he came here in '55, in perfect triumph, dearest Albert bringing him from Dover ... He is grown very stout and grey and his moustaches are no longer curled or waxed as formerly, but otherwise there was the same pleasing, gentle and gracious manner ...[42]

A number of Napoleon's most ardent supporters crossed the Channel to join him in Chislehurst. His old friend Dr Conneau came to attend him, bringing with him his own son, Louis, who had grown up with the Prince Imperial. Assorted Barons, Baronesses, Counts and Countesses resumed their roles as aides and equerries. Franceschini Pietri returned to his job as the Emperor's Secretary, while the Duc de Bassano assumed the role of Chamberlain. Things began to seem familiar and comfortable again.

And yet, and yet ... what role, really, was there for an ageing 'Man of Destiny' in those years immediately following a catastrophic war, which seemed to have shattered the Bonaparte legend as much as it had ravaged the nation?

For France, the turmoil remained. The Communist uprising had reached its logical conclusion in a welter of bloodshed and fire in the streets of Paris. The Republic had won back control, and the Prussians had withdrawn, yet the future scarcely seemed certain or secure. Already, the shame of Sedan was receding in the minds of many, blotted out by the greater shame of the commune, and the golden twilight of the Second Empire was wrapped in the rosy glow of nostalgia. A steady stream of exiles, envoys and petitioners made their way across the Channel to visit Camden Place. Some came to express loyalty, some to suggest secret schemes, some to spy, some to seek their fortune, and others just came out of curiosity. It was difficult to sift the false from the genuine, but the fact that they came at all helped to revive Napoleon's spirit. He saw in these visitors confirmation that, one day, France would again turn to him. It was merely necessary for him to wait, as he had done so often before.

And so life at Camden Place settled into a peaceful routine, of receiving guests, of walking to the village to watch the cricket, of rebuilding the Imperial library, of reading and writing. For Napoleon, it was a tranquil setting in which to hatch new plans; for Eugénie, however, it was desperately dull. There was none of the spark of the old Court, of the excitement of mixing with great people, and of being at the very heart of great events, which had been life to her in the old days, and she fretted at their isolation. More worrying still was the effect on Louis.

The Prince showed little sign of emerging from the emotional torpor into which he had sunk. England and the dreary little house at Chislehurst made no impression on him; he took little interest in what went on around him, even less in his studies, and could only be roused by some reference to the situation in France. 'He had not,' Filon observed, 'the soul of an *émigré*, and he was a Frenchman even before he was a Bonaparte.'[43] Indeed, he had been raised all his life

secure in the knowledge of who he was, and who he would be; and
nothing of that, it seemed, remained to him. He was cast adrift, with
none of the familiar certainties of his childhood left to cling to. One
day he would still take his rightful place at the head of the family
– but now he would become Emperor of nowhere. One taste of modern
war had, it seemed, quite stripped the Bonaparte myth of its veneer of
glory.

Napoleon III, with time on his hands, had marked the change in his
son. He decided that Louis needed to be drawn out of himself, and
it was arranged that he should be allowed to attend classes at King's
College, in the Strand. It was not a success; Filon considered that most
of the students were as socially inferior to Louis as they were intellectually advanced. Most were older than he, and had already passed exams
which, with his interrupted education, he was not yet ready to sit. There
was a problem, too, in that Louis was a devout Catholic, and King's
College was resolutely Anglican. Although an exception was made to
admit him, the college environment seemed to the Frenchmen inexpli-
cable and alien, as Filon recalled:

> We had a disagreeable impression that first day we penetrated
> the corridors of King's College, filled with students who whistled
> incessantly. As in France I had never heard whistling except from
> the lower orders, for the moment I had some doubt as to the young
> gentlemen's designs; but almost immediately I became convinced
> that they were whistling for their own pleasure. 'It's not a school,'
> said the Prince, 'it's a nest of Blackbirds.' The Prince never entered
> into conversation with any of them and no one ever approached
> him. He would always have remained an alien in England if he had
> spent several years in those surroundings.[44]

Yet if his brief time at the college did little for his intellectual development, it broadened his mind in other respects, for it allowed him for
the first time in his life to escape the claustrophobic environment of the
Court:

> A London street has more to teach a young man, and especially a
> young Prince, than one would readily believe. At every step, before
> every shop, he had a question to put to me, and I an answer to give.
> When at Charing Cross some individual in a greater hurry than the
> others knocked against him as he passed, he turned round, very
> much surprised and amused; for him it was quite the novel pleas-
> ure to be elbowed. What an adventure to make his way into a café,

to sit down at a marble-topped table and to order an ice or a cup of chocolate from a waiter! What delight, above all, to stare without being stared at, to be a spectator instead of a spectacle, and so to see some of the innumerable little dramas of the streets! All of this was teaching him life, I mean the life common to all, of which up to then he had known nothing …[45]

And therein lay a great truth. Louis undoubtedly understood the importance of popular support as a power-base to Bonaparte ambitions, and did his best to sympathise with the plight of individual Frenchmen, yet he could never truly be a 'man of the people' as his father had been. He was certainly bright enough to perfect the noble gesture – once, in his youth, he had heard of an old soldier who had lost his savings, and he made good the amount with a note 'From a Grenadier to a Voltigeur' – but in truth great gulfs separated him from the hopes and aspirations of the ordinary Bonapartist supporters, upon whom his future would depend. Nor did his exile ease the situation, for Louis would spend his entire adult life away from France. The course of the upheavals of much of the nineteenth century had left its mark on the character of Napoleon III, perhaps few more so. He had seen governments rise and fall, seen glittering ambitions and the proudest of family names trampled in the dust, then rise again; had been on the streets with the jostling, ranting crowds; had endured prison, and still turned it all to his advantage. Moreover, if his virtues were those of an Emperor, his vices were only too human – his women, his gambling, his cigars. Louis knew nothing of these things. He had been raised in the cosseted and worthy environment of Royal palaces, emotionally secure, protected from his father's shortcomings, aware that for many the world revolved around him. The only aberration was the terrible events of 1870; even then, his physical discomfort had been brief, and he had been sheltered by a devoted band of supporters who had worked hard to contain the emotional damage, and to restore the future. Nevertheless, Louis' reaction had been revealing, even allowing for his youth; he had withdrawn into his shell, and with no reserves of his own to fall back on, he owed his recovery to the resilience of others. The contrast with his father was marked; the Emperor was, of course, older and infinitely more experienced, but the fall had been all the greater because it had taken place at a time when the opportunities for recovery were running out. Yet, old and sick and outcast as he was, Napoleon had turned his thoughts to recovery within a few months of his arrival in England. It remained to be seen to what extent Louis would prove his father's son.

Louis spent scarcely a term at King's College. When the long summer holiday of 1872 came, his mother took him touring to Scotland, then to the Isle of Wight. Here he visited Carisbrooke Castle and pondered the fate of Charles I, once held captive there. He learned to swim, and enjoyed the hospitality afforded at Cowes by the English aristocracy on their yachts. By the time he came to return to his studies, it had already been decided that he should not go back to London.

The change had come about because of a chance suggestion by Colonel Manby, a friend of Napoleon from the old days. Why not send the Prince to the Royal Military Academy, Manby suggested? The RMA was one of two British military establishments which had existed to train young officers in their craft. The Royal Military College, then at Sandhurst, was the oldest – it was founded in 1799 – and for twenty years it had trained young men in the arts of being cavalry and infantry officers. The Royal Military Academy, situated at Woolwich, south of London, offered a more technical education for those who wished to enter the Royal Engineers or the Royal Artillery. These were, of course, less fashionable arms of service, but the great Napoleon himself had been a gunner, and Woolwich would offer Louis the chance to follow in family footsteps.

The Emperor was delighted at the thought. It would not hurt to give Louis a sound theoretical knowledge of the military technique, as he himself had once studied it, and, more importantly, the prospect of donning a uniform might re-awaken Louis' enthusiasm. Manby raised the matter with the War Office, who made no objection – although of course it was understood that a foreign Prince, and moreover a Bonaparte, could not be allowed to take up a serving commission in the British Army upon graduation. The Governor of the College, Major General Sir Lintorn Simmons, readily agreed. Louis was ecstatic, and rose unexpectedly to the challenge. His educational achievements were considerably below the required entry standard, but according to Filon, 'The prospect of entering a military school stimulated the Prince to a pitch that surprised me. I had never seen him work with so much ardour, so systematically and regularly'[46]. Louis was called before an examining body, and was required to sit an entrance exam. To everyone's surprise, he passed. In November 1872 he took up his place at Woolwich. It had been arranged that Louis Conneau, his boyhood friend, should also attend.

The Governor had arranged for a small suite of rooms to be made available to Louis as a study. It was, however, too restricted to accommodate even his limited entourage – Conneau, Filon and a servant, Xavier Uhlmann – and a house was rented for him in Nightingale Lane, within walking distance of the Academy.

In many ways, it was a curious arrangement. Louis, young, lonely, still unworldly in so many respects, had been given a privileged entrée into a quintessentially English institution. 'The Shop', as it was universally known, was home to 200 young cadets who were bound together by a web of common experiences and attitude which were very different to his own. Here were the sons of officers and minor gentry, steeped in the hearty virtues of cricket and rugby, who had gone through the mill of the public school system, and who were often as emotionally distant from their parents as Louis was tied to his. Perhaps above all, they were characterised by an intense commitment to the cause of the British Empire, and to a tradition of military achievement personified by the Duke of Wellington, who still, just a generation after his death, cast a long shadow over the British establishment. Filon, at least, was aware of the deep incongruity of such an environment for, of all people, a Bonaparte:

> What did he feel when he put on the English uniform? He thought no doubt of another uniform, a French one this time, which he had been obliged to put off in haste on that afternoon of September 4th, 1870, and that thought must have awakened a memory always bitter. But in any case it was a soldier's uniform, and in becoming a soldier once more, he seemed to come nearer to France.[47]

When Louis began his studies, however, he was in for a shock. Just a few days after the start of his first term, Filon found him depressed. 'I have entered here too soon', he explained. 'All my school-fellows have had at least three years' mathematics: I have had hardly a year.' And it was true; discussing the matter with Simmons, Filon was taken aback by the Governor's bland assumption that Louis would pass through the course by relying on his rank alone. 'There were precedents,' explained Simmons, 'and ... several young Princes had already been through the school without taking any pains to become great mathematicians ...' Filon was indignant:

> I answered him that this solution would not satisfy our Prince, whose ambition was to approve himself at all points an efficient pupil, and to go through his officers' training in all seriousness. I saw by his eyes that his sympathy for the Prince was greatly increased by this, and he promised me that the masters would do all they could to help him through his early difficulties.[48]

Louis' reluctance to adopt airs, and his willingness to undergo the same trials as other cadets, undoubtedly helped overcome the wariness of his companions. If he could not understand the English passion for outdoor games, or the philosophy of team spirit and character building which they embodied – 'he did not meddle' with cricket and football, for he 'could not see the advantage ... and had no liking for showing himself, when it could be avoided, inferior to his comrades'[49] – he was at least willing to put up with the inevitable bullying, which even he realised was a rite of passage. The military colleges had, of course, inherited many characteristics of the stifling masculinity of the claustrophobic public-school system, including the full psychotic array of physical torments which had produced many a real-life Harry Flashman. Sandhurst had its 'ragging' and Woolwich is 'roshing', and as ever it was the newest recruits – the despised 'Snookers' – who suffered most. It was not Louis' conspicuous Frenchness that made him a target; he merely suffered with all the rest. His hesitant grasp of English led inevitably to confusion, for which he paid the price. Told by his classmates that he was to reply 'Very good, sir!' when addressed by an officer, he could not understand why this response, given to an officer who had admonished him for having fluff on his uniform on parade, earned him extra drill. Noticing that some cadets wore their forage caps at a jaunty angle, Louis assumed this was merely fashion and took it up, not realising that it was an unspoken privilege of the senior classes. That earned him a dunking in a cold bath; an affront to the Imperial dignity which so affected the bewildered Conneau that he jumped in beside him. When their fellow Snookers were required to run the gauntlet in an after-dinner 'roshing', clambering over an obstacle course of chairs and tables, while their seniors lined up to whip them along with swagger sticks, canes, belts and toasting-forks, Louis and Conneau refused to be excused, and completed the course in such quick time that they were sent round to do it again.[50] They did so without complaining, to the glee of their tormentors. Such punishment at least elevated them to that traditional position of acceptance accorded to outsiders in the public-school philosophy – that of the 'sporting funny foreigner'.

Yet Louis had scarcely settled into a routine at Woolwich when a fresh blow struck. At 10 am on 9 January 1873 he was called out of class to find one of his father's ADCs, the Comte de Clary, waiting for him with a carriage. His father's health had taken a turn for the worse. It was a short drive from Woolwich to Camden, but even so Louis recognised in the faces of the assembled doctors he met in the hallway that he was too late. He went straight to his father's room, to find him already dead.

The end had come quite quickly. Throughout November and December the Emperor had continued to plan a triumphant return to France. He was to sail secretly by private yacht to Ostende, then enter France via the Belgian border. The date – 20 March 1873, four days after Louis' 17th birthday – had been selected to coincide with military manoeuvres in France, in the hope that the army could be provoked into a show of support. Yet even as he schemed, Napoleon had been reluctantly forced to admit that his health was not up to it. A consultation had been arranged with Sir William Gull, the Queen's physician, who approached Sir Henry Thompson, a leading urologist. Thompson was worried by the size of the stone in Napoleon's bladder, and urged that a series of operations begin immediately. The second operation took place on 8 January, and Filon noticed a turn for the worse:

> … distressing alternations were observed in the patient: clouds swept at times over that calm, strong reason; dreadful memories obsessed him. He was asked, during an interval of lucidity, if the Prince should be fetched from Woolwich. The patient murmured;
> 'He must not be disturbed: he is at work'.[51]

One thought in particular nagged at him, and in his moments of rambling he came back to it often, for the answer it begged seemed to undermine so many of the principles by which he had led his life.

'We did not behave like cowards at Sedan, did we, Conneau?'[52]

The following morning Eugénie was about to leave Camden to visit Louis when the doctors called her back. As she walked to his room, she heard someone calling urgently for the priest, Father Goddard. Napoleon saw her enter, and weakly blew her a kiss; a few minutes later, he was dead.

The death of Napoleon III produced an outpouring of Bonapartist grief which threatened to overwhelm the young Louis. The Emperor was laid to rest at the Roman Catholic Church of St Mary's in Chislehurst, in what was little short of a state funeral. At Camden Place the Emperor lay in state in all the inevitable panoply,

> … dressed in his general's uniform, with his sword by his side, his kepi at his feet, the ribbon of the Légion d'Honneur across his body. On his breast, with a mother of pearl crucifix, rests the Star of the Legion, the Military Medal for the Campaign of Italy, and the Medal of Military Valour, a Swedish order only awarded to those Sovereigns who have been victorious in battle …[53]

On the day of the funeral – the 15th – a huge crowd gathered to line the route, for public sympathy for the exiles was still strong, and hundreds of Frenchmen had crossed the Channel to be present. Indeed, the funeral procession was led by a party of Parisian workmen, carrying – in a manner which somehow symbolised Napoleon's life – a large Tricolour on an improvised stick; the Republican government had confiscated their original flag in an attempt to prevent them attending. The mood was sombre and restrained until after the funeral, when one of the workmen saw Louis close by, and took the opportunity to call out 'Long live the Emperor! Long live Napoleon IV!'. To Louis' confusion, the crowd took up the cry. The new age had begun.

Queen Victoria herself, with her youngest daughter, Princess Beatrice, travelled down from Windsor to see the coffin a few days later. She found the experience all too sad:

> To the right of the altar, or rather below it, behind a railing, in the smallest space possible, rest the earthly remains of the poor Emperor, the coffin covered with a black velvet pall, embroidered with golden bees, and covered with wreaths and flowers of all kinds, many of which are also piled up outside, to which Beatrice and I each added one. The banner of the French 'Ouvriers' was placed near the wreaths ...
>
> From thence [we] drove to Camden House, where at the door, instead of his poor father, who had always received me so kindly, was the Prince Imperial, looking very pale and sad. A few steps further on, in the deepest mourning, looking very ill, very handsome, and the picture of sorrow, was the poor dear Empress, who had insisted on coming down to receive me. Silently we embraced each other and she took my arm in hers, but could not speak for emotion. She led me upstairs to her boudoir, which is very small and full of the souvenirs which had been able to save ...[54]

Indeed, Filon saw those gatherings at Camden as more of a trial for Louis than the funeral itself. He was sixteen years old, and the full weight of Bonaparte tradition had descended upon him; he had no sooner buried his father than he found himself

> ... shaking hands with everyone, addressing a word of thanks and friendliness to those he recognised and doing his utmost to resist the infection of the sobs and weeping that greeted his coming. This terrible day was drawing near its close when at last he was able to go and weep in his mother's arms, the only one who remained to console him, to counsel and sustain him.[55]

And no sooner was the body cold than the political fall-out began. Plon-Plon, sensing an opportunity to re-assert himself within the family fold, descended on Camden Place. His manner was brisk and bullying, but if he had thought to seize the initiative by a show of authority, he had sadly misjudged the mood. He demanded to see Napoleon's will, and was appalled to see that it had been written as long ago as April 1865. The Emperor had left his entire estate to Eugénie; Plon-Plon was not mentioned. As usual, he took refuge in bluster, and accused Napoleon's aides of concealing an amended will. When Eugénie made an attempt at reconciliation, and offered to put aside their differences, Plon-Plon replied coldly that he would think about it, and left. A few days later he laid out his terms; he demanded that Eugénie acknowledge him as head of the Bonaparte party, and that he should become Louis' guardian until his majority. Eugénie exploded:

> He dared – would you believe it? – he dared demand that the person of the Prince Imperial should be confided to his sole care and surveillance! ... Do you realise the insult and all the threatening import of such a message? ... does the Prince, then, wish me to admit myself incapable and unworthy to bring up my son! What have I done to merit such an outrage?[56]

The die was cast. Plon-Plon had forfeited his last chance to influence the future of Bonapartist politics. When Louis returned to Woolwich in February, he was already, in the eyes of his followers, Napoleon IV. Before his father's death, he had signed himself 'Prince Louis-Napoleon'; now he took a simple title – *Napoleon*.

He did not return to Woolwich as he left it. The black crepe band that he wore round the arm of his uniform suggested an enforced maturity, and there were changes of life-style, too. A new, larger house – 51 Woolwich Common, a three-storey end-of-terrace – was rented, to allow for the addition of a page, a cook and a housemaid to the Imperial entourage. And almost immediately, life at Woolwich intruded on the closed world of Imperial grief. At 4 am on the day after Louis' return the household was awakened by the Prince's orderly; the Academy was on fire, and all the cadets were required to assemble on the parade ground.

In fact, fire had taken a firm hold of the Academy's central block, which housed the Library, archives and offices. It was a bitterly cold night, and cadets struggled to and fro, trying to salvage what furniture and records they could. When Louis returned to Filon the following morning, his hands and face were blackened with smoke. Indeed, Louis had apparently excelled himself in another regard, for at the height of the confusion it had occurred to the Governor that the most active and hard-working of the rescue party might appreciate a good breakfast. Turning to the nearest cadet – who happened to be Louis – he asked him to report to Lady Simmons, and tell her to prepare breakfast. Louis did so. Lady Simmons, not unnaturally, asked how many people would attend. Simmons had not thought to convey this thought to Louis, who resolved to show his initiative.

'All of them!' he replied, then saluted, and ran back to the fire. To his astonishment, when he repaired to his quarters with the blackened and tired work party at 8 am, Simmons found breakfast prepared for 200 people. Fortunately, his sense of humour was up to the occasion, and the cadets ate well that morning.[57]

Such excitements aside, Louis' remaining time at Woolwich was spent in the sobriety of routine and study. The day began with drill at 8 am (extra drill – 'Hoxters' – for defaulters was at 6.45 am). This lasted until 10 o'clock, after which there followed an hour and a half of lectures or study. At 11.30 there was a brief luncheon break – bread, biscuits, butter and a pint of beer – and two more hours of lectures, followed by Dinner Parade. Dinner followed, with more beer and a 'heavy duff', then recreation time, to sleep or work it off. An evening meal was available at the cadets' own expense, and two more hours of lectures followed in the evening. It was a brisk, healthy regime, which allowed Louis little time to dwell on his grief, and he thrived on it. Filon, indeed, recalled it as an idyllic time:

> In the long summer evenings, when the weather was fine, we used to go out and continue, under a sky full of stars, through the heart of the quiet countryside, the conversation that had begun in the little drawing room. We would follow the road from London to Gravesend, sometimes towards the great city, sometimes mounting towards Shooter's Hill ... the highwaymen that once infested the English roads have long ago disappeared, and no-one ever troubled our political speculations. Sometimes, the Prince would interrupt them by a word of admiration, a little start of artistic delight when at some turn of the road there appeared to us a corner of the landscape lit up by the setting sun or by the moon, the Thames, perhaps, smitten by a silver ray through the blueish mists that veiled it. One evening he stretched out his hand with a single word, 'Gustave Doré!'[58]

Louis had been accepted, too, by his fellow cadets, who had come to appreciate the charm of his Gallic mannerisms, and tolerated his un-English preference for individual distinction. His enjoyment of his own skill at fencing and horsemanship was so obvious and unaffected that it took the sting out of his tendency to 'show off'. Only in history lessons was there ever a conflict, and it required the Governor to address his sense of duty before Louis could be restrained from interrupting during accounts of the battle of Waterloo. No longer withdrawn, his buoyant manner and quaint accent had made him universally popular. Indeed, the P.I. – as everyone knew him – had not yet outgrown his taste for boisterous, dangerous, and usually rather pointless adventures. He was admitted to the clandestine Alpine Club – whose members were required to scale the Academy's roofs, and decorate the spires with chamber pots – and delighted in the sort of prank which still horrified Filon:

> We were crossing a bridge when the Prince left me suddenly, jumped upon the parapet, and from thence into space. I was terrified. I ran to the place where he had disappeared, and a happy outburst of laughter came up from the darkness. The bridge was not over a stream, but across a path that passed a dozen feet below. He speedily rejoined me, and evaded my scoldings by the cajolaries of a spoilt boy.[59]

Yet if Louis had come to appreciate something of the English life and landscape, his points of reference remained essentially French, while his future was entirely framed by his hope to return home as Emperor. A fashionable parlour game from the summer of 1873 has left an insight into his private thoughts. At smart dinner parties, guests were offered an album to sign, which 'demand your confession in the guise of answers to an unvarying set of questions'[60]. The English, of course, answered as a rule with a proper degree of flippancy, but Louis was typically earnest:

> What is your favourite virtue? *Courage.*
> Your leading Passion? *Patriotism.*
> Your idea of happiness? *To do good.*
> Your idea of unhappiness? *To live in exile.*
> If you were not yourself, who would you like to be? *Anybody!*
> Where would you like to live? *In France …*
> Your heroes in history? *Napoleon. Caesar.*
> Your heroine in history? *Joan of Arc …*
> Your present state of mind? *Sad.*

This sense of isolation from the mainspring of his life undoubtedly deepened as Louis' majority approached. It had been agreed that he would officially come of age on his eighteenth birthday – 16 March 1874. This would introduce him to a much wider involvement in the political affairs of the Bonapartists than had hitherto been the case – a possibility which had not escaped the Republican government in France. The Republic was losing popularity at home, and sympathy for the passing of Napoleon III, coupled with curiosity about the development of his son, had created an interest in the Imperial party of which the government was profoundly suspicious. As his birthday approached, the Republican press began a tirade of ridicule, aimed across the Channel. Louis they dismissed as *The Bullet Boy* – taunting him with the recollection of Saarbrücken – or *Napoleon Three-and-a-half*, or, on learning that he took an interest in cycling, *Vélocipède IV*. He was, they insisted, the class idiot at Woolwich (*le fruit sec*), and so unbearable in his airs that he was shunned by his classmates, who 'sent him to Coventry' (*en quarantaine*). Louis affected to ignore this abuse, but it clearly found its mark; he presented a photograph of himself, surrounded by his classmates, to Filon with the inscription *un fruit sec en quarantaine*.[61]

Under such circumstances, it was important to make a good impression on his 18th birthday, and a public ceremony was organised at Chislehurst. Despite a Republican prohibition, hundreds of Frenchmen again crossed the Channel, so that Chislehurst common

> ... looked like a Paris suburb on a holiday. Every kind of pedlary was going on: some sold papers, others photographs, medals, souvenirs, emblems. There was an alfresco café where the Prince's monument now stands. Thousands of English people enjoyed the sight, swelling the crowd and adding to the gay hurly-burly which kept increasing ...[62]

Invited guests were allowed into the grounds of Camden Place, where a large marquee had been erected. Here Louis was to make his political debut. A little nervous, he stood next to his mother on a platform at the end to make his speech. To everyone's relief, he spoke clearly and well, outlining the fundamental principles of Bonapartism, re-affirming his belief in the plebiscite, and dedicating himself to France. When he asked, rhetorically, 'Will France, if she is openly consulted, cast her eyes upon the son of Napoleon III?' there were inevitable cries of '*Oui!*' and '*Vive l'Empereur!*' At the end of the day, his supporters went home happy in the knowledge that this was no *fruit sec*.

Yet there were other, more subtle, reminders of the reality of his position. In the summer of 1874 his friend Louis Conneau was offered a place at the

French military academy of St Cyr. If he were not to place himself at risk of permanent exile, like Louis, Conneau was obliged to return; and in any case, as he passed into manhood, he too longed for the chance to return home. Louis did his best to make his congratulations sound genuine, but as he returned alone to the final term at Woolwich, where his English friends were eagerly pondering their future careers, his own prospects seemed as empty as ever. Two years later Conneau passed out of St Cyr and entered the French army as a sub-lieutenant, and Louis' reaction was telling. He sent him a sword, that ancient symbol of nobility, honour and courage, engraved 'Napoleon a L.N. Conneau. Passavant le Meillor' – 'Pass before the Best' – and a letter full of typically Bonaparte longing:

> If I have the happiness I long for, to fight side by side with you, I shall say, when I see you strike a good blow, 'Mon Dieu, that sword is Conneau, and Conneau's strength is in the sword'. And the sight of your courage will make me tremble for joy. If unluckily I have not the good fortune to share your peril, if I cannot strike some day in your good company – well, then, I shall comfort myself with the thought that this memorial to our close friendship will be with you wherever you go.[63]

Louis had taken his own final exams at the Academy in January 1875, and he tried hard to believe they marked not the end of a happy phase of his life, but a new beginning:

> I pass out of the School seventh, but I was first in the final examination. The Duke of Cambridge, as well as the Governor of the Academy, has been charming to me and my comrades have bidden me adieu in the warmest fashion. At length I have completed one section of my studies, and I am ready to begin others ...[64]

Louis was allowed to lead the Passing Out parade before the Commander-in-Chief of the Army, the Duke of Cambridge, and Eugénie was the guest of honour; she wept when the Governor, in his speech, singled out Louis for praise, and the cadets cheered their approval. His position among the graduates entitled Louis to a special privilege, for the top ten places traditionally secured a place in the Royal Engineers – the more fashionable of the Corps. But the great Napoleon had been a Gunner, and Louis turned down his place – to the delight of the eleventh man on the list. At a speech he made at a Royal Artillery Banquet a few days later, he explained why:

I hope the officers of this royal regiment of artillery will let me feel that I still belong to their corps. Thanks to England's kindness, I have been able to carry on the tradition of my family – always a family of gunners. I was denied an education in my own country, but I am proud to have had as my companions the sons of men who fought against us so bravely on many a field of battle.

Never can I forget these years spent at Woolwich, or cease to value the honour of belonging to a corps whose motto is *Ubique quo fas et Gloria ducunt*.[65]

With the end of his studies, it was time, too, for his faithful tutor, Augustin Filon, who had guided and taught him for more than seven years, to take his leave. 'When the wheels of the carriage that took me away sounded on the gravel at their first revolution', recalled Filon, 'it seemed that they were passing over my heart.' Yet for Filon, there was a consolation; he was free at last to return to France. For Louis, adulthood meant increased isolation, and the prospect of 'a special kind of university, the school of the Pretender'.[66]

What was he like, this young Bonaparte, on the eve of his 19th birthday, facing the world as his own man for the first time? Physically, he had matured, and sported his first thin moustache, but he was still below average height, rather slim and wiry, and short in the leg. On first impressions so many were struck by his lively, extrovert manner, but there was a trace of melancholy in the soulful eyes he had inherited from his mother, and it emerged in the earnestness which descended on him when he discussed France, and his future. One who met him about this time neatly summed him up:

As to appearance – photographs flatter him – bad complexion – legs too short – however, delightfully frank and winning.[67]

Physically, he was full of energy, but this was ill-suited to the life fraught with frustration and ambiguity which now lay before him. With no reserve of maturity to draw upon, he still sought an outlet in bouts of spontaneous and unpredictable skylarking. Vaulting into the saddle of his horse, leaping over chairs or tables, climbing the odd roof; it was if by commanding his courage and his body, he could somehow control his circumstances. Probably, as Adrian Greaves has observed, his suffocating childhood and the peculiar circumstances of his exile had made him a 'neurotic extrovert', with a need to compensate for his early under-stimulation and later insecurity by a conspicuous show of flamboyant behaviour.[68] Certainly, throughout his life, he delighted in attempting feats of physical daring which appalled more responsible temperaments, and indeed he seems to have secretly relished the disapproval of authority figures. It was, after all, one of the few statements of individuality available to him.

Yet in the first few years after his graduation, his life was particularly directionless. He watched his classmates from Woolwich take up their places in the British Army, and realised that – as a foreign national, and a head of state in exile – no amount of courtesy from the Queen or her government could ever open that route to him. Yet in some respects his time at Woolwich had merely served to highlight the futility of his position. If ever a man believed himself cut out to be a soldier, it was Louis; destiny propelled him, and his soul yearned for it. Perhaps, one day, with experience, he might even have been good at it; but his tragedy lay in the inescapable fact that by surrounding himself with soldiers, he merely confirmed that he was not one.

He did, at least, manage to secure an honorary position with a British battery. He approached the Duke of Cambridge to ask if such a position might be available, and the Duke did not object; the Queen, moreover, was rather touched. In 1875 and again a year later Louis was allowed to join G Battery, 24th Brigade, Royal Horse Artillery, for summer manoeuvres at Aldershot.

They were to prove happy times. Here Louis was free for the first time of the restraining influence of the Imperial household, and moved as an equal among British officers. He rode with the battery, supervised gun drill, and swapped professional observations in esoteric jargon with men who were too genuinely polite to point out that his role was largely superfluous. Here he made three lasting friendships, perhaps the only ones of his adult life which were based on common interests and mutual affection, which were free of the baggage of his past associations, and were not framed by his political aspirations. His friends were all young lieutenants with the battery – Arthur Bigge, a few years older than Louis and rather serious, who slipped easily into the role of elder brother; J.H. Wodehouse, and Frederick Slade. When the time came to share with them the dubious delights of life under canvas, Louis relished his first real taste of a soldier's life. To Eugénie he wrote:

Thank you so much for your affectionate letters I have just received, they have come to find me in middle of a horrible sea of mud. For the five days that we have been in tents, it has done nothing but rain; nevertheless, I find myself very well in this life, a complete novelty to me. Two days ago, the water invaded our canvas home, during the horror of darkest night; I found myself with my comrade, in the middle of a little lake, in which our belongings were floating about in a wretched state.

It was a painful waking ... I rescued our inundated chattels, made a pile of them on the canteen, the only thing that raised its head above the deluge, and went out of my tent ... Then armed with a shovel I dug a trench all round the tent, and in this way drained my dwelling at the expense of a shower-bath.

Our misfortunes have had no effect on the men's temper, they console themselves for the rain since they have a French cook. The cook is a delightful young fellow, endowed with the most exquisite qualities of body and mind ... This cook, you have already guessed from my description, is me ...[69]

From all the safety of peace-time soldiering, it was possible for Louis and his friends to indulge their fantasies of glory, and during the 1876 manoeuvres they posed for photographs in mock duel. There was a certain inevitability about the proceedings. Louis was one of the duellists and Slade the other; Louis, of course, was the victor – *Passavant le Meillor*. Even at play it would not do for a Bonaparte to be vanquished. Slade's elder brother, Captain J.R. Slade, acted as his second, while Lieutenant Richard Bannatine-Allason stood for the Prince. In the first photograph Louis waves a breezy salute to his foe; in the second, he runs him through, and in the third, wipes the non-existent blood from the blade. It is not clear if the sword he used for the photographs was one of those belonging to his great uncle, which he famously wore; if it was, it was the closest that blade would come in Louis' hands to the reality of the soldier's trade.

Moreover, that second summer saw an incident which had more than a touch of an omen about it. One evening Louis, showing off, tried to jump over a camp-fire; he tripped, and fell into it, burning his arm badly. He made light of the injury, and insisted on riding with the battery the following day, with the result that a doctor had to be called to attend him that evening. When he returned to Camden, his arm was in a sling.

In truth, the time spent with G Battery represented increasingly brief outbursts of adventure among the stultifying routine at Camden. Louis, of course, followed French politics no less obsessively than his father, and he was in close touch with M. Rouher, the head of the Bonapartist party inside France. With each fluctuation of Republican fortunes – the fall of the Thiers administration, the ascendancy of Marshal MacMahon, the Republican resurgency in the election of 1877 – dozens of sympathetic Bonapartists would scurry across the Channel to frame each new response. Louis was prepared to return to France by whatever means possible; he preferred the plebiscite, since he imagined himself returning on a wave of public adoration – but, if that were not possible, he was quite prepared to mount a coup. For all his eagerness, however, the fact remained that he was 'hardly known to the wider French electorate, to whom he seemed young and inexperienced, 'The Bullet Boy', and an unlikely candidate for real political power. He had much to prove if he were to earn the popular support he longer for, and the hard truth – which he never learned to accept – was that in the mid-1870s Bonapartism was largely peripheral to mainstream French political activity.

If Louis was not yet able to assume his rightful place in the world, however, he could at least enjoy his new adult status. He regularly accepted invitations to house-parties among the British, where his reputation for practical jokes spread. He rode with a number of English hunts, he frequented gentlemen's clubs, and he occasionally went out on the town with the Prince of Wales' Marlborough House set. Bertie, of course, set scant store by respectability, and was the subject of a good deal of scandalous gossip – about which, on the whole, he did not give a damn. At that time he was paying particular attention to the actress, Lillie Langtry. Once, during a particularly wild stay at Cowes, on the Isle of Wight, an attempt was made to stage a séance; it ended when Louis tipped a sack of flour over Bertie's head. On another occasion, Bertie and Louis dressed a donkey in women's clothing, hoisted it up to a first-floor window, then hid it in the bed of the son of the house.[70] The journalist, Archibald Forbes, recalled one particular bout of exuberance which would have a terrible echo in the years to come:

> [Louis'] craving for effect curiously displayed itself during a parade in Scotland of a number of Clydesdale stallions, at which were present the Prince of Wales and a number of noblemen and gentlemen. One horse, which was plunging violently, was described as never having allowed a rider to remain on its back. At the word the Prince Imperial vaulted onto the bare back of the animal, mastered its efforts to dislodge him, and rode the conquered stallion round the arena amid loud applause.[71]

Louis prided himself on his horsemanship, and had perfected the art of vaulting into a saddle; over the years, a number of commentators recalled his relish at performing this trick in public. Ironically, years later, his one failure in this regard would cost him his life.

Louis' association with Bertie inevitably raises an important question about his character; his relationship with women. Circumstances combined to prevent him forming a lasting relationship, with the result that rumours of affairs have persisted. Ten years after his death, *Le Figaro* suggested that Louis had enjoyed a secret mistress, Charlotte Watkins, a middle-class English woman whom he first encountered on a train, and who later bore him a child. When this child was later brought before Eugénie, however, she dismissed the story on the grounds that the baby had clearly been conceived several months after Louis' death.

A more persistent rumour concerned the possibility of a romance between Louis and Queen Victoria's youngest daughter, Princess Beatrice. Certainly, the two had met young, when Victoria first travelled to Camden Place in 1870 to visit the newly arrived exiles. Victoria, in her stern way, was a hopeless romantic, and may have enjoyed the possibility of an innocent friendship between two young teenagers. Yet in truth, there is little evidence that the relationship ever amounted to more. Beatrice cried on hearing of Louis' death in Zululand; but so, too, did the Queen herself, and many others, none of whom were in love with him. Beatrice's letters on first hearing the news betray a genuine sorrow, but not the desolation of one whose life's love has been taken. The Queen was, in any case, intensely protective of her daughters, allowing them to marry only after careful consideration. Beatrice she kept by her side, as her companion, for as long as possible; in the end, she did not marry until 1885, when she was twenty-eight, and nearly an old maid. There was, furthermore, one serious obstacle to any engagement; Louis was a devout Catholic, and Queen Victoria the head of the Anglican Church.

In fact, what little evidence there is suggests that Louis was shy of any sexual involvement with women. In all probability, he had been sheltered from the open promiscuity of his father, and had, in any case, been too young to understand it. The war of 1870 had removed him from the environment of the Imperial Court, with its ambiguous sexual morality, and he had spent his crucial teenage years either at Camden, or at Woolwich. By the time of his exile, Napoleon III was a spent and largely repentant force sexually, and for a short while, at this most impressionable age, Louis experienced the security of a monogamous family environment. Woolwich, of course, was an exclusively male affair, where sexuality was largely sublimated in intense physical activity. This remained something of a pattern with Louis, and perhaps explains his prolonged enjoyment of such essentially childish pursuits. Certainly, it was a love of pranks which he had in common with the Prince of Wales; the Prince's womanising probably served to underline the differences between them rather than the similarities. Bertie was fifteen years older than Louis, and there were gulfs between them which Louis had not yet learned to bridge.

Indeed, for much of his adolescence Louis had been dependent on his mother, and his arrested maturity probably had much to do with Eugénie's disdain for sex. Eugénie had learned to cope with her husband's infidelities by coming to regard them as a masculine frailty which was both inevitable and contemptible. In all probability, her view that sex was an unworthy distraction had affected Louis' own attitude. Certainly, he was said to have entertained a contempt for romantic intrigues, and at the age of twenty-three he commented significantly that 'I have not cared to let my wing be clipped by marriage'.[72] Louis had more important things on his mind, and as a Catholic he could not afford to let either his soul or his political ambitions be tarnished by an unworthy liaison. His tone to Filon in August 1878, commenting on such speculation, betrays a certain irritation:

> You speak to me of certain projects of marriage which excited friends have put forward. To marry was not the object … otherwise you would have been one of the first to know. It is possible that I may not wait till years have made me as bald as Corvisart, or 'pot-bellied' like Rouher, before entering upon marriage, but I have at present no definite intention of the kind. Doubtless I may not hope for the happiness of marrying according to my affections, but I know enough of life never to consent to marry against my inclinations …[73]

To Rouher he wrote, 'Marriage is a big question for a man who has made up his mind to fulfil all its duties'[74]. It may be that his obvious boyishness and physical exuberance, the need to impress in masculine rather than feminine company, concealed a prolonged adolescence, a sexual immaturity and inexperience which would persist to his death.

Certainly, the one dominant female in his life remained his mother. After Napoleon's death, Eugénie had accepted the inevitability of relinquishing many aspects of her direct influence over Bonapartist affairs. This was all the more necessary after Louis had come of age, for Eugénie was astute enough to realise that her own history might be a burden to him. While many Bonapartists now thought of her as a tragic figure, a martyr to the shattered dreams of the Second Empire – a view not entirely at odds with her own image of herself – many recalled her imperious manner and her influence over her husband, and blamed her for the Emperor's downfall. Those who had earlier resented her for her beauty and grand manner in secret now made little effort to hide their disdain. But if she was content to step back from the front rank of politics, she had no intention of abandoning her control over Louis. Filon captured something of her style:

She did not, indeed, renounce the right of giving advice; for instance, she would say, in connection with the visit of a new adherent, 'Do not speak much; let him speak and listen yourself. That is what your father would have done.' The tone suggests rather the mother who teaches than the Regent who commands, does it not?[75]

Thrown together in exile, Louis' tendency to depend on his mother – which had always been a strand in their relationship – grew more pronounced. Eugénie was the only member of Louis' close family upon whom he could rely to both understand his situation, and guide him through the murky waters of family politics. She represented, moreover, his one clear link with the Bonapartist traditions of the past. As a result he was torn by the dilemma common to many a devoted son of a dominant mother; he needed Eugénie's support and approval while at the same time he strove to establish his separate sense of identity. For Eugénie, the situation was largely true in reverse. Her sense of self, and what aspirations she retained, owed much to her role as the mother of a Bonaparte, of the next Emperor, of Napoleon IV, and it was impossible to disentangle her identity as Dowager Empress from her more intimate relationship with Louis, her son.

The situation was further complicated by Napoleon's will. Because he had made the will when Louis was a child, the Emperor had left everything to Eugénie, and nothing to his son. Louis was therefore called upon to act the role of Prince in exile without independent means. Camden Place remained his mother's house; while he lived there, he could not act as he saw fit without her approval, nor could he move out and set up his own establishment. While Eugénie gave him an allowance, Louis was always conscious that he remained financially dependent, and if Eugénie disapproved of his plans, she simply refused to pay for them.

To be tied to both his mother's purse and apron strings was an uncomfortable position for a Man of Destiny; it was all the more inescapable because she played so large and genuine a part in his emotional life.

Once the heady promise of Woolwich and Aldershot was spent, ennui settled over Camden Place. The occasional visits from Bigge, Slade and Wodehouse, the courtesy calls from English admirers, the constant trickle of schemers and dreamers from across the Channel, could not disguise the emptiness of the routine, and the over-familiarity of the Court in exile. In an attempt to escape it, Louis and Eugénie travelled. France was still closed to them, but they went several times to Arenenburg, where Louis drank in the heady Bonaparte atmosphere. They visited

Italy, and Louis paid his respects to the Pope, and pondered wistfully the great art of Florence. In July 1878 he went to Sweden, this time without Eugénie; he wrote to her with obsessive regularity. He struck up a rapport with the family of King Oscar, staying at his summer villa, and hiking and fishing in the woods with his sons. Everywhere, there were the same high spirits, and the same pranks. For the most part, he made a good impression, and the established heads of European royalty came gradually to accept the grand-nephew of the man their forebears had once considered the most dangerous of the age.

Yet at the end of it all, there was Camden again – and still no call from France. For a brief, significant moment, it seemed that he entertained hope of military service in Europe. In the autumn of 1878 Russia and Turkey were at war in the Balkans. Austria seemed poised to intervene, and Louis and his cousin, Napoleon Roccagiovine, hatched a plot to offer themselves to the Austrian army. The result was predictable, as Filon recalled:

> He dreamed of joining in that war, he and his cousin: hence the request sent to the Emperor Franz Josef, which the Empress, though much against her will, consented to transmit and support. She was greatly relieved to find that this request was not entertained; the Prince, on the contrary, was deeply disappointed, but speedily consoled himself when he discovered that the occupation of Bosnia gave rise to no incident of importance.[76]

Eugénie herself thought the whole idea unworthy of a Bonaparte, and her response had been scornful:

> If there is no war you will spend your time in an Austrian garrison playing billiards and making love to an Italian singer. If there is a war you will fight against the poor Turks, who are allies of France, or perhaps (for politics are liable to strange and sudden upheavals in the Balkans) against Russia, whose Sovereign welcomed you like a father four years ago at Woolwich.[77]

Yet Louis remained determined in his purpose. In a letter written at this time to Bigge, he revealed his real motives, and they had little to do with Balkan politics. 'I am,' he wrote, 'thirsting to smell powder'.[78]

For a Bonaparte, the true test of character lay in war, and any war, it seemed, might do. Within a few months, the smell of black powder and carnage would blow from a very different and entirely unexpected direction, and its allure would prove irresistible.

NOTES

1. King Dinuzulu kaCetshwayo and his uncles, the Princes Ndabuko kaMpande and Shingana kaMpande, were exiled on St Helena between February 1890 and December 1897. They had been found guilty of High Treason for an armed uprising directed against British authority in Zululand in 1888. Although forbidding from the sea, the interior of St Helena is sub-tropical.

2. Ironically, he may have been poisoned by arsenic introduced into his personal supply of wine – which was imported from the famous vineyards at Constantia, in the Cape. See *Napoleon; The Man Who Shaped Europe*, by Ben Weider with Emile Guegen, 1997.

3. Quoted in David Duff, *Eugénie and Napoleon III*, London, 1978.

4. Walter Geer, *Napoleon The Third*, 1921.

5. Victor Hugo, *The History Of A Crime*.

6. On the subject of Eugénie's parentage, see David Duff, *Eugénie and Napoleon III*. Manuela herself denied Villiers was the father, commenting 'the dates did not coincide.'

7. Quoted in Jane Stoddart, *The Life of the Empress Eugénie*, London, 1906.

8. *Uncensored Recollections*, Anon, 1924, quoted in Duff, *Eugénie and Napoleon III*.

9. Stoddart, *The Life of the Empress Eugénie*.

10. Eugénie to the Duke of Alba, 16 May 1843, *Lettres Familières de L'Imperatrice Eugénie*.

11. Stoddart, *The Life of the Empress Eugénie*.

12. Marie A. Belloc, *Eugénie, Empress and Exile*, Lady's Realm, 1897.

13. Cecil Woodham-Smith, *Queen Victoria*, 1972.

14. Lady Augusta Bruce to Queen Victoria, 31 January 1853, *Letters of Queen Victoria*.

15. Ivor Guest, *Napoleon III in England*, 1952.

16. Dr E. Barthez, *The Empress Eugénie and Her Circle*, London, 1912.

17. Ibid.

18. General Fleury, quoted in Stoddart, *The Life of the Empress Eugénie*.

19. Barthez, *The Empess Eugénie and Her Circle*.

20. Augustin Filon, *Memoirs of the Prince Imperial, 1856–1879*, London, 1913.

21. Ibid.

22. The action at Arcole (Italian campaign, 1796–7) is a good example of Napoleonic myth-manipulation. Antoine-Jean Gros' dashing study was one of a number which depicted Napoleon in heroic mode, attempting to rally French forces by carrying a Colour across a

fiercely contested bridge. In fact, the assault was not a success, and the French were driven off the bridge by an Austrian counter attack. Napoleon would have drowned in the marshy ground had his staff not rescued him.

23. Frank Richardson, *Napoleon; Bisexual Emperor*, London, 1972.
24. Filon, *Memoirs of the Prince Imperial*.
25. Ibid.
26. Ibid.
27. Augustin Filon, *Recollections of the Empress Eugénie*, London, 1920.
28. Eugénie to Manuela, quoted in Duff, *Eugénie and Napoleon III*.
29. Filon, *Recollections of the Empress Eugénie*.
30. Louis to Filon, *Memoirs of the Prince Imperial*.
31. Filon, *Recollections of the Empress Eugénie*.
32. Archibald Forbes, *Saarbrück; The Baptism of Fire*, in *Battles of the Nineteenth Century*, Vol. 1, London, 1896.
33. Archibald Forbes, *Memories and Stories of War and Peace*, London, 1898. Forbes was told the story by Louis himself when the two met, years later, in Zululand.
34. Filon, *Memoirs of the Prince Imperial*.
35. Filon, *Recollections of the Empress Eugénie*.
36. Filon, *Memoirs of the Prince Imperial*.
37. Stoddart, *The Life of the Empress Eugénie*.
38. Filon, *Memoirs of the Prince Imperial*.
39. Ibid.
40. Ibid.
41. Queen Victoria, 30 November, 1870, *Diaries*.
42. Queen Victoria, 27 February, 1872, *Letters*.
43. Filon, *Memoirs of the Prince Imperial*.
44. Ibid.
45. Ibid.
46. Ibid.
47. Ibid.
48. Ibid.
49. Ibid.
50. E.E.P. Tisdall, *The Prince Imperial; A Study of his Life Among The British*, London, 1959.
51. Filon, *Memoirs of the Prince Imperial*.
52. Filon, *Recollections of the Empress Eugénie*.
53. Ibid.
54. Queen Victoria, 20 February 1873, *Letters*.
55. Filon, *Memoirs of the Prince Imperial*.
56. Filon, *Recollections of the Empress Eugénie*.

57. Tisdall, *The Prince Imperial*.
58. Filon, *Memoirs of the Prince Imperial*.
59. Ibid.
60. Ibid.
61. Ibid.
62. Ibid.
63. Louis to Conneau, 29 June 1876; quoted in Stoddart, *The Life of the Empress Eugénie*.
64. Filon, *Memoirs of the Prince Imperial*.
65. Quoted in Tisdall, *The Prince Imperial*.
66. Filon, *Memoirs of the Prince Imperial*.
67. Augustus Hare, quoted in Tisdall, *The Prince Imperial*.
68. Dr Adrian Greaves, *A Psychological Portrait of the Prince Imperial*, Journal of the Anglo-Zulu War Historical Society, June 2000.
69. Filon, *Memoirs of the Prince Imperial*.
70. H.E. Wortham, *The Delightful Profession*, London, 1931.
71. Forbes, *Memories and Stories of War and Peace*.
72. Quoted in Duff, *Eugénie and Napoleon III*.
73. Filon, *Recollections of the Empress Eugénie*.
74. Filon, *Memoirs of the Prince Imperial*.
75. Filon, *Recollections of the Empress Eugénie*.
76. Filon, *Memoirs of the Prince Imperial*.
77. Filon, *Recollections of the Empress Eugénie*.
78. Filon, *Memoirs of the Prince Imperial*.

III

'a very disastrous engagement ...'

At first glance, there was nothing to trouble the Bonapartes in the news which reached Colonel Stanley, the British Secretary of State for War, in London on 11 February 1879. It was bad news, of course; and already nearly three weeks out of date. It had come from the Cape by telegram, but at the beginning of 1879 there was no direct telegraphic link from South Africa to Britain, and messages had to be sent first by steamer to Madeira, and the beginning of the wire. But Britain was a colonial power, the greatest Empire of the day, and her troops were stationed in distant garrisons across half the world – and empires did not grow by peaceful means alone. Bad news, under such circumstances, was to be expected now and then, and it had little impact on the aspirations of the Court in exile at Camden Place, who probably knew little of the intricacies of British colonial policy, and cared less. Yet the bleak tone of this particular telegram would galvanise the British government and public alike, and have entirely unexpected and quite devastating repercussions for the future of Bonapartist fortunes.

It had been written by the senior British commander in southern Africa, Lieutenant General Lord Chelmsford, and it brought news of an opening catastrophe in a 'small war' which had broken out, almost unheeded, in a little-known country far away:

I regret to have to report a very disastrous engagement which took place on the 22nd instant between the Zulus and a portion of No. 3 Column left to guard the camp about 10 miles in front of Rorke's Drift – The former came down in overwhelming numbers and, in spite of the gallant resistance made by the six companies of the 24th Regiment, 2 guns, 2 Rocket-tubes, 104 mounted men and about 800 natives, completely overwhelmed them. The camp, containing all the supplies, ammunition and transport of No. 3 Column, was taken, and but few of its defenders escaped. Our loss, I fear, must

be set down as 30 officers and about 500 non commissioned officers, Rank & File of the Imperial troops and 21 Non Commissioned
Officers Rank and File of the Colonial Forces.[1]

Chelmsford's telegram catapulted British policy in southern Africa to
the forefront of public consciousness. Written in the immediate aftermath of defeat, his despatches were inevitably clouded by the fog
of war, but the air of incomprehension which pervades them found
little sympathy with the British press, for whom military success overseas had become axiomatic. As *The Illustrated London News*, the most
sober and respected of the illustrated weekly papers, commented
darkly:

> ... Lord Chelmsford's account of this unhappy affair ... seems
> rather feeble, not at all like the relation of Sir Garnet Wolseley's
> and Lord Napier of Magdala's operations in similar warfare. The
> famous despatch of Julius Caesar has often been quoted, 'I came,
> I saw, I won a victory'; but Lord Chelmsford's might run thus, 'I
> went, I did not see, I suffered a defeat.'[2]

The news was all the more confusing because there had been little in
the press over the previous few months to suggest a crisis in Zululand
was imminent. Foreign news had been dominated by the implications
to British policy of the recent Balkan troubles, and by a fresh British
entanglement in Afghanistan. Indeed, when the story first broke that
British troops were poised to invade Zululand, *The Illustrated London
News*, which adopted a cautious note throughout, had been moved to
ponder the justice of the cause:

> It has been long brewing; not, indeed, in the intentions of
> King Cetewayo, but in the determination of the South African
> Colonists of European extraction. It is the combined result of sus-
> picion, of fear, and of greed. We are not, perhaps, warranted in
> saying that these motives have been consciously entertained by
> the Colonists, but they have certainly been provoked into activ-
> ity by causes which ought never to have been allowed to gain
> head.[3]

When news of the invasion was followed within days by reports of
disaster, the paper's tone became positively indignant, and with rare
perception its editors placed the blame squarely at the feet of the High
Commissioner to South Africa, Sir Henry Bartle Frere:

How far the determination of the High Commissioner at the Cape
– for determination it may be gathered from his despatches to have
been – may have been justified by local knowledge the British
public have yet to learn. No explanation he has yet given can be
held to demonstrate the necessity of an immediate invasion of
Zululand. He was cautioned more than once by the Government at
home who, however, left him to pursue his own course, on his own
responsibility.[4]

The road to war with the Zulu kingdom had indeed been a strange one,
which in retrospect reflected little credit on British policies. The origins
of European interest in southern Africa were entirely strategic, and it
had been the Dutch who had first established a toe-hold at the tip of
the continent in the seventeenth century, with the intention of servicing
ships on the long haul round Africa to the Indies. In the turmoil of the
Revolutionary and Napoleonic years, this enclave had taken on a new
significance for the rival European powers, and in 1806 the British had
taken the Cape by force – largely, it must be said, to stop the French
from getting it. Neither the British, nor the Dutch before them, had been
interested in active settlement, although the Dutch had established a
small farming community, which raised cattle and crops to provision the
passing fleets. These first settlers, originally Dutch, but mixed later with
religious refugees from France and Germany, had gradually expanded
their interests into the African hinterland, often in the face of opposition
from their own administration. Nevertheless, accustomed as they were
to surviving by their own resources, and isolated from new currents
of European thought, they increasingly turned their back on the wider
world, and looked inwards instead. By the beginning of the nineteenth
century they had assumed a distinct character of their own, and a
markedly conservative mind-set. They did not welcome the advent of
British authority, shaped as it was by a metropolitan and humanitarian
philosophy very different from their own, and in the 1830s many of these
frontier farmers emigrated from the Cape Colony into the interior, in an
attempt to place themselves outside British control.

   This movement, known as the Great Trek, had re-shaped the political
geography of southern Africa, and left a legacy of tension which has
continued unresolved to this day. The settlers – known by the Dutch
word for farmers, *Boers* – left a trail of conflict with indigenous African
societies in their wake, and had dragged British authority haphazardly
and reluctantly behind them. By the time the movement had finished,
the Boers had come to dominate the interior of southern Africa, while
the British, for whom maritime interests remained paramount, retained

control of the coastal seaboard. Sandwiched uneasily in between, clinging perilously to what remained of their authority and refusing to relinquish their claim to the land, were the independent kingdoms of the original African peoples.

This complex mesh of inter-European rivalry reached Natal, on the eastern coast, in 1824. At that time Natal lay several hundred miles beyond the borders of British administration, which ended at the Eastern Cape frontier. But rumours had reached the Cape of the emergence of a rich and powerful African kingdom to the north, and the merchants of Cape Town had speculated on an exploratory expedition, led by an unemployed ex-Navy Lieutenant by the name of Francis George Farewell. Farewell's goal was a masked inlet marked on the charts as Rio de Natal, or the Bay of Natal, and he braved the infamous sand-bar to establish the first deliberate contact with the Zulu kingdom, which dominated the region. Farewell's tiny settlement had flourished under the protection of the King Shaka, but his attempts to persuade the British government to assume formal control over it were not enthusiastically received. Only on the arrival of the Boer Trek, with its implied threat to British influence in the region, did the British react. Troops were despatched over-land to occupy the Bay and isolate the Boers from foreign support. The result was a bizarre little battle fought on the sand-dunes overlooking the lagoon, and eventually the British triumphed. In 1843 Natal became a British colony, to the disgust of the Trekboers, many of whom retreated to the interior rather than find themselves once more under British rule.

Colonial Natal grew slowly. The country offered excellent prospects to cattle-ranchers, while the sub-tropical coastal belt had potential for sugar and fruit farming, but the harsh landscape, the heat of the summer months, and the almost total lack of resources and communications made Natal appealing to only the most adventurous souls. Of course, like the rest of southern Africa, Natal was by no means empty before the British arrived, and the growth in the colonial administration was characterised by an unresolved tension with traditional African forms of government. As one observer put it drily, Natal was 'a British colony, so called, but in truth a native territory scantily occupied by Europeans'.[5]

Relations with the Zulu kingdom, the colony's northern neighbour, were generally good, however. Zulu influence south of the Thukela had ever been patchy, even at the height of the kingdom's power and authority, and many African groups took the opportunity afforded by the arrival of the whites to abandon their allegiance to the Zulu kings. This had been acknowledged by King Mpande in the 1840s, when an Anglo-Zulu accord recognised the line of the Thukela and Mzinyathi rivers as the border between the two states. Despite occasional political rifts and scares, no major conflict between Natal and Zululand erupted during thirty years of British rule in Natal.

For much of that time, indeed, British administration in southern Africa had been shaped by the desire to avoid unnecessary involvement or expense. Anglo-Boer rivalry, and the need to regulate the influence of British traders and missionaries, may have dragged the British government farther into Africa than it had at first wanted to go, but the fact remained that possession of the ports alone justified her presence. South Africa had brought very little return for the drain it had imposed on the British exchequer, and for the shed blood of the long-suffering redcoat who had policed it. Until the 1860s, whatever enthusiastic members of the settler community might have claimed to the contrary, South Africa remained to the British,

> ... never likely to compete with America or Australia in the Emigration market. They have to contend with every difficulty to which a country can be subject. There are harbours with sand-bars which it is improbable that any outlay will remove. There are rivers without water, plains without grass, hills without trees or shelter. There are, as in the Karoo, hundreds of square miles of sand separating one end of our jurisdiction from another, and defying all hope of improvement. Every article of life is more difficult to obtain, and worse when obtained, than in England.[6]

In 1867, however, two children discovered a diamond near Hopetown, north of the Cape Colony, and in the twinkling of an eye, the future of a continent turned. With typical adroitness, the British promptly re-drew the map of southern Africa to bring the area under British control, and the adventurers and speculators flooded in. By the early 1870s the new boom town of Kimberley was producing sufficient diamonds to cause Imperialist visionaries to reconsider southern Africa's potential. Not only was Kimberley itself offering the first hint for half a century of a financial profit, but the possibility existed that there might yet be scores of Kimberleys in the interior, waiting to be discovered. Together, they might fuel the economic penetration of the entire African continent, but the rub lay in the need to create, almost from scratch, an entirely new industrial infrastructure. Optimists in Durban suddenly saw themselves as the gateway to a world of opportunity, the hub which connected maritime trade routes to a network of roads and railways on land, which imported goods and equipment, and extracted mineral and material wealth in return.

Yet this heady vision begged a number of jagged political questions. It was assumed, of course, that any such economic development would be accomplished at the expense of vast numbers of under-paid African labourers. And while the attempt to make Africans work cheaply for whites was a characteristic of both British and Boer administrative systems, it was seldom easily accomplished, and indeed a wave of discontent which passed through South Africa's beleaguered black groups in the 1870s was partly the result. For many, it seemed that the final reduction of any lingering African independence was a prerequisite of economic expansion.

Nor were black Africans the only problem. The Boer republics of the interior – the Orange Free State and the Transvaal – remained grounded in the needs and attitudes of their white farming populations. Introverted and xenophobic, they resented attempts to draw them within the ambit of a broader geo-political economy, especially since it was clear that the dominant power would be Britain. And the bright new railways creeping painfully north from the Cape and inland from Durban were unlikely to be of much benefit if they stopped at Boer borders, while the free movement of African labour was not encouraged by the taxes and harassment to which migrant workers were exposed as they passed through Boer territory.

The solution, in British eyes, was a policy of Confederation – a bringing together of southern Africa's disparate groups under a loose form of British control, for their own ultimate good. The scheme had worked well in Canada – another region marked by deep rifts between its European settler groups – and from the mid-1870s the Colonial Office in London attempted to introduce it at the Cape. In 1877 British officials, escorted by troops, marched into the capital, Pretoria, and raised the Union flag. This high-handed move was accomplished on the pretext that the Transvaal Republic was economically bankrupt and at risk from its African neighbours. The takeover had been so sudden that the Boers had been bewildered, and the British misinterpreted their confusion as acquiescence – an error which would produce its own bitter crop of bloodshed in due course. The echoes of the British proclamation of annexation had hardly died away when a new High Commissioner arrived in Cape Town to force through the remainder of the Confederation package.

Sir Henry Bartle Frere was an experienced Imperial pro-consul who had earned his reputation in India. He brought determination and energy to his new job, but he was perhaps rather too influenced by settler and missionary opinion emanating from Natal. Within months he had begun to see the existence of the Zulu kingdom as the principal obstacle to his plans.

There were a number of both practical and ideological reasons for this. In assuming control of the Transvaal, the British had inherited a long-standing border dispute between the Republic and the Zulu kingdom, regarding title to sparsely populated land along the upper Mzinyathi and Ncome rivers. The Zulu kings had allowed Transvaal farmers to graze their stock in this region since the 1840s, but the Boers had pressed farther and farther into Zulu territory, to the increasing consternation of the Zulu, who vehemently denied ever granting settlement rights. Indeed, before 1877 it had suited the British to support Zulu claims against the Boers; now that they had assumed control of the Transvaal, they abruptly switched allegiance. This created a tension with the incumbent Zulu king, Cetshwayo kaMpande, which Frere chose to interpret as African belligerence. Moreover, Frere came to see the geographical position of the kingdom – lying squarely across Natal's potential line of expansion into the interior – as an economic obstacle to be overcome. By the middle of 1878 he had resolved to force a confrontation with King Cetshwayo. The home government, while acknowledging that friction with independent groups was an inevitable result of the Confederation process, was reluctant to sanction military activity, if only because it was committed elsewhere in the world. As the Colonial Office had observed following the annexation of the Transvaal:

> I hope it does not mean we shall have a great pressure put on us to annex Zululand. This must and ought to come eventually, but not just now. There are however signs of this tendency.[7]

Yet Frere gambled that he would be able to mount a quick and successful campaign against the Zulus, and that once he had achieved a victory, his superiors would forget their reservations. In one fell swoop he would destroy a conspicuous bastion of African autonomy, open the road to the interior, resolve the border dispute, and prove to reluctant republican elements in the Transvaal by a little judicious sabre-rattling that the British meant business – and all under the guise of protecting vulnerable British settlers and missionaries from the threat of a savage and unpredictable neighbour. 'If we make a speedy and satisfactory settlement with Cetywayo,' he commented archly, 'we shall have comparatively little trouble with anyone else'.[8] On 11 December 1878 Frere's representatives met with Zulu envoys on the banks of the Thukela river, and presented them with an ultimatum they knew the king could not accept. On 11 January 1879 the Anglo-Zulu War began.

The senior British commander in southern Africa was Lieutenant General Lord Chelmsford. Chelmsford was in his early fifties, an establishment figure with a good deal of experience behind him. Nevertheless, he was very much the product of a conservative outlook which still dominated the senior reaches of the British military, and which had not yet come to terms with new, and increasingly fashionable, progressive theory. Lord Chelmsford approached the coming campaign in a conventional manner, both overestimating the capabilities of his own men, and underestimating those of the enemy. Moreover, he was further constrained by Frere's political objectives, which required him to mount an offensive campaign, despite the fact that he had insufficient troops at his disposal, and was unlikely – because of the reluctance of the home government to support a confrontation – to be reinforced. Chelmsford had recently brought a messy little war against the Xhosa people to a successful conclusion on the Cape Frontier – the last gasp of a doomed century of Xhosa resistance – and his experience there had convinced him that the firepower of his regular infantry battalions represented an unbeatable asset on the battlefield. Aware that the Zulu army was more mobile than his own, his strategy was shaped by the need to pin down the Zulu, and bring them to battle.

As a result, he had initially hoped to invade Zululand in five separate columns, each advancing from a point equidistant along the Natal and Transvaal borders. The uncomfortable truth of his position had soon become apparent, however, when shortage of men and logistical support forced him to make do instead with just three offensive columns, with the remaining two in reserve. Each column consisted of roughly two battalions of infantry, an artillery battery, a small complement of volunteer cavalry, and several battalions of African auxiliary troops, raised in Natal, and known as the Natal Native Contingent – a total of roughly 3,000 men. While Chelmsford knew that the Zulu army had a nominal strength of 40,000 men, he had only the haziest idea when he crossed the border of its whereabouts, or of King Cetshwayo's defensive plans.

Chelmsford's shortcomings were woefully exposed on 22 January, just eleven days after the war had begun. Curiously, circumstances combined to force the Zulu to mount a determined response to the advance of all three British columns on the same day. While Chelmsford's flanking columns were subjected to harassing attacks, the main counter strike was directed against the Centre Column, which the General commanded in person.

The Centre Column had crossed into Zululand at Rorke's Drift, along the central reaches of the Mzinyathi, on 11 January. Bad weather slowed the advance to a crawl, and it was not until the 20th that Chelmsford moved forward to establish a new camp beneath a distinctive rocky outcrop known as Isandlwana, just seven miles from the border. By the time he arrived at Isandlwana, reports already suggested that a large Zulu army, marching direct from the king's main residence at oNdini, was operating in his vicinity. On the 21st, Chelmsford sent a large reconnaissance into hills on his right front, hoping to intercept this army; and when his patrols discovered Zulus some twelve miles beyond Isandlwana, late that evening, he thought he had done just that. News of this encounter reached him at the camp late that night, and he ordered about half his force to make ready to march out before dawn to confront the Zulu.

In fact, however, the main Zulu army, about 25,000 strong, had already slipped unnoticed across his front, and lay hidden much closer to Isandlwana. While Chelmsford was away, scouts from the camp stumbled across the Zulu bivouac, provoking an immediate attack. From the first, the British commander at the camp, Lieutenant Colonel Pulleine, underestimated the Zulu threat, and made his initial dispositions before the enemy came into sight. By the time the Zulu attack rolled down on him, it was too late; the Zulus outflanked him on both sides, and when Pulleine attempted to reposition his line, the Zulus first broke it up, then drove his men back through the camp. It was a classic Zulu attack, well conceived, and executed with great courage and determination. The Imperial troops under Pulleine's command had attempted to rally, but the Zulu cut the line of retreat, and the British stands were systematically broken up and overwhelmed. Pulleine and 1,300 of his men – British regulars, Colonial Volunteers and black Natalians – were killed; fewer than sixty whites escaped the carnage. The Zulu captured everything of value in the camp, including a thousand modern rifles, and 200,000 rounds of ammunition.

Chelmsford himself had been too far off to be much aware of the fighting, and by the time he realised something was wrong, the battle was over. That night his tired and unnerved command returned to Isandlwana, and bivouacked amidst the wreckage of the camp, taking what sleep they could on a field littered thickly with the bodies of men, and the carcasses of transport animals. On his way back to Natal the following morning, Chelmsford passed an equally exhausted detachment of Zulus, walking disconsolately in the other direction – the survivors of an unsuccessful attack on the border post at Rorke's Drift.

For the British, the dogged defence of Rorke's Drift provided the only piece of good news on a very bad day.

The disaster at Isandlwana devastated Chelmsford's plans. At one fell swoop, a third of his offensive capability had been destroyed or driven out of Zululand. The flanking columns were left unsupported, and as soon as they received the news, they had little option but to dig in; the entire offensive had ground to a halt. For hundreds of miles the frontier lay open, and there was nothing to prevent a Zulu counter attack beyond a handful of white volunteers, and a poorly trained African border levy. White civilians panicked and fled to the dubious security of the nearest towns, and the major metropolitan centres, Pietermaritzburg and Durban – many miles away from the border – made hasty preparations for their defence. For at least a fortnight after the battle, white and black Natalians alike quaked in their beds and on their sleeping mats, in nightly anticipation of a Zulu attack.

The disaster seemed all the more terrible because it was incomprehensible. 'I can't understand it', someone had heard Chelmsford say on the day of the battle, when the truth had at last become inescapable, 'I left a thousand men there'. And that same sense of numbed shock would characterise reaction in Britain. 'No such disaster as that at Isandula ought to have been possible with a disciplined force', thundered *The Illustrated London News*.[9] Many commentators, indeed, were at a loss to see how nearly 800 British troops, representing the full might of the most technologically advanced industrial economy of the age, could possibly have been defeated by men with black skins, armed primarily with shields and spears. Most took refuge in theories of treachery and betrayal, epitomised by a map of Isandlwana, published in one journal, which featured an entirely fictitious ravine by which the Zulus had sneakily entered the camp unseen.

Yet whatever the cause of the catastrophe, it clearly called for retribution. Despite an uneasy suspicion among the liberal press that Frere had cast Britain in the role of the aggressor, it was still necessary to restore British honour in the field before political complexities could be addressed. *The Illustrated London News* again summed up the tone:

[The Zulus] are to be defeated; their tyrant is to be deposed; their nation is to be disarmed; their country, for a time at least, must be subdued and held under British rule, though it be only for the safety of our adjacent provinces. But there is no right-minded and honourable man, with a soul of loyalty or patriotism and chivalry in him, who can think fit to hate the Zulus, as a nation, for having inflicted one temporary defeat upon our army in the defence of their own land, and under the command of their hereditary ruler.[10]

Nevertheless, the government sanctioned an immediate increase in military commitment to southern Africa. Chelmsford had modestly asked for 'three infantry Battalions, two Cavalry Regiments, and one Company of Royal Engineers' to restore his position.[11] In the event, he was offered an embarrassment of riches. As news of Isandlwana rippled across the Empire, reinforcements were hurried to the Cape from garrisons around the world. The 57th Regiment, about to return home after a tour of duty in Ceylon, was diverted instead to South Africa, while the garrison at St Helena – so small that it could scarcely make a difference – was promptly put aboard a passing warship, and sent to the Cape. All in all, Chelmsford would receive two cavalry regiments, two further artillery batteries, an ammunition column, six infantry battalions, and several companies of support personnel – Engineers, Service Corps and Hospital Corps. In addition, the losses sustained by the battalions already in South Africa were made good – which in the case of the 1/24th meant almost rebuilding it from scratch. Altogether, he received just under 10,000 men, so that by the end of the war, the total number of men under his command, including African auxiliaries, was equal to nearly half the theoretical strength of his enemy. As the redcoats were disgorged at Durban, and marched north to assemble menacingly on the Zulu borders, it became increasingly apparent, even to King Cetshwayo himself, that the Zulu stood no chance of winning the war by military means.

Most of the new additions – nearly 9,000 men – came fresh from the UK, and there was a frantic scramble to bring the selected battalions up to war strength. Officers' leave was cancelled, while natural wastage was made good from a pool of new recruits at training depots across the country. Many of these were young men who had enlisted under the army's controversial new 'short service' system, which attempted to attract a better class of recruit by offering a reduced period of enlistment and better living conditions. The 'short service' system was already under fire from conservatives within the military establishment who argued that it overloaded the ranks with young, unsteady men, who lacked the necessary experience to withstand the rigours of active service, and in a way the Anglo-Zulu War would prove them right. Yet the fault lay not so much in the system itself as in the hurry with which the reinforcements were assembled after Isandlwana, though the effect was disconcerting:

> Thus it came about that our battalions landed in Zululand full of incompletely trained men, a great proportion of whom had never fired a round of ball cartridge, while many had never fired a round of blank, before they embarked.[12]

Nevertheless, morale among those ordered to Zululand was generally high, particularly among the officers, for whom fresh campaigning offered a chance for adventure, and the possibility of promotions and awards. Moreover, despite the eminently reasonable tone of papers such as *The Illustrated London News*, there was a very real sense of indignation abroad in the country, and a desire to exact revenge from the Zulus. 'The men are all in high spirits,' observed *The Graphic*'s correspondent at the dockside, 'and apparently eager to take part in avenging the slaughter of their unfortunate comrades.'[13] Captain William Molyneux, one of Chelmsford's aides who happened to be recuperating in England from complications of dysentery and pneumonia contracted on the Cape Frontier six months before, captured the mood of the moment:

> Early that morning my man (Private Noot of the 2nd batt. 24th) rushed into my room with *The Times*. 'Oh, sir, the regiment has been cut up by the Zulus, and Mr Pope (who commanded Noot's company) and a lot of soldiers killed. Read this – do you think they will let us go out? – Don't let them send me to the depot.' The man was mad with rage. I read the account, ordered breakfast to be got ready at once, that I might be in Pall Mall as soon as possible. 'We will see if we can't go out together,' I added; and at this the good fellow began to look less mournful.[14]

Guy Dawnay, a gentleman adventurer whose brother, Hugh, Lord Downe, was a Captain in the Life Guards and had been ordered to Zululand as an ADC, decided on hearing the news to go out on his own account, in the hope of securing a commission with the volunteer forces. He had once hunted big game in Zululand, and had fond memories of the country and the Zulu people, but saw no contradiction in fighting them, and thought his experience might prove useful. His diary suggests something of the breathless haste with which the officer class prepared for war:

> On Wednesday February 12th, on coming down to breakfast at Baldersby, I first heard of the Isandhlwana disaster; and forseeing the chance of a rising in Natal, I got a few things ready for a hurried start, and ordered my rifle and cartridges to be packed, loaded &c. by Henry. On Saturday, the 15th ... I found a telegram from H., saying he was going to Zululand on General Marshall's staff, went up to London that night, settled next day to start on myself by if possible the very first troopship leaving for the Cape, and try to make myself of use as to getting horses for him &c., went back to Yorkshire again that night, packed up the few things I wanted on Monday morning, rode over to Beningborough that afternoon, found a telegram from E. saying he had got a berth for me on the 'Pretoria', to sail the next

day but one, went to London that night, had a very busy day on Tuesday, getting different things, ordering a carbine – which H. is to bring for me – and next morning, Wednesday 19th, said good-bye, and left Belgrave Square at 10.30 …[15]

Between 20 February – scarcely a week after the news arrived – and 1 April, no fewer than nineteen transport ships left the London docks, Portsmouth or Southampton carrying troops to the Cape. The spectacle was sufficient to cause the correspondent of *The Graphic* to positively glow with pride:

> If King Cetewayo could be transported on the magician's carpet, described in the Arabian Nights, from his native country to this island for an hour or two, he would speedily sue for peace. He would be fairly astonished by the bustle of preparation at barracks, arsenals, and docks, caused by his success at [Isandlwana], and he would begin to comprehend what savages very seldom do comprehend, that the forces opposed to him in South Africa are a mere advance-guard of what the Home Government can send out if they chose to put forth their strength.[16]

At the docks, the troops assembling for embarkation were the subject of a good deal of public attention, prompting one editorial to ponder philosophically:

> Although there is a sincere mourning for those who have been slain, it cannot be denied that the Zulu disaster with its consequences causes a pleasurable excitement to thousands of persons. In spite of that thin film of civilisation with which we are coated, we are still fighting animals, and where we cannot ourselves fight, we like to fight by proxy, and so we stare with all our eyes at soldiers bound on active service.[17]

Moreover, for all the ensuing patriotic fervour, the men's shortcomings did not go unnoticed:

> Crowds of people paid their pennies to get unto the pier for the sake of inspecting these warriors, who, though for the most part were very juvenile, were pronounced to be of 'the right sort'.[18]

At Camden Place, Louis saw the press reports, and 'was stupefied, like the rest of the world, to hear that a little English army had been surrounded, surprised, and all but annihilated'.[19] His reaction was unexpected, but not at all untypical:

> It was one evening after dinner, in this same month of February. The Prince seemed unable to sit still; he came and went, moved the chairs, sat down at the piano, where he tapped out a military call, became restless again, and showed the signs of a joyful excitement which could not escape the Empress' notice. 'What is the matter with you tonight?' she said to him. 'If I told you you wouldn't sleep all night.'
>
> An hour later, the Prince was alone with his mother and bidding her goodnight. 'Do you imagine,' said she, 'that I shall sleep after what you said to me? I shall conjure up terrible things; for instance that you have asked to go and serve in Africa against the Zulus.'
>
> The Prince, delighted at being discovered, confessed that that very day he had sent to the Duke of Cambridge a request for permission to serve in Africa.[20]

Even now, more than 120 years after the event, this seems a curious decision. France had little interest in British policy at the Cape, and Bonapartist political ambitions even less. As Filon ruefully observed, 'it is unlikely that the Prince had scrutinised English doings in South Africa very closely';[21] indeed, he had probably never heard of the Zulus before the news of Isandlwana broke. He was, moreover, a foreign national, whose associations with the Royal Artillery were entirely honorary, and by no stretch of the imagination could it be considered his quarrel.

Yet his response was typical of Louis' character. It was an impulsive decision, an instinctive reaction to a sudden opportunity for fresh adventures, which can only be understood against the background of his recent frustrations. Since the embarrassment of his failure to enlist in the Austrian forces in the Balkans the previous year, he had clearly been looking for a war to join, and in many way the Anglo-Zulu War suited his purpose ideally. It was mercifully free of the political complications which had refused him entry to the Balkans, while even his enemies in France could scarcely object to his involvement in a colonial campaign, when France herself had large colonial possessions in Africa. And while the Zulu victory at Isandlwana offered the very real spice of danger, it was widely assumed throughout Britain that the flood of reinforcements would inevitably turn the war in her favour. They were going out not just to fight the war, but to win it, and Louis could be there to smell the powder – with very little real risk, and very few repercussions. Later, with typical candour, he admitted:

I asked no one's advice, and I made up my mind in forty-eight hours; if my resolve was swift, it was because I had reflected at length on such a contingency and made my plans.

Neither my mother's fears nor the despair of the people about me, nor the exhortations of M. Rouher and my supporters, caused me to hesitate a minute or lose a second of time; this will only seem natural to those who know me, but how many are they?

... I have had proof that no one will be followed but a man of known energy, and my care has been to find a way of making myself known.

... When one belongs to a race of soldiers, it is only sword in hand that one gains recognition ...[22]

What apparently decided him to go was the knowledge that his friends from G/24 Battery were already involved in the campaign. Indeed, both Bigge and Slade had resigned their home service appointments a year before, and had been in South Africa since early 1878. There was a short-age of artillery batteries at the Cape at that time, with just two – N/5 and 11/7 – being required to fulfil a heavy commitment in the closing stages of the Cape Frontier War. The campaign was fought out in difficult terrain, broken and wooded, and both batteries had found it necessary to work piecemeal, with their guns distributed in sections among the scattered British units. As a result, officers had been moved around more than was common, and Bigge in particular had enjoyed a variety of appointments. It was here that his relationship with Colonel Wood had begun, and Wood had employed him for a while as an aide. 'He came to me with a good rep-utation,' recalled Wood, 'and I saw a great deal of him in Camp, although on the lines of march but little, having chosen him to make a road sketch from King William's Town to Maritzburg, which he did very well.'[23]

When the troops were moved up to the Zulu borders, the batteries were reassembled, and while N/5 was attached in its entirety to the Centre Column, 11/7 was spilt between the two flanking columns. The Headquarters section, under the command of Major Edmund Tremlett, was attached to Wood's Left Flank Column, and both Bigge and Slade were destined to serve with it throughout the Anglo-Zulu War. Indeed, they had already been in action; on 24 January, just two days after Isandlwana, Wood had attempted to disperse a Zulu concentration cen-tred upon a natural stronghold, Hlobane mountain. Following tactics perfected in the Cape Frontier War – ironically the same ones employed at Isandlwana – he had mounted an infantry attack in open order, under cover of 11/7's guns. He had been forced to break off the action when a rider arrived with the news of the Centre Column's fate.

It is unlikely that Louis knew anything of Bigge's and Slade's adventures when he applied to go to South Africa, but their presence in the field can have only added to the impact of the news from the front. The final straw undoubtedly came when Josceline Wodehouse – his other great friend from Aldershot days – came to tell him that he had secured a placement with another battery, N/6, which was about to embark at Southampton with the reinforcements. 'While even one of the officers in my battery stayed in England,' Louis explained,

> I might have honourably remained here myself. When Wodehouse came in his turn to say goodbye to me, my mind was made up. How could I show myself again at Aldershot when they will all be out there?[24]

Needless to say, Eugénie was appalled. Her first instinct was to restrain him by the one means which had consistently succeeded in the past – a call to his duty as a Bonaparte. 'If anything happens to you,' she accused him, 'your adherents will not weep for you; they will have a grudge against you!'[25] Yet his mother's opposition probably just served to strengthen Louis' resolve; the war would, at least, allow him to step away from her apron-strings, and the hothouse atmosphere at Camden Place. 'Do you want me to remain always the "little Prince" to everyone?' he retorted, 'Do you want me to fade away and die of sheer *ennui* ...?'[26]

In the event, Louis' first application was refused outright. He needed permission from the Commander-in-Chief, the Duke of Cambridge, before he could be allowed to accompany British forces, and the Duke turned the idea down flat. Not used to being thwarted, Louis was crushed, to the extent that Eugénie, to comfort him, promised to withdraw her objection.

This change of heart, from a woman whose future focused entirely upon her son, requires some explanation. In an interview given two months later, Eugénie rationalised her position. 'I could not fail to realise the justice of many of my son's remarks,' she said, 'and this will explain to you why, although I still argued with him, I resigned myself at last to the inevitable.'[27] Yet there was probably more to it than this. Eugénie was undoubtedly devoted to her son, and her first instinct was often to control, curb or shape his actions; but above all she needed him to grow into the role she had nurtured all her life, that of a Bonaparte, of the Great Napoleon's natural successor. She was realistic enough to recognise that he could not live behind his mother's skirts forever. If she despised the Zulu campaign as unworthy of his blood, she at least saw in his ardour a strength of purpose worthy of a Man of Destiny. Whatever risks he might run, they could only add to the honour of his reputation. And if the worst happened? There are perhaps echoes here of Eugénie's attitude during the Franco-Prussian War. She could weep with pride for Louis dead or a prisoner, as she said then; but what of a man who never had the wit or courage to seize his chances, to prove himself, as they both knew that he must, before the world's hard gaze?

When Louis wrote once more to the Duke, he could not entirely contain his self-pity:

> I have just received the letter you wrote me. Before telling you how much it distressed me, I must thank your Royal Highness for the flattering approval it gives to the motives that led me to this step. I should have been glad to share the fatigues and dangers of my comrades, who all have the happiness of being on active service. Though I am not so conceited as to think that my services can be useful to the cause I wished to serve, I nevertheless looked upon this war as an opportunity of showing my gratitude towards the Queen and the nation in a way that would be very much to my mind. When at Woolwich and, later, at Aldershot, I had the honour of wearing the English uniform, I hoped that it would be in the ranks of our allies that I should first take up arms. Losing this hope, I lose one of the consolations of my exile. I remain none the less deeply devoted to the Queen and deeply grateful to Your Royal Highness for the interest you have always displayed in me. I beg you to believe in the feelings of sincere attachment of your very affectionate,
>
> Napoleon.[28]

This letter, however, struck just the right note. The Duke of Cambridge passed it on to the Queen, for comment, and Victoria was clearly moved:

> ... thank you for ... these very nice letters from the young Prince Imperial. I am very touched at the kind and gratifying expressions he makes use of, and cannot but admire his desire to go out and serve with my brave Troops. But I am glad I am not his mother at this moment.[29]

This tacit nod of Royal approval was crucial. The Duke was prepared to reconsider his position, but in the hurried consultations with the Cabinet which followed, it was clear that Disraeli would have nothing to do with the idea, and refused to allow the Prince to join Chelmsford's forces in any official capacity. The solution was simple enough; the Duke gave permission for Louis to go on the understanding that he was there in a private capacity, and held no official rank or standing. He was to be, in effect, no more than Lord Chelmsford's private guest; a celebrity tourist in the war zone. Disraeli found the situation exasperating:

> I am quite mystified about that little abortion, the Prince Imperial. I thought we had agreed not to sanction his adventure? Instead of that he has royal audiences previous to his departure … What am I to say on this? H.M. knows my little sympathy with the Buonapartes.[30]

In a letter to Frere, which Louis took with him by way of an introduction, the Duke made this quite clear:

> I am anxious to make you acquainted with the Prince Imperial, who is about to proceed to Natal by tomorrow's packet to see as much as he can of the coming campaign in Zululand in the capacity of a spectator. He was anxious to serve in our army having been a cadet at Woolwich, but the government did not think that this could be sanctioned; but no objection is made to his going out on his own account, and I am permitted to introduce him to you and to Lord Chelmsford in the hope, and with my personal request, that you will give him every help in your power to enable him to see what he can. I have written to Chelmsford in the same effect. He is a charming young man, full of spirit and energy, speaking English admirably, and the more you see of him, the more you will like him. He has many young friends in the artillery, and so I doubt not, with your and Chelmsford's kind assistance, will get through well enough …[31]

The Queen was more to the point:

> Heard from George C that the Prince Imperial is determined to go. Difficulties were made, but George suggested his going out on his own hook … expressed a great wish to serve me … to start on Thursday.[32]

Louis was delighted at the turn of events, and though it is clear he had been made fully aware of the conditions of his approval, he did not seem unduly troubled by them:

> I've had all the trouble in the world to get leave from the English Government. Today I've got it at last, but with all kinds of restrictions. I'm supposed to be sailing for the Cape as a traveller, and

only when there am I to put on a uniform and attach myself to the
general in charge of artillery. So we must be careful to warn our
journals not to say I start with my battery – it will be alright for
them to say that I am hastening out to share the toils and perils of
my comrades. They are too definite about my rank in the English
Army, for it is quite unofficial.[33]

There is nothing in this letter which suggests that Louis regarded the
reservations about his standing as anything other than a formality – or
indeed that he intended to take any notice of them whatever. War, the great
adventure for which his soul had cried out since childhood, had now begun
in earnest; a small war, perhaps, but he had every intention of emerging from
it a great man. Small wonder that he took little notice of Queen Victoria's
stricture – that 'he must be careful not unnecessarily to expose himself, for
we know he is very venturesome'[34] – from the very beginning.

As soon as the news came, Louis threw himself into the necessary
preparations. He arranged a passage on the *Danube*, which was scheduled to leave Southampton on the 28th, carrying two companies of
the 3/60th Regiment and a number of volunteer officers to Durban.
The Prince had no intention of taking an entourage with him – 'some
devoted men had offered to go with him to Africa; but, though touched
by their devotion, the Prince did not consent to accept it, for he could not
take a bodyguard (it is his own expression) into an English camp'[35] – and
intended to sail with only his valet, Xavier Uhlmann. Nevertheless, there
were things to be done. Like his British counterparts, he needed to buy
new equipment and prepare his weapons – including at least one family
sword – and make arrangements for his two favourite horses to sail with
him. His affairs, too, had to be put in order, and he needed to write to
his friends and supporters, explaining his reasons and outlining what
he hoped to achieve by joining the campaign. Finally, on his last night
at Camden Place,[36] he took the precaution, like many another soldier
departing to war, before and since, of drafting his will.

The will remains a touching document, a glimpse into Louis' most
private aspirations and loyalties at a time when, not yet twenty-three,
he was forced, perhaps for the first time, to confront his own mortality.
Under the circumstances, it is scarcely surprising that he thought most
of his mother, yet there is an unusual degree of fatalism and a touch of
melancholy in his apparent readiness to accept the possibility that he
might die before her. Moreover, underlying all the assumptions upon
which the will is based, is the implacable weight of Bonaparte tradition,
which for Louis, at least, seemed to offer no easier alternatives than
glory, or death:

This is my Last Will and Testament

1). I die in the Catholic, Apostolic and Roman religion, in which I was born.

2). I desire that my body may be laid near that of my father, until the time comes when both may be transferred to the spot where the founder of our house reposes among the French people, whom we, like him, dearly loved.

3). My latest thought will be for my country; for which I would wish to die.

4). I hope that my mother, when I shall be no more, will maintain for me that affectionate remembrance which I shall cherish for her to the last moment.

5). Let my private friends, my servants, and the partisans of the cause which I represent, be assured that my gratitude to them will only cease with my life.

6). I shall die with a sentiment of profound gratitude towards Her Majesty the Queen of England, the entire royal family, and the country in which for eight years I have received such cordial hospitality. I constitute my mother my universal legatee, subject to the payment of the following legacies ...

... To MM. Conneau, Espinasse, Bizot, J.N. Murat, A. Fleury, P. de Bourgoing, S. Corvisart, my arms and uniforms, except those I may last have worn, which I leave to my mother ...

... I need not recommend to my mother to neglect nothing to defend the memory of my great uncle and father. I beg her to remember that as long as a Bonaparte lives the Imperial cause will be represented. The duties of our house towards the country will not be extinct with my life. When I die the task of continuing the work of Napoleon III will fall to the eldest son of Prince Napoleon, and I hope my beloved mother, by supporting him with all her power, will give to us who shall be no more this last crowning proof of affection,

Napoleon.[37]

For the most part, the individual bequests were predictable, generous gifts to the small circle of friends and supporters who had sheltered him all his life. Only the reference to his last uniform, a dashing, sentimental flourish, would prove to carry a sting in the tail.

On the morning of the 27th Louis rose early, and went to the Catholic Church in Chislehurst, to take the sacrament, and pay his respects at his father's tomb. Then there followed a rather gloomy breakfast at Camden with his mother, with most of their aides in attendance, before Louis and

Eugénie set off together on the train to Southampton. 'I had the sweet comfort', Eugénie recalled, 'of seeing him feted all the way, and all the people blessing him as he passed.'[38]

Indeed, the arrival of the Imperial party at the docks caused quite a stir among the crowd who had gathered to see troops and munitions loaded aboard the SS *Danube*. *The Graphic* saw much in the incident to confirm both the smug superiority with which the English traditionally regarded their neighbours across the Channel, and the air of romantic melancholy which lingered around the Imperial family:

> Prince Louis Napoleon … As our French neighbours are at present in possession of a Republic which shows greater promise of durability than either of its predecessors, it is, perhaps, more courteous to call the son of the late Emperor of the French by this title than to style him the 'Prince Imperial', a phrase which implies that there is an Empire in posse. Since that disastrous year when he received his ill-omened 'baptism of fire' at Saarbrück, this enterprising young gentleman has seen no real fighting. But he has received a careful education at the Royal Military Academy, Woolwich, and hence it has been thought advisable by himself and his friends that he should gain some lessons in war, albeit a war conducted against a savage leader … should the whirligig of time in France ever again give the Empire a chance, the Prince's prospects of success will be improved by the fact of his having undergone some privations and dangers of a campaign. The Prince and his mother, who accompanied him, were warmly cheered both at Waterloo and at Southampton terminus on Thursday … The ex-Empress walked on board the 'Danube' leaning on her son's arm. She was dressed in partial mourning, and looked anxious and careworn. In her hand she carried a bunch of violets. As she stepped on the deck two young ladies each tendered her a bouquet, but as her hands were already full, the Prince, who was in private clothes, received them on her behalf, and raising his hat in recognition of the cheers which went up on all sides, said, in the best of English, 'Thanks, very much. Indeed, I am very grateful to you for your kind reception.'[39]

Eugénie was certainly anxious. She found her position impossible, and she thought herself tragic as a result, a feeling intensified by Louis' obvious excitement. 'In spite of his grief at parting with us,' she wrote,

> … he is overflowing with joy at the thought of the campaign. May God protect him! Have prayers said for him, that he may find an opportunity to distinguish himself, and return safe and sound.[40]

To her mother Eugénie summed up her predicament with an accuracy that touched on the prophetic:

> My life already crossed by such a variety of agitations is now to pass yet more painfully, hanging on the telegraph wire! Pity me, dear mother, for nothing is so terrible as suspense and it will be the companion of my days and nights. I haven't the courage to write more, for I must preserve all my courage to the end.[41]

At last the gangplanks were hauled in, the engines started, and the *Danube* was under-way. As the last of the spectators' cheers died in the distance, there was for the passengers an inevitable moment of anti-climax, a hint of the weeks of boredom to come on board ship, and Louis took the opportunity to collect his thoughts. At Plymouth, where the *Danube* made its last landfall on British soil, Louis scribbled a hurried note to his mother:

> For the seven hours I have been on board, I have nothing particular to tell you, except that I find myself very comfortably settled in my cabin, and that the sea is as calm as Lake Constance. However, there is a thick fog that only allows us to get along very slowly.
>
> I can say to you in writing what I did not wish to tell you *viva voce*; how much the grief of leaving you is mingled in my heart with the delight of being on active service. To tell you all I felt while bidding you good-bye would have been to agitate you to no purpose, for you must know me well enough to read my heart ...[42]

Then there was nothing to be done but resign themselves to the tedium of the voyage. It would take the best part of a month to reach Cape Town, where the *Danube* would stop to refuel for a day or two, then it was several days more to Durban. The gradual change in the weather, the occasional strange sights and distant shores, the novelty of ship-board life and the forced gaiety of home-made entertainments, could not entirely obscure the fact that the passengers were destined for a month of utter boredom, to be endured in cramped and uncomfortable conditions. Moreover, the reinforcements were being shipped abroad during the last blustery spasm of the European winter, and there was a risk that the weather might make life very uncomfortable indeed. One young officer, writing on board the *Dublin Castle*, which made the passage a week ahead of the *Danube*, describe his initiation to life on the ocean waves:

... when we started we were lustily cheered by crowds on the shore: the band played 'Should old acquaintance', etc, and we soon lost sight of England. Friday night everybody was ill, as the sea was rough. Saturday in the Bay of Biscay it was awful, the waves were mountains high – a grand sight – so much so that the upper decks were washed over by the sea all day. I was awfully ill, in fact so was everybody. Our cabin, which is on deck, was turned upside down, portmanteaus and everything flying about, we had to hold tight to stay in bed at all ... Saturday night the storm continued, the hatches were battened down to prevent the water going down to the lower decks. You know the boats slung up by the side of the ship actually touched the sea when we rolled; also the sea broke over into the engines. On Saturday morning at 4 a.m., I was on watch, luckily for me it was much calmer, I found two of the horses had died in the night, and that several hammocks, and other things had been washed overboard. I was awfully glad when we got out of the Bay. I'll never go to sea again if I can help it ...[43]

The *Danube* touched at Madeira – 'one sees,' wrote Louis, 'things that are novelties to civilised folk' – but after that there was nothing but 'sky and sea for twenty days'.[44] Nevertheless, the sense of excitements looming ahead was enough to keep Louis cheerful:

From Madeira down the Line we had fine weather.
The heat under the tropics was overwhelming, and nothing but the flying fishes, whose portrait you see could distract us from our compulsory idleness.
From the Equator, the sea was extremely rough, and though the old ceremony of crossing the Line has fallen into disuse aboard steamers, the Atlantic himself saw to it that we were baptised.
The days are long between sky and sea: and so every means of diversion is sought after.
Among the passengers are a great number of officers on leave or retired, militia captains, or simple adventurers who like myself are going to the Cape to make war or seek their fortune. They call themselves 'volunteers' and each of them flourishes a sword a little. We thought it would be amusing to break the monotony of the voyage by having a grand parade on board, to which each man should come in full dress and equipment.
Chosen Commander-in-Chief, I gave the order for a great review, and it was thoroughly diverting to see that line of Fradiavolesque

uniforms rise and fall with the roll of the ship. This farce had a serious side, that of allowing us to improve our equipment and our uniforms by comparison.[45]

For many of the volunteer officers en route to South Africa, the passage offered perhaps their first opportunity to become familiar with the weapons upon which their lives might very soon depend. Many had purchased swords, revolvers or even expensive hunting rifles just days before embarkation. Indeed, army training of the day paid little attention to officers' weapons proficiency, and while the War Office advised officers to procure revolvers at their own expense, it did not insist they practise with them. As a result, there was a sudden flurry of target practice, even on board ship, whenever any targets tempted their sportsmen's instincts. The results were not encouraging, as Guy Dawnay recalled – a fact which no doubt accounted for the poor standard of revolver marksmanship throughout the Zulu campaign:

> Yesterday afternoon there was a great deal of revolver practise, an old shark coming right up alongside during it and getting a heavy fire, though I don't think he was any the worse for it.[46]

Whether Louis himself took the opportunity to practise his shooting skills is not known; in the light of subsequent events, the evidence suggests he did not. For him, the sword was always a much more gallant weapon.

Nor were the officers alone in need of such practice, as Major Bindon Blood RE recalled:

> ... great trouble was taken on the voyage in the instruction of recruits on board the transports, so that in the harbour at St. Vincent's, for instance, where our ship anchored for about twenty-four hours, the bullets were frequently heard singing unduly near our ears! And the same thing happened at Simon's Bay ...[47]

There was to be one disappointment for Louis before the journey was over. The sea-lanes to the Cape took him within striking distance of that austere rock in the Atlantic which held a particular place in the heart of every true Bonapartist, but,

> I counted on writing you this from St. Helena, where I should have liked to make a pilgrimage before going on my first campaign ... My steamer did not stop there ...[48]

On 26 March, however, the *Danube* reached Cape Town, and Louis was granted his first glimpse of Africa. To men fresh out from the cold and damp of an English winter, the heat of the Cape, and the strangeness of the landscape and the exotic cosmopolitan population, threatened to overwhelm the senses. 'Cape Town was a horrid place,' thought one young officer,

> ... very hot and dirty, and there has been no rain there for some months, consequently everything has burnt up. Over the town an enormous mountain called Table Mountain towered, almost a perpendicular rock, some four or five thousand feet above the sea, and quite surrounding the town ... I went to some botanical gardens, and a museum there, which were the only things worth seeing there. The inhabitants were perfectly hideous, most of them niggers, did nothing but make faces and jabber ...[49]

Louis, however, was delighted to be off the cramped ship, and to be active again. 'The moment the Danube came into the roadstead,' he wrote to Eugénie,

> a naval officer in Lady Frere's suite came to meet me and invite me to accept the hospitality of Government House.
> I went in a carriage, acclaimed by a many-coloured population who had draped the windows with flags of as many different hues.
> Lady Frere has just taken me to Constantia, where I have eaten some of the famous grapes. I must declare that they surpass those of Arenenburg, and I was delighted with the varied landscape that presented itself to my eyes, tired of a watery horizon ...[50]

Yet for all Louis found much to reflect his gaiety in his new surroundings, there was a sombre air hanging over Cape Town in March 1879. It was, of course, hundreds of miles from Zululand, yet it had not gone untouched by the disaster at Isandlwana. It had taken just three days for the news to reach the town barracks, where the wives of many of the soldiers of the 24th Regiment had been left when the battalion had moved up to Natal, and a shudder went round the town at the sight of,

> About fifty women whose husbands, it is feared, have been slain, were bewailing bitterly the sad bereavement they had sustained, and their sobs were calculated to unman the sternest soldier that ever faced death upon the field of battle.[51]

The slaughter seemed to confirm all of the deepest subconscious fears of the settler community, and it raised the spectre of a united African rising across southern Africa. For Frere, it was immediately apparent that all hope of bringing the war to a quick and successful conclusion, and avoiding the censure of the home government, had gone, and he went to Natal to try to contain the damage. Although no general rising occurred – in reality, there was never any likelihood that it might – the flow of reinforcements through Table Bay kept the war to the forefront of Capetonians' minds. Indeed, by March a number of Chelmsford's agents were at work in the town, trying to raise recruits for the irregular corps, or buying up horses and stores. They brought with them a detailed knowledge and first-hand experience of the war which was eagerly devoured by the officers on the transports, and the effect of their reports was sobering. Guy Dawnay, whose previous experience of Zululand had given him a healthy scepticism of the Cape Town rumour-mill, was nonetheless disturbed when he bumped into one veteran:

> Commandant Lonsdale,[52] who escaped from Isandhlwana, and is now raising some cavalry volunteers ... The slaughter was far greater than we first stated, 51 European officers and 786 men being killed, and they say nearly 1000 of our native contingent. A great number of the dead ripped open, and the poor little band-boys stuck on the camp meat hooks.[53]

The story of the 24th's drummer boys, although largely apocryphal,[54] passed like wildfire among the troops in the crowded transports lying off Cape Town, together with equally lurid – but rather more reliable – stories of Zulu treatment of the British wounded and dead. 'They always kill the wounded,' one officer was told, '(because they think that our doctors can cure any wounds), by assegaing their entrails out'.[55]

It was not a prospect guaranteed to instil raw recruits, fresh out from England and scarcely trained, with confidence. Even before many of the reinforcements set foot in Zululand, they were showing distinct signs of nervousness.

Louis, of course, was merely excited. 'Tomorrow I leave for Durban,' he wrote to Eugénie, 'where I am eager to arrive, for a battle is expected.'[56]

NOTES

1.   Lord Chelmsford to the Secretary of State for War, 27 January 1879.
       Chelmsford Papers, National Army Museum, London. Published in

John Laband (ed.), *Lord Chelmsford's Zululand Campaign 1878–1879*, Army Records Society, 1994.

2. *The Illustrated London News*, 8 March 1879.
3. *The Illustrated London News*, 1 February 1879.
4. *The Illustrated London News*, 8 March 1879.
5. *Graham's Town Journal*, 21 August 1871.
6. *The Illustrated London News*, 1 February 1879.
7. CO/179/123; minute to Lord Carnarvon, 27 April 1877.
8. Frere to Theophilus Shepstone, 15 and 20 November 1878. Shepstone Papers, Natal Archives.
9. *Illustrated London News*, 8 March 1879.
10. *Illustrated London News*, 22 February 1879.
11. Chelmsford to Secretary of State for War, 27 January 1879. British Parliamentary Papers, C. 2252, enc. 2 in no. 22.
12. Sir Bindon Blood, *Four Score Years and Ten*, 1933.
13. *The Graphic*, 22 February 1879.
14. Major General W.C.F. Molyneux, *Campaigning in South Africa and Egypt*, London, 1896.
15. *Campaigns; Zulu 1879, Egypt 1882, Suakim 1885; Being the Private Journal of Guy C. Dawnay*, London, c.1886.
16. *The Graphic*, 1 March 1879.
17. *The Graphic*, 22 February 1879.
18. *The Graphic*, 1 March 1879.
19. Filon, *Memoirs of the Prince Imperial*.
20. Ibid.
21. Ibid.
22. Louis to Louis Conneau, Pietermaritzburg, 20 April 1879. Quoted in Filon, *Memoirs of the Prince Imperial*. Filon does not name the friend, but he is identified by Stoddart – who clearly had access to the letter, and offers a slightly different translation – in *The Life of the Empress Eugénie*.
23. Wood, *From Midshipman to Field Marshal*.
24. Filon, *Memoirs of the Prince Imperial*.
25. Ibid.
26. Filon, *Recollections of the Empress Eugénie*.
27. Eugénie, interview with Raoul Duval, 12 May 1879, quoted in Filon, ibid.
28. Louis to the Duke of Cambridge, 21 February 1879, quoted in Filon, ibid.
29. Queen Victoria to the Duke of Cambridge, 24 February 1879, reproduced in Edgar Sheppard, ed., *George, Duke of Cambridge*, 1907.
30. Disraeli to Lord Salisbury, 28 February 1879. Reproduced in Stanley Weintraub, *Disraeli: A Biography*, 1993.

31. Duke of Cambridge to Bartle Frere, 25 February 1879. Reproduced in Sonia Clarke, *Zululand at War 1879*, 1984.

32. Queen Victoria's Journal, 24 February 1879.

33. Prince Imperial to d'Espeuilles, February 1879, quoted in Katherine John, *The Prince Imperial*, 1939.

34. Queen Victoria to the Duke of Cambridge, 24 February 1879, in Sheppard, *George, Duke of Cambridge*.

35. Filon, *Memoirs of the Prince Imperial*.

36. 26 /27 February 1879, ibid.

37. *The Illustrated London News*, 5 July 1879.

38. Eugénie to her mother, quoted in Katherine John, *The Prince Imperial*.

39. *The Graphic*, 8 March 1879.

40. Quoted in Katherine John, *The Prince Imperial*.

41. Eugénie to Mme Montijo, ibid.

42. Filon, *Memoirs of the Prince Imperial*.

43. *Letters and Diary of the Late Arthur C.B. Mynors, Lieut., 3rd Batt., 60th Rifles*, privately published, Margate, 1879.

44. Louis to Eugénie, Cape Town, 26 March 1879. Reproduced in Filon, *Memoirs of the Prince Imperial*.

45. Ibid. Use of the phrase 'like myself ...' is revealing.

46. Dawnay, *Campaigns*.

47. Blood, *Four Score Years*.

48. Louis to M. Pietri, quoted in Filon, *Memoirs of the Prince Imperial*.

49. *Letters and Diary of Arthur C.B. Mynors*.

50. Louis to Eugénie, 26 March 1879, Filon, *Memoirs of the Prince Imperial*.

51. *The Graphic*, 22 February 1879.

52. Rupert LaTrobe Lonsdale commanded the 3rd Regiment, Natal Native Contingent in January 1879. He had been present with Lord Chelmsford at the time of the battle, but feeling ill had ridden back to the camp at Isandlwana. He was close to it before he realised it had already been over-run by the Zulu.

53. Dawnay, *Campaigns*.

54. The average age of the drummers killed at Isandlwana was twenty-four. See Ian Knight, *Zulu; The Battles of Isandlwana and Rorke's Drift*, London, 1992.

55. *Letters and Diary of Arthur C.B. Mynors*.

56. Louis to Eugénie, Cape Town, 26 March. Filon, *Memoirs of the Prince Imperial*.

IV

The Soldier's Dream of Glory

The *Danube* left Cape Town on 27 March, and five days later she entered Durban harbour without incident.

She was lucky. In many ways, for troops en route to Zululand, the stretch of coastline from Table Bay to Natal represented the most dangerous part of the entire journey. Scores of ships over the years had been driven ashore or onto submerged rocks by the unpredictable weather and dangerous currents which characterise an area still known as the Wild Coast – and troop transports were by no means immune. Indeed, one of the most famous shipwrecks in British maritime history had occurred in these waters, and in very similar circumstances, just a generation before.

On 25 February 1852 the steamship *Birkenhead* left Simon's Town, on the eastern side of the Cape Peninsula, heading for Algoa Bay, on the Cape frontier. Aboard were over 600 troops, drafts from a number of cavalry regiments and infantry battalions, intended as reinforcements for the bitter war Sir Harry Smith was then waging against the Xhosa people. At 2 am on the 26th, two miles off Danger Point, near Cape Agulhas – the southernmost tip of the African continent – the *Birkenhead* struck an uncharted rock, which ripped a great hole in her bow. Thousands of gallons of water instantly flooded the forward compartments, where at least a hundred troops were drowned in their bunks. The rest scrambled desperately onto the deck, only to find that many of the lifeboats had either been damaged on impact, or were rusted in place. It was a hot night, and in the airless conditions below decks many of the men had been naked or only partly clothed, and there had been no time to dress before their officers had called them to attention. There were a number of women – soldiers' wives – and children on board, and these were loaded into the surviving boats. Once the boats had pushed away from the side, the civilian captain suggested that every man should save himself, but the officers, afraid that the boats would be swamped, refused. There was no time to think of an alternative plan; within minutes, with the men still lined up on deck, the *Birkenhead* broke up around them, and sank.

The ship was wrecked close to the shore on a calm night, but most of the men could not swim, and those who tried found the sea clogged with weed and teeming with sharks and barracuda. Of 638 people on board the *Birkenhead*, over 400 died; all of the women and children survived, however, and in the story of this wreck lay the origin of the tradition of 'women and children first'. The courage and discipline of the troops in the ship's last moments came to epitomise the best tradition of British self-sacrifice. Even the Duke of Wellington was moved to express his approval, and the story passed into army folklore as the 'Birkenhead Drill' – a by-word for a cold acceptance of a hard and hopeless bargain. And if the reality behind the incident did not quite stand up to the romantic myth to which it gave birth, it was potent enough, as one survivor recalled:

> The old king of Prussia commanded that the story of the Birkenhead drill and fortitude should be read to every regiment in his army; artists have painted pictures of the troops drawn up in steady ranks on deck, and poets have sung of the way the bugles rang and the drums beat; but there was no sound of bugle and no roll of drum; there was none of the stiffness of parade which the pictures show – and yet there was a falling-in, a last muster, a standing shoulder to shoulder as the end came, and many a handshake, and many a sobbed farewell ...[1]

The story of the *Birkenhead* still echoed among the reinforcements who arrived at the Cape in March 1879, and with reason, for the risk of shipwreck was still very real. Indeed, two of the transports carrying troops to Zululand came to grief, and in the same waters as the *Birkenhead*. If the outcome of each case was very different, that was due as much to luck, and the heavy presence of Navy vessels cruising off the coast, than to improved safety conditions. On 21 March the transport *City of Paris*, carrying the 2nd Bttn. 21st Regiment, was caught in a sudden squall at the entrance to Simon's Bay, and driven onto rocks at the foot of the Roman Rocks Lighthouse, two miles offshore. The damage was not serious, however, and HMS *Tamar* was on hand to offer support. The battalion was put ashore without loss.

More serious was an incident involving the SS *Clyde*, which occurred on 3 April – less than a fortnight later. Although the wreck of the *Clyde* lacked the sheer human drama of the *Birkenhead* story, the incident is not without interest, for it marks the first appearance in South Africa of a man whose fortunes would prove inextricably bound up with the fate of the Prince Imperial.

The *Clyde* was an iron steamship of 2,283 tons, and she had set out from Woolwich on 1 March, travelling a week behind the *Danube*. Like the *Birkenhead*, she too had called into Simon's Bay rather than Cape Town to refuel, an operation she had accomplished in good time due to the enthusiasm of the officers on board. She was carrying 120 tons of ammunition, four Gatling guns, and over 500 men, mostly drafts to replace the losses of the ill-fated 1/24th. These were short-service men and raw recruits hastily cobbled together from no fewer than eleven home battalions, and under the temporary command of Colonel H.F. Davies of the Grenadier Guards. The ship set off again on the 2nd, but at 4.35 the following morning, just before dawn, she

> ... was enveloped in a fog; but, as the officer on duty supposed, quite clear of the coast, when suddenly rocks and breakers appeared out of the fog before her. The ship was then but a few lengths from the breakers. The only thing to do was to reverse the engines, and this was done on the instant. She was then going at from ten to eleven knots an hour, and before she was stopped a grinding sound was to be heard under the bows and extended amidships, when she stuck fast upon what was believed to be a bar of sand.[2]

The *Clyde* had struck a reef a mile from Dyer Island – three miles offshore, between Danger Point, where the *Birkenhead* went down, and Quoin Point, in an area known to modern eco-tourists as Shark Alley, owing to the number of great whites which feed there. A quick survey showed that she was holed and taking in water, but that there was no immediate danger; three hours after the collision, there was still no more than two or three feet of water in the hold.[3] The young soldiers of the 24th were to be spared the 'Birkenhead Drill', at least, but Davies paraded them on deck and, no doubt conscious of their youth and the potential for indiscipline, ordered a guard to be placed over both the rum ration and the lifeboats.

The ship's captain, Captain Luckhurst, had plenty of time to organise an orderly evacuation. While the lifeboats were made ready – at about 5.25 am – breakfast was prepared for the troops. The first two companies[4] to go ashore were ordered to make ready their weapons and accoutrements, and together with the sick were loaded into the boats at about 6.20. They set out for the shore in two parties, under the command of Captain W.M. Brander, 24th, and Lieutenant J.B. Carey, a special service officer from the 98th Regiment. As the survivors of the *Birkenhead* had discovered, to get away from the ship in boats did not necessarily mean an end to their troubles. To reach the shore the boats would have to pass though a thick belt of weed, which grew right up to the surface of the water, then brave an awesome line of breakers which crashed onto an open shore. Indeed, one of the *Birkenhead*'s boats had become foaled in this weed to the extent that it had been trapped for hours, unable to land, though the beach was only a few hundred yards away.

On this occasion, however, the survivors were in luck, and the worst that happened was that the two parties became separated, and came ashore out of sight of one another. Nevertheless, it was hardly a welcoming introduction to the African continent, for the shoreline was a bleak, windswept reach of sand dunes, with little vegetation, and no obvious fresh water. Lieutenant Carey took the initiative and he soon organised parties to search for water – 'I got the men to scrape together with their hands for water'[5] – and to begin constructing shelters. By the time further boats arrived from the wreck, they found a serviceable bivouac under construction, and the kettle already on. Nevertheless, it was an unnerving and uncomfortable experience. 'We lost everything what we had on us,' lamented a Private of the 24th, Isaac Morris:

I was able to keep my rifle, but lost everything else. I was fortunate to have my life. The ship sank out of sight, leaving no trace except for a little of the mast. We came ashore in a very desolate place, without a house within scores of miles ...[6]

There was, however, one consolation. Whatever demons the bloodthirsty stories of Isandlwana, current at the Cape, might have conjured up in their imaginations, there were no fearsome African warriors waiting on shore to disembowel them – just a solitary Boer farmer named Albert van der Byle, who put his wagon at Carey's disposal, and, with an eye to the main chance, offered to sell food to the troops. Throughout the morning, the remaining men were put safely ashore. Colonel Davies stayed on board with a work party until the last of them had gone, then supervised the destruction of the rum ration. Shortly before noon the ship began to break up, and the last of the officers abandoned it. On landing, Davies was delighted to find that Brander and Carey

... had chosen an admirable spot, [with] plenty of wood and water and a certain amount of brushwood and grass which preserved it from being dusty, all the ground round being sandhills. The bivouac was well-sheltered.[7]

By 8.30 that evening the men had been fed, and were under cover for the night. When they awoke the next morning, they found that the *Clyde* had sunk during the hours of darkness, and only the tops of her spars were visible above the water. While the men had managed to salvage a quantity of food, tons of supplies, spare uniforms and weapons, and thousands of rounds of ammunition, had all sunk with her. Of the ship's crew and passengers, however, not one man had been lost.

Moreover, rescue was at hand. The *Clyde*'s Chief Officer had set out for Cape Town in a long-boat to alert the authorities, and HMS *Tamar* hurried to the scene. By mid-morning on the 4th, the men were embarking in the *Tamar*'s boats. Davies was pleased with the way they had behaved, and his glowing report was later endorsed by Colonel Bellairs, Lord Chelmsford's Adjutant-General. Among the officers singled out by Davies for recommendation were Brander and Carey,

> ... for the great judgement they showed in selecting a landing place and camping ground, and to the latter officer for the excellent huts which he so quickly constructed for the troops.[8]

When the news reached England, the Duke of Cambridge himself, no doubt mindful of the contrast with the *Birkenhead* disaster, was equally full of praise:

> If there had been the slightest confusion, the slightest irregularity – if there had been any forgetfulness on the part of the officers concerned, or any want of attention on the part of the non-commissioned officers and men, the chances are that very few of the men would have been saved; but such was the devotion to duty and discipline that ... I firmly believe that the English soldier is ready to do anything he can be called upon to do.[9]

All in all, the *Clyde* affair had reflected well upon all concerned, and, for an ambitious officer like Lieutenant Jahleel Brenton Carey, to be mentioned in despatches before even setting foot at the front could hardly be more encouraging. Carey must have looked forward to the coming campaign with optimism and confidence.

Not that Carey was new to such a serious level of responsibility, since he was already an experienced officer, and more than used to acting on his own initiative. This was not, however, reflected in his rank, largely because for officers with ambition but no personal wealth or contacts – and Carey fitted both categories – it was still a struggle to rise in the Army of the 1870s by merit alone. Carey was born at Burbage, in Leicestershire, in July 1847, the son of a country parson, Adolphus Carey, later Vicar of Brixham, in Devon.[10] On his mother's side, Carey's grandfather was Admiral Sir Jahleel Brenton, who had commanded a frigate in the war against Napoleon, and 'received a baronetcy for his blameless career'.[11] Carey had inherited Sir Jahleel's splendid Biblical name,[12] and perhaps some of his martial spirit. He had spent much of his youth in France, and was educated in French schools, before entering Sandhurst to train as an infantry officer. On graduation, he received a free commission, and in 1865 joined the 3rd Battalion of the West India Regiment, a regiment of black troops commanded by white officers, based in Jamaica.

The spur to his choice of commission was undoubtedly the genteel poverty to which the Carey family was subject. The church and the Army were the traditional refuge for the second and subsequent sons of the middle and even upper classes in Victorian Britain, since the law of primogeniture ensured that only the eldest son inherited the family fortunes – and both institutions featured heavily in Carey family history. Colonial regiments, such as the 3rd West India, were deeply unfashionable in Army circles, and it was well known that officers joined them largely to acquire a comfortable standard of living in the colonies, to which they could not aspire at home. This prejudice – ironic in an institution dependent upon colonial troops to defend the Empire upon which its power and prestige relied – lasted throughout the Victorian period. As late as the Anglo-Boer War – that first great and terrible crucible, when the conventions of nineteenth-century warfare ground up against the realities of modern war – the curiously obsessive division between the Army establishment at home, and the Anglo-Indian faction, hampered cooperation at senior levels to the extent that operations in the field were often compromised. When Carey first took up his commission, regiments composed of black troops stood lower in the social scale than even those of British Indian regiments. Moreover, the 3rd West India spent much of their time in garrison duties on the 'gold coast' of Africa, a spot so unhealthy that it was traditionally known as the White Man's Grave. To have chosen such a commission, Carey must either have been broke, desperate, or extremely determined to make the most of his opportunities. Probably, he was all three.

For all the many thousands of words written later about Carey, his character remains elusive. It is true that his surviving letters suggest that he was both devoutly religious and rather sentimental about his family, traits which have been presented by some authors as unusual or obsessive, and attributed to his upbringing in France. Yet such an assumption is misleading. Victorian society was overtly devout in the 1870s in ways which a century of cynicism since have made it hard to understand, and the strong links between the Church and officer class often carried into the field. Living with the prospect of sudden death has ever been the soldier's lot, and the appeal of religious faith under such circumstances is obvious enough. For all its legendary rough edges, the Victorian army was no different. This was particularly true of the educated officer elite, although the effects of educational reform, the temperance movement and religious evangelism had left their mark, too, among the Other Ranks. Church services for Christian denominations were regularly held among British troops on campaign, and this would certainly prove to be true in Zululand. Moreover, small but dedicated elements were prepared to go further, and organise extracurricular religious activities. During the siege of the mission station at Eshowe, for example, regular Bible readings were organised:

> ... we meet four times a week; between thirty and forty soldiers and blue-jackets attend.
> ... The men seem to enjoy our little meetings very much, as they show by coming to them after very hard work and in hot weather, and under circumstances not altogether comfortable.[13]

References to religious observance can be found throughout the letters and diaries of the Anglo-Zulu War, suggesting that Carey, far from being isolated in this regard, was in fact part of a mainstream pattern of belief and practice. Evelyn Wood and his staff regularly offered up individual prayers most nights before retiring; the Prince Imperial, devoutly Catholic, said his nightly prayers aloud.[14] The letters of another veteran of the Eshowe campaign, Captain Warren Wynne RE, reveal an overriding commitment to religious belief and family affection which was in fact commonplace. Duty, God and the sanctity of the family were the very pillars of Victorian morality, and many officers took these responsibilities seriously. Nor were they at all self-conscious in expressing them, for by 1879 the open sentimentality of the early Victorian period had not yet given way to the more restrained outlook of the 1890s. Wynne's writings, no less than Carey's – and dozens of their contemporaries – are redolent of an open personal and spiritual devotion:

> We have Holy Communion next Sunday. How I am looking forward to it in the midst of all this work and anxiety. May our dear Lord make Himself very fully known to me in the breaking of bread, and may I be enabled to realise the blessedness of the Communion of the mystic Body of Christ, even His Holy Church, His saints on earth and in Paradise ...

... Give my father my kindest love, and thank him for all his great kindness and consideration; and also very much love to my sisters, and Skeff and Charley.

Abundance of love to the dear little mother and all our dear ones. Kiss our pets for me very fondly.[15]

In his photographs Carey appears alternately wistful or lugubrious, but the conventions of formal Victorian portraiture make any great insight into character difficult. Later – after the event – his colleagues in Zululand suggested that Carey was a withdrawn man, and something of a loner, but this too might be misleading. Carey's position as a special service officer inevitably isolated him from the camaraderie of the regimental mess, and he spent much of his time with a small coterie of staff officers who surrounded Chelmsford, most of whom were senior to him. He had little time to meet with equals in relaxed circumstances, and few opportunities to make new friends in Zululand. As Colonel Richard Harrison, Carey's immediate senior in Zululand, recalled, a staff position inevitably threw a man on his own resources:

> I left England and landed as a Regimental officer. My rations were drawn by the quartermaster-sergeant, my cooking was done by the company cooks, my baggage was carried in regimental transport, my tent was pitched and trenches dug by a regimental fatigue party; but when I became a Staff officer, and was liable to march and pitch my camp either by myself or with others, it became necessary to make oneself entirely independent.[16]

Under such circumstances, it is scarcely surprising that in the six weeks between his arrival in Zululand and the affair if 1 June, Carey seems to have formed no lasting friendships.

Carey had spent time in Africa before. The British West India regiments were widely employed to police British possessions not only in the Caribbean islands, but across the nearest continental possessions – in West Africa and Central America. Carey was to become familiar with all three theatres, and in the course of his service would be exposed to some of the more uncomfortable realities of British colonial policy. When he took up his commission, the 3rd West India were based at Sierra Leone, in the very heart of the White Man's Grave, and within a year found himself not only leading a company, but posted in sole command to the old British fort at Accra, on the Gold Coast. He was not then twenty. Even in an age when junior officers regularly held field commands in their teens, this was an unusual responsibility, and suggests something of the scarcity of resources which the British at that time commanded in the region. Unfashionable or not, the 3rd West India probably gave Carey more testing and varied experience than he might have enjoyed in a Line Regiment at home.

Carey survived – not entirely unscathed – the wide and exotic array of diseases which traditionally decimated Europeans on the Coast, and in 1866 the battalion returned to its headquarters in Jamaica. Just a year later, in response to friction in British Honduras, detachments of both the 3rd and 4th Battalions were ordered to Central America, and Carey volunteered to join them.

The Honduras campaign of 1867 has made little impact on the history books, and indeed amounted to little more than occasional bouts of skirmishing, conducted in a remote and desperately inhospitable terrain. British territorial claims comprised a narrow strip of land on the eastern seaboard of Central America – modern Belize – bordered on all landward sides by largely unsympathetic Spanish colonial or independent neighbours. The principal economic justification for the British presence lay in the extraction of mahogany timber, and indeed much of British Honduras consisted of dense rain forest. So difficult, indeed, was this landscape to administer that in places the borders were ill-defined, and local settlers had taken advantage of this to establish logging camps in areas to which their title was, to say the least, dubious. As one surprisingly frank contemporary account put it, this

> ... gave rise to endless disputes and complications, fostered, in great measure, by renegade settlers within our territory, and fanned into a flame by unfair trading practices.[17]

In April 1866 a party of Indians under a chief named Canul, protesting against incursions into territory they claimed as their own, attacked a logging camp on the remote Hondo river. Two visiting Englishmen were captured, and only released after the payment of a substantial ransom. This was the first indication that the usual frontier tensions had reached a critical juncture, and over the next few months further attacks on logging establishments took place, to the extent that the industry along the Hondo was largely paralysed. The British response was to send an envoy, Civil Commissioner Rhys, to try to negotiate with Canul's supporters. Rhys was escorted by 140 men of the West India Regiment, under the command of a Major MacKay. Most of the men were from the 4th Battalion, but there was a small detachment from the 3rd – and among them was Lieutenant Jahleel Carey.

From the first, it is clear that there was something rotten at the heart of this expedition. MacKay seemed reluctant to take to the field at all, and when at last he did, he was criticised for leading his men to the front by the most roundabout means possible. The result for the men under his command was at first uncomfortable, and then terrifying:

> ... they entered upon what resulted in a terrible and unfortunate march. All night the soldiers toiled manfully through mud and slush, under an almost incessant downpour of rain, and in the morning were met by a force of the enemy variously estimated, and a fight ensued. Volleys were interchanged, resulting in eighteen or twenty casualties on our side, and probably the like on the part of the enemy; for the Indians invariably carry off their dead and wounded as they fall. Both sides, however, retreated from the field, leaving the action indecisive, while the unfortunate Commissioner, by some unexplained chance possibly, falling into the hands of the enemy, no doubt, added another to the victims of their cold-blooded cruelty.[18]

In the recriminations which followed, MacKay was accused of losing his head, and abandoning the field at the first shots, leaving his men to their fate. His junior officers, Carey among them, could only cover the retreat as best they could, and an open rout had been narrowly avoided. The bodies of the dead were abandoned on the field, and no attempt was made to rescue Commissioner Rhys.

News of the fiasco swept through Honduras. Loggers abandoned their exposed camps in the forests, and carried their panic into the town of Belize, where

> ... one night in particular, a false alarm of the approach of Indians caused a general rush to the boats, and a panic prevailed [which was] simply indescribable, and certainly discreditable to a city of 6000 inhabitants, built in a defensible position on the delta formed by the mouths of the river Belize.[19]

So unstable did the situation become that local officials appealed to Jamaica for support, and the Governor himself, Sir James Grant, hurried to the mainland with a detachment of troops under the command of Colonel Harley. Harley organised a punitive column of 300 men, Carey among them,[20] and promptly plunged into the forest,

> ... at one time literally strung up by rope-like parasites – now struggling in the grasping embrace of creeping tendrils, anon slipping into deep holes, or plunging recklessly along the narrow paths, panting from the exertion and the stifling heat, drenched with

torrents from above and saturated in the nether extremities while fording numerous creeks, without breakfast or the likelihood of supper, the troops toiled on uncomplaining through a perfect labyrinth of trees ... Words are insufficient to enumerate the misfortunes of that line of march, until at night, wet and wearied officers and men lay down together in dripping uniforms ... without food or drink, with no protection from the ground beneath, or the sky above, covered with insects, and worried with flies ...[21]

Harley's objective was the village of San Pedro, which had been sustaining Canul's incursions. To Harley's disappointment, when his men reached the village on 9 February and attacked it, they found it deserted. They razed it to the ground anyway, and to make their point destroyed several other neighbouring villages. They then visited the site of the MacKay fiasco, and recovered and buried the bodies still lying there. There was little in the way of opposition; most of the rebels simply disappeared into the forest. By the end of March, order was restored, and the loggers returned to denude the forest once more. The sequel to this unhappy story was entirely predictable:

We understand that Major Mackay, late in command of a detachment of the 4th West India Regiment at Honduras, has been ordered to report himself at headquarters in [Jamaica], to undergo examination before a court of inquiry, touching his conduct when in command against the Indians at Orange River. Lieutenant Carey and Ferguson, who were with the detachment, have also been ordered to Jamaica to give evidence before the Court ... It will be remembered that the major was in command of a detachment which ... met Indians near San Pedro, and the major, apparently believing that he was being surrounded by overwhelming numbers, ordered a retreat, which speedily produced a panic ... It is to establish the truth or falsity of the conduct attributed to the major that the inquiry, we understand, will be instituted ...[22]

MacKay was duly censured – in curiously prophetic terms Lieutenant Governor Austin described the action as 'an affair more discreditable to the service has never, I apprehend, occurred'[23] – but his junior officers were exonerated, and indeed Carey probably emerged with as much credit as anyone from the fiasco. In particular, he was commended for his thoroughness and efficiency, and 'was mentioned in despatches by Lieutenant Colonel Harley for the maps and plans which he then prepared'.[24]

Nor were there any reasons to question his personal courage. He had retained his self-control and some measure of authority throughout a particularly terrifying baptism of fire on the Hondo, and there was no suggestion that he had been unnerved, despite his youth at the time. Later, he had remained cool and resourceful throughout the *Clyde* incident, despite the very real dangers involved. 'That Lieutenant Carey was wanting in personal courage', recalled one officer who met him in Zululand, 'I cannot believe'.[25]

Indeed, perhaps the most significant theme to emerge from Carey's career before 1879 was his determination to succeed by conspicuous professionalism. In this, he was part of a trend within the Army which was only then becoming fashionable. In the 1850s British officers of any social standing had often affected to despise their craft, trusting to their luck as gentlemen and amateurs to see them through, and believing that too great a degree of professionalism carried with it the vulgar taint of trade. Although the Staff College had been established with the specific intention of training officers in their craft, senior figures within the Army establishment, including the Duke of Cambridge himself, continued to regard it as a passing fashion, and to dismiss its graduates as officious and over-ambitious. Nevertheless, a new school of younger officers was on the rise, who championed reform, and placed great emphasis on a proper degree of technical skill. They were epitomised by Sir Garnet Wolseley, whose own campaigns in West Africa in 1873–4 had achieved remarkable results by thorough planning and careful logistics. For many, Wolseley's methods pointed the way ahead, and indeed as Wolseley's personal star rose those who hoped to shine with him, and sought posts in his high-profile commands, were expected to share his level of commitment. Lacking money or influential contacts, Carey relied for preferment on his skills as an administrator and draughtsman. Nor were his goals unrealistic; there were many, like him, who came from the impoverished minor gentry, and yet rose to distinguished rank. Evelyn Wood's father was also a parson; and he commanded one of Chelmsford's columns in Zululand.

Carey left Honduras suffering from the effects of fever and rheumatism brought about by exposure to the difficult terrain. He returned to England on leave, and when he had recovered he took the opportunity to attend the Musketry School at Hythe, in Kent. This earned him a first class certificate, so that when he returned to his regiment he was appointed Musketry Instructor. And at about this time he married one Anna Isabella Vine at the town of Falmouth, in Jamaica.

For a man still in his early twenties, it must have seemed to Carey that his life was comfortably established on the road to the status and security to which he aspired.

Then disaster struck. In June 1870 the 3rd West India Regiment was disbanded. Carey was 'nearly at the head of the List of Lieutenants, [and] the disbandment of his Regiment was a cruel reverse'.[26] He and most of the other officers of the regiment were placed on the half-pay list – that professional oblivion to which the government consigned all those officers for whom it had no immediate use, but whom it wished to retain on tap. Carey found himself without a commission, and with little more than the good will of his old commanding officer. 'Whenever I wanted a difficult, unpleasant task well and thoroughly accomplished', wrote Colonel Chamberlayne, 'I employed Lieutenant Carey.'[27] It was scant consolation for a young officer suddenly deprived of his prospects. Carey, however, reacted with characteristic determination. He returned to the UK to seek out an appointment in a Line Regiment, and had not been home long when news broke in the British press of the Franco-Prussian crisis in Europe. Carey promptly volunteered for service with the English Ambulance – a voluntary group which crossed the Channel to offer medical aid and supplies to both sides.

His motives were probably mixed. Humanitarianism was undoubtedly one of them, and Carey, of course, knew France, and could speak French. But perhaps equally important was the realisation that the Franco-Prussian War was likely to have a significant impact on British military thinking. It was, it seemed, the most challenging war of the age, in which traditional French elan was ranged against steely Prussian efficiency. If the American Civil War had been the first conflict to suggest the terrible changes wrought on the battlefield by the technological and industrial improvements of the mid-nineteenth century, it had been largely condemned by military theorists in Britain as a war waged by amateurs. This was, perhaps, true; though of course such a response missed the point that future wars would be increasingly difficult to contain within professional bounds. In 1870, however, the speed of the Prussian mobilisation struck a chord with many progressive thinkers within the British Army, and many ambitious officers sought excuses to reach the front as observers.[28] To have been in France could have harmed Carey's career not at all, especially as he would emerge with 'special thanks, with a cross and ribbon, for his conduct in the relief of French wounded'.[29]

It is probably no coincidence that at about the time of his return, Carey was able to purchase an exchange into the 81st Regiment – a British line Regiment – and thereafter transfer into the 98th (Prince of Wales') Regiment, who were then stationed in his old haunts, the West Indies. He seems to have made a good impression in his new posting, since he was appointed Garrison Adjutant, and held the position of Brigade Major for several months. Three years later, the 98th were moved to Malta, and in 1878 Carey was accepted into the Staff College. He passed out 'with high testimonials',[30] and in the same flush of national enthusiasm which had sent Louis to South Africa, he had volunteered for service in Zululand.

When the first reinforcements began to arrive at Durban in the middle of March, they received a euphoric reception from a community which had been living under daily anticipation of a Zulu attack for nearly six weeks:

> ... the welcome which they were accorded was exceedingly appropriate, and evidently appreciated by both officers and men ...
>
> As they marched up the Point road they were welcomed by the residents, who rushed to their doors, and, in many cases, heartily cheered the new arrivals. The scene was a most interesting one, the troops being followed by a large crowd of townspeople both on foot and on horseback.[31]

But even by the time the *Danube* arrived on 1 April the Durban crowd was growing used to the spectacle, and the sight of exotic military equipment being brought ashore at the docks, and of brightly coloured uniforms in the streets, had lost its novelty. 'During the past few days', wrote one local correspondent, 'there has been one continuous busy scene at the Point', but 'very few people gathered ... to witness the landing of the troops there.'[32] Even Louis' arrival prompted little comment in the local press, which by that time had turned its attentions to fresh developments inland, on the Zulu border.

Nevertheless, Louis was exuberant at arriving at last so close to the theatre of war, and the cheers of the rather bored group of bystanders at the Point convinced him that Durban was equally delighted to see him:

> Since my last letter, that is to say since I left Cape Town, I have lived in a state of anxiety and impatience, comparable to that of an old troop horse yoked to a plough when he hears the trumpet sound the charge ...
>
> ... My regret is not to be with those who are fighting; you know me well enough to judge how bitter this is. But all is not over and I shall have my revenge on my ill-luck.
>
> I was received on my arrival in Natal like a crowned head, though I wore a lieutenant's uniform. The ships were dressed with flags and the military authorities came to meet me ...[33]

In fact, Louis was deeply disappointed to find that most of the senior officers, including Lord Chelmsford and his staff, were not in Durban, but rather at the front, where a new wave of fighting was underway.

Louis carried with him a letter of introduction to Lord Chelmsford from the Commander-in-Chief, but etiquette made it impossible for him to travel to the front until he had received Chelmsford's permission. 'I had to resign myself,' he wrote to General Simmons, 'to my fate and wait here until the General comes back'.[34]

Captain Baynton, of the Union Steamship Company, made his house available to the Prince, and Louis took the opportunity to see something of Durban. He called in to the offices of a Durban photographer, and had several portraits taken of himself. He had had his hair cropped short for convenience in the field, and together with his carefully cultivated moustache, and the blue Artillery undress uniform he wore, he appears more mature in these last photos than he actually was – very much the young officer off to war. He had just turned twenty-three.

The enforced wait at least gave Louis the opportunity to attend to some last-minute practicalities. Sadly, one of his magnificent horses had died on the voyage out – by no means an unusual occurrence – and he needed to buy a new one.[35] Good horseflesh was almost impossible to find in Durban at the time, since the influx of officers en route to the front had pushed prices sky-high, and even the most inadequate farm nag commanded a premium. According to local tradition, Louis was visiting the Royal Hotel in Durban with Uhlmann one day when he glanced out of the window, and saw a civilian riding past on a handsome grey. Louis immediately sent Uhlmann to buy the animal. The owner, Meyrick Bennett, the managing director of Randles Brothers & Hudson, was reluctant to sell, but Louis, typically, would not be thwarted.[36] He offered £75 – well over the odds – and Bennett at last succumbed.[37]

Since this horse was apparently to play a crucial role in subsequent events, it is interesting to ponder its character. After Louis' death it was claimed that the animal was highly strung, nervous, skittish and unpre-dictable,[38] but the earliest evidence suggests that the opposite was in fact the case – and that, if anything, he was placid to the point of stubborn-ness. An officer who saw him frequently later in the war noted that he was 'very quiet and easy to mount ... I see [him] mounted by Clifford's aide-de-camp, Lieutenant Westmacott, every day of my life'.[39] Years later, when the horse was put out to pasture, a relative of his new owner remained puzzled by the reputation he had acquired:

It was truly strange that he should have been restive on that ill-fated day when his master was killed, for a more good-tempered animal it is not possible to imagine. He was, of course, very old when I knew him, but he showed what a grand horse he had been. I drove him once in a pair ...[40]

Another observer, who also claimed a family connection, merely recalled that 'it took some effort to get him to move. My father used to say that the horse was a really stubborn brute'.[41]

Nor is the horse's name entirely clear. Dr George Campbell, a great collector of Durban lore, told the historian Donald Morris that the horse was named Percy, but if so this was probably Meyrick Bennett's name for him, and there is no record that Louis ever referred to him as such.[42] Indeed, despite the notoriety which the horse later achieved, there is remarkably little contemporary reference to his name, suggesting perhaps that Louis had made little impact outside the close-knit group of staff officers with whom he served. Louis, it seems, called him Tommy, revealing an unexpected flair for wry humour.[43] He also bought another local horse, a roan which he called Fate – a name far more in keeping with Louis' sense of destiny;[44] presumably, like many of the new arrivals, he had come to realise that while local animals were unprepossessing by European standards, they were far more suited to conditions in the field. The grey was not unduly large – between fifteen and sixteen hands – though he may sometimes have seemed so, when ridden by a slim young man with short legs.

During his few days in Durban, Louis began to form an impression of the people among whom he was now living. Despite his limited experience, his inquisitive mind and readiness to hold an opinion had already led him to question the corrosive effects of European contact on local African groups, and to absorb many of the opinions current among the troops about their enemy:

I have already been struck in Africa by a fact that justifies this idea: it is the difference between the Cape natives and the natives of Natal. The latter are still half warriors – living in kraals and following their ancient customs; the former have adopted European habits. The Kaffirs of Natal have kept some of the noble qualities that characterise man in nature, while those of the Cape Colony have lost all those qualities, and have learned nothing from the whites except to drink, to smoke, and to cover themselves in rags. As for the Zulus, they are certainly the finest black people in the world; among the soldiers there is no feeling of vengeance towards them, nothing but admiration for such bold warriors ...[45]

In that last respect, he was deluding himself. In fact, by the end of March the imminence of a new wave of fighting had begun to exaggerate the nervousness among the troops which had prevailed since Isandlwana. The wild stories current in Cape Town took on a new significance once the reinforcements actually arrived in Natal, and were exposed not only to the proximity of the enemy, but to the strange sights, sounds and unsettling experiences of Africa itself. The letters of one young officer suggest something of the extent to which the Zulu had come to be regarded as bogey-men, credited with scarcely human powers of ubiquity, endurance and savagery:

> No one knows where the Zulu armies are; one day they are seen at one place, another at another; one meal lasts them for three days; and the bush they can creep through like snakes. Being nothing but Zulus (natives) about the country here, they come and watch us; in fact, they know everything that goes on. They are awfully wily; they are never to be caught in an open country, and never will be unless at Undini; the only time they will attack their enemy is before daybreak, and at night when we encamp ...[46]

Indeed, as Frances Colenso, the wife of the Bishop of Natal, who with her family was bitterly opposed to British policies in Zululand, nonetheless noted, 'the spirits and courage of the army are flagging, and they seem to be beginning to *fear the Zulu*'.[47] Lord Chelmsford himself, reviewing the 60th Rifles at Durban after their arrival in the middle of March, had unconsciously reinforced these fears:

> The impression left on our minds was that the Zulus were very formidable foes, and we soon found out that this unfortunate sentiment prevailed on all sides, and that hesitation and vacillation were the natural result. Our men, especially the young soldiers, were not slow to share the general feeling of uneasiness which the disasters at Isandlwana and elsewhere had caused.[48]

The effects of this unease were not confined to the new arrivals, however, and had been apparent since news of Isandlwana had first spread throughout the invasion force. A series of incidents had occurred – in themselves by no means unusual in any war – which had gone some way to establishing a climate of fear among British troops in Zululand. In the field, morale in the British Army often depended upon the confidence which the ordinary soldiers held in their officers; not so much in their skills or professionalism, but in a sense that they would stand by them, and not let them down, no matter how dangerous the circumstances. Huge social gulfs separated the officer class from the men under their command, and while these could not easily be bridged, they were to some extent mitigated by the carefully cultivated rituals of regimental tradition.

Nevertheless, the Victorian Army reflected the wider social assumptions about the responsibilities of the ruling elite, and imposed a duty of courage and self-sacrifice upon the officers in particular. Any individual aberration, particularly by an officer, had a potential consequence which went far beyond a particular incident, and threatened to undermine the effectiveness of the institution as a whole. What this meant in practical terms was that rather too much often depended on a split-second instinctive response by a potentially inexperienced or isolated individual, usually in desperate and terrifying circumstances. For both the army establishment, and the British public at home – thrilling to the adventures of the 'thin red line of heroes' in the weekly illustrated papers – it was a necessary article of faith that the line between courage and cowardice in action was clear cut. Yet in Zululand, after Isandlwana, that was far from the case. And as Carey would later discover, the establishment response to individual failings often had little to do with the realities of combat in this most vicious colonial war.

The incident which had done most to damage confidence in serving officers had occurred on 12 March, while both Louis and Carey were still at sea. On Zululand's troubled north-western borders, the British had established a small garrison of five companies of the 80th Regiment at the small German settlement of Luneburg, in the heart of the disputed territory. These men had originally been part of Lord Chelmsford's projected No. 5 Column, based on the Transvaal border, but despite the fact that that column had largely been broken up after Isandlwana, they still received their supplies from depots in the Transvaal, rather than Natal. This meant that regular supply convoys had to make a long and arduous journey from the town of Middleburg, nearly 130 miles away to the north. The last part of this journey, near Luneburg itself, was the most dangerous, since the road passed through the territories of a number of semi-independent chieftains along the upper Phongolo river, who had proved themselves to be tenacious and resourceful guerrilla fighters in the Zulu cause. In particular, only about five miles from the garrison at Luneburg, the track crossed a steep, narrow river called the Ntombe, within sight of a hill which was known to be a refuge of the most able Zulu commander in the region, a disaffected Swazi prince named Mbilini waMswati.

At the end of February a convoy of eighteen wagons, loaded with supplies and ammunition, left Middleburg for Luneburg. The commander of the Luneburg garrison, Major Tucker, well aware of the danger they faced nearby, sent a company of troops to meet them at the hamlet of Derby, half-way. But the progress of the convoy was delayed by bad weather, and a misunderstanding of Tucker's orders led the troops to

THE SOLDIER'S DREAM.

With a little of the Romance rubbed off.

The satirical magazine Fun *saw little glory in the Anglo-Zulu War; here the fearsome 'cat of nine tails'—a biting comment on the harsh discipline enforced among British troops in Zululand—rides over the hopes of the young soldier, represented by Louis' body.*

abandon it on the road, and march into Luneburg alone. On 7 March a fresh detachment was sent out from Luneburg under Captain Moriarty, to bring the convoy in. They found that the leading wagons had reached Myer's Drift on the Ntombe, but that the rest of the convoy was scattered over several miles of track beyond. Moreover, the proximity of Mbilini's stronghold, and the absence of any armed escort, had made the civilian wagon drivers extremely nervous.

Moriarty's party escorted the wagons to the drift, but persistent rain had turned the track into a quagmire, and the river itself had risen above its banks, to the extent that only two wagons had been able to cross to the southern bank in safety. Moriarty positioned the rest of the wagons on the northern bank in a loose defensive arrangement, and for several days the command waited miserably for the river to subside. It rained almost continuously, turning the inside of the enclosure into a sea of mud, while the men were scarcely ever out of their wet clothes. At one point the river rose, flooding half of Moriarty's encampment; on another it dropped, so that his defensive arrangement was suddenly several yards short of the water's edge. Concerned about the delay, Major Tucker rode out from Luneburg, and was disconcerted to find that morale in the camp was low. Urged to bring the convoy in as soon as he could, Moriarty merely replied that he would do so when he could. Moreover, despite the suspicion of some of the wagon drivers that Zulu civilians who entered the camp to sell food were in fact spies, no attempt was made to put it on a proper defensive footing.

The evening of 11 March saw Moriarty and seventy of his men on the north bank, with a Lieutenant H.H. Harward[49] and thirty-four men on the southern bank. It rained heavily during the night, and a thick mist rose up from the river. At about 4 am the men on the south bank heard a shot fired off in the darkness, from somewhere beyond Moriarty's position. Harward had his men dress and stand to, and sent a messenger across the river to ask Moriarty for instructions. Moriarty merely ordered the sentries on his side of the river – just two of them, posted close to the wagons – to be alert, and suggested that Harward send his men back to sleep.

About forty-five minutes later, the men on the south bank heard another shot, and a sentry's urgent cry, 'Sergeant Johnson!' They stumbled out from their tents just in time to see about 800 Zulus sweeping down on Moriarty's position.[50] The British target had been too tempting to ignore; after days of careful observation, Prince Mbilini had seized his opportunity. The Zulus had advanced under cover of the mist to within just twenty or thirty yards of the camp without being spotted; they then fired a volley, threw down their rifles and charged. Most of Moriarty's men had been asleep, and stumbled out naked and half-equipped to find the Zulus already in among the tents. The horror of that moment was vividly captured by a civilian wagon driver who survived:

> As I emerged from the wagon I heard Captain Moriarty cry out, 'Fire away, men, I am done!' I then went to the adjoining wagon to call Whittington … and I told him the [Zulus] were around. He immediately came out and jumped down, but was caught almost as soon as he got to the ground, and assegaid on every side. The poor fellow shrieked out, but without avail, as no assistance was at hand. Seeing that I was powerless to do anything, having no arms of any kind, I ran down between the oxen and made for the river, which was about 60 yards off. I found the Zulus shooting and stabbing the people in all directions. The sight was a most horrifying one, and never to be forgotten. I had to dodge about to save myself, and am now surprised to find that I managed to get through at all. As soon as I got to the river, I jumped in and made a dive, as swimming was too dangerous, the Zulus standing on the banks and at the edge of the river, as thick as thieves, throwing assegais and aiming their guns wherever they saw a head. I came up about the middle of the river, but the moment my head was out, I saw several Zulus pointing their guns, ready to fire. I therefore dived again, and came out on the other side … I now found that fighting was going on on all sides of me, and that it was almost impossible that I could get on any farther, and in my desperation I contemplated throwing myself in the water, to be drowned peaceably, rather than suffer the death by torture of many of those I saw around me. I, however, got into a courageous spirit again, and dashed off, keeping as much out of the way of the enemy as l could … [51]

On the south bank, the commotion gave Harward's party a few moments' grace. He assembled his men, and, according to his official report:

> I ordered them to retire steadily, and only just in time to avoid a rush of Zulus to our late position. The Zulus came on in dense masses and fell upon our men, who being already broken, gave way, and hand to-hand fighting ensued. I endeavoured to rally my men, but they were much too scattered, and finding re-formation impossible, I mounted my horse and galloped into Luneburg at utmost speed, and reported all that had taken place.[52]

When Harward arrived at Luneburg, 'on his knees, the picture of death',[53] Tucker ordered all available men to march to the Ntombe. Pressing ahead with a handful of mounted officers, he saw the Zulu already retreating in the distance, driving away the cattle from Moriarty's transport wagons. The camp site itself presented a scene of utter devastation, typical of the aftermath of Zulu warfare:

> As we approached the Intombi Drift a fearful and horrible sight presented itself, and the stillness of the spot was awful; there were our men lying all about the place, some naked and some only half clad. On the opposite side of the drift I need not attempt to describe to you what I saw; all the bodies were full of assegai wounds and nearly all were disembowelled. This is the custom of the Zulus, arising from a superstition that unless they do so their own stomach will swell and burst. I saw but one body that I could call unmutilated ...
>
> ... Nearly everything had been broken or torn to pieces, the tents being in shreds, the ammunition boxes broken to atoms, the mealies and flour thrown all over the place. They had killed all the dogs save one, and that we had found with an assegai wound right through its neck ...[54]

Over sixty men of the 80th were killed in the incident, together with seventeen civilian wagon-drivers and team-leaders. Those who managed to get away survived only because the senior NCO on Harward's bank, Sergeant Booth, had rallied a handful of men to cover the rout.

But if Booth's actions were exemplary – he was later awarded the Victoria Cross – the actions of the senior officers were questionable. Much of the blame for the disaster fell on Moriarty, who was responsible for the poor siting of the camp and lax security, but he had paid for his mistakes with his life, and could not be called to account. Harward's position was more ambiguous. By his own account, he had done his best to ensure the safety of his men, and had only left the field to seek help once it was clear that no proper stand was possible. Nevertheless, his actions were clearly open to other interpretations; as Booth himself put it, 'Lieutenant Harward saddled his horse and galloped away leaving us to do the best we could'.[55] But if the Regiment entertained any doubts about his conduct, Harward must at least have enjoyed the support of his senior officer, Tucker, for despite a court of inquiry held within days of the disaster, Harward was not to be tried by Court Martial until nearly a year later. During that time he had continued to serve with his battalion throughout the remainder of not only the Zulu War, but the subsequent campaign against King Sekhukhune of the Pedi as well.

Harward was Court Martialled at Pietermaritzburg on 20 February 1880 on two charges, that of failing to take proper precautions for the defence of the camp, and of 'riding off at speed and abandoning his men'. In his defence he argued that he had only arrived at Ntombe from Luneburg to join Moriarty the night before the attack, and that he could not have been expected under such circumstances to have taken charge of its defence. Regarding the desertion of his men, he pointed out simply that his was the only horse in the camp. The Court acquitted him on both charges – a fact which probably reflected a degree of sympathy among troops serving in Zululand over his predicament.

When the verdict was passed to higher authority for confirmation, however, Harward suddenly found himself sternly rebuked by the senior officer in South Africa. By that time, Lord Chelmsford had long since resigned his command, and his successor, Sir Garnet Wolseley – who had not been present during the Isandlwana campaign, and had no direct experience of the conditions which prevailed in its immediate aftermath – took an unforgiving view of any apparent lapse of personal courage. Indeed, Wolseley held little regard for the way Chelmsford had conducted the campaign, and attributed many of the war's disasters to a climate of incompetence and cowardice which had been tolerated at the highest levels. As a result, he refused to confirm the not guilty verdicts on Harward, and explained his reasons in a deeply revealing summation which was read at the head of every Regiment in the British Army:

Had I released this officer without making any remarks upon the verdict in question, it would have been tacit acknowledgement that I concurred in what appears to be a monstrous theory, viz., that a regimental officer who is the only officer present with a party of soldiers actually and seriously engaged with the enemy can, under any pretext whatever, be justified in deserting them, and by so doing, abandon them to their fate. The more helpless the position in which an officer finds his men, the more it is his bounden duty to stay and share their fortune, whether for good or ill. It is because the British officer has always done so that he occupies the position in which he is held in the estimation of the world, and that he possesses the influence he does in the ranks of our army. The soldier has learned to feel that, come what may, he can in the direst moment of danger look with implicit faith to his officer, knowing that he will never desert him under any possible circumstances.

It is to this faith of the British soldier in his officers that we owe most of the gallant deeds recorded in our military annals; and it is because the verdict of this Court-Martial strikes at the root of this

1. Imperial exiles: Napoleon III and Louis, photographed in England in 1871, shortly after the Emperor's arrival.

2. The Empress Eugénie, photographed in the 1880's.

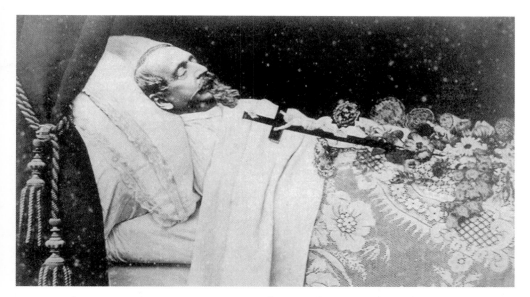

3. The passing of an Imperial dream. A photograph purporting to show Napoleon III on his death bed at Chislehurst. (Ron Sheeley Collection)

4. A remarkable photograph of the Prince Imperial with officers of G/24 Battery, RHA, at Aldershot, 1875/6. From left to right, they are Captain T. Carr, Louis, Major Ward-Ashton, Lieutenant A.J. Bigge, Lieutenant J.H. Wodehouse and Lieutenant R.C.E. North. (Ron Sheeley Collection)

5. The 'Salute'; Louis (right) and Frederick Slade pose in a mock duel, Aldershot, 1876. (Ron Sheeley Collection)

6. 'The end of the duel'. Louis, of course, is victorious. (Ron Sheeley Collection)

Above: **7.** Officers at the Staff College, 1877/8; Lieutenant J. Brenton Carey, 98th Regiment is seated far left. (MOD/Rai England)

Right: **8.** One of the last photographs taken of Louis in Durban, April 1878. Despite his unofficial status, he is wearing an Artillery officer's undress patrol jacket.

9. Carey, photographed on his return from Zululand in 1879. (Ron Sheeley Collection)

10. Lieutenant-Colonel Richard Harrison, who authorised Louis' patrol on 1 June. Photograph *c.*1874. (MOD/Rai England)

11. Surgeon-Major F.B. Scott, who was attached to Chelmsford's Headquarters' Staff to look after the health of the Prince Imperial, and who later conducted the medical examination of his body. (Ron Sheeley Collection)

12. Captain H.M. Brander, 24th Regiment, who was present with Carey during the wreck of the *Clyde*, and who served as prosecuting council at his trial. (Keith Reeves Collection)

13. Major Bettington, right, and one of his men. Bettington's Horse provided the escort for Louis' patrol on 1 June. (National Army Museum)

14. A modern aerial view of the donga on the Tshotshosi where Louis was killed. The monument stands among the trees to the left. Sobhuza's homestead lay more to the right of the present settlement. The effects of Major Stabb's attempts to deflect the course of erosion can clearly be seen in the silted channels, left.

15. Sobhuza, the Zulu headman at whose homestead the Prince was killed. (Cape Archives Depot)

16. Perhaps the most accurate representation of the scene in the Zulu homestead on 1 June, minutes before the attack, based on information supplied by Carey. Louis is sitting foreground, with Carey behind him, the Zulu scout left, and the escort in the background.

17. French artist Paul Jamin's picture – perhaps the best-researched of the many paintings produced to commemorate his death – captures Louis' last moments, 'fighting like a lion'. (La Réunion des Musées Nationaux)

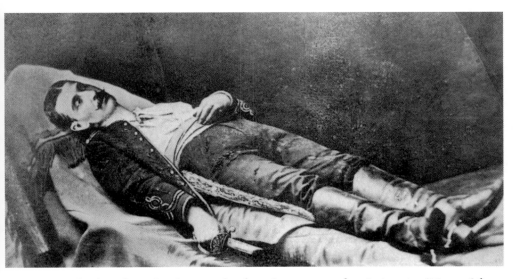

18. In death, at least, Louis seemed to have been true to the glorious traditions of the Bonapartes, as this fake image of the fallen hero, produced by his supporters, suggests. The reality of his brutal end in the donga was very different. (Ron Sheeley Collection)

Above: **19.** The recovery of Louis' body from the donga, 2 June 1879.

Below: **20.** Louis' uniform, patiently collected by Col. Villiers in September 1879, and later cleaned of bloodstains. The holes left by the spear-thrusts which killed him can clearly be seen in his patrol jacket, waistcoat and shirt. (By kind permission of the Compiègne Collection and Winston Ramsey, Plaistow Press. From *The Zulu War; Then and Now*)

Right: **21.** The fateful saddle. Louis was clinging to the stirrup and near holster in front of the saddle when the strap between the holsters tore, and he fell. (Compiègne / Winston Ramsey)

Below: **22.** The funeral at the Thelezeni camp, 2 June 1879. Louis' body is strapped to a gun carriage and draped with a Tricolour. Lord Chelmsford and his

Above and below: **23.** and **24.** Men of the 21st Regiment pose among the ruins of Sobhuza's homestead, 3 June 1879.

25. The grey horse, Tommy, which Louis was riding on the day of the attack, photographed in Pietermaritzburg at the time of the funeral procession.

26. The Catholic Cathedral in Pietermaritzburg, photographed while Louis' body lay there in state.

27. The scene at Durban docks when Louis' body was taken on board the steam tug *Adonis*. Note the horse Tommy among the troops, right.

28. Major Stabb's party pose behind the completed monument at the Tshotshosi, March 1880. Stabb stands to the left of the cross, Colonel Bowker to the right; Sobhuza and Jabez Molife stand between them.

faith, that I feel it necessary to mark officially my emphatic dissent from the theory upon which the theory has been founded.

In communicating to the army the result of this Court-Martial, the Field-Marshal Commander-in-Chief desires to signify his entire approval of the views expressed by the commanding officer in respect of the principles of duty which have always actuated British officers in the field, and by which, His Royal Highness feels assured, they will continue to be guided.[56]

Wolseley's intervention, of course, destroyed Harward's career, and he resigned his commission the following year.

Yet Harward was not the only one to fall short of Wolseley's exacting standards, who in private called into question a number of incidents which had elsewhere been lauded as heroic:

Heroes have been made of Melvill and Coghill who taking advantage of their having horses bolted from the scene of the action [at Isandlwana] to save their lives. If the 24th had been well-handled and had behaved well then the disaster could never have occurred, much as Chelmsford by his ignorance of Zulu tactics, had left them exposed to attack, and it is monstrous making heroes of those who saved or attempted to save their lives by bolting or those who shut up in the building at Rorke's drift could not bolt and fought like rats for their lives which they could not otherwise save.[57]

It comes as a surprise to find that such views were not entirely out of keeping with prevailing opinions in Zululand in 1879. The case of Melvill and Coghill, in particular, had a number of parallels with that of Harward. Lieutenant Melvill was adjutant of the 1/24th, and had taken the Queen's Colour of his battalion during the closing stages of the Battle of Isandlwana. To lose a Colour in action was a regimental disgrace, and Melvill had left the camp just as the British position collapsed. Together with Lieutenant Coghill, he had reached the Natal border, only to lose the Colour in the Mzinyathi river before both he and Coghill were overtaken and killed. Asked whether Melvill might have deserved the Victoria Cross, Chelmsford replied in careful terms which fully recognised the ambiguity of his position:

I am again puzzled how to reply … I feel sure that Melvill left the camp with the colours under orders received. He was too good a soldier to have left without. In being ordered to leave, however, he no doubt was given the best chance of saving his life which must have been lost had he remained in camp. His ride was not more daring than that of those who escaped. The question, therefore, remains had he succeeded in saving the colours and his own life, would he have been considered to have deserved the Victoria Cross?[58]

As to the famous defence of Rorke's Drift, one staff officer wrote,

> ... until the accounts from England came out nobody had thought of the Rorke's Drift affair except as one in which the private soldiers of the 24th behaved so well. For as a matter of fact they all stayed there to defend the place for there was nowhere else to go, and in defending it they fought most determinedly.[59]

Yet the opinions of the military were by no means the determining factor which shaped the lottery of courage and condemnation in Zululand in 1879. The image of Melvill and Coghill, clutching the Colour, and cutting their way dramatically through the encircling Zulu hordes at Isandlwana, had offered such a potent image of heroism that the press had already immortalised it in a dozen dramatic engravings. Among the general public, at least, no one sought to question the direction in which they were riding. Moreover, the undeniably heroic stand at Rorke's Drift had offered just the sort of example of resolute courage against the odds with which to offset the catastrophe at Isandlwana, and restore morale. Whatever the private reservations of many officers in Zululand, the public would have its heroes; no fewer than eleven of the defenders of Rorke's Drift received the Victoria Cross, and it was announced that Melvill and Coghill would have received the award had they lived.[60]

The Ntombe affair had only served to exaggerate the prevailing fear of the Zulu, and even as Louis was waiting impatiently at Durban for Lord Chelmsford to return, there were further ugly manifestations at the front. On 2 April the 3/60th – whom Chelmsford had so unsettled with his welcome address when they arrived in Durban just a fortnight before – went into action for the first time. They formed the front face of Lord Chelmsford's square at the Battle of Gingindlovu, during the Eshowe Relief Expedition, and during a particularly determined attack on their sector, these 'half-baked nervous boys', as one colonial officer called them, became 'worse than wobbly'.[61] Even one of their officers admitted:

> Our men were awfully frightened and nervous at first, could not even speak and shivered from funk, so we – the officers – had enough to do to keep the men cool ...

... I myself did not quite like the first few shots as they whizzed over our heads; but found I had such a lot to do to keep the men in order and telling them when to shoot, that I did not mind a bit.[62]

In the event the 60th stood their ground and the Zulus were defeated, but the incident gave rise to a grim sequel four days later. By that time, Chelmsford was returning to Natal, having achieved his object in relieving the beleaguered force at Eshowe. Despite their recent successes, however, the troops under his command remained very wary of the Zulu. On the night of 5 April Chelmsford formed a defensive laager near an abandoned mission station at eMvutsheni. Picquets were placed in advance of the lines for the night, with African allies in groups beyond. At about 3.30 on the morning of the 6th, one of the picquets issued a challenge, and receiving no reply fired a warning shot. The picquets of the 60th promptly abandoned their positions in panic and fled back on the lines, where the men turned out and fixed bayonets to repel an attack. When figures rushed out of the darkness and tried to enter the camp they were met with shots and the bayonets, despite frantic cries of 'Friend! Friend!' Only when Chelmsford himself furiously called a halt to the chaos was it realised that the intruders were actually the advanced picquets of their own African allies. One man was killed, and thirteen wounded – including five of the 60th. A sergeant of the 60th was subsequently Court Martialled, and sentenced to five years penal servitude, and reduction to the ranks. Later, the conviction was quashed, apparently because it seemed to some inappropriate that a sergeant should be punished when so many officers had been found wanting.

In Durban, meanwhile, Louis remained undaunted, and was increasingly frustrated at his inability to reach the front. To keep him amused, Major Butler, the Acting Adjutant General on the lines of communication, had offered him a temporary attachment to an Artillery battery camped in the staging depot at Cato Manor, outside Durban.[63] This at least gave Louis the opportunity to mix with men going up to the war – 'at all events I shall not follow the operations as a newspaper reporter'[64] – without undue hardship;

... there they made themselves very comfortable, one of the large Indian tents which had been sent from Ceylon with the 57th Regiment making a capital officers' mess tent. The Prince himself was still often seen at Mrs Baynton's and the Natal Club.[65]

Chelmsford returned to Durban on 9 April, and Louis hurried to meet him the following day. One of Chelmsford's staff, Captain Molyneux, left a telling impression of Louis at the time of that interview:

The Prince then and afterwards always wore the uniform of the Royal Artillery; he was not very well at this time, with a slight touch of fever. On his arrival the Chief thought it would be as well to have a medical officer attached to the Headquarter Staff, and Surgeon-Major F.B. Scott was accordingly appointed to the post. The Prince was a charming young fellow, burning to distinguish himself, a capital rider and swordsman; but of course, like all high-spirited young men, a little difficult to manage, and I think the fever never quite left him while he lived.[66]

Louis was carrying a letter from the Duke of Cambridge which explained his position in much the same casual terms the Commander-in-Chief had used to Bartle Frere:

My Dear Chelmsford,
    This letter will be presented to you by the Prince Imperial, who is going out on his own account to see as much as he can of the coming campaign in Zululand. He is extremely anxious to go out and wanted to be employed in our Army; but the Government did not consider that this could be sanctioned, but have sanctioned my writing to you and to Sir Bartle Frere to say that if you show him kindness and render him assistance to see as much as he can with the columns in the field. I hope you will do so. He is a fine young fellow, full of spirit and pluck, having many old cadet friends in the Artillery, he will doubtless find no difficulty in getting on, and if you can help him in any other way, pray do so. My only anxiety on his account would be that he is too plucky and go-ahead.
            I remain, my dear Chelmsford,
                Yours most sincerely,
                    George[67]

In truth, Louis' arrival was a fresh burden of responsibility which Chelmsford could have done without. The war had reached a critical phase and the situation was changing almost daily. The successful actions of late March and early April had begun to turn the tide in Chelmsford's favour, and there was much work to be done in transforming the huge influx of reinforcements into an effective force with which to take up the campaign. Chelmsford had very little time or energy to devote to Louis' welfare, the more so because Cambridge had been deliberately vague when it came to the question of what Louis might actually do. Only Sir Lintorn Simmons had hinted at what might be appropriate; Eugénie had no particular role in mind for her son, except that it must be worthy of him. 'The Empress would not,' observed Simmons, 'like him to be attached to a native corps.'[68] The implication, however, was clear enough, and Disraeli had guessed the outcome from the first. 'I fear,' he told Lady Chesterfield,

> ... that some indiscreet friends, in very high places, gave him privately letters to Ld Chelmsford, begging that General to place the Prince on his staff.[69]

In any case, Louis' charm worked as well on Chelmsford as anyone else, and the general took the line of least resistance. He offered him a post as an extra ADC on his staff. As he wrote to Cambridge:

> I have asked the Prince Imperial to accompany my Head Quarters, which I am glad to find is what he himself was anxious for. I should feel much obliged if your Royal Highness would assure the Empress that I will look after the Prince to the best of my ability, and that I am convinced I shall find him a very valuable addition to my Staff ...[70]

To Lintorn Simmons, Chelmsford explained further:

> The Prince Imperial has consented to accompany me into the field, and without putting him in orders, I have arranged with him that he shall be considered as one of my staff.
>
> I hear that he is quite delighted at being so employed; and at all events his desire to serve under my command is a set-off to the criticisms of those who consider that I am quite unfit for my present command ... I have already begged the Duke of Cambridge to assure the Empress that I will take every care of the Prince. He will have to rough it with all of us, but the climate is a healthy one and the out-of-door life we lead is one which seems to agree well with all of us.[71]

Nevertheless, some confusion remained even at Headquarters about Louis' true position. Chelmsford was, in any case, notoriously casual about staff matters. At a time when the importance of a properly appointed and responsible staff was seldom recognised, Chelmsford was reluctant to delegate, had appointed no chief of staff, and dispensed staff duties on an informal and ad hoc basis. This compounded Louis' already ambiguous position, and Captain Molyneux was later to admit that he had never really understood what Louis' duties really were.[72]

Still, the post appeared to confer a degree of responsibility upon him, and the Prince was delighted, especially when Chelmsford and the staff left Durban for Pietermaritzburg on 17 April, en route to joining a column assembling in northern Zululand.

Yet it seems likely that the illness noted by Molyneux had affected Louis more than he cared to admit. From the first, Chelmsford had expressed doubts that the Prince's constitution was up to the demands of life in the field. Whatever his military pretensions, Louis had little experience of it, and was as vulnerable as any raw recruit to the fevers and stomach complaints which plagued new arrivals in Natal. Certainly, Chelmsford did not think him robust; 'I hope his health will stand it,' he wrote from Durban on the 14th, 'as it would be a serious responsibility if he broke down.'[73] These concerns were confirmed on his arrival in Pietermaritzburg:

> He had been unfortunately laid up with fever in Durban, and the jolting of the carriage and the heat of the sun rather knocked him up. I am afraid he is not naturally very strong, and I very much doubt that he will be able to stand the long rides we have in store for him if he follows me wherever I go.[74]

Louis's reaction was typical. Feeling his reputation wilt in the eyes of his colleagues, he attempted to demonstrate his mastery of the situation with an act of physical daring. The result was not what he had hoped for:

> At Maritzburg the Prince Imperial, whose health had not bettered by the rough travelling (for the rail did not run all the way), met with an accident, which necessitated his being left behind for a time. We were all saddled up and ready for a start on the morning of the 22nd, when the horse ridden by Longcast the interpreter bucked him clean over his head. The Prince, who was standing by, caught the beast, rearranged its bridle, and, before we could stop him, vaulted on to its back. He was still weak from fever, but regardless of that and having no stirrups, he stuck to it for some time, till in the end he was also shot over its head, and unfortunately landed upon a heap of stones. This so knocked him out of time that the General had to insist on his stopping behind with Dr. Scott until better. With a salute, and a sorrowful face, he said 'as it is your wish, sir', and shook us all by the hand as we rode off. However, he was able to join us again at Ladysmith on the 27th, having driven up in the Lieutenant-Governor's carriage. He looked better, but we could see

at meals that he was hardly yet up to the mark to face our rough fare.[75]

Chelmsford made no comment on the incident, but merely observed that 'for the first time since I held this command I am going to take a doctor with me, in order that he might look after the Prince. His name is Dr. Scott'.[76]

This final delay was deeply frustrating for Louis. He had arrived in Durban just too late to join the Eshowe Relief Expedition; now, it seemed, he might miss out on a fresh offensive. Even at Cato Manor, at the mess of N/6 Battery, he had found it difficult to constrain his impatience, and even found himself questioning his family loyalty to the artillery:

He showed no great content with his position in the Artillery, remarking in conversation that the Artillery was from its very nature unsatisfactory to serve with, as it gave no opportunity for close personal contact with the enemy.[77]

By the time he finally reached the troops assembling on the Zulu border, his yearning for that opportunity – as his officers would discover – could hardly be contained.

NOTES

1. Corporal W Smith, 12th Regiment, *The Wreck of the Birkenhead*, Royal Magazine, August 1905.
2. *The Illustrated London News*, 17 May 1879.
3. Colonel Davies' report on the wreck, WO 32/7729.
4. A and D Companies.
5. Carey's report, WO 32/7729.
6. Private I. Morris, letter, 6 May 1879, published in *Y Gwyliedydd*, 26 June 1879. Reproduced in Frank Emery, *The Red Soldier*, London, 1979.
7. Davies, report, WO 32/7729.
8. Ibid.
9. Duke of Cambridge, speech to the Royal Academy dinner, reported in *The Illustrated London News*, 17 May 1879.
10. Biographical notes on Carey appeared in *The Illustrated London News* on 12 July 1879, and *The Graphic* on 6 September 1879.
11. *The Illustrated London News*, ibid.
12. Perhaps his first name was rather too extravagant for his liking; like

many Victorian officers, Carey preferred to refer to himself by his middle name – he signed himself J Brenton Carey.

13.   Anonymous 'Staff Officer', quoted in *The Queen's Colours*, published by The Religious Tract Society, London, c.1880.

14.   Agnes Carey, *The Empress Eugénie in Exile*, London, 1922.

15.   Captain Wynne to his wife Lucy, 7 February 1879. Published in Howard Whitehouse (ed.), *A Widow-Making War; The Life and Death of a British Officer in Zululand 1879*, Nuneaton, 1995.

16.   General Sir Richard Harrison, *Recollections of a Life in the British Army*, London, 1908.

17.   *Our Latest 'Little War', or, Campaigning in Honduras*, United Services Magazine, September and October 1868.

18.   Ibid.

19.   Ibid.

20.   Carey 'was present at the storming and capture of San Pedro', *The Graphic*, 6 September 1879.

21.   *Our Latest 'Little War'*.

22.   *The Jamaica Gleaner*, 5 March 1867, quoted in Donald Featherstone, *Captain Carey's Blunder*, London, 1973.

23.   Austin to Governor Sir J.P. Grant, Belize, 15 January 1867. CO 123/127.

24.   *The Graphic*, 6 September 1879.

25.   Sir H.M. Bengough, *Memories of a Soldier's Life*, London, 1913.

26.   *The Graphic*, 6 September 1879.

27.   Ibid.

28.   British humanitarian aid in the Franco-Prussian War was co-ordinated, for example, by Captain Henry Brackenbury, Royal Artillery, an advocate of Army reform, a member of Wolseley's school, and later General Sir Henry Brackenbury, GCB, Director-General of Ordnance. Herbert Kitchener also volunteered, but holding an active commission at the time was rebuked by the Duke of Cambridge.

29.   *The Illustrated London News*, 16 August 1879.

30.   Ibid.

31.   *The Natal Mercury*, 18 March 1879.

32.   *The Natal Mercury*, 1 April 1879.

33.   Louis to Eugénie, Durban, 2 April 1879. Reproduced in Filon, *Memoirs of the Prince Imperial*.

34.   Louis to General Lintorn Simmons, quoted in Katherine John, *The Prince Imperial*.

35.   The surviving horse was apparently called Stag. See Agnes Carey, *The Empress Eugénie in Exile*, 1922.

36. *The Natal Mercury*, 9 June 1879, confirms the name of the original owner, but not the name of the horse.

37. '... he bought [the horse] at the base for £75 to replace one he had brought out and had died'. Captain James MacSwinney, 94th Regiment, letter to his sister, Louisa Mason, 1 June 1879. National Army Museum Collection, London.

38. See, for example, *The Story of the Zulu Campaign* by Major Ashe and Captain E V Wyatt-Edgell, London, 1880, which set the scene by describing this horse as 'big, awkward-looking, but [a] very powerful animal, but an inveterate buck-jumper, and, moreover, excessively timid under fire'. It is interesting that this description – from information supplied by officers who served in Zululand – does not name the horse. Any suggestion of nervousness on the part of the horse tended to absolve Louis of the charge of poor horsemanship.

39. Letter reproduced in Featherstone, *Captain Carey's Blunder*.

40. Rosamund Southey, *Storm and Sunshine in South Africa*, London, 1910.

41. Letter from Mrs N Fisher, unidentified Durban newspaper, 10 July 1964. Cutting in the Old Court House Museum, Durban.

42. See Donald R Morris' *The Washing of the Spears*, London, 1965.

43. A Mr Camille Helleputte, who had accompanied troops into the field, met the Prince and Carey as they started their patrol on 1 June; 'The Prince was riding a grey horse he named "Tommy"'. *Natal Mercury*, 9 June 1879. Tommy Atkins was the nickname of the ordinary British soldier. It is possible of course that oral tradition has merely confused the names Tommy and Percy.

44. 'Isn't it strange that his horse should be called "Fate"?'. Unidentified newspaper cutting, Prince Imperial files, Royal Archives, Windsor Castle.

45. Louis to General Simmons, reproduced in Filon, *Memoirs of the Prince Imperial*.

46. *Letters and Diary of Arthur C.B. Mynors*, privately published, 1879.

47. Frances Colenso to Mrs Lyell, 22 June 1879, reproduced in *Colenso Letters from Natal*, ed. Wyn Rees, Pietermaritzburg, 1958.

48. 'Some Recollections of the Zulu War, extracted from the unpublished reminiscences of the late Lt. General Sir Edward Hutton', *Army Quarterly*, XVI, April 1928. Hutton was then a captain in the 3/60th.

49. Curiously, Harward's career was very similar to Carey's; he had also begun his service in the (1st) West India Regiment, and had served in Sierra Leone, on the Gold Coast, and in Jamaica. Although

born the same year as Carey, however, he was not commissioned until 1871. Most of the dates of his overseas service do not coincide with Carey's, although it is just possible they might have met in Jamaica in the early 1870s. See Robert Hope, *The Zulu War and the 80th Regiment of Foot*, Leek, 1997.

50. Contemporary British accounts placed the number of Zulus much higher, as many as 4,000 men. This, it seems, was an over estimate, and the lower figure is more in accordance with Zulu capabilities at the time. See John Laband, *Mbilini, Manyanyoba and the Phongolo Frontier* in Laband and Thompson (eds), *Kingdom and Colony at War*, Pietermaritzburg, 1990.

51. Letter, *Natal Mercury*, 19 April 1879.

52. Dated Luneburg, 12 March 1879. Published in the *Natal Mercury*, 21 March 1879.

53. Major Tucker, letter to his father, 19 March 1879. Reproduced in Frank Emery, *The Red Soldier*.

54. Ibid.

55. Sergeant Booth, letter to Lucy Booth, 14 March 1879. Reproduced in Hope, *The Zulu War and the 80th Regiment of Foot*.

56. Reproduced in the official *Narrative of Field Operations Connected with the Zulu War*, Intelligence Dept. of the War Office, London, 1881.

57. Private journal, entry of 19 March 1880. Preston (ed.), *Sir Garnet Wolseley's South African Journal, 1879–80*.

58. Chelmsford to Sir Alfred Horsford, 14 May 1879. Chelmsford Papers, NAM; reproduced in French, *Lord Chelmsford and the Zulu War*.

59. Major C F Clery to Lady Alison, Wolf's Hill, Zululand, 16 May 1879. Reproduced in Sonia Clarke, *Zululand at War*, Johannesburg, 1984.

60. There was no provision for the posthumous award of the VC in 1879. When the rules were changed in 1907, VCs were awarded retrospectively to both Melvill and Coghill.

61. Colonel G Hamilton-Browne, *A Lost Legionary in South Africa*, London, c.1912.

62. *Letters and Diary of the Late Arthur C. B. Mynors.*

63. N Battery, 6th Brigade, under the command of Major F T Le Grice, which had arrived in Durban on 31 March.

64. Louis, letter to Simmons, quoted in John, *The Prince Imperial*.

65. Captain W H Tomasson, *With the Irregulars in Zululand and the Transvaal*, London, 1881.

66. Major General W C F Molyneux, *Campaigning in South Africa and Egypt*, London, 1896.

67. Duke of Cambridge to Lord Chelmsford, 25 February 1879. Published in Hansard, 23 June 1879.

68. Sir Lintorn Simmons, letter to Lord Chelmsford, reproduced in Katherine John, *The Prince Imperial*.
69. Disraeli to Lady Chesterfield, reproduced in Weintraub, *Disraeli*.
70. Chelmsford to the Duke of Cambridge, Durban, 11 April 1879. Chelmsford Papers, NAM; reproduced in Major The Hon. Gerald French, *Lord Chelmsford and the Zulu War*, London, 1939.
71. Chelmsford to Simmons, reproduced in John, *The Prince Imperial*.
72. Molyneux, Court Martial Proceedings, WO 71/343.
73. Chelmsford, letter dated Durban 14 April 1879, quoted in *The Illustrated London News*, 16 July 1879.
74. Chelmsford, letter dated Pietermaritzburg, 20 April 1879, quoted in *ILN*, ibid.
75. Molyneux, *Campaigning in South Africa and Egypt*.
76. Chelmsford, letter dated Pietermaritzburg, 20 April 1879. Reproduced in *The Illustrated London News*, 16 July 1879.
77. Tomasson, *With the Irregulars*.

V

'... a real terror'

Those few days that Louis spent languishing at Pietermaritzburg in April 1879 were made all the more frustrating because it was obvious to the army at large that the war was moving into a new and significant phase.

Despite heavy casualties and some setbacks, the Zulu army had been entirely successful in checking the initial British offensive at the beginning of the year. This had been most apparent at Isandlwana, where the attack of 22 January had destroyed the old Centre Column as a fighting force. In fact, just half of the column's effective strength had been present during the action, but the casualty rate had been so high among them – almost all the regular troops wiped out, and nearly half the auxiliaries – that, combined with the loss of transport equipment, tents, food and reserve ammunition, the column could simply no longer function in the field. The implications for British morale had been enormous, undermining faith in both Chelmsford's personal leadership and the army's capabilities in general, and damaging the fragile relationship between the military and the civilian administration in Natal. Whatever the propaganda value of the heroic defence of Rorke's Drift, in the aftermath of Isandlwana, the truth was that Lord Chelmsford had been ignominiously chased out of Zululand, and his strategy was in tatters.

Yet even this was not the end of Chelmsford's worries, for the attack on Isandlwana had clearly been part of a concerted Zulu response which had challenged the advance of all three columns. While the full weight of the Zulu army had descended upon the camp at Isandlwana, local elements living in the northern and coastal sectors had harassed the flanking columns. With the destruction of the Centre Column, Zulu strategists were now able to concentrate on the remaining British positions, which were too separated to support one another. While northern groups such as the abaQulusi had skirmished with Wood throughout February and March, the coastal column had been isolated at the abandoned mission station at Eshowe. King Cetshwayo had forbidden his commanders to make a direct attack on fortified positions – 'Do not put your face into the lair of a wild beast', he is said to have told his army, 'for you are sure to get clawed'[1] – and instead the Zulu simply cut off all communications between the Eshowe garrison and the outside world. For three months, between the end of January and the beginning of April, the Zulu had neutralised a column of over 1,700 men – an achievement which was arguably a more effective use of manpower than the attack on Isandlwana.

For most of that time, the British had remained painfully vulnerable, too, to a counter-thrust into Natal. Apart from a few small, isolated and demoralised garrisons, the border lay open for much of its length, and the settler population hurriedly abandoned outlying districts and hurried to the dubious safety of the towns. Natal's African population, whose conspicuous support for the British invasion had made them equally vulnerable to Zulu reprisals, were left to fend for themselves – a decision which undermined their faith in the colonial administration.

In retrospect, the British position was never again as precarious as it was after Isandlwana, but in fact the Zulu were unable to exploit their advantage due to very real limitations which shaped their strategy throughout the war. Unlike its British counterpart, the Zulu army was not a full-time professional body, but rather the manpower of the nation mobilised for its defence. The battles at the end of January had caused enormous casualties – at least 3,000 dead and thousands more injured – and the army had been exhausted by them. The men needed time to recover, and once the immediate threat posed by the first wave of fighting had passed, they needed time, too, to return to the every-day responsibilities of their civilian lives. Moreover, the options available to the Zulu high command were further limited by a lack of political will to carry the war forward into colonial territory. The king and his advisers were aware that the British had far greater resources than their own, and were nervous of provoking a damaging escalation of the fighting. Indeed, the king was already beginning to doubt that the war could be won by military means alone, and he hoped instead that by fighting only in defence of his own territory he might persuade the British to re-evaluate the cost of the invasion.

This was a valid response to the crisis which threatened the kingdom's very existence, but it underestimated British Imperial pride. While the British government might indeed question the worth of prolonging the war, it could not allow the lasting blow to its prestige which would result if Isandlwana was not avenged. Only once the military situation was restored would the government be prepared to consider a political settlement; its first reaction was to make sure Chelmsford had sufficient resources to bring the campaign to a successful conclusion.

The Zulu thereby let slip their one opportunity of discrediting Chelmsford completely; by the middle of March so many reinforcements had arrived that he felt able to take the first tentative steps to regain the initiative. His first objective was to relieve the beleaguered garrison at Eshowe, and in order to distract the Zulu, he asked Wood to make a diversion in northern Zululand. The build up of British troops on the border was only too obvious to Cetshwayo, who responded by reassembling his own forces.

The result was a second wave of fighting, fought over a period of just a few days, at either end of the country, and with no less savagery than the January battles. But the time it was over, however, the strategic balance had tilted spectacularly in favour of the British.

Prompted by Chelmsford's instructions, Wood made an attack on the Hlobane complex, which had served as a focus for Zulu resistance in his area. The attack was delivered at dawn on 28 March, but was badly conceived and co-ordinated, and was thrown into confusion by the sudden and unexpected arrival of the main Zulu army, direct from oNdini. With the coastal column neutralised at Eshowe, the Zulu high command had identified Wood's column as the main remaining threat, and had decided to attack it before Chelmsford's reinforcements could cross the border; attracted by the sound of firing from Hlobane, the Zulu army had arrived in time to turn Wood's foray into a rout. The next morning, however, when the Zulu army assaulted his base at Khambula, Wood was ready for them. For an entire afternoon the Zulus made repeated attacks against his fortifications, but were finally driven off with heavy casualties.

Chelmsford, meanwhile, had crossed the Thukela, and on 2 April at Gingindlovu had dispersed a Zulu force which had gathered to contest his advance to Eshowe. The beleaguered garrison was relieved, and over the following week Chelmsford reorganised his forces in the coastal sector, abandoning the forward position at Eshowe, and taking up a much stronger position closer to the border.

These two British successes were hugely damaging to Zulu prospects. For the first time in the war, the king's main armies had been heavily defeated, and the losses were equal or greater than those of the earlier battles. This was particularly disheartening in the case of the Khambula *impi*, which had included all the regiments who had previously triumphed at Isandlwana, and which was led by the king's most trusted commanders. Moreover, the fact that at both Khambula and Gingindlovu the army had brought about its own destruction by attacking entrenched positions, in direct defiance of the king's orders, made the defeat all the more depressing.

If it was clear to the Zulu that the tide of war had turned against them, however, the same was not entirely apparent to the British. While British troops took heart in the recent victories, the disaster at Hlobane afforded a grim reminder that the Zulu were still a dangerous enemy, and a nagging fear of their capabilities remained. The net result was that, after three months of fighting, Lord Chelmsford seemed no farther forward than when he started; his troops were once again massed on the borders, and Zulu intentions remained as obscure as ever. The whole process of invasion had to begin again.

Chelmsford's response was to formulate a new offensive plan, which retained elements 'of his original strategy, but recognised the need to operate in greater strength. The troops concentrated in the coastal sector were formed into a new column, called the 1st Division, whose objectives were to suppress any remaining resistance on their front, and to destroy the centres of royal administration there.

For a renewed advance on King Cetshwayo's capital at oNdini, Chelmsford relied on a combination of Wood's column, and the remnants of the old Centre Column, reinforced by fresh troops from home. Wood's determination to continue forward operations in the dark months after Isandlwana had earned him Chelmsford's admiration, and his success at Khambula made it difficult in any case to relieve him of an independent command. Chelmsford, moreover, had noted the nervousness of the reinforcements in action at Gingindlovu for the first time, and was reluctant to let them carry the weight of the new invasion unsupported. He recognised that they 'will not be of much use, as they are certain to be composed of boys',[2] and was keen to allow them time to mature in the field.

His solution was to retain Wood in his present position, but to reconstitute his command as a Flying Column, which was instructed to move south from Khambula to rendezvous with a new column, which was to be assembled on the middle border. This new column, called the 2nd Division, was to be commanded by Edward Newdigate, one of five Major-Generals fresh out from England, and would consist of the survivors of the old Centre Column, supplemented by reinforcements. Chelmsford intended to accompany this column in person. The 2nd Division and Flying Column would then advance in tandem towards oNdini, and if attacked would fight as one body.

Although this plan enabled Chelmsford to mass a far greater concentration of troops than had been possible hitherto, it begged a number of crucial logistical questions. Where should the new column assemble, by what route should it advance, and where should it join up with Wood? In fact, as Chelmsford had recognised in January, the number of practicable entry points into the Zulu kingdom was limited, especially for an army encumbered with hundreds of transport wagons, and Chelmsford had used the obvious viable routes then.

The Rorke's Drift road, which boasted one of the best tracks, remained open to him, but for a number of reasons this route had fallen into disfavour. It was fed by a line of supply which ran from Pietermaritzburg, through Greytown and thence to Helpmekaar – the old assembly point for the Centre Column – before dropping into the Mzinyathi valley, towards the Drift. Yet in the aftermath of Isandlwana this line – which at times ran very close to the Zulu border – had proved vulnerable to counter-attack, to the extent that civilian wagon-drivers had refused to travel it, and traffic had been paralysed. Instead, Chelmsford intended to use a line of communication farther to the west, which was more distant from the border, and which passed through Ladysmith, striking the border near the village of Dundee, north of Rorke's Drift. This route would allow Chelmsford to concentrate his reinforcements quickly and safely, and it allowed a forward base closer to Wood's command, but it by-passed the old entry point, which meant that Chelmsford would have to find a new track into Zululand.

There was another reason – largely unspoken but all the more potent for that – to avoid the Rorke's Drift road. For two months Chelmsford had felt himself too vulnerable to risk sending an expedition to bury the dead at Isandlwana, and 1,300 men, together with the carcasses of hundreds of oxen and horses, still lay out at the foot of that mournful crag, exposed to the elements and to the attentions of scavengers. From time to time adventurous British patrols had ridden out from Rorke's Drift to scout the old battlefield, but most had retired in the face of the appalling spectacle and smell. Chelmsford himself had no wish to see the place again, and he was certainly unwilling to expose his fresh troops to that particular experience at the very start of a new campaign.

Yet the fact remained that, if he avoided the Rorke's Drift road, there was no very obvious entry point into Zululand from Dundee. Chelmsford's plan would require moving an entire column into terrain dominated by the confluence of two major river systems – the Mzinyathi and Ncome – and which had hardly been touched by British operations in January. Military intelligence of this area was negligible, while the reports of civilian traders were confusing, as Chelmsford admitted:

> ... it has been [impossible] to obtain any really reliable information regarding the country even from those who know it well – They

have never been accustomed to look at any of the roads from any but a trader's point of view, and are therefore quite unable to give detailed information which is so important when movements of troops are concerned.[3]

Ideally, Chelmsford hoped to find a route which crossed into Zululand close to Dundee, which would allow him to join with Wood's force as soon as possible, and which then struck out towards oNdini. There was one existing track which might have proved useful, but it meandered by a more northerly route, crossing the headwaters of the White Mfolozi river, then approaching oNdini by way of iNhlazatshe mountain. While this was reputed to be a good road, it would hugely increase Chelmsford's line of communication, and force him to operate farther from the border, as he explained to Wood. Instead, he hoped to find a short-cut, which would enable him to by-pass Isandlwana, and strike the old Rorke's Drift road in the vicinity of Babanango mountain:

If ... we take the Northern road and a raid be made into Natal I feel sure that I should be blamed for my strategy, and very properly so – Kindly consider then how we can best work to the south of Inhlazatye, and yet not leave the frontier North of that mountain unprotected.

I am willing to admit that the Babanango road is the worst of the two, but I am certain that I am right in determining that our main line of advance shall be made upon it – and with the force at our disposal, and at this season of the year we ought to have no difficulty in making any lines practicable for our convoys.[4]

Despite the fact that these issues had not been entirely resolved, Chelmsford designated Dundee as the assembly point for the 2nd Division, and by the middle of April the first reinforcements had arrived there from Durban. Dundee in 1879 was little more than a hamlet – it consisted of two churches, a ramshackle hotel, and half-a-dozen stores and farm-houses – and it was soon dwarfed by the military camps which sprang up around it. The logistical effort required to feed and transport the troops was immense, and Chelmsford's staff was scarcely adequate for the purpose. Furthermore, the indecision regarding the precise direction of the advance added to their frustrations. To ease the burden, Chelmsford decided at the beginning to create a forward supply depot at Conference Hill, on the border, which lay half-way between Dundee and Wood's base at Khambula. Here huge quantities of supplies could be concentrated to support both columns when the advance began.

Yet Chelmsford hoped not to commit the 2nd Division to an actual advance via Conference Hill, which lay too far north for the projected Babanango route. Instead, he hoped that a route via Landman's Drift – which crossed the Mzinyathi much closer to Dundee – might lead directly eastwards across the Ncome, and thence into Zululand. The search for this route was already a priority when Chelmsford moved his headquarters to Dundee at the end of April.

After just a few days' rest in Pietermaritzburg, Louis had caught up with the staff in Ladysmith, much to his delight. They could hardly fail to be impressed by his enthusiasm, but, as Lieutenant Colonel Crealock, Chelmsford's Assistant Military Secretary, noted, he was by no means fully recovered:

> The Prince Imperial and Milne, A.D.C., are both the worse for fever … the Prince is very sharp, and he could not have done better than to come to us. All the A.D.C. are very nice clever fellows and as kind as it is possible to be to him, without any sort of toadyism in their composition.[5]

By the time they reached Dundee, Louis was caught up in the infectious atmosphere of the impending advance. Making light of his illness, he wrote excitedly to Eugénie:

> I am writing to you from Dundee where we arrived yesterday with the general staff … In a week at the furthest we shall have reached the extreme line of our outposts near Conference Hill. All continues to go on well here: though my comrades on the staff are all much older than I am, their society is very agreeable, and will help to make my life as pleasant as it can be in Zululand. My health is excellent and I should have nothing to wish for if the distance that separates us allowed me to hear from you oftener …
>
> If you saw the extraordinary posture in which I am writing to you, crouching on my heels and using my saddle as a desk, you would, I am sure, excuse my bad writing.[6]

In fact, Chelmsford did not linger in Dundee. On 2 May he rode to the Khambula camp, to discuss the impending invasion with Evelyn Wood. Louis was exhilarated; at last he was on enemy soil, and at Khambula he sought out his old Aldershot friends, Arthur Bigge and Frederick Slade, whose battery was under Wood's command. Both men had played a prominent part in the battle a month before, and they walked Louis over the site, pointing out the positions of Wood's entrenchments, and the ground over which the Zulu had attacked. For much of the battle the artillery pieces had stood in the open, on sloping ground between the earthwork fort and a wagon laager – a position which enabled them to direct their fire as the Zulu attacks had developed. At one point, a particularly determined rush had almost overwhelmed the guns, and several warriors had been shot down as they tried to snatch the reins from the limber-teams. Wood had been full of praise for the gunners, and had described Bigge and Slade as 'unsurpassable'.[7] Probably, even by the beginning of May, there was still good evidence of the fight on the ground, for the battle had been particularly fierce close to the British perimeter, and the work of cleaning the site afterwards had been gruelling. Even after the immediate confines had been cleared of Zulu dead, the air remained tainted for days by the pools of blood and brains which lay on the rocky slopes where the destruction had been greatest.[8] Farther off, along the line of retreat, Zulu corpses lay hidden in long grass or in dongas until the shifting winds revealed their presence. Louis did not record his feelings on this, his first real exposure to Zulu warfare, but no doubt they were mixed; had he arrived in Zululand a week earlier, he might have been standing beside Bigge and Slade during the attack.

Even so, the open-air life he was now living – a telling contrast to the cloistered years at Camden Place – thrilled his soul, and he was intensely fascinated by the sights and sounds of army life in the field. He discovered that Wood's irregular cavalry units – many of whom were recruited from among the hard-bitten adventurers and soldiers of fortune who had gathered on the Cape frontier, or gravitated towards the diamonds fields at Kimberley – contained a number of Frenchmen. He sought them out, keen to hear their stories, and to discover their politics – though of course he could not quite bring himself to meet with them on equal terms:

> For two days we have been sleeping in our clothes, ready to leave our tents at the first alarm. Since we crossed the Buffalo River, we have been in the enemy's country and yesterday I thought we should meet some parties of Zulus, for we were following with a small escort the line of Blood River which bounds the space occupied by the belligerent forces.
>
> I found to my great surprise several Frenchmen among the volunteer cavalry corps that covers the frontier. They are all old soldiers who do not know what to do in France since the profession of arms was abolished by the recruiting laws.
>
> They all come to find me and are enchanted to find me.
>
> They are not, as you may well imagine, the cream of the nation, but that did not prevent me from fraternising with them ...

The French are sometimes quaint fellows. Lord Chelmsford's late cook was a Frenchman. He cooked very badly, but he wrote verses. This poor devil, named Laparet, who had followed the General 'for love of war', was killed at Isandhlwana, fighting like a lion.[9]

Yet Louis may have deluded himself as to the true impression he made on his compatriots, as an officer of the irregular corps ruefully noted:

... the Prince asked for the Frenchmen of the Regiment, and with these he shook hands and chatted, giving them sovereigns: two of the men taking a matter-of-fact view of the business, came and offered a sovereign for a bottle of brandy. We gave them two other sovereigns in exchange for their two; I am sorry to say we gave them brandy also, though I believe we laid ourselves open to a severe punishment; we little thought at the time how soon we should prize these relics ...[10]

At least Evelyn Wood took to him. 'The young Prince impressed me much by his soldier-like ideas and habits', he wrote, 'and was unwearied in endeavouring to acquire knowledge and military experience.'[11]

But Louis' hopes were to be frustrated for a while longer. For one thing, his first hard ride across country had brought on a recurrence of his illness. 'The Prince accompanied me to Kambula', wrote Chelmsford, 'which soon knocked him up, and he had a slight attack of fever.'[12] Indeed, over the next few weeks a distinct pattern in his health emerged, and each bout of energetic activity would be followed almost immediately by exhaustion.

On 6 May, moreover, Chelmsford moved his headquarters once more, this time out of Zululand, and away from the front, and established himself at Utrecht in the Transvaal. Utrecht – slightly larger than Dundee, and predominantly Afrikaans in character – was in the heart of the 'disputed territory', and offered Chelmsford an ideal position from which to ponder the new advance, and co-ordinate frontier defence. Louis lodged in a house on the outskirts of town, and one of his fellow ADCs, Captain Molyneux, described something of the life of the staff there as they made their personal preparations for the coming campaign;

I, in common with many others, had to get a new packhorse; my sick nag had to be sent up from Maritzburg; the mess had to be reorganised and the stores collected for the campaign. This last business, by the way, proved a somewhat costly process; beer was selling at four shillings a bottle, brandy or champagne at the comparatively moderate figure of twenty shillings. Then I had to find the variation of my compass, rate my watch, fix the latitude, and draw maps. But Utrecht is certainly not a very pleasant place of residence, being built along the edge of a marsh, its altitude, three thousand five hundred feet above the sea, alone preventing malaria. It is liable also to Indian 'devils' on hot days; to whirlwinds, that is to say, of black dust spinning through the camp and covering everything with filth.'[13]

At least Utrecht was able to offer Louis some diversions. A few miles outside the town was the temporary residence of Prince Hamu kaNzibe, King Cetshwayo's half-brother, and one of the most powerful *izikhulu*[14] in northern Zululand. Prince Hamu represented the one success of British diplomatic attempts to split the Zulu Royal House; in the middle of March he had defected to Wood's column with 1,300 of his followers. Wood had settled him a safe distance from the border, and many of Hamu's warriors had been drafted into Wood's auxiliary units. They had fought at Hlobane, where they had been recognised by Zulu loyalists, and had suffered heavily as a result – an experience which in itself can hardly have encouraged further defections.

Nevertheless, Hamu's presence in British territory was something of a propaganda coup for Wood, and the Zulu Prince's household was the subject of much curiosity among the British. In the middle of May Chelmsford paid a visit to Hamu to discuss his future role in the war. His staff were fascinated by Hamu's entourage, and in particular by his large number of female attendants. On the way back, as Captain Molyneux recalled, a curiously prophetic exchange took place:

One day the Chief, with a large party of us, visited Uhamu's people, who were at some distance from Utrecht in a bit of country intersected with dongas. On his way back, Colonel Reilly could not get his English horse up a steep bank, and as we helped him out the Prince said, 'How would you have liked it, Colonel, if we had ridden away and left you to the mercy of those savage ladies?' It was a curious coincidence, considering that within a fortnight some of our people rode away and left the poor boy to his fate in another donga.[15]

At Utrecht, too, Louis had the opportunity to catch up on the news from France. In Durban he had made a fleeting acquaintance with a young French reporter, Paul Deleage, who had come to South Africa to cover the war – and Louis' involvement in it – for *Le Figaro*. Deleage inclined towards Republicanism, and his expectations of Louis were shaped by

Republican propaganda. He had expected to find *le fruit sec* of the gossip columns, or – worse – a dull young man corrupted by English manners and attitudes. Instead, he melted before Louis' charm, and declared him 'not a young man but a prince, with all the simplicity and charm of an *esprit supérieur et distingué*' and, moreover, 'a Frenchman with all the qualities of his race'.[16] Deleage at once became an admirer, and focused all his professional interest upon Louis, relegating the English and their dull little quarrel with the Zulus to its proper place. Louis, in turn, was delighted to have the opportunity to play host to a fellow Frenchman, and to discuss the news from the home he had not seen in years. At Utrecht they gossiped about Hamu together, and visited the hospital, where Louis chatted to a handful of Frenchmen he found among the patients. Louis even allowed himself a conspiratorial joke at the expense of the stolid Boer farmers who had come to the town from the outlying areas for protection. 'Do you suppose,' he asked the sophisticated Parisian Deleage, 'they were like this in the time of William the Silent?'[17]

At Utrecht, Chelmsford appointed the staff who would be responsible for deciding the exact route to be taken by the 2nd Division. As a conservative and a member of the Indian school, Chelmsford shared the Duke of Cambridge's wariness of Staff College graduates, and during the first invasion had appointed his staff on the basis of personal acquaintance rather than professional expertise. Even after the arrival of the reinforcements, this select group included no one who was trained in staff duties, and no chief of staff. It was not until May that Chelmsford even recognised the necessity of appointing a proper Intelligence Department; he had appointed a Natal civil servant who knew something of Zululand, the Hon. William Drummond, as its Head. The organisational effort to prepare for the new invasion was enormous, and the burden inevitably fell therefore, in an almost haphazard way, on a small and insufficient group of untrained officers.

Singled out for a particularly onerous duty was Brevet Lieutenant Colonel Richard Harrison. Harrison, a Royal Engineer, had been sent to South Africa at the head of the 30th Field Company after Isandlwana, and had arrived at Durban on the transport *Palmyra* on 5 April. To his disappointment, he had been taken from his company and attached instead to Chelmsford's staff. Harrison was a practical and thorough officer in his early forties, with a good deal of active experience behind him – he had served in the Indian Mutiny, in China and Canada. He was, nevertheless, taken aback when,

> On the morning of May 8 Lord Chelmsford came into my tent and told me that he had determined to appoint me acting

Quartermaster-General of the Army, pending approval from England. Of course I was much honoured by the confidence thus shown in me, and I said I would do my best; but I was well aware of the difficulties that had to be faced. At that time there was no Quartermaster-General's department in the country. The work was supposed to be done by the Adjutant-General's Staff and a new organisation which had charge of the base and the lines of com-munication, of which General Clifford was the head.

The troops were scattered along a line of communication over 300 miles, which had to be kept up chiefly by runners or special order-lies. No road reports or military sketches of the country existed. There was very little information regarding the enemy, and I had no office whatever, only Lance-Corporal Martin, whom I had brought with me from Pietermaritzburg, and my own private sketching case and stationery.[18]

Harrison at least had a realistic view of the enormity of the task that faced him:

I knew that three matters were urgent, viz. First, the completion of the organisation of the forces; second, the collection of supplies and transport; third, reconnoitering the enemy's country.

That same afternoon an officer, Lieut. Carey, 98th Regiment, was appointed to assist me in military sketching; and the Prince Imperial was lent to me to collect and compile information in regard to the distribution of troops and depots ...

... The next day I was put under orders as Assistant-Quartermaster-General attached to Headquarters, and it was clearly laid down that I was to be the head of a department, distinct from the Adjutant-General, and having authority and instructions to all officers of the Army by means of memoranda. Work began to pour in from all sides, and from that date until I handed over to an officer sent out specially from England I spent the greater part of every day in the saddle, and the greater half of every night writing letters and instructions in my tent. My lamp was the only one allowed to be kept alive after hours.[19]

Carey's appointment in this capacity was certainly appropriate. After his adventures on the *Clyde*, Carey had apparently been considered for a post with the 1st Division,[20] but instead he had marched up to Dundee with the drafts of the 1/24th, and arrived on 4 May. Along the way, he had been commended for 'surveying the route for the troops, and in the

selection of camping grounds, all the way up the country'.[21] Now he was
appointed Deputy Assistant Quartermaster-General to the 2nd Division,
as Harrison's assistant.

Harrison had met his other new assistant, Louis, before, in Ladysmith,
but this was probably the first time Carey and Louis had met. Much has
been written about the close friendship which apparently sprang up
between them; most of it almost certainly exaggerated.

It is true that Louis probably found that he had more in common with
Carey than with most in the British camp, although he must by then
have been well used to the British officer class. Carey, however, knew
France well, spoke French, and had also seen something of the horrors of
the Franco-Prussian War, albeit from a very different perspective. And in
return, Carey undoubtedly found Louis' youthful exuberance charming,
and was flattered by his company, which could only enhance his career
prospects. When bored by the harassed and phlegmatic British types
who surrounded him, Louis could at least take refuge in a discussion
with Carey of the Great Napoleon's victories.

Yet if there was the spark of a genuine affection between them, it
hardly had time to develop in the busy weeks of May 1879. Although
both were attached to Harrison's department, Carey and the Prince had
specific and often very different duties to perform, and they did not
always work from the same base. Louis' position was inevitably flexible,
for he remained nominally part of Chelmsford's staff, based at Utrecht,
but moved between camps and patrols as Harrison required him. Carey,
however, was based at Conference Hill, at least until the column moved
forward to the border.[22] Both Carey and Louis took part in a number of
reconnaissances before the invasion began, but prior to 1 June they had
only been on one together. Nor did they mess together in camp, for Louis
dined with the General's staff, and Carey in Harrison's mess.[23]

When they first met on 8 May, Louis had just three weeks left to live.
It is unlikely that he spent more than a handful of those days in Carey's
company.

Of the tasks allotted to him, reconnaissance occupied most of Harrison's
time, for until the invasion route was decided it was impossible to
plan a projected chain of supply. Harrison summed up the situation
succinctly:

It was known that the country between the Black and White
Umvaloosi Rivers was difficult, if not impracticable. At the same
time it was known that there were tracks practical for wagons
between Rorke's Drift and the capital. What was required was to
ascertain if sufficiently good roads could be made between the

rendezvous of the 2nd Division and Wood's column, to enable these forces to join hands and then advance as one army towards Ulundi.[24]

Already, General Newdigate and the Headquarters of the 2nd Division had moved forward from Dundee, and on 2 May had established themselves at Landman's Drift on the Mzinyathi. Landman's Drift proved a good camping ground, as the country was open on all sides, while the slopes of the nearby Doornberg were covered in bush, and provided ample firewood, even for the large concentration of troops who now gathered there. Once the camp was in place, Chelmsford made preparations to scout the terrain ahead. While the country beyond the Mzinyathi, as far as the Ncome, presented no problems, the lie of the land on the Zulu side of the border remained unknown. Before any advance could begin, it would be necessary to thoroughly scout the Zulu of the Ncome, in a swathe stretching from the confluence with the Mzinyathi in the south, as far north as Wood's base at Khambula.

Such a reconnaissance had two important functions. Firstly, it was still necessary to establish the line of advance, and secondly it was important to gain some impression of the Zulu presence in the border districts. Since the British victories at Khambula and Gingindlovu, the movements of the Zulu army had not been at all apparent to Chelmsford's intelligence staff. The country seemed ominously quiet; all along the border Zulu homesteads were deserted, where the women and children had gone into hiding, taking their cattle with them. The whereabouts of the young men of fighting age remained uncertain. While Chelmsford was confident that the recent battles had severely damaged the Zulus' capacity to resist in the long term, such was the awe with which the enemy were regarded that he could not afford to assume that his advance would be unopposed. It was necessary for the British to reassure themselves that for the early stages, across unknown territory, the country would be free of significant Zulu concentrations.

The first sweep across the border took place on 13 May. A battalion of auxiliaries – the 2nd Battalion, NNC, under Major Bengough – had marched north from Landman's Drift to Koppie Alleen on the Ncome river, where they had rendezvoused with a unit of irregular horse, who had come down from Conference Hill. Together these units crossed into Zululand, and had moved southwards down the border, heading towards Rorke's Drift, burning Zulu huts and skirmishing with small parties of Zulus along the way. This was the first major incursion into Zululand along the Mzinyathi front since Isandlwana, but while it raised the spirits of those who took part, it suggested, too, just how nervous were the troops fresh out from England. When Bengough's battalion crossed back into Natal at the end of the raid, British scouts watching the Mzinyathi drifts mistook them for Zulus, and panic spread along the border at the prospect of a raid. Fortunately the true identity of Bengough's men was realised before any damage was done, but the reaction of the Imperial troops was sufficient to throw doubts on the advisability of using auxiliary troops in such a role again.

In fact, there should have been ample troops available to the 2nd Division to mount such forays, since two regiments of British cavalry had just arrived at Dundee. The 17th Lancers and 1st Dragoon Guards had been sent out with the reinforcements after Isandlwana specifically to redress Chelmsford's chronic shortage of cavalry. In fact, however, their limitations had become apparent even before they reached the border. Their impressive English horses were out of condition after the long sea journey, and, accustomed to being fed on cut fodder from bags, they had difficulty adjusting to local grasses. They were, moreover, suffering from the extremes of temperature – in May 1879 the weather along the Mzinyathi alternated between baking hot days, bitter winds and driving rain – and proved far less sure-footed over the rough terrain than local horses. Despite the fact that they had marched slowly to the front to allow the horses time to acclimatise, they were still not fully effective by the middle of the month.

They were beset with other problems, too, of a largely psychological nature. The irregular cavalry units who already had some experience of Zululand had learned that survival often depended on alertness and flexibility. The regular cavalry, however, placed greater reliance on discipline, as Captain Molyneux discovered:

> It was then that I first noticed what an unhandy lot as a rule our cavalry were. One day we were out reconnoitering some fifteen miles over the border with a squadron of our own men and about as many Irregulars, and while the party were off-saddled on an open down, I was sent with two troopers to make a report on a neighbouring valley. We rode to the top of a hill overlooking it and all the country for miles round, where I gave my horse to one man, telling him to hold the three and let them feed, while the other kept his eyes open in every direction. My sketch took me, I suppose, half an hour, and on my return there were my two men, both mounted and both looking the same way, as rigid as rocks; they had never stirred from their saddles, nor let the horses have a bite of the grass. 'Why did you not dismount and let your horses graze, as I told you?' 'Beg pardon, sir; regimental standing orders say vedettes are not to

dismount; and if the horses graze they bust their breastplates.' The last remark is quite true enough, provided you have not the sense to slacken the breastplate ...[25]

The unsuitability of the newly arrived cavalry threw the responsibility of scouting the border back on the existing irregulars. Harrison, as usual, saw the problem clearly:

> The troops available for escort duty were the Cavalry Brigade at Dundee, the mounted troops of Wood's column under Lieut-Colonel Buller, and Bettington's Natal Horse, at that time at Conference Hill. The Cavalry Brigade were still somewhat unfit for work after their long voyage from England, and they had not yet learned the ways of campaigning in South Africa, while Wood's mounted troops were in good condition, thoroughly acquainted with Zulu customs, and moreover under the command of an officer who had an eye for country second to none in the Army, and who was an exceptionally good leader of men. So I arranged that for the first reconnaissance I should accompany a mounted patrol led by Buller ...[26]

Harrison might have added another factor, which would have a bearing on subsequent events. The Cavalry Brigade was commanded by Major General Sir Frederick Marshall, one of five generals sent out after Isandlwana to support Chelmsford. Both Marshall and his Brigade Major, Captain Herbert Stewart, were disappointed to find that the Brigade was not expected to act independently, but was attached to Newdigate's command, and that Chelmsford seemed to have no very clear role in mind for the cavalry. As Stewart rather tetchily observed en route to Dundee:

> ... we ... have been passing our time en route to the frontier absolutely in the dark and although questions of the highest importance have apparently been decided with regard to our future in the forthcoming advance, I think I may safely say that neither General Marshall, nor Colonel Lowe or any other cavalry soldier has ever had the opportunity of expressing his opinion with regard to the possibilities of the cavalry – either as to marching requirements or in any other particulars.[27]

Nor were the Brigade commanders mollified once they reached the border, as one of Marshall's intelligence staff admitted:

I am afraid things again look like a probability of splitting up our brigade, the idea now being to leave the K.D.G. at Kopje Allein on the Blood River. It seems lunacy; and this, too, while Wood's 1,200 irregular pony cavalry are allowed to go on. Wood gets everything; he is to go on in front, and advance at once; he has got all our provisions, forage etc., and all the gatlings are to be sent to him; that is, he will have six, while we have none. He has a separate command entirely, which is what neither Marshall nor Newdigate now have; it naturally gives rise to a good deal of jealousy.[28]

Yet in truth the irregulars were probably best suited in any case to the work Harrison required of them. Although none were then attached to the 2nd Division, Wood's column was now closer and easier to co-operate with, since on 5 May he had moved south from his old base at Khambula to Segonyama hill. There were, moreover, irregulars stationed at Conference Hill. These were the No. 3 troop, Natal Horse, under Captain Bettington, who had been there since 21 April. Both Bettington and his men had had a chequered history. Rowland Albemarle Bettington – who had a brother, Claude, also serving in Zululand – had knocked about the world before settling in South Africa in 1872.[29] He had given up farming to serve in the 9th Frontier War, and had been adjutant of the 2nd Battalion, 1st NNC, until the NNC had been reorganised after Isandlwana, and he had been offered his own command.[30]

Bettington enjoyed a good reputation as a commander of irregulars, although it is difficult at this distance to see why, since his experience in Zululand before April 1879 was limited.[31] His unit, inevitably known as Bettington's Horse, had been formed in February, largely from the white NCOs of the 3rd Regiment, NNC, which had been part of the old Centre Column, and which had been disbanded for poor performance during the Isandlwana campaign. Many of the men had had first-hand experience of the demoralisation which set in after Isandlwana, though their showing in their new incarnation was generally considered good. Like most of the irregular corps – and indeed the NCOs of the black auxiliary units – the men wore buff corduroy jackets and trousers, which were in plentiful supply in government stores, and wide-brimmed hats, wound round with a red rag. They were armed with carbines, while only a few of their officers carried swords, which were generally considered more of a hindrance than a help in irregular warfare.[32]

No sooner had Wood begun his advance than he began to sweep the country in front of him, towards a possible junction with the 2nd Division. On 10 May he had accompanied 150 men led by his energetic and resourceful cavalry commander, Redvers Buller, in an extended

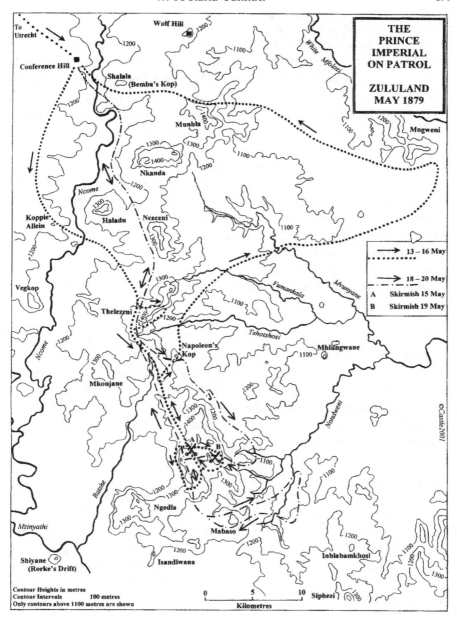

THE
PRINCE
IMPERIAL
ON PATROL

ZULULAND
MAY 1879

patrol which rode from his camp at Segonyama past Munhla hill. Passing through a narrow defile beyond Munhla, they were ambushed by a party of Zulus who tried to rush the rearguard, but Buller's men met them with a heavy fire, and drove them off. Wood returned satisfied that his own column could find a road towards Babanango without difficulty.

The Zulu response to this patrol is of interest, because it demonstrated that despite the fact that the countryside appeared deserted of non combatants, small groups of warriors were still operating in the area. For the most part, these were scouts and followers of local chiefs, who had remained near their homes to watch British movements, and to protect what remained of their property. Unable to resist strong British incursions, they were nonetheless prepared to attack smaller patrols whenever the opportunity presented itself. Over the next few days, there would be several more such incidents.

On 13 May Harrison himself took part in his first extended patrol into Zululand. 'The General officer commanding, with his Military Secretary,' he recalled,

> ... left the Headquarters camp at Utrecht for a trip to Newcastle, and I went off to take part in the reconnaissances in Zululand. I was accompanied by two officers of the Headquarters Staff, viz. The Hon. J. Drummond, Chief of the Intelligence Department, and the Prince Imperial, extra aide-de-camp to Lord Chelmsford. Each of us took one servant and three horses; all our requirements were carried in saddle-bags.[33]

Harrison's party rode to Conference Hill, where they were to meet Buller. Wood had moved his camp again on the 12th, and was now less than twenty miles from Conference Hill. Buller arrived on the 14th accompanied by nearly 170 mounted men – sixty Frontier Light Horse, under Captain D'Arcy and Lieutenant Blaine, forty men of the Natal Native Horse under Lieutenants Cochrane, Raw and Henderson, and sixty of Baker's Horse.[34] Harrison's account captured the flavour of life on such expeditions:

> ... we went together to Koppie Allein, where we bivouacked in a deserted farm. The horses were knee-haltered and turned into a mealie field for the night. Fires were lit and food prepared, each one for himself, and then we lay down and slept, in great coats and blankets, on the mud floor of the farmhouse.
>
> At daylight on the 15th we were off in a southerly direction, Buller leading. At about 10.35 we halted to rest the animals, and boil water

for tea or coffee. All meals on these occasions are much the same – a little tinned meat, some ration bread or biscuit, occasionally as a treat a little potted meat or, perhaps, jam, and then the fragrant and soothing cup of tea or coffee, after which a talk round the smouldering fires, and, if there is time enough, a pipe or cigar ...[35]

The party was moving south, through the open, grassy country on the left bank of the Ncome. This was the same area scoured by Bengough's foray just a few days before, and the patrol reached the foot of Thelezeni hill without encountering any opposition. Here the patrol divided in two, the Native Horse moving along the base of the hill while the irregulars drove up the sides, hoping that any Zulu sheltering there would bolt towards the Native Horse. In fact, there was no sign of the enemy, and the patrol continued southwards. It was only when the stop was made for breakfast that they encountered the first signs of a Zulu presence. 'We off-saddled at a kraal where the Zulus had been over-night,' recalled one of the party, 'in fact a few of their number had been there that morning, but did not wait for us'.[36] Ahead of them, the country rose up again towards the northern edge of the Nquthu ridge; this was almost familiar territory, for the old track from Rorke's Drift was now only a few miles off to the right, while Isandlwana was less than a dozen miles away to the south. The first shots of the war had been fired at the southern end of the range, when Lord Chelmsford had attacked Chief Sihayo's followers on 12 January; now, a few Zulu scouts were spotted scrambling up the rocky slopes ahead. The result, when they reached the top, was electrifying:

I saw them making off up Sihayo's Hill, just opposite, and they did not stop till they reached the top, when they took instant proceedings to call a gathering of the clan. The town-crier, on a grey horse, gave due notice to all the citizens living in kraals; and very soon we beheld, from our halting place below, a respectable assembly of blackskins on the ridge above. The man on the grey horse acted as general as well as town-crier, and divided his forces judiciously. He posted his infantry on the left and the cavalry on the right of the pass. The infantry numbered fifty, while the horsemen could only number eight. Opposed to this army was Colonel Buller's Irregular Horse. Some of the young hands thought a bloody conflict was about to be fought out on the hill-side; the older hands calculated that the Zulus would disappear as soon as we moved upwards.

The older hands were right. When Lieutenant Raw, who had been sent on ahead with six of his Basutos, reached the summit, he found himself in undisputed possession of the field. After galloping about from point to point, the Prince espied a Zulu on a distant kopje, and went for him. Off went Lieutenant Raw and the six Basutos after the impatient Prince, and on came Baker's Horse in the wake of the Basutos. The kopje was reached in time for them to see a few scared Zulus making off across country, far down on the plains below. In the hope that one bullet out of fifty might find a billet in a black man's body, Baker's Horse opened fire upon the flying specks beneath. There were no casualties.[37]

Harrison himself made light of this incident, merely remarking that:

… we saw a few Zulu scouts among the hills, some on foot and one or two mounted. We pursued them for some distance, and then gave it up, because they did not go in the direction that we wanted to spy out.[38]

Yet the significance of the skirmish was not lost on some of the others present. This had been Louis' first taste of action in Zululand, and he had revealed himself to be courageous, daring – and utterly irresponsible. For the first time since arriving in South Africa, he had been within reach of the enemy, and he had acted instinctively, all the years of frustration and inactivity bursting out of him in that wild, exuberant charge. Years later, it was this blissful disregard of authority which one young trooper of the Frontier Light Horse still remembered:

When we were on the move during the day, riding in half-sections, he was a real terror; if any Zulus were seen – and they were usually on the slope of a hill – he would dart out of the rank, his servant behind him, and race sword in hand to get them. His great ambition was to come to close quarters, and try his sword against shield and spear. He did not appear to care whether he was obeying orders from Buller or not. He wished to get at the Zulus, and was not waiting for orders from anyone. Probably, being a visitor to Wood's column, he did not think that he was under the direct orders of Buller or anyone else.

Twice on that patrol I was ordered – being a light-weight and having a fleet horse – with several others to head him off with orders from Buller to return to the ranks. After a long chase, we would gallop up on either side of him, shouting 'Halt!' He would draw rein, smiling sweetly, and say, 'Thank you, thank you!' replace the sword in the sheath, and calmly ride back with us. The wigging he was going to receive from Buller did not appear to trouble him in the least. All the men loved him. He was so clean, neat, and natural. One sort of officer will have you know he is an officer; not so the prince. He was only a happy young fellow.[39]

It is clear from this incident that Louis never had the slightest intention of adhering to the conditions by which he had been allowed at the front, nor was he paying attention to the promises he had made to his mother, to Queen Victoria, and to the rest. Irregular warfare on the Zulu frontier had much in common with his romantic ideas of combat; he saw in it the chance to engage in personal duels, the steel of his sword against the steel of the stabbing spear, a test of courage and honour, with all glory going to the winner. He chose to disregard the fact that the patrols had a practical purpose far more important than his personal distinction, and that by his reckless behaviour he exposed not only himself to danger, but risked the lives of the men sent to recall him. For a young man obsessed with the profession of soldiering, he had proved himself to be a dangerous amateur; Buller was furious.

The rest of the patrol passed off without incident. Buller spotted several large homesteads below them at the foot of the ridge, and the party descended to investigate. They were all deserted, although one contained a large quantity of shelled mealies. These were given to the horses, and those that remained were put to the torch, along with the homesteads themselves. It was by now afternoon, and there was little more to be achieved. Rather than bivouac in the broken ground at the foot of the ridge, Buller ordered the patrol to turn back towards Wood's camp. They spent that night near Thelezeni:

The wind blew cold, most bitterly so; and for those who had no blankets there was no sleep that night. The prince was among the forlorn and coverless ones, and he wandered up and down disconsolately. Next day nothing occurred. We breakfasted, we dined: we saw no Zulus, killed nothing; met with no accidents, and got into camp as quietly as you like ...[40]

The journalist Archibald Forbes added another detail to the story of that uncomfortable night:

During the night, which was bitterly cold, and during which the Prince's excitement continued, he tramped up and down constantly, singing at intervals 'Malbrook s'en va-t-en-guerre', not wholly to the contentment of the phlegmatic Britons around him ...[41]

The party returned to find that Wood had moved south again, to a position near Wolf Hill. According to Harrison:

> ... the three days' march that we had just accomplished, under the guidance and direction of Buller and his mounted men, had no doubt been useful to all of us, and it had established certain facts in connection with the Zulus; but it had not discovered a route for the 2nd Division, and so I determined to make a second reconnaissance. This matter I discussed with Colonel Wood when we got in, and we had a long talk regarding plans for the campaign, and then I wrote to Lord Chelmsford and others until far into the night.[42]

It was probably on this occasion[43] that Wood recalled a prophetic conversation between himself and Louis:

> I observed at dinner, 'Well, you have not been assegaid, as yet?' 'No; but while I have no wish to be killed, if it were to be I would rather fall by an assegai than bullets, as that would show we were at close quarters'.[44]

The following morning exhaustion set in. Wood had invited Louis to join him for breakfast, but Louis failed to appear, and on going to investigate Wood found him fast asleep. Reluctant to risk the Imperial dignity by shaking him awake, Wood stepped outside the tent, and called in a loud voice,
'Here are the Zulus!'
The result was predictable; Louis emerged, bedraggled but sword in hand.
'Now sir', said Wood with a bow, 'I hope you'll consent to breakfast with me'.[45]
Harrison returned to Conference Hill, taking Louis with him; Drummond returned to the Headquarters staff at Utrecht. Harrison had arranged for the second patrol to begin that same day, the 18th. The plan was for his party to set out from Conference Hill, and meet a strong escort under Buller near Thelezeni. They had both covered this country two days previously, and such a rendezvous would spare Buller's men the additional ride to Conference Hill from Wolf's Hill. 'My immediate party for this expedition', recalled Harrison, 'consisted of the Prince and his servant, Captain Carey, D.A.Q.M.G., Captain Bettington with five of his men leading spare ponies, and twenty Basutos under an officer.'[46] Louis noted that the 'men took with them three days' provisions (tinned meat and biscuits), the horses having to be fed exclusively on the veld'.[47]

The party left Conference Hill at about 8 am, travelling down the valley of the Ncome, then angling up the side of the Thelezeni ridge. At the southern end of the ridge they paused to look eastwards, down into the watershed of the Tshotshosi river. It was here that they were supposed to meet Buller, but there was no sign of him, and the landscape, as usual, seemed deserted. Harrison led his party down the side of the ridge towards the river, hoping to find a good route for wagons, but the descent was steep, and the hillsides scarred with dongas. Instead, the party turned southwards towards the Nquthu range, but after several hours' difficult riding, there was still no sign of a track – or Buller.[48]

It was now late afternoon, and Harrison decided to risk bivouacking for the night. The patrol retired to a suitable piece of ground, then ringed their horses, and kept them saddled all night. No fires were lit; according to Bettington:

Even to strike a match or to say a word, except in a whisper, was strictly forbidden. In front, in the rear, on the right and left, Basutos were stationed as sentinals with orders to walk towards each other. Then the men could take some rest; the Prince was stretched upon the ground like the others, sharing his scanty covering with Lomas, his orderly ... So the night passed, troubled only by false alarms given by one of the officers, Lieutenant Carey.[49]

This last comment is interesting, and has often been quoted to suggest that Carey was nervous by nature. Yet Bettington's account was probably written after Louis' death, and perhaps for Eugénie's benefit – by which time Carey had already been marked down as responsible for what had followed. In fact, neither Harrison nor Louis mentioned any nervousness on Carey's part in their reports of that night, and it may be that Bettington's remarks actually reflected a tension that naturally was common to them all. Certainly, if Carey had revealed himself as unduly anxious, it is unlikely that Harrison would have trusted him with authority on future patrols – or that Louis, for whom courage in the face of the enemy was everything, would have been keen to accompany him.

The next morning, the patrol faced a dilemma:

... after a further fruitless search for Buller's men, we had to make up our minds what to do: should we return to Conference Hill or get back onto the Ingutu Range, and, proceeding eastward along the ridge, endeavour to find a road leading into the valley of the Nondweni River, and so to Ibabanango Mountain? Captain Bettington told me that he had frequently been in that part of the country with quite a few men, and that safety lay in proper precautions rather than the size of the escort. So I agreed to go on. The Prince and [Lieutenant] Carey were both sketching, and Captain Bettington took immediate command, under me, of the mounted men.

Our order of march was as follows: Bettington leading; in front and on the flanks, guided by their leader's hand, Bettington's troopers; close behind, taking notes on the ground as we went along, the Prince Imperial; then myself; and behind me Carey and the Basutos. Our direction was south-east, and our objective to find a way up to the top of the Ingutu Ridge.[50]

The patrol was now somewhere on the northern edge of the Nquthu hills, east of the middle reaches of the Batshe river. As they tried to pick their way up the slopes, they noticed 'some sixty Zulus whom we had already chased some days before, and who were supposed to be scouts and spies, and not inhabitants of the neighbouring kraals'.[51] The Zulus seemed to be watching their progress, but when they began a desultory and ineffective sniping, Bettington, worried by 'the danger of leaving them on our flank and rear while we were surveying the ground' urged Harrison to allow him to drive them off.

The result was nothing if not predictable:

The Prince dismounted and drew his sword; Bettington passed on in front, his men firing as they went; and I waved my helmet to urge on the Basutos. Two of the latter galloped up at once, and joined us in the attack, but the rest hung back a little and did not come up again until we had won our way to the top. The Zulus began their tactics of trying to surround us, but the side of the hill, except on the path, was too steep even for them. Moreover, I think they were surprised by our rapid attack, and did not know what our strength was. Anyhow, they gave way in the centre as we mounted the path, and then the Basutos came up and completed their discomfiture.[53]

'Neither the Prince nor Bettington was touched,' wrote Filon, 'and as they opened up the plateau, they charged at the head of the other horsemen.' The Zulus scattered, and 'after a brief pursuit' Bettington reined his men in. On the top of the ridge there was a large deserted homestead, and Harrison allowed the men to off-saddle there and take breakfast. Exploring the huts, they discovered several saddles and other items which had clearly been looted from the camp at Isandlwana. Bettington suggested that they call it 'Napoleon Kraal' in honour of the Prince. Relaxed and elated after their brush with danger, Louis had warmed to

Bettington, whose life seemed to sum up a spirit of adventure which, in their very different ways, had brought them both to Zululand:

> ... he took the greatest interest in hearing from Captain Bettington how he had spent his early life in New Zealand, driving cattle, assisting as a dispenser, keeping a livery stable, and for a time even acting as 'boots' in a hotel, until he found himself in Natal at the time of the Zulu War, and obtained command of the irregular mounted corps which bore his name.[56]

Louis had noted that Bettington, like many irregular officers, did not carry a sword, and had only used his revolver in the skirmish. This may have been practical, but it did not seem to Louis at all romantic:

> 'For myself' said he, 'I make a point always of having mine, not so much to attack, as to defend myself if I were surrounded. I should die fighting, and then death would have no pangs.'[57]

Carey, it seems, had made no particular impression on anyone.

At about 9.15 the patrol started off again, and almost immediately Harrison had an adventure of his own:

> I had started slightly ahead of the escort, when I saw three men in redcoats advancing towards me. They were coming along in a leisurely manner, evidently returning to the kraal in ignorance of the skirmish that had taken place there, and thinking that it was still occupied by their own people. Their only arms, as far as I could see, were assegais.
>
> Not realising at first who they were, whether Natal Kaffirs in British service or followers of Ketchwayo, I approached nearer to them, at the same time changing direction slightly to the right in order to avoid being caught on the path they were using. Which ran along the steep northern edge of the Ingutu Ridge. At that moment I heard a shout behind me, and saw Bettington, the commander of my escort, coming along the path at a gallop, with his revolver in his hand. Clearly he did not want any nearer approach to show him who my three friends were, and, riding past me, he shot one of them, while the other two jumped into the bush on the mountain side and disappeared.[58]

The patrol then continued westwards along the top of the hills, until it reached the far end. Opening up to their left was the valley of the Nondweni river, leading north towards Wood's position; ahead of them

lay Babanango mountain, and the old road from Rorke's Drift towards
oNdini. 'It seemed to me,' recalled Harrison with some satisfaction, 'that
we had found the road that we wanted for the 2nd Division.'[59]

Their objective accomplished, the patrol returned towards Thelezeni.
It was dusk by the time they reached it, but after their experiences in the
morning, Harrison was reluctant to bivouac so near to the site of their
skirmish:

> Towards evening we found some wood in a kraal, and were able
> to cook. Then, leaving our fires alight, we went on again. Some
> Zulus followed us, and when they came to one of our fires they
> danced around it, making a hideous noise.[60] So we did not think
> it safe to stay long anywhere, but worked our way by stars and
> compass throughout the night, and early the next morning reached
> Conference Hill.[61]

The patrol reached Conference Hill at dawn. This was a dangerous time,
because it was usual for British troops in camp on the borders to stand
to just before dawn in case of a surprise attack, and Harrison was well
aware of the prevailing nervousness:

> We were aware also that many of the troops were young and inex-
> perienced, and did not always await their officers' orders to fire. So
> we approached the laager at Conference Hill with caution. It was
> well we did so. The men were lining the trench that had been dug
> around the encampment, and we could hear their colonel talking to
> them. 'Now, boys, be ready – when I give the word to fire, fire low
> – I see them coming – look out, boys – remember to fire low'; and
> so on, until, by signals, without showing our bodies, we convinced
> the gallant defenders of the post that we were not Zulus, but only
> hungry and tired comrades anxious to obtain food and rest.[62]

On the whole, Harrison considered himself well satisfied with the results
of the week's work:

> Since we had left, we must have ridden over 200 miles. During
> the last thirty-six hours we were twenty-five in the saddle, but the
> Prince enjoyed it immensely ...[63]

Indeed he had. Back in camp he bumped into Deleage again, and the
Frenchman was indignant that the English had so thoughtlessly risked
the life of the heir to the Imperial throne. Louis had laughed him off:

I enjoy these little outings; they suit me perfectly – but if I had to be killed, I should be in despair at the thought of falling in one. In a great battle, very well; it's for Providence to decide; but in an obscure skirmish – ah, no, that would never do![64]

Deleage was hardly reassured. He took consolation by complaining bitterly to Carey, who could at least sympathise with him in French.

Yet Harrison was in for a disappointment. The afternoon of their return he and Louis rode to Utrecht, 'leaving our companions at Conference Hill',[65] to report to Chelmsford in person. Harrison was discussing his findings with the General when Buller arrived. There had clearly been some confusion over the exact rendezvous point; Buller explained that he had waited at what he thought was the spot but, not seeing Harrison, he had reconnoitered 'on his own account'.[66] He had led his patrol into the valley of the Tshotshosi to the east of Thelezeni, then followed the more open country to the north of the Nquthu, towards Babanango. The country had appeared to be thickly populated, but the homesteads were all deserted, and the only Zulu Buller encountered were a few old and infirm non-combatants who had clearly been too frail to evacuate.

Buller, too, was convinced that he had found a route for the advance of the column. Wood had already moved the Flying Column farther south to Munhla Hill; Buller suggested that the 2nd Division should cross the Ncome into Zululand at Koppie Alleen, heading towards the nek between the Thelezeni and Incenceni hills, and then down into the valley of the Tshotshosi – a route which would intersect the projected line of advance of the Flying Column. It was a more northerly route than Harrison had considered, but it had the advantage of avoiding the Nquthu hills altogether, while at the same time making it possible to effect an almost immediate junction with Wood's column. Chelmsford was inclined to accept Buller's advice, and Harrison was philosophical: 'His recommendations in regard to the route for the 2nd Division differed to mine,' he recalled, 'and as he had had considerable experience in the country, and I had had none, the General naturally inclined to his.'[67]

It may also have been on this occasion when Buller voiced his concerns about Louis' recklessness in the field. He had not approved of the way Louis had put himself at risk on the first patrol, and he would not, he said, 'allow the Prince Imperial to go again with him on ... reconnaissance as he considered it too dangerous'.[68] Chelmsford had more things on his mind than the foolishness of a high-spirited young man, and without directly confronting Louis, ordered Harrison to confine him to safer duties around the camps:

By direction of Lord Chelmsford I gave the Prince written instructions that he was never to leave the immediate precincts of the camp without a proper escort. His ordinary work was to sketch the camps occupied by Headquarters, and the roads they traversed when on the march.[69]

Since Chelmsford had decided that the Headquarters Staff would accompany the 2nd Division, this work was both mundane and safe. Louis' precise duties consisted of 'the construction of the map of the country compiled from the various reports that I received';[70] the work of sketching in the field now fell solely to Carey. As Chelmsford himself put it:

The Prince Imperial went on a reconnaissance and very nearly came to grief. I shall not let him out of my sight again if I can help it.[71]

This routine work would last for ten days, allowing Louis little chance to see anything of the country beyond the camps at Utrecht and Conference Hill. 'Since my last letter,' he wrote to Eugénie on the 26th,

my life has been most sedentary, especially in relation to the nomad habits one gets into here. A week spent in my tent affects me like a week spent in a feather bed, for the canvas ceiling has its charms in comparison with the vault of the sky. But, as I have already many times written to you, the life I am leading here pleases me and does me good. Never have I felt so strong and energetic.[72]

Louis' story of his recent adventures soon circulated among the staff. Major F.W. Grenfell, 60th Rifles, whose work as Deputy Assistant Adjutant-General to the Headquarters staff brought him into close contact with Louis, recalled somewhat sardonically:

The Prince Imperial is with us, and was in great danger last Tuesday. He, and Colonel Harrison, our Q.M.G., joined a reconnaissance of Buller's, missed their escort, and went on with only five men. The Zulus caught them on top of a hill, where they came under fire. The Prince drew his sword and charged up the hill, shouting. His ferocious yells (and I conclude his likeness to his great uncle) alarmed the Zulus, who fled, but they had to pistol a Zulu before they got out, which they did all right, but slept two nights in the open, very cold and miserable.

He is a very plucky little chap, and will, I think, get himself shot before the campaign is over.[73]

Deprived of the hope of any more such excitements, Louis took an almost fevered interest instead in the preparations for the coming campaign:

> The Prince's passion for information was boundless, and the questions he used to put searching in the extreme. For instance, he would ask 'How many biscuits in a bag?' Of course, the unhappy commissariat officer thus tackled broke down; the next question would be 'How many in a barrel?' then: 'Are there more in a barrel than a bag?' To all the answer would be the same; the Prince would then remark, 'Great want of organisation', and down would go the whole thing in his note-book. Then perhaps he might begin to query about the difference between sweet and sour veldt, what animals would do best on the former, and what on the latter ...[74]

Nevertheless, Louis was clearly frustrated by the forced inactivity, and told Forbes that he 'hated desk work'.[75] Indeed, Deleage recalled that 'Lieutenant Carey found the Prince's work done with so much haste and inattention that he had to sit up all night correcting it'.[76] What's more, this sense of frustration seems to have had a bad effect on his health, and indeed Deleage's description of him suggests that his earlier fever was still troubling him:

> ... the Prince complained that he had had to toil at the desk all day, and said he had a pain in his back; his eyes had a rather haggard expression, which showed that he had over-tasked his eyes, which were somewhat weak ...[77]

At least the ten days spent in camp on the eve of the invasion allowed Louis to mix more freely with the army around him. For most of his time on the border he had been moving around, either with the Headquarters, or with Harrison in Zululand, and both duties had kept him away from the assembling army. He had, it's true, found time to walk over the battlefield of Khambula with Bigge and Slade, and to accept an invitation to dine at the mess of N/5 Battery,[78] but in fact – for all the glowing testimonials to his popularity published after his death – he had little time to mix with anyone outside the staff. In camp, he was naturally a focus for the curious, and the journalists who had also assembled for the coming invasion inevitably sought him out. He met Archibald Forbes, the correspondent of *The Daily News*, and found common ground in their shared adventures in the Prussian war. Forbes, who had been contemptuous of the pretensions of the Imperial family in 1870, relented now; 'the boy of the Empire when the shackles of the Empire had fallen from his limbs,' he wrote, 'was no longer a buckram creature but a lively natural lad'.[79] Deleage was on hand, too, to discuss French politics, while Louis' interest in the work around him brought him into contact with fresh faces in the officer corps. Many, like Horace Smith-Dorrien – then a young transport officer, and one day to become a General in the First World War – were won over by his charm:

> The Prince Imperial, wearing the undress uniform of the Royal Artillery … endeared himself to all … he was especially friendly to myself. He took a deep interest in the organisation of every branch of our force … he was in my tent up to 11 p.m. on the night before going out on his last patrol … extracting from me a promise to write him a treatise on bullock transport …[80]

Yet not everyone was impressed, and Grenfell, for one, admitted finding Louis too Gallic for his own very English tastes, and too self-absorbed:

> … while courteous and respectful, he was always somewhat cold and dignified. His craving for effect was shown in various ways. He seldom used his stirrup to mount his horse, but generally vaulted into the saddle … He was ardent for opportunities of distinction, and on two or three occasions he had displayed rash gallantry which alarmed the officers told off to attend him.[81]

The army at large, where it was aware of him at all, regarded him with little more than polite and uncomprehendable curiosity, reflected in a remark by an anonymous officer to Deleage:

> After all, what's the Prince supposed to be doing in this row? He'll get no credit from us, and I can't see what good it's to do him in your own country, unless he goes back a cripple – and even then![82]

Indeed, the attitude of the rank and file may have been even less sympathetic, and a comment made in a stage whisper outside Louis' tent suggests that the attitudes of Wellington's day had not entirely passed away. 'Do you know that saying,' he asked Deleage one day,

> … that an Englishman is worth five Frenchmen – I won't go into the number of other nations? … The other day I was in my tent and heard it just outside. I was very angry – and I've been anxious to speak to you about it. You might hear it at any time and think it was

meant for you – whereas it is only a byword; it has no weight except what people might choose to give it ...[83]

While Louis worked for Harrison, safe at camp, meanwhile, the sweeps into Zululand continued. The Cavalry Brigade at last made its first major incursion into enemy territory. Still stationed at Dundee, it set out for Rorke's Drift on the 19th, and at dawn on the 21st crossed the Mzinyathi into Zululand. The force was under the command of General Marshall, and neither Chelmsford nor his staff were present. Burning Zulu homesteads as they went, the cavalry advanced cautiously to Isandlwana, but the Zulu did not dare to oppose so large an expedition. The old battlefield was a deeply disturbing sight, for while the Zulu had removed most of their dead, the remains of Lord Chelmsford's command still lay scattered amongst the long grass, mixed up with animal carcasses and the rotting and rusting debris of the camp. Some of the bodies were mere skeletons; others, held together by their uniforms and desiccated by the sun, still had skin drawn over their features, and were recognisable. The cavalry hastily covered over some of the remains, but Colonel Glyn of the 24th had asked to be allowed to bury his own dead, and the redcoats were left where they were. There was, in any case, a more practical purpose for the visit; Lord Chelmsford needed any serviceable wagons still on the site to boost the transport for the 2nd Division. The cavalry was back at Rorke's Drift by mid-afternoon, bringing with it forty of the ill-fated Centre Column's wagons.

By the end of the third week in May, then, the British had effectively scoured a wide band of country on the Zulu side of the border, extending from Conference Hill on the Ncome to the north, as far south as Rorke's Drift on the Mzinyathi. There were clearly no large Zulu concentrations in the region, nor indeed many civilians, while the systematic destruction of homesteads and crops had deprived the scouts still lingering in the area of food and shelter. When Lord Chelmsford was ready to make his advance, he could be confident that for the first few days he would be advancing through something of a scorched-earth zone, and that he was at no immediate risk of attack.

As the 2nd Division's preparations progressed, so such activity increased. Wood himself went on another patrol, to seek out and bury some of the dead from the Hlobane battle. Although his route took him farther north, he, too, found the countryside deserted.

On 27 May the 2nd Division began to move forward from Landman's Drift towards an advanced post at Koppie Alleen, on the banks of the Ncome. The start of the new invasion was now only a few days away, and Chelmsford rode down with the Headquarters Staff to join the column. Although the broad details of the route to be followed had now been agreed, it was still necessary to plan the exact route and to select camping sites, and Harrison's staff were as busy as ever. Carey, in particular, undertook another patrol,[84] and, to Chelmsford's relief, he was able to confirm Buller's original suggestions.[85]

By the 29th there was a tangible sense of excitement among the troops of the 2nd Division, and in a day full of portents a number of officers crossed the border to make a final examination of the terrain ahead. Chelmsford and his staff rode into Zululand, escorted by some of the Dragoons and Buller's irregulars; Louis went with them, allowed into enemy territory for the first time since Harrison's reconnaissance. So too did Carey. Herbert Stewart and a group of officers from the Cavalry Brigade also crossed the river 'on a private reconnaissance'.[86] Indeed, the border area seemed to be alive with British patrols, but while it was inevitable that they should encounter and support one another, the lessons of the day were unsettling.

Chelmsford and his staff crossed the Ncome valley, and climbed up onto the nek below Thelezeni, looking out for several miles across the valley of the Tshotshosi below them. From their viewpoint the prospective route seemed 'plain sailing', but Chelmsford resolved to 'send out an officer to make good of this track'.[87] He sent Carey, accompanied by a squadron of Dragoons,[88] and the staff then returned to camp. On the return journey, Molyneux witnessed a telling incident, which suggested Louis had learned nothing from his recent experiences:

As we rode home that day, the Prince Imperial and I were walking our horses a little behind the rest, talking over all sorts of things, while half a mile away in all directions were scouting parties of Irregulars. Some days before, when out with Colonel Harrison and Bettington's men, the Prince had gone straight for some Zulus on a hill, who luckily had bolted. Reverting to this, I asked him why he had risked his life, when the death of one, or even a dozen Zulus would not affect the course of the campaign. 'You are right, I suppose', he said; 'but I could not help it. I feel I must do something.' Just at this moment a shot was fired on our left. I looked across, and saw the man who had fired riding on quietly, reloading. If he had fired at a Zulu, he had killed him; if he had fired at a buck, he had missed it; he was neither hurrying nor dismounting; the conclusions were plain enough. Yet there was the Prince, going, sword drawn, at full gallop for the man; I could have no chance of catching him, and in the dusk he might break his neck in the wild ride. 'Prince, I must order you to come back!' I shouted. He pulled up at once, saluted, returned his sword, and said nothing for a minute; then broke out, 'It seems I am never to be without a nurse'; and a moment after, 'Oh, forgive me; but don't you think you are a little too phlegmatic?' I reminded him what he had just owned about the affair with Bettington's men, and he laughed, saying that I had answered him rather neatly ...[89]

Sir William Beresford, another special service officer acting as Buller's ADC, noticed something else about Louis that day:

[Beresford] held his horse (the same one he was riding on the fatal day) he [i.e. Louis], who had been wonderfully active had some difficulty in mounting, and Lord William said to him, 'he's too high for you, Sir' – to which he observed – no, his trousers were too tight, and prevented him from getting on – [90]

Carey, meanwhile, had earned himself a rebuke. Stewart's party had met with Chelmsford somewhere below Thelezeni, then had ridden in a different direction, entering a number of homesteads, 'all used lately, some within a day or two'.[91] Here they came across 'Carey, D.A.Q.M.G., and Jones, and a squadron of KDGs, surveying.'[92] Stewart was clearly surprised to find them, and either then or later, and making use of Marshall's name, he reproached Carey for using Dragoons in such work, and said that he would not allow them to accompany Carey again.[93]

This is an important incident, which has often been quoted to suggest that Carey was over-cautious, and had over-reacted to the Zulu threat by taking too large an escort. In fact, Stewart's concerns were if anything exactly the opposite. There is nothing to suggest that Carey was at all unnerved at this stage, nor was the ultimate responsibility for the use of the Dragoons his – both were, after all, acting under Chelmsford's orders.[94] The escort – fewer than 150 men – was not large compared to the numbers employed by Buller ten days earlier, and indeed the following day Major Bengough of the Native Contingent met Carey sketching in a similarly advanced position with no escort at all.[95] Stewart, moreover, had known Carey at Staff College, where he had been the senior officer of Carey's batch of students; so far from being critical of Carey, he knew him to be 'a most conscientious and hard-working officer'.[96]

What bothered Stewart, in fact, was the casual use of Dragoons in a potentially dangerous expedition at a time when their role had yet to be decided, and without Marshall's express sanction. Both Marshall and Stewart were still smarting from the apparent indifference with which Chelmsford regarded their command, and indecision about the role of the Dragoons had not helped matters. A few days before, Chelmsford had proposed sending the entire regiment to garrison duty in the Transvaal;[97] he had recently changed his mind, but had decided instead to relegate them to a supporting role, patrolling the lines of communication – a decision one Brigade officer privately condemned as 'lunacy'.[98] That his reasons were probably influenced by the poor showing of the regular cavalry in comparison to the irregulars of Wood's command had hardly improved the temper of the Brigade's officers. It was clearly the presumption of the staff which had irritated Stewart, and Marshall would remain touchy about the unauthorised use of his troops throughout the war. As late as 9 July, five days after the Zulu army was effectively broken up at the Battle of Ulundi, he would still admonish an officer who had taken it upon himself to,

> ... divert a large portion of the Cavalry for an expedition, which to say the least of it, is all in the air ... I must request during this time, which I hope will be very short, of my providing supplies to the front, that you will not divert the Cavalry from the line of communications. I have already informed you un-officially of my wish to keep the Cavalry until this very important duty of supplying was performed on or near the roads on which the convoy travels, but as you appear to either misunderstand or take a different view of the situation, I now request you to retain the Cavalry for the escort of all convoys guarding the line of communication ...[99]

The net result of this breach of etiquette, for which Chelmsford was ultimately responsible, was that Carey would receive no further escort of Dragoons for his sketching work over the next few days. Moreover, those who overheard Stewart's remarks, unaware of the tensions which lay behind it, took his criticisms at face value; on his return to camp, Carey would be teased unmercifully.

By 30 May Chelmsford was able to tell Wood that he hoped that the 2nd Division would finally cross into Zululand on 1 June'.[100] He estimated that it would take two days to reach Thelezeni nek and descend into the valley of the Tshotshosi; the Flying Column, then camped at Munhla Hill, would arrive on the Tshotshosi at about the same time.

On the last day before the new invasion began, the tension in the 2nd Division camp was almost palpable. There was a false alarm before dawn, but with no Zulu in sight the various formations were free to make their preparations for the advance. Louis was elated at the thought of being in action; 'Tomorrow we shall sleep in Zululand,' he told Dawnay, 'I hope'.[101]

That evening, Louis approached Harrison with a request, as Harrison recalled:

> ... he came to me and asked that he might extend his sketch beyond the camp to be occupied the next day, and make a reconnaissance of the road to be traversed the following day. I saw no objection to this, provided he took with him the usual escort. Many of us had been over the ground, and we knew there was no 'impi' in the neighbourhood. Moreover, I thought that the cavalry which accompanied the division, would be extended over the country far in advance of the camp, so I gave my permission. Shortly afterwards Captain Carey came to my tent, and asked that he might go with the Prince's party, as he wished to verify his sketch of the country, and I said 'yes', and added that he could look after the Prince, and see that he did not get into trouble.[102]

It is interesting to note from this account – and Harrison was, of course, writing years after the event – that it was Louis who instigated this expedition from the beginning. Indeed, it seems that there was little enough justification on military grounds for a further patrol. Harrison had clearly not felt the need to make a fresh reconnaissance, while Carey merely wished to verify his existing sketches. Carey had been over the ground on the 29th and again on the 30th; even Lord Chelmsford himself had already examined it. The camping ground for the first night's halt – on 1 June – had already been selected, as had the approximate position for the second. Carey, of course, was particularly zealous when it came to sketching duties, at which he excelled; he was no doubt buoyed up by the knowledge that Chelmsford had already noted his diligence. As an ambitious man, it must have occurred to him, too, that the opportunity to be seen working closely with the Prince could only help his career.

It is difficult, now, to avoid the conclusion that this expedition was little more than a jaunt, thought up by Louis as an excuse to escape the boredom of camp routine, and be in the forefront of the advance. It was indulged by Harrison out of a sense of sympathy for Louis' recent inactivity. Over the previous few days, recalled Harrison, Louis had 'continually asked me to let him go out, as he preferred the more active to the sedentary part of our duties',[103] and according to Forbes Louis was 'dead tired of routine desk-work', and had that evening 'begged' to go.[104] After the event, Harrison claimed that he had given Louis written orders for the patrol – which implied a degree of justification on military grounds – but that they were conveniently lost with his body.[105] Carey understood that Louis was going 'on his own request' to allow him the

honour of choosing 'a camp for the forces for the 2nd June and that I was
to allow him to do it entirely himself'.[106] There was, of course, every reason to believe that the countryside was safe, providing the party did not
stray beyond the extensive cavalry screen. It had been swept many times
over the previous few days – there was no sign of even the Zulu patrols
who had been on the Nquthu hills ten days before. The prevailing opinion in the camp was that the Zulus would not contest the advance until
the column reached Babanango mountain.[107] Harrison did not bother
to inform Chelmsford that he had given Louis permission to leave
the camp; he no doubt thought that Chelmsford's own reconnaissance
on the 29th, during which Louis had been present, and the imminent
advance had both rendered the earlier ban out of date.

It is interesting to note, too, that Harrison did not trouble to impose a
proper chain of command, presumably because the patrol had no very
real purpose, and was not thought to be at risk. Though he could hardly
admit it later, he was simply allowing Louis to see something of the fun
of the first day's advance; Carey's presence at least meant that there was
an officer to keep an eye on him. Harrison's tone suggests that he hardly
thought it necessary.

The following morning – Whit Sunday, 1 June 1879 – Carey approached Harrison on the subject of an escort, and was given a request to
take to the Cavalry Brigade HQ. For the first time since it had arrived at
the front, the Brigade was extensively employed securing the Zulu side
of the border in preparation for the advance. Most of the regular cavalry
were already deployed;[108] Harrison had only specified a small escort,
perhaps because he knew that in any case Stewart had refused to allow
regular cavalry to accompany Carey again. Harrison had asked for men
from Bettington's Horse and the Natal Native Horse, and Stewart did
not demur. According to Forbes, who was present in Stewart's tent at
the time:

> … Carey came to him with Harrison's warrant for an escort. Carey
> did not mention, nor did the document state, that the escort was
> for the Prince Imperial. Stewart ordered out six men of Bettington's
> Horse – a curiously mixed handful of diverse nationalities – and
> he told Carey that he would send Captain Shepstone an order for
> the Basuto[110] detail of the escort; but that time would be saved
> if Carey himself on his way back to headquarters would hand
> Shepstone the order and give his own instructions. Carey chose the
> latter alternative and departed. An hour later, while I was still with
> Stewart, the six Basutos paraded in front of his tent. Either Carey or
> Shepstone had blundered in the instructions given them, that was

clear; but nothing could now be done but to order the Basutos to hurry forward and try to overtake the other instalment of the escort. Meanwhile the Prince had been impatient; and he, Carey and the white section of the escort had gone on.[111]

According to Carey:

I went for Captain Bettington's men myself and they paraded at 9.15 a.m. at the Headquarters Camp. We then started taking with us a friendly Zulu furnished by the Hon. W. Drummond to give us the names of the hills.[112] Before crossing the Blood River I sent the order to Captn. Shepstone who was encamped on the Zulu side, with a verbal message to send on the men as soon as possible. The messenger, one of Bettington's men, returned saying they would meet us at the ridge between the Incenceni and Itelezi mountains. I sent the man back to bring them on himself, but he returned telling me they had started with Captn. Shepstone and would join us. As the Prince was anxious to get on, and we could see two large bodies of Basutos riding in parallel directions on our flanks, I did not consider it my duty to persuade the Prince to await them.[113]

The muddle was typical of the confusion which reigned over small matters on a day when an army was entering enemy territory for the first time.

While Louis was waiting for Carey to organise the escort he had scribbled a note to Eugénie, and handed it to Forbes, who was riding back to Conference Hill. His thoughts, as ever, were on the coming adventure, on France, and his mother:

Koppie Allein, June 1st, 1879

My dear mother,

I am writing hurriedly on a leaf of my note-book; in a few minutes I am off to select a camping-ground for the second division on the left bank of the Blood River. The enemy is concentrating in force, and an engagement is expected in a week's time. I do not know when I shall be able to send you any news, for the postal facilities leave much to be desired. I did not want to let slip this opportunity of embracing you with all my heart.

Your devoted and dutiful son,

Napoleon

P.S. I hear of M. Godelle's splendid election. Pray tell him from me how delighted I was at this good news.

When the party was finally assembled, it consisted of Louis, Carey, the Zulu guide, and Sergeant Robert Willis, Corporal J. Grubb, and troopers Robert Cochrane, Nicholas Le Tocq, W. Abel and G. Rogers, all of Bettington's Horse. Cochrane was an old soldier who had sixteen years' experience in the Royal Artillery behind him, and had served in two minor South African campaigns. Trooper Le Tocq was a Channel Islander, who spoke French with a heavy regional patois, and Grubb spoke Zulu. Bettington later testified to the good character of all the escort, commenting that 'they are four of the most trustworthy men I have got';[114] Le Tocq, at least, had served as an NCO in the old 3rd NNC, and had been through the unnerving experience of the Isandlwana campaign, although his old commander judged him 'a cool hand under fire, albeit by no means a smart soldier'.[115] The troopers took with them two spare horses, and one of the pets which had attached itself to Bettington's camp – a small white terrier.[116] Louis was riding his favourite horse, Tommy, and Rogers, too, was riding a grey.

That morning, Melton Prior, the 'special artist' for the most prestigious of the English weekly papers, *The Illustrated London News*, was outside his tent on the outskirts of the camp,

> when I saw the Prince Imperial on horseback coming from the laager, and as he passed me he said, 'Goodbye, Mr Prior.'
> 'Goodbye, sir. I hope you will have a jolly morning', I replied, as he rode away to join Lieutenant Carey and his escort.

Later, it struck Prior that he was probably the last man in the camp to see Louis alive.[117]

NOTES

1. Account of Sofikasho Zungu, iNgobamakhosi ibutho. Bowden Papers, Natal Archives. Reproduced in Ian Knight (ed.), *Kill Me in the Shadows*; *The Bowden Collection of Anglo-Zulu War Oral History in Soldiers of the Queen*, Issue 74, September 1993.
2. Chelmsford to Evelyn Wood, Pietermaritzburg, 22 April 1879. Chelmsford Papers, NAM; reproduced in John Laband (ed.), *Lord Chelmsford's Zululand Campaign 1879*, Gloucestershire, 1994.
3. Chelmsford to the Duke of Cambridge, Durban, 11 April 1879. Chelmsford Papers, ibid.

4. Chelmsford to Wood, Escort, 25 April 1879. Chelmsford Papers, ibid.

5. J.N. Crealock to Sir Archibald Alison, Pietermaritzburg, 25 April 1879. Reproduced in Sonia Clarke, *Zululand at War*.

6. Louis to Eugénie, 30 April 1879. Reproduced in Filon, *Memoirs of the Prince Imperial*.

7. Wood, *From Midshipman to Field Marshal*, 1906.

8. Report from a correspondent with Wood's Column, dated 31 March 1879; published in *Natal Colonist* for 11 April 1879.

9. Loins to Eugénie, 4 May 1879, quoted in Filon, *Memoirs of the Prince Imperial*.

10. Tomasson, *With the Irregulars in the Transvaal and Zululand*.

11. Wood, *From Midshipman to Field Marshal*.

12. Chelmsford, letter dated Dundee, 6 May 1879, reproduced in *The Illustrated London News*, 16 July 1879.

13. Molyneux, *Campaigning in South Africa and Egypt*.

14. 'Great ones'; members of the Royal House and important regional chiefs.

15. Molyneux, *Campaigning in South Africa and Egypt*.

16. Deleage, quoted in Katherine John, *The Prince Imperial*. Curiously, Louis struck most of his British colleagues as more Spanish than French; Forbes wondered 'whether there was in his veins a drop of Bonapartist blood (remembering the suspicions of King Louis of Holland with regard to Queen Hortense) is a problem now probably insoluble. Certainly neither he nor his father had any physical feature in common with the undoubted members of his race ...' (Forbes, *Memories*), while Grenfell thought 'the blue blood of the Montijos was strongly developed. He was a Spaniard from top to toe'. (Grenfell, *Memoirs*).

17. Deleage, quoted in John, ibid.

18. General Sir Richard Harrison, *Recollections of a Life in the British Army*, London, 1908.

19. Ibid.

20. Chelmsford Papers, NAM (15) Nos. 50 & 59.

21. *The Illustrated London News*, 16 August 1879.

22. Harrison, *Recollections*.

23. 'He was really extra A.D.C. to Lord C. & messed with us, & not with the Quarter Master Genl. Department'. Hon. William Drummond, letter to his father, HQ Camp, 'Ipoko Stream', 11 June 1879. Royal Archives, RA VIC/R5/29. Lt. Colonel J.N. Crealock, letter of 2 June 1879, confirms this arrangement. RA VIC/R5/20.

24. Ibid.

25. Molyneux, *Campaigning in South Africa and Egypt*.
26. Harrison, *Recollections*.
27. Herbert Stewart to General Allison, Ladysmith, 8 May 1879. Allison Papers; reproduced in Sonia Clarke, *Zululand at War*, Johannesburg, 1984.
28. Guy C. Dawnay, *Campaigns*; *Zulu 1879, Egypt 1882, Suakim 1885*. Privately published *c*.1886.
29. Sonia Clarke, *Zululand at War*.
30. John Laband and Pain Thompson, *The Buffalo Border 1879*, Pietermaritzburg, 1983.
31. There were other views. On 23 June Guy Dawnay, attached to the Cavalry Brigade, noted that Bettington's Horse had 'reported hills "black with Zulus". It is only Bettington, though'. Dawnay, *Campaigns*.
32. Speaking of the patrol on 1 June, Trooper Cochrane recalled that the men were armed with 'Carbines and ammunition. No swords'. Court Martial proceedings, WO 71/343.
33. Harrison, *Recollections*. Note that Carey was not included in the party.
34. Cochrane, Raw and Henderson were all survivors of Isandlwana. The composition of this force is given by an unnamed participant in a letter dated 16 May, published in *The Illustrated London News* on 28 June 1879.
35. Harrison, *Recollections*.
36. Letter of 16 May 1879, *The Illustrated London News*. It is interesting to note, in the light of subsequent events, that on this occasion even Buller had allowed his men to off-saddle at a deserted homestead, despite signs of recent occupation.
37. Ibid.
38. Harrison, *Recollections*. Presumably Harrison was reluctant after Louis' death to admit that the Prince had shown obvious signs of recklessness on his first patrol.
39. George Mossop, *Running the Gauntlet*, London, 1937.
40. Letter of 16 May, *The Illustrated London News*.
41. Archibald Forbes, *Memories and Stories of War and Peace*, London, 1898.
42. Harrison, *Recollections*.
43. Wood suggests that this conversation took place on 21 May, which would date it to the end of Harrison's second patrol; but Harrison makes no mention of a meeting with Wood on that occasion, and says that the second patrol returned not to Wood's camp, but directly to Conference Hill.

44. Wood, *From Midshipman to Field Marshal*.
45. John, *The Prince Imperial*.
46. Harrison, *Recollections*.
47. Louis, report on reconnaissance of 17/18 May. Royal Archives, RA VIC/R5/13.
48. Buller's continued absence is indeed curious, and suggests that perhaps he did not particularly want to be found. His own objectives were to scout the route for the Flying Column; after his experiences of the previous few days, he may have come to regard Louis' presence as a burden.
49. Augustin Filon apparently used Bettington's notes as a source for his *Memoirs of the Prince Imperial*, and quotes passages from it. The original document has yet to come to light.
50. Harrison, *Recollections*.
51. Louis, report, RA VIC/R5/13.
52. Ibid.
53. Harrison, *Recollections*.
54. Filon, *Memoirs of the Prince Imperial*. His source is presumably Bettington.
55. Harrison, *Recollections*; Louis, report. This was at least the second occasion on these patrols when permission had been given to off-saddle at a deserted *umuzi* (Zulu homestead).
56. Harrison, *Recollections*.
57. Filon, *Memoirs of the Prince Imperial*. The source is presumably Bettington again.
58. Harrison, *Recollections*.
59. Ibid.
60. This description is suggestive of a preparatory ritual. It may be that the Zulu party included an *inyanga* – specialist diviner – who used debris left by the patrol to perform a ceremony aimed at securing supernatural ascendancy over them.
61. Harrison, *Recollections*.
62. Ibid.
63. Ibid.
64. Deleage, quoted in John, *The Prince Imperial*.
65. Harrison, *Recollections*.
66. Ibid.
67. Ibid. Ironically, on 5 June Chelmsford grumbled that Harrison's route might after all have been 'very much shorter than the one we are now taking'. Chelmsford to Wood, 'Camp right bank Ityontyozi R. 5 June 1879'. Chelmsford Papers; Laband, *Lord Chelmsford's Zululand Campaign*.

68. Account of Lord William Beresford, given in conversation to Queen Victoria, Osborne House, 26 August 1879. Royal Archives, RA VIC / R8 / 56.

69. Harrison, *Recollections*.

70. Harrison, report of 1 June 1879. Royal Archives RA VIC / R5 / 17.

71. Chelmsford, letter dated Utrecht, 21 May 1879. Reproduced in *The Illustrated London News*, 16 July 1879.

72. Louis to Eugénie, 26 May 1879. Reproduced in Filon, *Memoirs of the Prince Imperial*.

73. *Memoirs of Field-Marshal Lord Grenfell*, London, 1925.

74. Tomasson, *With the Irregulars*.

75. Forbes, *Memories and Stories*.

76. Deleage, quoted by Forbes, ibid.

77. Deleage, report quoted in *The Illustrated London News*, 16 July 1879.

78. 'We had the young Prince Imperial to dine at our small and rough mess and I think he enjoyed himself. He is most devoted to the RA'. Colonel Arthur Harness, letter from Landman's Drift, 3 May 1879, reproduced in Sonia Clarke, *The Invasion of Zululand 1879*, Johannesburg, 1979.

79. Archibald Forbes, *Souvenirs of Some Continents*, London, 1890.

80. General Sir Horace Smith-Dorrien, *Memories of Forty-eight Years Service*, London, 1925.

81. Grenfell, *Memoirs*.

82. Deleage, *Trois Mois Chez Les Zoulous*, quoted in Katherine John, *The Prince Imperial*, London, 1939.

83. Ibid.

84. On 27 May two squadrons of Dragoons under Major Marter, having arrived at Koppie Alleen that day, made a reconnaissance into Zulu territory (J.P. Mackinnon and S.H. Shadbolt, *The South Africa Campaign 1879*, London, 1880). In the light of the subsequent wrangle over the use of Dragoons for such work, it is possible that Carey may have been present with this patrol. Certainly Chelmsford referred to Carey's report the following day.

85. 'I send you Carey's reconnaissance report which leads me to believe that our road from here does run between the Incenci and Itilezi'; Chelmsford to Wood, Stony Koppie Camp, 28 May 1879. Chelmsford Papers, NAM; reproduced in Laband (ed.), *Lord Chelmsford's Zululand Campaign*.

86. Guy Dawnay, *Campaigns*.

87. Chelmsford to Wood, pencil note, dated 'Malafelegu Kraals', 2.30 pm. East of range between Telezi and Incenci, 29 May 1879'. Chelmsford Papers, NAM. Reproduced in Laband (ed.), *Lord Chelmsford's Zululand Campaign*.

88. Chelmsford to Wood, Stony Hill camp, 30 May 1879. 'Carey has verified the track I wrote to you about yesterday'. Chelmsford Papers, NAM, reproduced in Laband, ibid. Note, however, that Carey was sketching on both 29 and 30 May; it is not entirely clear on which day he verified this route.

89. Molyneux, *Campaigning in South Africa and Egypt*. Molyneux is vague about the date on which this incident took place; the conclusion that it occurred on the 29th is mine.

90. Queen Victoria's conversation with Beresford, RA VIC/R8/56.

91. Dawnay, *Campaigns*.

92. Ibid.

93. Notes by Brevet Major Viscount St Vincent, 7th Hussars, published in Clarke, *Invasion of Zululand*.

94. 'One day we [i.e. the Headquarters' Staff] were reconnoitring some fifteen miles over the border with a squadron of our own men and as many Irregulars'; Molyneux, *Campaigning*. Molyneux confirms this was the same patrol on which he had cause to recall Louis.

95. Bengough, *Memories of a Soldier's Life*.

96. Stewart, evidence at Carey's Court Martial, WO 71/343.

97. Dawnay, *Campaigns*.

98. Ibid.

99. The officer was Colonel Davies, of *Clyde* fame, then in command at Fort Newdigate, Zululand. Memo dated Landman's Drift, 9 July 1879. Ron Sheeley Collection.

100. Chelmsford to Wood, Stony Hill Camp, 30 May. Chelmsford Papers, NAM; reproduced in Laband, *Zululand at War*.

101. Dawnay, *Campaigns*.

102. Harrison, *Recollections*.

103. Harrison, report dated 'Camp, Etelezi ridge, June 1st 1879'. Royal Archives, RA VIC/R5/17.

104. Forbes, *Memories and Stories*.

105. Harrison, evidence at Carey's Court Martial, WO 71/343.

106. Carey, report to Harrison, dated 'Itelezi Ridge Camp, Zululand, 1 June 1879'. Royal Archives, RA VIC/R5/18.

107. See Dawnay, *Campaigns*, entry of 29 May 1879; 'Report from Wood that impi is within thirty miles, and will attack us probably before we reach Ibabanango'.

108. '... the whole of the cavalry, 5 squadrons besides Basutos, were ordered to the front'. J.N. Crealock, letter, 2 June, Royal Archives.

109. Carey, report to Harrison, 1 June 1879. Royal Archives.

110. The British habitually referred to all the men of the Native Horse as 'Basutos'. In fact Shepstone's Horse, commanded by Captain

Theophilus Shepstone Jnr, which had been created when the auxiliary units were reformed after Isandlwana, consisted of men from a number of different groups, none of them BaSotho. They included amaNgwane from the Drakensberg foothills – who had previously fought at Isandlwana – amaBomvu, and Christian Africans from Driefontein. Paul Thompson, *The Natal Native Contingent in the Anglo-Zulu War 1879*, Pietermaritzburg, 1997.

111. Forbes, *Memories and Stories*.
112. This man was a member of the 2nd Battalion, NNC; Bengough, *Memories*. This passage makes it clear that he was selected for his prior knowledge of the country, rather than for security purposes; the NNC units included a number of political refugees from Zululand. No one bothered to note his name.
113. Carey, report to Harrison, 1 June 1879, Royal Archives.
114. Bettington, evidence to Carey's Court Martial, WO 71/343.
115. Commandant G. Hamilton-Browne, *A Lost Legionary in South Africa*, London, *c*.1913. Hamilton-Browne does not name Le Tocq, but incidents in the story told to him mirror Le Tocq's account.
116. Some contemporary reports suggested that this was a pet of Louis', but there are no references to him owning a dog in Natal prior to 1 June. Trooper H.S. Powers of Bettington's Horse described it as 'our pet fox terrier, which had accompanied the patrol'. *The Natal Mercury*, 22 January 1929.
117. Prior, *Campaigns of a War Correspondent*.

VI

'... for Providence to decide'

After the trials of a summer which was both hot and wet, winter had
come early to Zululand. The rain of the last days of May had cleared the
air so that the morning of 1 June was 'bright, crisp, cold'.[1] On the left
bank of the Ncome, across the river from the camp at Koppie Alleen, the
hillsides were alive with groups of cavalrymen. After the wet weather,
the grass was long and greener than was usual for the time of year, and
the British uniforms added a splash of colour to the monotonous tones
of the landscape – the dirty yellow of the irregulars, the deep blue of the
lancers, topped by the fluttering red and white pennons of their lances,
and the scarlet of the Dragoons.

If there were any Zulu scouts watching the British activity, however,
they were nowhere to be seen.

A civilian with the column encountered the patrol just as they crossed
the Ncome into Zululand. Louis was in the vanguard of an army at war
– *passavant le meillior* – and clearly enjoying himself hugely:

> The Prince was in the uniform of the Royal Artillery, and seemed
> to be in very high spirits, laughing and talking with his comrades,
> as he went along. Mons. Helleputte was on horseback and about to
> take the wrong road, to join the first division of the column, when
> he was hailed by [Lieutenant] Carey, and informed of the course he
> had better take, and after a few kind and cheerful words from the
> Prince bade him 'Bonjours' and 'Au Revoir'. The Prince was riding
> a grey horse he named 'Tommy'.[2]

The party rode through the valley along the now familiar route, and
wound up onto the northern slope of the Thelezeni ridge, halting about
seven miles from Koppie Alleen. They were close to the area picked out
for that night's camp, and it was here that they were supposed to meet
the men from Shepstone's Horse; there was no sign of them nearby, but

looking back 'one of the men said he saw them coming up the valley'.[3] If
so, it would be a while before they arrived, and Louis and Carey took the
opportunity to dismount to verify their reports and 'to fix the position of
several hills'.[4] They were still there a little while later when first Harrison
and then Grenfell found them.

The two staff officers had ridden out early that morning to mark out
the position of the camp, ready for the column to come up later that day.
Harrison pointed out the location, and left Grenfell to the mundane duty
of marking out the sites to be occupied by the wagon laagers while he
went off 'to see to the watering arrangements':

> While so engaged I came across Carey and the Prince, and found
> that they had with them the European part of their escort, a detach-
> ment of Bettington's Horse, but none of the Basutos, whom I had
> specially ordered to be detailed, because they have a much keener
> sense of sight and hearing than Europeans, and consequently made
> better scouts. They told me that they were to get their Basutos
> from the regiment that was out scouting in front of the camp, and I
> enjoined them not to go forward without them.[5]

Having thus reinforced his earlier instructions, Harrison, who was
clearly preoccupied, rode off to prepare for the advance with the remark
that 'General Marshall's cavalry was coming up scouting'.[6] Shortly afterwards Grenfell appeared. He, too, was surprised to find the patrol
accompanied by only Bettington's men, but when Louis suggested that
the patrol should move forward, Grenfell decided on the spur of the
moment to accompany them:

> As my work for the morning was over until the arrival of the col-
> umn, which would not take place for some two or three hours, I told
> the Prince I would ride with him part of the way and look at the
> position of the camp in the Ityotyozi Valley and we rode away – the
> Prince and I together, Carey behind.[7]

Before they left, Carey 'suggested to the Prince waiting for the Basutos
but he said "Oh no we are quite strong enough"'.[8]

It was now late morning, and already the pattern of relationships
within the patrol had established itself. Louis, despite holding no formal
position within the army, was issuing all the commands, and was impatient, as ever, to press on. Despite the fact that Harrison had entrusted
Carey with the order to arrange an escort, Carey seems from the first to
have felt no responsibility of command, and the reasons for this had little

to do with the officer's undress uniform Louis habitually wore. Carey had been around Louis long enough to observe the courtesy with which even senior officers treated him, and whatever the technicalities of their respective military positions, he understood only too well the difference in their social standing.

Although Carey was by far the more experienced officer, he had not so far managed to establish his authority in Zululand, as his most recent reconnaissances had demonstrated; the ease with which Louis was accustomed to command those around him, on the other hand, was obvious enough. It had always been Louis' patrol, moreover, and Carey had only joined as an afterthought; a feeling which Harrison's instructions – that Carey should allow Louis to choose the new camp-site without interference – can only have encouraged. Carey, moreover, seems to have genuinely liked the Prince, and to have been caught up by Louis' infectious charm – a charm which Louis had always shame-lessly exploited to get his own way, and which made it very difficult to contradict or overrule him. Carey was flattered at the opportunity to spend time in Louis' company; and as an ambitious man, he can hardly have overlooked the social advantage which might be won by being on nodding terms with the future Emperor of France. All in all, it would have taken a man very confident in his rank and authority to stand up to Louis that bright winter morning; even Buller had balked at a direct confrontation a fortnight before. Lieutenant J. Brenton Carey was lost from the start.

Throughout the day, whenever Carey's professionalism and experi-ence prompted him to speak, he did no more than offer suggestions and advice – which Louis cheerily ignored.

Any reservations Carey may have had about the safety of the patrol at this stage were in any case undermined by the readiness of Major Grenfell – a senior officer – to fall in with Louis' plans. Indeed, Grenfell, too, seems to have treated Louis as the commanding officer, riding to the front with him, leaving Carey trailing behind, relegated psycho-logically to a very definite second place. Despite the fact that Grenfell knew Harrison's reservations about the missing auxiliaries, he made no attempt to prevent the patrol riding on without them. The appar-ent emptiness of the landscape, and the proximity of an entire British column, seems to have created a pervasive sense of over-confidence, as Grenfell himself admitted:

We rode seven or eight miles on a ridge which runs out into the Valley; it was bare of trees or cover, and therefore, as the Zulus had no horses, even with the smallest of escorts, it was perfectly safe.

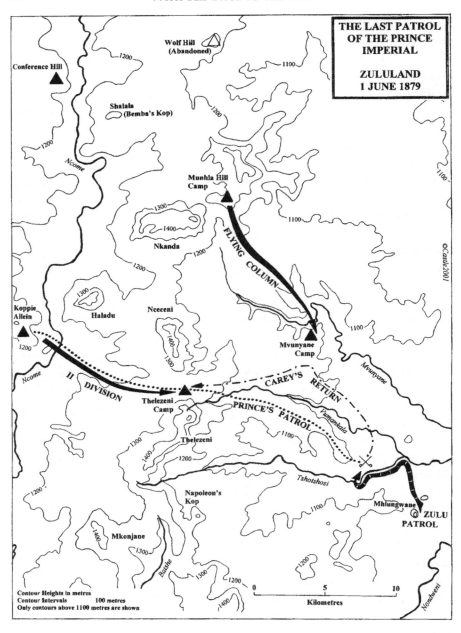

We had a long talk, and before reaching the crest of the hill descending into the Ityotyozi Valley I thought I could hear the whips of the teams approaching the camp we had just left, I therefore said 'Goodbye' to the Prince, and turned my horse around to return to the camp. The last words I said were 'Take care of yourself Prince, and don't get shot.' He replied, pointing to Carey, 'Oh no! he will take very good care that nothing happens to me.'[9]

Later, Deleage would wonder bitterly why the patrol had gone so far forward of the column,[10] yet this intention was clear from the beginning. Both Harrison and Grenfell knew that the patrol intended to examine the Tshotshosi valley; when Grenfell left them, he expressed no doubts about the wisdom of their continuing, and his attitude can only have encouraged the prevailing complacency.

Some time after Grenfell's departure the patrol reached an open, flat-topped space in the centre of the ridge. The view from the top was spectacular; below them the ground fell gently away eastwards into the broad, open valley of the Tshotshosi, framed in the distance by a chain of hills rising above the Nondweni river beyond. Off to the right lay the spurs of the Nquthu range, and the slopes where Louis had hunted Zulus a fortnight before. The countryside was an undulating sea of grass, rippling in the breeze, scarred here and there by erosion gulleys, but almost devoid of bush and trees. Here and there the grey domes of thatched Zulu huts stood out darkly in clusters against the hillsides, suggesting that the area was thickly populated, but there was no sign of life. The sun was now directly overhead, and the heat was stifling, all the more so by contrast with the recent cool, overcast weather. On such days the air hangs heavy and torpid in Zululand, and a tired silence settles over the countryside, broken only by the mechanical whir of insects and the occasional monotonous cry of a bird. Perhaps the heat dulled their senses; if Carey and the troopers were conscious of danger, they did not act upon it. 'Here', recalled Carey,

I suggested 'Off Saddling', but the Prince said he preferred to do so nearer the river and merely ordered the men to loosen their girths. We remained here ½ an hour sketching. This hill occupies a commanding position and we could see the country for miles around: I narrowly searched it with my telescope but could see no signs of the enemy in any direction.[11]

Thinking that it might be possible to run the road down the slope of the ridge, the patrol left the sky-line and descended towards the river. When they were just two or three hundred yards away, they saw a deserted *umuzi* in front of them – six neat huts, surrounding a stone cattle pen. It appeared to be deserted, but 'the Prince sent the [Zulu guide] to get down and look in the kraals to see if there was anybody in',[12] when he returned to confirm that 'there was nobody', 'the Prince gave us the order to off-saddle'.[13]

In the light of subsequent events, the decision to halt at this homestead was the subject of savage criticism. Certainly, in retrospect, it was not an ideal spot. It belonged to an *umnumzane*[14] named Sobhuza, but Sobhuza and his family, like most Zulus locally, had gone into hiding to avoid the British patrols. There was no palisade around the perimeter of the homestead, but instead it was hemmed in by long grass, which grew five or six feet high all round, except at the entrance, which was rather more open. Less than a hundred yards away in front of the huts was a donga, which emptied into the Tshotshosi downstream. The patrol hardly noticed this donga at first, masked as it was by the long grass, but while the banks were not particularly steep, they were in places five or six feet high. After the recent rains there was a trickle of water flowing through the bed of the gulley, and lying here and there in pools. At the head of the donga, and in patches down by the river, Sobhuza's mealie crop grew six feet tall, the stalks dry, brown and brittle with the onset of winter.

The decision to halt at this spot was Louis', and his reasons were the proximity of water and the presence of 'plenty of mealies for our horses'.[15] He was, of course, following the precedents set in his earlier expeditions into Zululand, where it had been common to explore deserted homesteads and to off-saddle, to take advantage of shelter and food for the horses. No doubt he thought he had learned the lessons of those patrols well; if so, however, he had overlooked the fact that in experience and judgement, he was not yet in Redvers Buller's league. Nevertheless, if Carey had any doubts about the choice of spot, he did not voice them, and indeed the atmosphere within the patrol remained relaxed and confident. No lookouts were posted; having searched the countryside through telescopes from the ridge, Carey admitted, 'As no Zulus were in sight, and we had the friendly Zulu with us, we did not consider it necessary to take any particular precautions.'[16]

It was usual for the men to carry their carbines unloaded when on horseback for safety reasons, and no attempt was made to load them now.

In more recent times, it has been suggested that the Prince's party had another motive for visiting this particular homestead.[17] According to this version, based on local tradition, the Prince's party had spotted several Zulu girls among the huts from the ridge above, and had approached them to try their luck. Although such stories should not be discounted out of hand – casual encounters between British troops and Zulu girls almost certainly did occur, but went largely unrecorded – it is very unlikely in this case, for a number of reasons. For one thing, both British and Zulu accounts agree that the countryside was deserted, and women, children and cattle, in particular, had gone into hiding. Generally, the Zulu neither used their womenfolk for bait, nor exposed them to risk in the enemy's presence. Louis himself was not a womaniser; he was a devout Catholic and indeed rather immature sexually. He was unlikely to compromise his status as a Man of Destiny with a casual encounter, the more so with an African girl, given his assumptions about class and race. Carey was perhaps more worldly, but he too was religious, devoted to his family, and unlikely to hazard his career on such an adventure. Moreover, any such encounter could only have occurred with the complicity of Bettington's men, which would have transgressed the strict codes of behaviour which defined the respective positions of Victorian officers from their men. Both Louis and Carey were too conscious of their positions to let their guard – let alone their trousers – down in front of their men.

It was now 2.40 pm, and an air of languor descended over the patrol. The party had ridden more than fifteen miles across country, and in the heat Louis seemed subdued. According to Carey, 'the Prince being tired laid down against a hut'[18] to doze, and he may even have taken his jacket off.[19] Other officers with the 2nd Division were to comment that the weather that day was 'hot and fine [and] made all our heads ache after the four rainy days'.[20] In all probability, Louis was suffering from the exhaustion which still plagued him after bouts of intense activity, a legacy of his recent fever. If so, it cannot be discounted that his judgement was impaired as a result.

While Louis rested, the Zulu guide was sent to the river to fetch water, and he, Corporal Grubb and Trooper Le Tocq made coffee. Carey himself 'walked about searching the hills and neighbouring kraals with my telescope'.[21] Although one or two of the escort later claimed to have been uncomfortable at the lack of precautions, none of them voiced these fears at the time to either Carey or Louis.[22] Corporal Grubb noted some fresh peelings of *imfe* – indigenous sugar cane – near one of the huts, but no one seemed concerned at the implications.[23] Although Carey stated that 'we knee-haltered the horses which, however, remained nearby the whole time in the kraal eating mealies',[24] it is clear that some at least wandered farther afield.

At about 3.20 – fifty minutes after they had first arrived – Carey sat down beside the Prince,[25] and for a few minutes the two chatted about the great Napoleon's Italian campaigns of 1796 and 1800.[26] Then, at 3.35 Carey,

> ... suggested that we should saddle up and be off as it was getting late. He said 'wait another ten minutes' but in 5 minutes' time told me to saddle up. I gave the order and went to fetch my horse from the mealies.[27]

By this time, some of the horses had wandered away from the huts, and it took the escort a few minutes to round them up. According to Le Tocq:

> I and Mr Carey went down to look for three horses at the river and met the native with the horses about half way up. While we were saddling the native said that he had seen a Zulu at the river.[28]

This news does not seem to have caused any alarm among the party, for the Zulu guide's manner was quiet and calm,[29] but the mood became brisk and business-like. By the time the party had finished adjusting their saddles, they were spread out in a straggling line on the western side of the homestead, in the open space between the huts and the cattle-pen. Carey, standing beside a hut at the entrance to the homestead, was nearest the way out; Louis was next to him to his right, nearer the pen. Most of the escort were to Louis' right, farther into the homestead, but one or two were nearer the entrance. It was now shortly before 4 pm, and Louis gave the order 'Prepare to Mount'.[30]

What happened over the next few seconds would haunt the survivors for the rest of their lives. In the following days, they were called upon to relive it time and time again in minute detail, and their accounts now read like a slow-motion sequence in a movie, in which moments of intense fright and horror come suddenly into focus amidst the blur of frantic action.

At the command 'Mount!', the men began the swing into their saddles. Corporal Grubb was a second or two slow, bending to help his foot into his stirrup, while Trooper Rogers had difficulty with the spare horse he was leading, and missed the command. As Le Tocq put it simply, 'some of us was in the saddle – and some of us was still down'.[31] Carey was up, and looked towards the escort, to see if they were in their saddles, and his description of what he then saw beyond them has a strange, dream-like quality about it, heavy with a sense of shock and unreality:

> ... my eyes fell upon a number of black faces rushing through the grass, behind the troopers. I saw the puffs of smoke, heard the

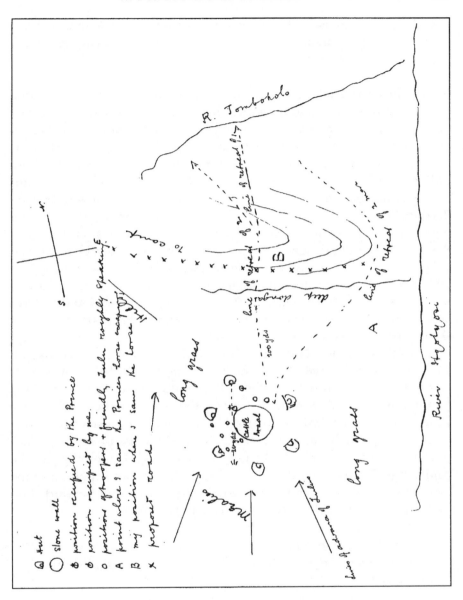

An official copy of Carey's sketch of the skirmish of 1 June; the first attempt at mapping the incident in which Louis died. (Reproduced by Gracious Permission of H.M. the Queen. Royal Archives, Windsor)

volley fired into us, and saw the Zulus rush forward with a shout.
They were then about twenty yards off. There was then a general
rush ...[32]

In fact, the party had been under observation since they had descended
the ridge more than an hour before. They had been spotted by a warrior
named Mthethe, who had been sitting among some rocks on the slopes
of Mhlungwane, a round-topped hill across the river.[33] Mthethe was
part of a scouting party consisting of members of the iNgobamakhosi,
uMbonambi and uNokhenke regiments, who were watching for signs
of the British advance. The exact size of the party remains unknown;
Bertram Mitford, a traveller who interviewed Sobhuza shortly after
the war, thought it numbered sixty men,[34] but Mnukwa, an officer of
the king's household who was present – and probably in command
– thought it closer to '40 or 50'.[35] The men were typical of the groups who
still lingered in the border regions, members of the younger, most active
regiments, and with strong local ties. Some of them were said to have
been members of Sobhuza's family;[36] others had taken part in the very
skirmishes in the northern Nquthu hills in which Louis had fought.[37]
They were not acting under the direct orders of the king, but like all
such groups they served to gather information on British movements,
and to harass British patrols where they could. When they realised the
patrol was vulnerable, Mnukwa called the men together, and 'as we
were many, we determined to attack'.[38] Making good use of the cover
and keeping widely separated, the Zulus had filtered down the slopes
of Mhlungwane and into the bed of the Tshotshosi. Under cover of the
banks, they had worked their way upstream, and had slipped into the
long grass to the south of the homestead. They had crept forward close
to the ring of huts without being noticed, but

> ... were scarcely in position when the word was given to mount,
> but fearing lest their prey should escape them after all, they made
> the attack.[39]

A warrior named Mphalazi fired the first shot,[40] and it took the patrol so
much by surprise that for a second Corporal Grubb thought 'that one of
our men had fired accidentally, and I only realised any danger when I
saw Zulus running through the mealies'.[41] That first shot was followed
immediately by 'perfect volleys',[42] and by a great shout of the war-cry,
'uSuthu!' And in the sudden shock of that terrible moment, all the
deep-seated fears of the Zulu menace which lurked in the heart of every
British soldier in Zululand, fuelled by the awful myths of Isandlwana,

rose to the surface in terrifying reality. The patrol promptly fell apart.

The sudden din panicked the horses, and they stampeded away from the source. Carey was firmly in the saddle, and so too were Abel and Cochrane, and all three were carried away towards the donga as the horses 'bolted'.[43] Sergeant Willis' feet were not in the stirrups, but he managed to cling on as his horse followed the rest.[44] Corporal Grubb was up, but could not control his horse properly because he did not have the correct bit.[45] Rogers never got into the saddle at all; Grubb saw him 'by the side of [the huts] running along with his head down. He levelled his carbine at something – it must have been a Zulu as they were fifteen yards off'.[46] Then Grubb flashed past him, and he saw him no more. Le Tocq had just mounted, but at the sound of the shots:

> The horse jumped and I nearly went over his head, and the rifle fell down. I dismounted and got the rifle. After that I could not get my leg over the horse. I was resting my stomach on the saddle ...[47]

Louis, too, was in trouble. Le Tocq passed him as they cleared the huts, and saw that he had not mounted, but was running along beside Tommy, and appeared to be clinging to the stirrup leather or part of the holster.[48] He had tried to vault into the saddle, but either the tightness of his trousers or the sudden panic of the horse had defeated him; no horse will be willingly left behind in a rush, and Tommy would not respond to the Prince's efforts to control him.[49] Le Tocq could do nothing to help; he called out '*Dépechez vous de monter sur votre cheval, Monsieur*', but Louis 'did not answer'.[50]

The Zulus by now were only a few yards away, running forward very quickly. Whatever the total size of the attacking party, only about a dozen broke cover near the huts, mostly on the eastern side, to the right of the entrance; the rest were spread out over several hundred yards, keeping to the grass, and firing heavily. Some emerged to the west, and began to head off to the left, to cross the donga upstream and try and cut the fugitives off from their line of retreat.

Sergeant Willis was only just leaving the huts at this point; he was one of the last out, and later claimed to have seen Rogers lying against a hut, already 'quite dead', apparently shot.[51] Zulu sources suggest, however, that Rogers was still alive when a warrior named Zubalo ran up to attack him; the two were struggling when another Zulu, Mshingishingi, went past and ran Rogers through.[52] In the confusion, no one noticed what became of the Zulu guide; Willis thought he was 'the last of all' to leave the *umuzi*.[53]

Halfway towards the donga, Grubb and Abel were riding close together when Grubb heard 'a bullet … whizzing past – and it struck something, and I saw Trooper Abel throw up his arms and fall back. He was riding about half a horse's length ahead of me'.[54] Grubb was adamant that a Martini-Henry bullet had struck Abel 'full in the back about an inch below his bandolier',[55] but there is some doubt about this, for Abel was certainly not dead when he hit the ground.[56] Grubb probably could not have helped him in any case, even had he wanted to, as his horse was out of control, and galloping after the others. A warrior named Mtunzi – who thought Abel's horse had put its foot in a hole, and thrown him – ran up and threw a spear which struck Abel 'as he was rising'.[57] Mnukwa, the *induna*, running up close behind Mtunzi, and knowing that the king had urged his warriors to take white captives, 'caught [Abel] by the arm, and wished to save him'[58], but several men – Dabayane, Gwabakana and Nyadana – stabbed him in the back as they rushed past after the others.[59] Abel's horse was still nearby, and was also stabbed. After Abel fell, Grubb's horse lurched off to the right, and Willis, close behind, followed him. At about this time Le Tocq, still lying across his horse, rode past, and called to Grubb, 'Put spurs to your horse, boy, the Prince is down'. Grubb

> gave a sharp look round and saw the Prince hanging on to something below his horse. I think it was the wallet or stirrup leather. He dropped and the horse seemed to trample him …[60]

Grubb was by now close to the lip of the donga, and tried to steady his horse to take a shot at the Zulus running close to the Prince, but 'the horse jumped into the donga and threw me on his neck. I was forced to let my carbine drop to cling to my horse'.[51] Grubb left the carbine where it lay, and rode on; as he crossed the donga downstream of the other survivors, the grey, Tommy, suddenly appeared beside him. There was no one in his saddle.

Carey, Cochrane and Le Tocq had crossed the donga close together, upstream of Grubb and Willis. As they scrambled out on the far side, Cochrane looked back and saw Louis on foot, off to his right, 'running in the donga, and about 14 [Zulus] as far as I could judge after him close up to him'.[62]

It was the last glimpse any of the escort were to see of him alive.

In those first few seconds of stampede, Louis had clung with one hand to the near-side pistol holster, in front of his saddle, and to the stirrup leather, as Tommy had crossed fifty or sixty yards of open ground between the huts and the donga. Near the edge of the bank the ground grew rough, however, the lurching of his weight put an unbearable strain on the holsters, and the stitching on the strap between them gave way – and Louis fell. One of the Zulus, Mwunzane, saw Louis bounce off Tommy's belly, 'and [he] fell back winded, and holding himself'.[63]

In one ghastly second, Louis faced the true nature of his obsession, and an awful truth rose before him. Personal combat, stripped of all the gloss of European knightly pretension, was not at all a romantic affair; in that instant Louis was no longer the noble heir of the House of Bonaparte, but a winded and trampled 23-year-old, facing his enemies alone, in a war which was none of his business. And as if to emphasise the point, fate had already robbed him of that most precious symbol of his family honour; his sword belt had broken in the wild ride from the huts, and even as Louis struggled to his feet, Mnukwa was picking up the blade from the grass twenty or thirty yards away.[64]

As he caught his breath, Louis turned towards a group of seven or eight Zulus who were by now only twenty yards away. Armed with just his revolver, Louis fired at the man, nearest to him, a warrior of the uMbonambi named Xabanga, who ducked down into the grass and threw a spear at close range which struck Louis 'either [in] the chest or inside the left shoulder'.[65] The spear must have fallen out, for Louis rushed at Xabanga, who turned away and dodged behind a warrior coming up behind him, a man named Gwabakana, who just moments before had stabbed Abel. Gwabakana had a gun, and he pointed it at Louis and fired, but even though he was only ten yards from him, he missed.[66] Louis stood for a second and fired back at Gwabakana; Mwunzane was close enough to observe the chilling detail that 'a look of surprise' passed over 'his face that he had hit nothing'.[67] Gwabakana then threw a spear which hit Louis, who promptly turned and ran towards the donga, with Xabanga, Langalibalele, Dabayane and others in pursuit.[68] As he reached the bottom of the donga, he turned to face the men behind him, and fired two shots 'more slowly, and still he hit nothing'.[69] Another warrior, Klabawathunga, now appeared over the lip of the donga on Louis' right. Langalibalele threw a spear which struck Louis in the thigh, but it either fell or he pulled it out, and with this spear in one hand, and his pistol in the other, he managed to keep his attackers at bay for a second.[70] At least two more warriors, Nyandana and Mphalazi, had now run into the donga, and Mphalazi saw

... the Prince seize Langalibalele's assegai and wield it. Langalibalele said that he hit the Prince first and on the thigh. I saw the Prince twist as he turned to face his pursuers, he then advanced quickly on Xabanga, and paused only on seeing a Zulu approach him on his right rear. When he fell he had an assegai in his right hand and a pistol in his left. He had just tried to change them from one hand to the other. In defending himself, he put his left foot into a hole, and slipped a little, on which the men rushed on him ...[71]

'Just then,' agreed Langalibalele, Louis 'put his left foot into a hole', and as he sat down backwards onto his hips, the Zulus rushed forward. 'Xabanga stabbed him', said Langalibalele, 'and he fell on his back, after which I stabbed him.' By now Klabawathunga and two or three others were close to him, and Klabawathunga stabbed him too, probably in the side, for in the final flurry of blows Mwunzane recalled that one Zulu 'stabbed him in the side [and] two others got him in the back'.[72] He was already lying on his back, and probably dead, when someone stabbed him in the right eye.[73]

Louis' struggle had been desperately brave, but it had been over in less time than it takes to read about it. Klabawathunga told Wood that he had been killed 'less than a minute' after he turned to fight,[74] and the entire skirmish can hardly have lasted more than three or four minutes. Indeed, it was not over yet; no sooner had Louis fallen than Klabawathunga ran off to pursue the Zulu guide, who was still trying to escape, presumably on foot. Another warrior, remembered only as Tom, snatched up Louis' fallen helmet, and without stopping chased after the survivors, who were 'riding away as fast as they could'.[75]

In the confusion of the rush from the huts, it was clearly impossible to retain any control over the patrol. According to Carey, the thought of rallying on the more open ground beyond the donga did cross his mind:

> I followed two men through the donga, though I was only able to get one man by me beyond, though I shouted 'we must form up on the other side to see to the retreat of everyone'. I now looked round and saw the Zulus coming after us through the grass and a party of them appeared to be endeavouring to cut off our retreat up the ridge. All this time we were under heavy fire from the grass. The man close to me remarked 'I fear the Prince is killed Sir'. I paused and looked round, and he pointed to the Prince's horse galloping the other side of the donga. I asked this man, who was, I believe, an old serjeant, whether it was any use returning, but he remarked that the Zulus were passing over the ground and he must be dead. He also shewed me the enemy creeping round our left. I now saw two men on my right about 500 yards off and one man in front, and as I saw no other loose horses fancied the other men must have returned up the ridge the way we came ...[76]

According to the Zulu accounts, the survivors continued riding hard on the other side of the donga, and did not slow down until they reached a patch of rocks which Wood – with relentless precision – noted was 820 yards away.[77] Carey may indeed have tried to call the men together, but if he did they did not hear him over the sound of the shooting. When they first cleared the donga, they were of course widely scattered – Carey, Cochrane and Le Tocq on the left, Grubb and Willis on the right – and after Grubb had lost his carbine they had only three carbines and Carey's revolver between them. Louis, Abel and Rogers were probably already dead by this point, and it is quite true that any attempt to rally could not have saved them, and would only have exposed the survivors to further attack.

Yet in letting the moment pass, without so much as a gesture, without even a parting shot in defiance, Carey would later discover a shocking truth – that the appearance of courage was sometimes more important than courage itself. By doing something, he could achieve nothing; but by doing nothing, he had thrown himself to the wolves.

As the men rode up the ridge, Wills and Grubb lagging behind, Grubb 'took off my hat and beckoned to them [Carey's party] to stop. They did not, but after a while they drew up into a walk.'[78]

Grubb's horse was exhausted, and Carey suggested he ride Tommy instead. At this point Grubb confirmed Cochrane's observation that the Prince had indeed fallen, and Carey was clearly shocked. 'When you heard the Prince was down,' recalled Grubb later, 'you seemed hardly to believe it, and asked me two or three times if it was true'.[79] In the awfulness of that realisation, Carey could suggest nothing but that they return as quickly as possible to camp.

The Zulus gave up their pursuit once it was clear they had no hope of catching the survivors, and returned to the site of the skirmish. The three dead white men lay close to the *umuzi*, where they fell; Rogers and Abel between the huts and the donga, and Louis in the donga itself. The Zulu guide had eventually been intercepted by a Zulu named Wopomane, and killed some way off.[80] The white terrier belonging to Bettington's Horse was sitting quietly near Abel's horse.[81]

In the aftermath of Zulu combat, it was necessary for warriors who had shed blood to undergo various purification rituals. These were required to prevent them suffering from the supernatural consequences of their actions. In particular, it was necessary to cut the belly of a fallen enemy, in the belief that this allowed his spirit to escape; failure to perform this rite would make the killer vulnerable to a chilling variety of spiritual and physical torments. It was also necessary for a man who had killed in battle to remove the clothing of his victim, and to wear it to *zila*

– to observe the abstentions and purification rituals which would allow him to return to normal life without fear of contaminating his family and friends. It was also common for warriors engaged in a dangerous fight to *hlomula* their fallen enemies, to stab the bodies repeatedly after death, each man marking his own participation in a victory over a gallant foe.[82] This ritual had its origins in the hunt, and was observed in recognition of the corporate effort required to kill dangerous game like lion; in 1879 white men were considered such a dangerous species.

Louis' body had already been speared several times as it lay on the ground, and Klabawathunga – who had returned from chasing the guide, and cannot have left the corpse very long – stripped it of the uniform. While Dabayane held the clothes, Klabawathunga 'cut the body in the Zulu fashion' up the stomach.[83] Each of the men who had stabbed Louis was entitled to wear part of his clothing, and it was divided up between them. 'There was some blood running from the Prince's wounds'[84] one man noticed, 'and the ground was much trampled on.'[85] Around Louis' neck the warriors found a gold chain with a medal of the Virgin Mary, and this they left because, as they explained later,

> the custom is not universal, but when a man is killed after fighting very bravely, many Zulus like to leave anything worn round his neck on the body.[86]

Abel and Rogers were treated in the same way. Dabayane noticed that, by the time he returned to Abel's corpse 'the Zulus who were behind him had stabbed him, in order to say "I put my assegai into a white man's corpse"', though he commented somewhat sourly that 'we would however sooner have killed one white man standing up to fight than two running away'.[87] Search parties the following day would find Rogers' corpse in the donga, some distance from where Willis claimed to have seen him dead. Perhaps he had run farther before being caught, but the Zulus had in any case dragged his body by the jacket, probably to avoid the ritual pollution caused by the presence of death in a living space.[88] A warrior named Luabaqazi saw the dog by Abel's body, and speared it, because 'we had been told by [Cetshwayo] to spare nothing, and when a Zulu is told to "make all clear" he kills all the dogs and fowls in a kraal'.[89]

Once the rituals were performed, the Zulus collected up trophies from their victims. The British weapons were gathered in; a warrior named Mpanzi kaNjojo took Louis' revolver,[90] and Mnukwa had already picked up his sword. Walking back between the donga and the homestead, Langalibalele came across the scabbard near the spot where Louis had fallen from his horse; when the party returned to the Mhlungwane hill

Mnukwa sheathed the sword 'to see if it would fit'.[91] Later, Mnukwa took the sword and scabbard to King Cetshwayo.[92] Ngagane found Louis' watch, and broke it open to see if it contained anything interesting.[93] The Zulus were never asked what happened to Abel's and Rogers' things.

All in all, it had been a very successful attack. The Zulus had killed four of the enemy, captured several horses, a number of firearms and some curios, and all without loss to themselves.[94] When they had collected up everything of value, they returned across the river. It was evening, 'the sun was just going down',[95] and they left the foreign dead to the coming night, and to the scavenging wildlife which haunted it.

The survivors of the patrol crossed the Vumankala river, keeping away from the ridge by which they had first descended into the valley. Their route took them in a more northerly direction, towards the line of advance of the Flying Column. It was late in the afternoon by the time they spotted their first British patrol, riding ahead of the column; it was their misfortune that the first man they met on their return was Redvers Buller.

The exchange which then took place has become part of the lore of Louis' death, but it should not be accepted without question. The best known version can be traced to an account given by Sir George Colley, who was later to serve in Zululand on Wolseley's staff:

> ... Wood ... and Buller were riding ahead of the column as usual to look out for good camping ground, when suddenly they saw an officer riding furiously towards them – so furiously that Buller observed, 'Why, the man rides as if he thought the Kaffirs were after him.' As he came nearer he gesticulated wildly and beckoned them to go back, but they rode on until they met him. 'Whatever is the matter with you?' said Buller. 'The Prince – the Prince Imperial is killed,' was all the man could gasp out, breathless and wild. 'Where? – where is his body?' asked Buller sharply. The man could only gasp and point to a hill about three miles off, from which they could see some twenty Kaffirs going away in the opposite direction with three led horses. 'Where are your men, sir? How many did you lose?' said Buller sharply and sternly, now thoroughly roused. 'They are behind me – I don't know,' stammered the unfortunate man. 'Then,' said Buller, turning on him savagely, 'You deserve to be shot, and I hope you will be. I could shoot you myself', and turned his back on him.[96]

There are aspects of this account which do not ring entirely true. For one thing, Colley was reporting the conversation second hand; he was not even in South Africa when it took place. Captain Molyneux was told much the same story, claiming as his source that 'escorts have ears', but he was careful not to name the officers concerned.[97] While most of the survivors later reported that they met both Wood and Buller, they do not necessarily suggest that they were together at the time. Wood himself does not mention the incident, merely remarking that 'at sunset the British officer and four survivors of the party rode into the 2nd Division camp.'[98] Certainly, Carey's behaviour in this version of the story seems unlikely; although he was undoubtedly in deep shock, he was only too aware by that time of how many men he had lost.

The most probable sequence of events was that Carey and the survivors first met Buller, and at some point later Wood. Buller's response need not be doubted; his manner was famously abrasive, particularly towards those who had fallen short of his own high standards of personal courage. Even he, however, did not suggest attempting to recover Louis' body that evening.

The significance of the incident lies not so much in the encounter itself, however, but in the way in which the story was then allowed to circulate. 'It may have been true; it may not', reflected Molyneux, 'at any rate it was the talk of our camp afterwards'.[99] By allowing himself to be associated with such a story, and by taking no steps to contradict it, Wood effectively distanced himself from the events of the day. For all his amiable manner, Wood was instinctively political, and throughout the Anglo-Zulu War he sought to dissociate himself from aspects of Lord Chelmsford's handling of the campaign which had attracted fierce criticism, whilst at the same time remaining on good terms with Chelmsford himself. His close relationship with Buller, moreover, provided a powerful tool with which to exclude any officer who threatened the pre-eminence of his inner circle; more than one officer who had earned a good reputation elsewhere in Zululand found himself marginalised by a whispering campaign when transferred to Wood's command. Over the next few days it was the Flying Column, rather than the HQ Staff or the newcomers of the 2nd Division, who would emerge as Carey's harshest critics.

From Wood's camp the survivors returned to the 2nd Division, and they reached the new camp below Thelezeni after dark that evening. Carey went straight to Harrison's mess, while the troopers returned to Bettington's camp. According to Grenfell:

> In the evening I dined with Colonel Harrison and some of the officers of the Headquarters Staff in our tent on the Itelizi Hill. Carey, who was a member of the Headquarters Mess, had not arrived, but no anxiety was felt regarding him, as we dined at sundown. To

complete his sketch and return to Itelizi would have taken some hours. I, therefore, ordered some dinner to be kept for him, and was alone in the tent when he came in. I said in a chafing way, 'Carey, you are very late for dinner, we thought you had been shot.' He replied, 'I am alright, but the Prince is killed.' I said, 'Good Heavens! Have you reported it?' He said, 'No, I have only just come in.' He was greatly agitated, and evidently had been riding hard. I then said, 'You must come immediately to Lord Chelmsford'. I met, if I remember rightly, Colonel Harrison on the way, and told him the dreadful news, and he then took Carey to the Commander-in-Chief'.[100]

Harrison's initial reaction was typical of those Carey would receive that night:

I said, 'You don't mean to say you left the Prince?'
And he replied: 'It was no use stopping; he was shot at the first volley.' And I said: 'You ought to have tried, at all events, to bring away his body'.
Much overcome by what I had said to him, he told me, as far as he could remember, the story of what had happened, accepting full responsibility for what had taken place. Immediately afterwards I went to see Lord Chelmsford, and asked him to allow me to go at once and look for the Prince. After what Carey had said I hardly expected to find him alive, but anyhow I thought I might bring home his body. The Chief, however, would not let me go; all he said was 'I don't want to lose you too.'[101]

To Chelmsford, the news was crushing. He had not asked for the burden of responsibility Louis' presence had imposed on him; he had done his best to accommodate him, but on the eve of the new invasion Chelmsford had been preoccupied with far more important matters. He had not even been aware that Louis had left the camp that day. Now the consequences to his own reputation, only just recovering from the Isandlwana debacle, were all too obvious. That night Grenfell saw him, 'in his tent with his head on the table in a state of absolute despair'.[102]

Word passed quickly around the camp. At Bettington's camp, the men were,

sitting smoking around the camp fires when a figure I recognised as Bob Cochrane stopped at the edge of the fire light, and as he pulled up he made the remark, 'Bad news lads'. I asked, 'What is it, Bob?'

To which he replied, 'The Prince is killed and Abel and Rogers.' We all laughed at this, and I said 'Tell us another, Bob,' thinking it was the usual sort of camp joke.

As his horse moved another pace towards the fire I could see then by the look on his face that it was no joke, and that his words were only too true. Just at this moment also there was a humming over at the Headquarter Staff tents and sooner than one can tell it the whole camp was alive to what had happened ...[103]

Harrison himself had stopped to break the news at the Cavalry Brigade Headquarters, and Forbes was among those who heard him:

Colonel Harrison, the quartermaster-general, put his head inside the tent door, and called out in a strange voice, 'Good God! The Prince Imperial is killed!' Harrison, though stolid, sometimes jested, and for the moment this announcement was not taken seriously. Lord Downe, Marshall's aide-de-camp, threw a crust of bread at his head, and Herbert Stewart ... laughed aloud.

But, sitting by the door, I discerned in the faint light of the dying day the horror in Harrison's face, and sprang to my feet instinctively ...[104]

Forbes, his journalist's instincts aroused, promptly sought out the survivors of the escort. 'They were all bad witnesses,' he decided, 'and I could not help suspecting that they were in collusion to keep something back.'[105] They probably were; all four had, after all, deserted not only Louis but their own comrades in the panic, and they were hardly likely to admit it. They all agreed upon one point, too – 'that Lieutenant Carey headed the panic flight'.[106] The next day Forbes examined Louis' saddle, and found that the strap between the two holsters was torn nearly through. To his disgust he found it 'no leather at all, but paper-faced – so that the Prince's fate was really attributable to shoddy saddlery'.[107]

Deleage heard the news from a passing officer, and rushed to the Headquarters tent for confirmation. He was, recalled Dawnay, 'in a tremendous state of mind',[108] and could not understand why no attempt was made to look for Louis that night. Harrison explained that it was too dark. 'But,' countered Deleage, 'the moon will rise presently and the country will be nearly as light as day.'[109] Harrison could not reply, and Deleage left him, bitterly damning the English for their cold-heartedness. Yet in fact Chelmsford had been right; on a dark night, at the beginning of an invasion, it would have been an unpardonable risk to send inexperienced troops into an area occupied by an unknown number of the enemy, simply to look for a man who was surely already dead.

There was nothing to do but wait until morning. Carey completed a formal report of the day's events for Harrison, but when it was done he could not sleep for shock, his mind spinning with the horrors of the day, and all the terrible ifs and buts. The loneliest man in the camp that night, he poured out his feelings in a long letter to his wife:

My Own One,
    You know the dreadful news, ere you receive this, by telegram.
    I am a ruined man, I fear, though from my letter which will be in the papers you will see I could do nothing else.
    Still, the loss of the Prince is a fearful thing. To me, the whole thing is a dream. It is but eight hours since it happened.
    Our camp was bad, but then, I have been so laughed at for taking a squadron with me that I had grown reckless and would have gone with two men.
    To-morrow we go with the 17th Lancers to find his body. Poor fellow! But it might have been my fate. The bullets tore around us, and with only my revolver what could I do?
    The men all bolted and now I fear the Prince was shot on the spot as his saddle is torn as if he tried to get up. No doubt they will say I should have remained by him, but I had no idea he was wounded and thought he was after me. My horse was nearly done, but carried me beautifully.
    My own darling, I prayed as I rode away that I should not be hit and my prayer was heard. Annie, what will you think of me! I was such a fool to stop in that camp; I feel it now, though at the time I did not see it.
    As regards leaving the Prince, I am innocent, as I did not know he was wounded, and thought the best plan was to make an offing.
    Everyone is very kind about it all here, but I feel a broken-down man. Never can I forget this night's adventure! My own, own sweet darling, my own little darling child, my own little Edie and Pelham! Mama darling, do write and cheer me up! What will the Empress say? Only a few minutes before our surprise he was discussing politics with me and the campaigns of 1800 and 1796, criticising Napoleon's strategy, and then he talked of republics and monarchies!
    Poor boy! I liked him so very much. He was always so warm-hearted and good-natured. Still I have been surprised; but not that I am not careful, but only because they laughed at all my care and foresight.

I should have done very differently a week ago, but now I have ceased to care.

Oh, Annie! How near I have been to death. I have looked it in the face, and I have been spared!

I have been a very, very wicked man, and may God forgive me! I frequently have to go out without saying my prayers and have to be out on duty every Sunday.

Oh! For some Christian sympathy! I do feel so miserable and dejected! I know not what to do!

Of course, all sorts of yarns will get into the papers, and without hearing my tale, I shall be blamed, but honestly, between you and me, I can only be blamed for the camp. I tried to rally the men in the retreat and had no idea the poor Prince was behind. Even now I don't know it, but fear so from the evidence of the men. The fire on us was very hot, perfect volleys. I believe thirty men or more were on us. Both my poor despised horses have now been under fire. The one I rode today could scarcely carry me, but did very well coming back.

Oh! I do feel so ill and tired! I long for rest of any kind ...

If the body is found at any distance from the kraal tomorrow, my statement will appear correct. If he is in the kraal, why then he must have been shot dead, as I heard no cry. *Enfin, nous verrons.* Time alone will solve the mystery.

Poor Lord Chelmsford is awfully cut up about it as he will be blamed for letting him go with so small an escort.

The *Times* and *Standard* correspondents have been at me for news, also the *Figaro* ...

My own treasure, I cannot write more. Good night, my own one; I will try and let you know a few words tomorrow. I will now try to sleep, till reveille at 5 a.m; and it is now nearly one and so very cold![110]

Dawn brought no respite from the consequences of his actions. Reveille sounded before daylight, and an expedition was assembled to recover the bodies; Carey, as the senior survivor, was required to lead them to the spot. The expedition was a large one – two squadrons of the 17th Lancers, one of Dragoons, a screen of Bettington's and Shepstone's Horse, and the 2nd Battalion, NNC. It was to be commanded by Marshall himself, and both Stewart and Colonel Drury-Lowe – the senior officer of the 17th – were present. It took some time to make the necessary preparations, and long before it was ready to depart Deleage had worked himself into a frenzy of frustration and misery. Officially, the size of the party was intended as a mark of respect, but there was a very real concern that the attack heralded the long awaited Zulu response, and Chelmsford was taking no chances. Chelmsford could not bring himself to go in person, and he sent Molyneux, one of his ADCs, to represent him. The party was accompanied by an ambulance wagon drawn by six white horses, but no one had any real hope that Louis could have survived over night; the wagon was intended as a hearse. Surgeon Scott went out to identify the remains. For the host of newspaper correspondents who had hurried out to South Africa in the wake of Isandlwana and were present in the camp in force, the new invasion could hardly have begun on a more dramatic note. 'They were,' recalled Melton Prior proudly,

the French correspondent of the Paris *Figaro*, Archibald Forbes of *The Daily News*, Francis Francis of *The Times*, Mackenzie of the *Standard*, Charles Fripp of the *Graphic*, and myself.[111]

The expedition set off about 7 am, the regular cavalry in column, screened by the irregulars. Although the spot was less than ten miles from the Thelezeni camp site, the 'march was very slow, with much trumpeting'.[112] After about an hour, Molyneux and Scott rode to the front, and as the expedition descended the ridge into the valley of the Tshotshosi, they could see a few miles away to their left irregulars from the Flying Column winding down the slopes to join them. A few Zulus were visible on the hills nearby, but they retired when a party of Lancers was despatched to clear them away. As they drew near the homestead, the Lancers swung round in a line to face it, while the Staff and journalists rushed forward to look for the bodies. As they approached, 'some bearded vultures, hawks, falcons, and secretary birds ... mounted on the wing from the long, dank grasses.'[114]

The party soon made a find in the upper part of the donga. 'Hardly had we got down the slope,' recalled Deleage,

when one of the horses stopped itself before a naked corpse; it was fearfully mutilated, the viscera having been torn from the body: although the features were concealed by a flannel shirt wrapped around the head, we saw at a glance it could not be the Prince, from the tall structure of the body. On uncovering the features we understood why the Zulus, contrary to their custom, had not taken away the flannel garment. The face was convulsed by the agonies of the assegai stabs that it presented a picture so unearthly and terrible that the savages themselves had been terrified and hidden it from their gaze.[115]

In fact, the strange appearance of the body was due to the fact that

> his cord jacket and woollen shirt were drawn up around his neck, so
> high that they did not at once show. It appeared as if the Zulus, after
> killing the unfortunate man, had dragged him along the ground by
> his jacket and shirt, and left them where they had pulled them up.
> He had a number of wounds in the upper part of his chest, which
> were plainly visible, and one through the right hand, showing that
> he had fought for his life at close quarters.[116]

The body was Rogers', and one of the burial party noted that he was also
still wearing a pair of leather gaiters on his bare legs, and guessed that
'the effort of getting the gaiters off was evidently too much trouble for
the Zulus'.[117] The body of Abel was lying where he fell, 'stark naked in
the long grass, riddled with assegai stabs in the upper part of the chest,
and with a gash in the abdomen which always concludes the bloody
work of Zulu slaughter'.[118] Captain Tomasson of the irregulars note
that Abel's horse was a few yards away, 'not yet dead, though unable to
rise or do more than move his head and forequarters, thus the incarnate
fiends had left him in his agony, the earth all torn with his ineffectual
struggles to rise'.[119] The horse was put out of its misery.

It was now about 9 am, and as the troops spread out across the donga
Captain William Cochrane of the Native Horse[120]

> ... called the attention of Surgeon Major Scott and myself to another
> body at the bottom of the donga, which, on reaching, we discovered to
> be that of H.I. Highness.
> It lay 200 yards (about) north-east of the kraal, and about half a mile
> south-south-west of the junction of the streams.
> The body was stripped, with the exception of a gold chain with medal-
> lions attached, which was still around the neck.
> The sword, revolver, helmet, and clothes were gone, but in the grass we
> discovered his spurs with straps attached, and one sock marked 'N' ...[121]

Once it was confirmed that it was indeed Louis' body, there was something of a rush to see it. Marshall and his staff came over to examine the
remains, while Prior recalled that

> I was riding by the side of Forbes, when, a short distance on our left,
> we saw one of the troop holding up his rifle and calling out loud.
> Forbes immediately said, 'There it is, Prior. Come on, ride for it!',
> and a magnificent rider he was.

I followed hard on his heels, and was the fourth man on the spot ...[122]

The bodies of Rogers and Abel had given fair warning of what to expect, and sure enough it was immediately clear that Louis' body was 'riddled with assegai wounds'.[123] He was lying on his back, with one arm folded slightly across his body, and there was a macabre reassurance in the fact that there were so many conspicuous wounds in front. Carey's account had left the exact circumstances of his death open to doubt, and there was an unspoken dread that Louis might be found with a bullet wound in the back – suggesting that he, too, had been running away. At least it was clear that he had died defending himself, and in a brave death his reputation would be secure; a code of loyalty and respect would prevent too public an examination of Louis' own role in the tragedy.

Deleage was overcome by this proof of Louis' desperate courage:

> I felt a moment of pride at this discovery, and bending over the Prince I touched his cold hands with my lips. That was a true Frenchman who alone, deserted by all, had known how to die like a Frenchman, with his face to the foe.[124]

Melton Prior saw the Parisian lean tenderly over the body, and

> ... with tears streaming down his face [he] took an English penny from his pocket and placed it over the Prince's eye (the one which had received a spear-thrust) in the hopes of closing it.[125]

It was a moment of almost unbearable pathos, and several of those who witnessed it, tough and experienced soldiers though they were, were close to tears. Surgeon Scott stepped forward to formally examine the body, and his report leaves little doubt how Louis had died. Only in regard to the wounds found in Louis' back was he ambiguous:

> To the best of my belief the body had not been moved when I got there. I think he died where I found him. He was lying on his back, with the left arm across him, in the position of self-defence. I counted 18 assegai wounds, all in front. It is true that there were two wounds found on his back – but from their nature, I am convinced that they were the terminations of wounds inflicted in front. Any one of five of the wounds would have proved mortal. There were no bullet wounds on the body. My reason for believing that the Prince's body had not been dragged is that there were no

wounds or abrasions about the body to indicate that he had been dragged …

There was a patch of blood, underneath the head and neck, which appeared to me to be caused by wounds received on the side of the neck, and also a wound through the right eyeball. The Prince's body was entirely stripped …

I think the patch of blood was there overnight, because it was saturated in the ground, and had congealed.[126]

If the body had been damaged by scavengers during the night, no one mentioned it. One of the bystanders noticed, however, a wound in the right thigh – caused by Langalibalele's spear – and that 'there was a long gash in the abdomen, exposing the intestines, which were, as in the case of the trooper, uninjured':

The gash … in the abdomen is not I feel assured inflicted with any idea of mutilating the corpse of the slain enemy, but simply because it is a belief amongst them, that if this fiscal coup is not given, and the body swells, as it would by the generation of the gasses of decomposition, the warrior who has neglected this precaution is destined to die himself by his body swelling. Apart from this gash, which in every case is inflicted after death, for no blood had flowed, there was no mutilation whatever. Many of the wounds were so slight that I think they, too, must have been inflicted after death, all the members of the party probably 'washing their spears' in pursuance of some ceremonious regulation on the subject of a dead enemy.[127]

His examination complete, Scott ordered 'the body enveloped in a white cotton blanket that had been used as a saddle cloth, and then a bier was improvised by roiling a couple of lances long-wise in the sides of a horse-blanket, two more lances being then lashed with reims crosswise at the head and feet for the bearers.'[128] The ambulance wagon had not been able to descend the hill, and the body was carried towards it by,

Major-General Marshall, Captain Stewart, Colonel Drury-Lowe, and three officers of the 17th Lancers, Scott, Bartle Frere, and myself, with M. Deleage, correspondent of the Figaro, who expressed a wish to assist, which was immediately granted. It was not long before we met the ambulance, in which the body was then laid and escorted back to camp by officers' parties of the Dragoon Guards and Lancers.[129]

No sooner had the body been moved than the nearest journalists and troops hurried to snatch up souvenirs. One artilleryman boasted that 'before leaving I got some of the grass with the Prince Imperial's blood on it – quite a rush was made for it.'[130]

Once Louis' body had been recovered, it fell to a party of Bettington's Horse to bury the remains of Abel and Rogers. The bodies were carried to a spot above the donga, and buried close to where Louis' body had been found. It was not an easy task, as the burial party 'had only one shovel, and as it was the dry season the ground was extremely hard'.[131] While the work was under way, a party of Zulus were spotted on the slope of Mhlungwane, 'six or eight mounted men, one on a grey horse, and twenty or thirty foot-men'.[132] The general feeling was that this was the same Zulu group who had killed the Prince, and perhaps they were; some Troopers of Bettington's Horse fired shots at them, but the range was too great to do any damage.[133] Before they left the spot, a party of Dragoons piled up stones into a cairn, to mark the spot where Louis fell.

The body reached the camp at Thelezeni at about 2 pm, Newdigate and his staff riding out to meet it. Chelmsford's first inclination had been to bury Louis in the field – as British war dead traditionally are – but his Staff urged the importance of sending the body back to England, and to his mother.[134] Accordingly, it was decided to hold a funeral service that evening, without interment, to be conducted by the Catholic chaplain to the forces, Father Bellard.

The funeral was a melancholy affair, made all the more poignant by the circumstances of the attack. If Louis had been largely unknown to the camp in life, there were few who were not moved by his death:

As the afternoon drew to a close and early evening approached, the troops marched silently away to an open space without the camp. The 21st, 58th, 94th, the artillerymen dismounted, Dragoons and Lancers carrying their lances, wheeled regiment after regiment into line until three sides of a great oblong square were formed; and as the gun-carriage bringing the covered body of Prince Louis Napoleon, preceeded by Artillerymen with reversed carbines, moved slowly into the centre, the gloom that had pervaded the camp since the mournful news was received grew deeper and sterner. The dull murmur of voices was hushed. Amid us, simply wrapped and stretched on a gun carriage, was the Prince's dead body ... The Catholic priest read out the funeral service, and his words increased the universal gloom. Beyond the ranked soldiers and bareheaded multitude was a strange sky; dull, leaden clouds hung about, and nearer the mountains seemed dark and distant in mist. Just about them, in a small space, lingered the after-gloom of the setting sun, drawing slowly down cloud-curtains in the west.[135]

Louis' body was draped in a Tricolor, and Chelmsford and his Staff walked behind the gun carriage; among the pall-bearers was Louis' friend from Aldershot days, Lieutenant Wodehouse. For Deleage, the experience was almost unbearable:

The funeral ceremony took place before the whole camp ... Never shall I forget that simple field-gun, on which was laid the Prince's body, wrapped only in a blanket with which we had covered him that same morning; a Prince's death had been needed to take that gun from the line of defence, and we could see the gap its absence made in the enclosure of the laager.

And the procession! Around the body, the officers of the Royal Artillery, that is to say, nearly all the comrades of the Prince's studies, and a little farther off, leaning sadly on his cane, with red-dened eyes and heavy heart, that unfortunate General who has been spared no misfortune since the day of his arrival in South Africa, and then a few paces from Lord Chelmsford, the officers of the General's staff, the comrades of yesterday, that military fam-ily of the Prince, the only family that could mourn for him at the moment of these obsequies.

And on either side, those two red lines of soldiers, old and young, fixed and motionless, leaning on their rifles, some think-ing of their comrades whose blood had already been drunk by the soil of Zululand; others dismayed to see, at their first step upon that wild land, so many high things laid low by the assegai of the Zulu.

For myself, who alone in that sad procession had the civilian's privilege of walking bare-headed, seeing as we passed the flag of England droop slowly to the ground, a royal salute, before this corpse wrapped in the tricolor, I thought how deeply shall they repent whose insults drove this unfortunate Prince to prove his manhood even at the cost of his life, when history shall relate how, in this far-off land, the last of the Napoleons brought honour by his very death to the banner of France.[136]

When the ceremony was complete, the body was passed over to Surgeon Scott, and a guard placed upon the tent. Scott was required to embalm the body as best he could, to withstand the rigours of the journey back to England. There were no proper embalming materials available, and Scott was forced to improvise; the viscera were removed and buried in a biscuit tin, while the body was 'pickled in salt'.[137] The operation lasted until 4 am, when:

> The Prince's remains were then carefully wrapped up, and placed in a zinc box hastily put together. A coffin is a luxury unknown in an army campaigning so far from home: the Engineers made one as well as they could out of tea cases ...[138]

Alone in his tent that night, Melton Prior, the special artist of *The Illustrated London News*, realised that the story of Louis' death would break on the world as his body passed back down the line. Of all the journalists who had been present when the body was recovered, only one – Charles Fripp of the *Graphic* – was a fellow artist. Prior realised that if he were to scoop Fripp, his drawings would be the first images the world would see of Louis' death:

> I went to General Newdigate and told him that I wanted to work all night, and asked permission to have a light in my tent. I assured him that I would cover it round with a blanket, and that it should not be seen outside in the smallest degree. He informed me that it was against the rules of the camp, but that under the circumstances, and on this special occasion, he would grant me the permission, and an order was written so that the sentry near my tent should not interfere with me.
>
> Once alone I lighted my lamp and sat down and pitched into work, and by five o'clock in the morning I had made nine sketches in connection with the Prince Imperial's end.
>
> My best horse was saddled, and my man, with my sketches in the regulation red envelope of the office, was only waiting for daylight to start and gallop to Landman's Drift to save the post, which he succeeded in doing, and my sketches were the only ones that appeared in London in connection with that sad event.[139]

Prior was not the only one sketching that evening. Chelmsford's military secretary, Lieutenant Colonel John Crealock, was an enthusiastic artist, and sketched Louis' portrait as the body lay in Scott's tent:

> I took a likeness of the poor lad's face for his mother ... One eye was stabbed out. The face was undisturbed and a placid look in

the face and in the fixed eye – as if it were far away in its thoughts. How often I have seen the same in his eye when alive. His face was sunk, and my likeness became without my knowledge so like the Napoleon 1st … I can't talk and write more about it; we are all in great sadness.[140]

The following morning the 2nd Division returned to its real business. Reveille sounded before dawn, and the troops had marched away from Thelezeni camp by 7.30 a.m. Shortly afterwards, the ambulance wagon carrying Louis' body set out back down the road towards Koppie Alleen. It was escorted by a squadron of the 17th Lancers, and accompanied by Deleage, Arthur Bigge, and the Prince's servants, Lomas and Brown.[141]

'Thus,' commented Crealock, 'sets the sun of the Bonapartes'.[142]

For Carey, however, the trial was just beginning.

NOTES

1. Account by H.S. Powers, then a trooper in Bettington's Horse. *The Natal Mercury*, 22 January 1929.
2. *The Natal Mercury*, 11 June 1879.
3. Carey, report to Harrison, 'Itelezi Ridge Camp, Zululand, 1 June 1879'. Royal Archives, RA VIC/R5/18.
4. Ibid.
5. Harrison, *Recollections*.
6. Carey, report 1 June.
7. Grenfell, *Memoirs*.
8. Carey, report 1 June.
9. Grenfell, *Memoirs*. One wonders if Louis would have expressed such confidence in Carey if Bettington's remarks about Carey's nervousness on the patrol of 17/18 May were justified.
10. 'How is it that they went farther, and that at the very time when I was looking for the Prince near the Itelezi Mountain he was being attacked eleven miles farther off?' Deleage, report in *The Illustrated London News*, 16 July 1879.
11. Carey, report 1 June.
12. Trooper Le Tocq's evidence at Carey's Court Martial, WO 71/343.
13. Corporal Grubb, evidence at Carey's Court Martial, WO 71/343.
14. Family head. Sobhuza's exact social standing is obscure, though he seems to have been a man of some influence locally, though apparently neither a Chief nor an *induna*.

15. Carey, report 1 June.
16. Ibid.
17. 'Ghosts who wear redcoats', *Northern Natal Courier*, 7 June 1996.
18. Carey, report, ibid. The account in Ashe and Wyatt-Edgell's *The Story of the Zulu Campaign* (London, 1880), partly based on unnamed first-hand reports, is even more suggestive – 'The Prince, who did not appear very strong, now complained of being very tired'.
19. 'The Prince had discarded his tunic in the heat'; account of Mrs Glencross, whose (unidentified) brother was part of the escort. *Natal Mercury*, 20 December 1957.
20. Guy C. Dawnay, *Campaigns; Zulu 1879, Egypt 1882, Suakim 1885*. London, *c*.1886.
21. Carey, report 1 June.
22. Hamilton-Browne, *A Lost Legionary*.
23. Corporal Grubb, evidence at Carey's Court Martial, WO 71/343.
24. Carey, report 1 June.
25. To wake him?
26. Carey's letter to his wife, evening of 1 June 1879. Reproduced in Morris, *The Washing of the Spears*.
27. Carey, report 1 June.
28. Evidence of Trooper Le Tocq, Court Martial, WO 71/343.
29. Evidence of Trooper Cochrane, Court Martial, WO 71/343.
30. Carey, report 1 June. When questioned about this at the Court Martial, the survivors of the escort agreed that Louis issued the order.
31. Evidence of Trooper Le Tocq, Court Martial, WO 71/343.
32. Carey, report 1 June.
33. Account of Mthethe, evidence collected at the Tshotshosi by Evelyn Wood, 30 May 1880. Wood Collection, Natal Archives Depot, Pietermaritzburg, II/1/2.
34. Bertram Mitford, *Through the Zulu Country, Its Battlefields and Its People*, London, 1883.
35. Account quoted in Cornelius Vijn (translated and edited by Bishop Colenso), *Cetewayo's Dutchman*, London, 1880. There is a suggestion that Sitshitshili kaMnqandi, an officer of the uKhandempemvu regiment and a prominent *isilomo*, or royal favourite, was among the party. See letter by Sir W. Wyndham, who visited the site in January 1882, quoted in C.T. Binns, *The Last Zulu King*, London, 1963. If so, however, Wood made no mention of the fact, despite going to great lengths to secure Sitshitshili's assistance in finding the body of Captain Barton at Hlobane in May 1880. Perhaps Sitshitshili preferred to keep his involvement quiet; perhaps Wyndham was mistaken in his information. None of Wood's informants mentioned Sitshitshili.

36. Captain W.E. Montague, *Campaigning in South Africa; Reminiscences of an Officer in 1879*, London, 1880.

37. 'Many of the people with whom the white men skirmished on the Nqutu, five days [sic] before the Prince was killed, were the same who attacked the reconnoitring party'. Statement of Mboza, interviewed by Wood, 27 May 1880. Wood Papers.

38. Account of 'Luabaqazi', Wood Papers, 30 May 1880.

39. Mitford, *Through the Zulu Country*.

40. Statement of Mnukwa, Wood Papers, 3 June 1880.

41. 'Memorandum of conversation with Mr Grubb on the 21 June 1880', Wood Papers, ibid.

42. Carey, letter to Mrs Carey, 1 June; Morris, *Washing of the Spears*.

43. Trooper Cochrane, evidence at Carey's Court Martial, WO 71/343.

44. Sergeant Willis, ibid.

45. Corporal Grubb, ibid.

46. Ibid.

47. Trooper Le Tocq, ibid.

48. Ibid.

49. My thanks to Nick Steele, the distinguished Zululand game conservator and author of *Take A Horse To The Wilderness* (Cape Town, 1971) for explaining this aspect of equine psychology.

50. 'Hurry up and mount your horse, sir'. Le Tocq, evidence at Court Martial, WO 71/343.

51. Sergeant Willis, evidence at Court Martial. Willis may of course have been reluctant to admit that he saw Rogers' predicament, and that he failed to help him.

52. Statement of Mshingishingi, 30 May 1880, Wood Papers. There is some doubt about where Rogers was killed, as his body was apparently moved after death. Tomasson is the most adamant source that Abel's body was found near the homestead, with his horse nearby, while Rogers lay in the donga. This confirms the circumstantial evidence of the survivors, and the exact details of individual deaths rest on this identification. See Tomasson, *With The Irregulars in the Transvaal and Zululand*.

53. Sergeant Willis, Court Martial.

54. Corporal Grubb, Court Martial.

55. Corporal Grubb. Evidence before Court of Inquiry, 2 June 1879. Published in *The Illustrated London News*, 16 July 1879.

56. Trooper Powers was adamant that 'neither man nor horse showed any signs of bullet wounds'. *Natal Mercury*, 22 January 1929. An injury from a Martini-Henry bullet fired at close range would have been quite conspicuous. Guy Dawnay commented somewhat

ambiguously that the dead were 'all assegaid'. Dawnay, *Campaigns*. By insisting that Abel was shot, of course, Grubb absolved himself of any responsibility to go to his aid.

57. Mtunzi, statement 26 May 1880, Wood Papers.
58. Statement by Mnukwa, 3 June 1880, ibid.
59. Statements of Nyadana, 27 May 1880, Dabayane, 1 June 1880, and Gwabakana, 24 June 1880, Wood Papers.
60. Corporal Grubb, Court Martial, WO 71/343.
61. Ibid.
62. Trooper Cochrane, Court Martial, WO 71/343.
63. Statement of Mwunzane, Bowden Papers, Natal Museum; published in Ian Knight (ed.), *Kill Me In The Shadows*; *Soldiers of the Queen*, 74 (September 1993). This evidence was collected in the 1930s, and is confusing in some aspects, but offers a startling vision of Louis' last moments.
64. Statements of Mnukwa and Mtunzi, Wood Papers.
65. Statement of Langalibalele, 1 June 1880, Wood Papers.
66. Statement of Gwabakana, 24 June 1880, Wood Papers.
67. Statement of Mwunzane, Bowden Papers.
68. Statement of Gwabakana, Wood Papers.
69. Statement of Mwanzane, Bowden Papers.
70. Statement of Langalibalele, Wood Papers.
71. Statement of Mphalazi, Wood Papers.
72. Statement of Mwunzane, Bowden Papers.
73. Statement of Langalibalele, Wood Papers.
74. Statement of Klabawathunga, Wood Papers.
75. Statement of Tom, 26 May 1880, Wood Papers.
76. Carey, statement, 1 June 1879. Cochrane confirms that he made these remarks to Carey; evidence, Court Martial, WO 71/343.
77. Statements of Klabawathunga and Tom, 26 May 1880, Wood Papers.
78. Corporal Grubb, Court Martial, WO 71/343.
79. Ibid.
80. Statements collected by Wood, 26 May 1880, Wood Papers.
81. Statement of Luabaqazi, 30 May 1880, Wood Papers.
82. On the subject of post-combat purification rituals, see Ian Knight, *The Anatomy of the Zulu Army*, London, 1995.
83. Statement of Dabayane, 1 June 1880, Wood Papers.
84. Statement of Mphalazi, 28 May 1880, Wood Papers.
85. Statement of Mthethe, 27 May 1880.
86. Observations of nine of Wood's informants, 27 May 1880, Wood Papers.

87. Statement of Dabayane, Wood Papers.
88. Evidence of Sergeant Willis, Court Martial, WO 71/343.
89. Evidence of Luabaqazi, 30 May 1880, Wood Papers.
90. Statement of Mphalazi, Wood Papers.
91. Ibid.
92. Statement of Mnukwa, 3 June 1880, Wood Papers.
93. Statement of Ngagane, 28 May 1880, Wood Papers. See also Magema's comment 'they thought that it was a case for money, and expected to find coins inside it', Vijn, *Cetshwayo's Dutchman*.
94. Klabawathunga, Langalibalele, Mnukwa and Gwabakana all confirmed that 'no Zulu was hurt that day'. Wood Papers, 1880.
95. Statement of Mthethe, Wood Papers.
96. Letter from Sir George Colley, quoted in Walter Jerrold's *Sir Redvers Buller VC; The Story of his L and Campaigns*, London, 1900.
97. Molyneux, *Campaigning*.
98. Wood, *From Midshipman to Field Marshal*.
99. Molyneux, *Campaigning*.
100. Grenfell, *Memoirs*.
101. Harrison, *Recollections*.
102. Grenfell, *Memoirs*.
103. H.S. Powers, *Natal Mercury*, 22 January 1929.
104. Forbes, *Memories and Stories of War and Peace*.
105. Ibid.
106. Ibid.
107. Ibid.
108. Dawnay, *Campaigns*.
109. Filon, *Memoirs of the Prince Imperial*.
110. Carey to Annie Carey, Thelezeni camp, 1 June 1879. Reproduced in Morris, *The Washing of the Spears*.
111. Melton Prior, *Campaigns of a War Correspondent*.
112. Molyneux, *Campaigning*.
113. Major Ashe and Captain Wyatt-Edgell, *The Story of the Zulu Campaign*, London, 1880. Wyatt-Edgell was present with the 17th on this occasion.
114. Ibid.
115. Deleage, quoted in *The Times*, 14 July 1879. In fact the contorted expression may equally have been due to muscle contraction after death.
116. Letter from a correspondent, 'Nongwini River, June 4th 1879'. Reproduced in the *Natal Mercury*, 11 June 1879.
117. Trooper H.S. Powers, *Natal Mercury*, 22 January 1929.

118. Letter written 'Nongwini River, 4th June', *Natal Mercury*.

119. Tomasson, *With The Irregulars in the Transvaal and Zululand*.

120. Capt. W.F.D. Cochrane, 32nd Regiment, attached to the mounted auxiliaries, was a survivor of Isandlwana.

121. Molyneux, report dated 'Camp between Inceni and Itelezi Hills, Zululand, 2 June 1879'. Royal Archives, RA VIC/R5/19.

122. Prior, *Campaigns*.

123. Trumpet Major Henry Wilkinson, 17th Lancers. Account published in *The Royal Magazine*, July 1911.

124. Deleage, *The Times*, 14 July 1879.

125. Prior, *Campaigns*.

126. Surgeon Major Scott, Court Martial, WO 71/343. If the Zulu evidence is correct, and the wounds to the back were inflicted in the general mêlée, Scott's description should be taken to confirm a total of twenty wounds.

127. Letter from an anonymous correspondent dated 'Nongwin River, June 4th, 1879'. *Natal Mercury*, 11 June 1879.

128. Ibid.

129. Molyneux, *Campaigning*.

130. Anonymous gunner, writing on 6 June 1879; published in the *Aberystwyth Observer* on 26 July 1879, and reproduced in Frank Emery's *The Red Soldier*, London, 1977.

131. Trooper Powers, *Natal Mercury*, 22 January 1929.

132. Letter, 'Nongwin River June 4th', *Natal Mercury*, 11 June 1879.

133. Trooper Powers, *Natal Mercury*, 22 January 1929.

134. 'We send the body away preserved – I pressed the point and so did Harrison.' Lieutenant Colonel J.N. Crealock, letter to Major General H.H. Crealock, 'Neck between Itelezi and Ncenceni', 2 June 1879. Brenthurst Collection; reproduced in Clarke, *Zululand at War*.

135. *The Times Weekly Edition*, 4 July 1879.

136. Deleage, quoted in Filon, *Memoirs*.

137. H.C. Lugg, *A Natal Family Looks Back*, Durban, 1970. Lugg's source was W.J. Clarke, who was a Corporal in the Natal Mounted Police in 1879, and claimed to have been present 'when the body of the Prince Imperial was recovered and removed to Durban'. Clarke is also apparently the source of the story that when Eugénie visited Zululand in 1880, the box was exhumed, and Louis' heart was found to have dried, and shrivelled to the size of a walnut. According to this story, the heart was returned to France and buried in the Arc de Triomphe. No official confirmation of this has been found, despite the extensive documentation on the 1880 expedition, and it is probably no more than romantic myth. Remains are not normally

interred at the Arc; Napoleon I is buried at Les Invalides. The anti-Bonaparte sympathies of the republican government would have made any such move difficult, so if any remains were recovered in 1880, they were more likely to have returned to England with Eugénie.

138. Filon, *Memoirs*.
139. Prior, *Campaigns*. In fact, Prior flattered himself; his sketches were published in the *ILN* on 16 July, in an issue devoted to the death of the Prince. Charles Fripp's sketches appeared in the rival *Graphic* just ten days later.
140. J.N. Crealock to H.H. Crealock, 2 June 1879. Clarke, *Zululand at War*.
141. Filon, *Memoirs*.
142. J.N. Crealock, letter 2 June, Clarke, *Zululand*.

VII

'... a most unfortunate business'

The 2nd Division resumed its advance on 3 June, ironically following the route Carey and Louis had travelled two days before, down the ridge from Thelezeni and into the valley of the Tshotshosi. The Flying Column had moved south the day before, and had already established a camp on the banks of the river; for the first time, the two columns were now operating in plain sight of each other.

That afternoon the 2nd Division camped just a few hundred yards away from Sobhuza's homestead, in the open ground beyond the donga. There was an intense curiosity about the spot, and whenever they found an excuse both officers and men made their way across to explore it for themselves, to gossip about the skirmish, or hunt for souvenirs. Some evidence of the fight still remained on the ground; a torn and bloody shirt was found in one of the huts – it was believed at the time to be Louis', but was probably in fact Trooper Abel's[1] – and nearby, someone found a wallet with stamps in it. The body of the dead dog was recovered by a soldier who 'skinned it, intending, I believe, to stuff it'.[2] Members of the Natal Native Contingent walked around the homestead, tapping the ground with the butts of their spears, looking for the underground grain-pits which were generally concealed beneath the cattle enclosure, but they turned up nothing more of interest.

To the surprise of the column, the huts were no longer deserted – three elderly Zulu women were found among them. They had chosen an odd time to return from hiding, or perhaps they had been concealed in the huts all along; it is possible that Louis' patrol had missed them in the darkness of the huts. In any case, they seemed undaunted now by any prospect of retribution afforded by the arrival of an entire British column. According to Guy Dawnay, 'two of the old women [were] speechless with age, the other a violent scold, who poured out a torrent of abuse on our colonial policy'.[3] This old lady claimed her sons had been among the attacking party, and she did not try to hide her scorn for the invaders:

They killed your great Inkoss [Chief]. Now they are gone to the king's kraal to fight you white men. What do you come here for? We don't want you. This is Zululand. Keep to your own side![4]

Of the others, one was simply so 'poor, old, and blind [that she] manifested the greatest indifference to the questions which were eagerly put to her'.[5]

The body of the Zulu guide – whom none of the survivors had seen since the attack began – was also found that day, about three-quarters of a mile from the huts. He had clearly been run to earth, and had turned to face his attackers. His leg was broken – probably from a gunshot wound – and several broken weapons lay nearby, evidence of a stiff fight.[6] Presumably his remains were buried, although no one in the British camp bothered to record the fact.

Chelmsford had issued a standing order prohibiting the burning of Zulu settlements, but after the troops had satisfied their curiosity, men of the 21st Regiment pulled Sobhuza's homestead apart, and posed triumphantly for a photographer among the ruins. The following day, that order was rescinded, and before the column moved off men of Shepstone's Horse put the remains to the torch.[7] The following night the 2nd Division camped on the Mhlungwane hill, and on 5 June the British finally left the Tshotshosi valley, with all its melancholy associations, behind them.

For the first few days after the attack, Carey had attempted to continue with his duties. For the most part the Headquarters Staff and officers of the 2nd Division were sympathetic to his predicament, but the Flying Column was becoming increasingly vociferous in its criticism of his conduct. Now that the two columns were working so closely together, it became impossible for him to avoid the hints and slights by which many of his colleagues revealed their contempt for his actions, and which increasingly undermined his position on Harrison's staff.

There were a number of reasons why the officers of the Flying Column had assumed such a stance. For the most part, morale within Wood's column was high, and officers and men alike believed that their commander was superior to Lord Chelmsford in both luck and judgement. Most of the troops were veterans not only of the opening stages of the Zulu campaign, but also of the Cape Frontier and Sekhukhune expeditions; they regarded themselves as veterans, and were openly dismissive of the nervousness of the new arrivals of the 2nd Division. And if Hlobane had been a fiasco – the worst butcher's bill of the war, after Isandlwana – the victory at Khambula had largely displaced it in their minds. As a result, it was commonly held that such an incident would never have occurred in Wood's column. Wood, they felt, would never have placed the Prince in such a vulnerable position – and the officers of the Flying Column would certainly not have behaved as Carey had.

Wood himself, moreover, was keen to distance himself from Chelmsford's conspicuous bad luck, and his opinion of the incident was coloured by men directly under his command who had known Louis personally, chiefly Arthur Bigge and Frederick Slade. Both were naturally upset by Louis' death, and indignant at the way the escort had apparently left him to his fate. Slade's views, expressed in a letter home, reflected the wider opinion of his column:

> Neither Carey nor his men made the slightest attempt to stand, and in plain words they ran away, and left the poor dear little Prince to die fighting on foot, single-handed. I cannot tell you what we all think of Carey's behaviour, but will tell you what Buller told him to his face yesterday when they met – 'You ought to be shot.' I think I may safely say that this is the opinion of every man in the column. To think that a British officer should leave any man, much more the Prince Imperial of France, to fall into the hands of the Zulus without making the slightest attempt to save him is disgraceful ... I hope he will be tried by court-martial and kicked out ...[8]

Among the 2nd Division, however, the mood was generally more sympathetic. The column was composed of men with very different levels of experience of Zulu warfare, but all had arrived at a healthy respect for their enemy. The survivors of the old Centre Column had seen the devastated field of Isandlwana, and knew what the Zulu could do; for the untried drafts fresh out from England, the stories about it had been enough. Major Phillip Anstruther of the 94th Regiment spoke for many when he admitted:

> I only thank God I was not placed in his position. I hope I should have done differently but really one can't say. The whole disastrous affair was over so to speak in a moment.[9]

The fact that the entire patrol – Louis included – had made no attempt to stand, but had simply tried to escape, led many to feel uncomfortable at the degree of personal criticism levelled at Carey. Colonel Arthur Harness – whose N/5 Battery RA had lost two guns at Isandlwana – considered it 'a painful affair, and one cannot help feeling that people at times must think of his being made rather a scapegoat.'[10]

Nevertheless, Carey's position on the staff hardly reflected well on Chelmsford, and Crealock noted with some embarrassment; 'the fact that his escort made no attempt to see [the Prince] away – as far as I can judge – will have an ugly effect.'[11]

Just three days after Louis was killed, Carey was forced to request an inquiry into the incident, in the hope that it would clear his name. The court met within sight of the ruined homestead on the morning of 4 June, as Arthur Harness observed:

I am writing from the door of my tent and can see, some four hundred yards off, the very spot where the poor young prince was killed. There is a court of inquiry ordered to assemble today 'on such matters as may be brought before it'. We all know it is to inquire into the circumstances of his death ...[12]

General Marshall himself sat as President, with Colonel Malthus of the 94th Regiment and Major Le Grice RA, as members, and any hopes Carey entertained of a quick end to his predicament were soon to be quashed. There was a good deal of evidence to hand, most of it superficially damning. Carey himself had written a report on the evening of the incident, and had been able to offer little to counter the impression that the patrol had simply panicked. Bettington had interviewed the escort the following day, and their reports were if anything more damaging, since all of them were adamant that Carey had been among the first away. The bald fact was that no attempt had been made to save any of those unhorsed in the first moments of the attack. If only Abel and Rogers had been killed, any reservations about Carey's conduct might have been overlooked – as had occurred in similar incidents elsewhere in Zululand – as a misfortune of war. Given the high profile of one of the victims, however, Carey could not expect to escape without a thorough investigation, and the reports submitted to the court of inquiry were clearly sufficient to establish a *prima facie* case of 'misbehaviour before the enemy'. As the only surviving officer, he found himself squarely within the frame. The court summed up the issue with depressing clarity, and the findings were inevitable:

The Court is of the opinion that Lieutenant Carey did not understand the position in which he stood to the Prince, and in consequence failed to estimate aright the responsibility which fell to his lot. Quartermaster-General Harrison states in evidence that Lieutenant Carey was in charge of the escort; while Lt. Carey, in alluding to the escort, says 'I do not consider that I have any authority over it'. After the precise and careful instructions of Lord Chelmsford, stating, as he did, the position that the Prince held, and that he was invariably to be accompanied by an escort in charge of an officer, the Court considers that such a difference of opinion should not have existed between officers of the same department. Secondly, the Court is of the opinion that Lieutenant Carey is much to blame for having proceeded on duty with part of the escort detailed by the Quartermaster-General. The Court cannot admit the plea of irresponsibility on Lieutenant Carey's part, inasmuch as he himself took steps to obtain the escort, and failed; moreover, the fact that the Quartermaster-General was present at Itelezi Ridge gave Lieutenant Carey the opportunity of consulting him on the matter, of which he failed to avail himself. Thirdly, the Court is of the opinion that the selection of the kraal where the halt was made, surrounded as it was by cover for the enemy, and the adjacent difficult ground, showed a lamentable want of military prudence. Fourthly, the Court deeply regrets that no effort was made to rally the escort and show a front to the enemy, whereby the possibility of aiding those who had failed to make good their retreat might have been ascertained.[13]

The court recommended that Lieutenant J. Brenton Carey be tried by general court martial.

At that point, however, the war intervened, and proceedings were delayed for several days. Indeed, on the very day the court of inquiry met, irregulars scouting ahead of the combined columns detected the presence of a large Zulu force in a line of hills on the far side of the Ntinini (uPoko) stream. From the beginning, the British had expected the Zulu to oppose their advance a few days into the march, and they had taken the early presence of Zulu scouts on the Nquthu range – and the skirmish on the 1st – as proof of this. To some extent, they were right; while the Zulu had largely abandoned a broad swathe of country along the border, they had assembled in some numbers beyond the Nondweni river. Here a broken range of hills east of the river gave some hopes of catching the British columns at a disadvantage. Nevertheless, they were not part of an army appointed by the king, but were for the most part men belonging to local chiefdoms, who had remained in their areas to try to prevent the invaders from devastating their crops and homesteads. Chief Sihayo kaXongo, an important border chieftain whose main homestead lay on the very border, at Rorke's Drift, maintained a cluster of homesteads on the banks of the Ntinini stream, known as eZululeni, *The Wanderer's Rest*, and it was here that the warriors had assembled.

Whether the Zulu had any real intention to attack the columns or not, the British were keen to bring them to fight. Some sort of victory was needed to stiffen the resolve of the new arrivals, and to diminish the exaggerated reputation of the Zulu threat. Moreover, the regular cavalry were still smarting from the generally negative comments their presence had aroused, and were keen to demonstrate their worth. The result was that when Marshall heard on the evening of the 4th that scouts had encountered the enemy on the Ntinini, he ordered the Cavalry Brigade to be ready to advance at 4.30 the following morning. To his disappointment, by the time he reached the Ntinini he found that Buller's irregulars from the Flying Column had beaten him to it, and were already in action.

Indeed, Buller's men had had an exciting time. They had run into a body of Zulu in the open country west of the stream, and had promptly attacked, dispersing them, and chasing them across the stream towards the homesteads beyond. The irregulars had followed up, and set fire to several of Sihayo's settlements, but the Zulu had raffled in rocky, bush-covered country beyond, at the base of a hill known as eZungeni. Buller's men had engaged them in a long-range fire-fight, but, deciding nothing could be gained, Buller had just begun an orderly withdrawal when Marshall's regulars arrived. Colonel Drury-Lowe, leading the 17th Lancers, was reluctant to miss the opportunity to give his men some practical experience in Zulu warfare, and despite the fact that the skirmish was largely over, he ordered his men to cross the river and deploy for the charge. They made a fine spectacle, their lance pennons fluttering gaily above the bush and mealie fields, but their charges struck air; the Zulu remained under cover at the foot of the hill, sniping at them. The only casualty was the adjutant of the 17th, Lieutenant Frith, who was struck in the shoulder by a particularly well-aimed shot which passed through his heart. The Lancers reluctantly broke off the engagement, and returned to the column, carrying Frith's body over the saddle. The Zulus promptly came down to occupy the ground they had abandoned.

This had been the first real engagement of the new invasion, and there was an uneasy feeling among the columns that the Zulu had got the better of the occasion. The effect on the morale of the 2nd Division was unsettling. Carey had been present during the action, and had ridden forward with Melton Prior to watch the skirmish unfold in the distance; in the light of his own predicament, what happened next must have seemed to him particularly ironic.[14] Frith's body was buried at a new camp established on the Nondweni river, and the following day a stone earthwork – Fort Newdigate – was built close by. Fort Newdigate was intended as the first of a chain of secure depots on the line of communication, but so far from being a reassuring sight, its construction merely heightened the sense of anxiety which had prevailed since Louis' death. A sense of unease pervaded the 2nd Division, given substance by the need for the fort, and the mournful presence of Frith's solitary grave in the empty veld nearby.

On the evening of the 6th, the 2nd Division experienced one of the worst scares of the war.

Guy Dawnay experienced the confusion and panic at first hand:

> The English mail came in in the evening, and we were just in the middle of our letters when at 9 p.m. we heard three single shots from the 58th sentries, on east of camp, then two regular volleys, then the alarm sounded, and musketry began all round the laager, a regular blaze of rifles now going on round the laager, and men firing wildly, under, and on the wagons. I felt sure that it was all humbug, and managed to make the men on my right cease firing, a bullet from somewhere inside the camp whizzing past my head as I was talking to them. Never saw anything so dangerous, and it was from beginning to end a false alarm ...[15]

In all, seven men were wounded before order was restored, and several horses killed. One regiment alone fired over 1,200 rounds of ammunition; among the most at risk was Major John Chard, the defender of Rorke's Drift. Chard had been on picquet duty with a party of Engineers who were caught in the cross-fire, and had spent his time crouched behind one of the low stone walls of the new fort, with bullets whistling over his head. One artillery battery had fired six rounds of canister – rounds intended only for use when the enemy were at close range – into the darkness, without having seen a single Zulu. Melton Prior – who had himself nearly been shot by men of the NNC – was indignant. 'A more disgraceful scene I have never witnessed,' he blustered.[16]

The panic at Fort Newdigate – which was promptly nick-named 'Fort Funk' – formed an uncomfortable back-drop to Carey's court martial. The advance was due to halt here for several days, while the Flying Column returned to the border to collect supplies, and the delay afforded an opportunity to convene the trial. The officers appointed to the court had just a few days to prepare themselves, and general courts martial on such serious charges were so unusual that Major Anstruther – the judge advocate – admitted that they were both ill-prepared and inexperienced:

> The nuisance besides is that I can't get a book of references on court-martials anywhere. There is not one in camp, so I have to do the best

I can, in fact bring common sense to bear on the technicalities. You
will see it all in the papers ...[17]

Meanwhile, as Carey prepared for his defence, Louis' mortal remains
had made the long journey down to the coast. The ambulance wagon
and its escort passed through Dundee on the 3rd, and was escorted
to Ladysmith by men of Carbutt's Rangers, an irregular unit with a
decidedly ambiguous reputation. They arrived in Ladysmith on the
5th, where the garrison turned out formally to meet them. Carbutt's
men escorted the wagon to the banks of the Klip river on the outskirts
of the town, and a new escort of the 58th Regiment under Lieutenant
Hill took command on the other side.[18] The body was now officially
in the care of Major General Clifford, commanding the line of communications, and each step of the journey towards Pietermaritzburg was
heralded by a flurry of official telegrams between the military and civil
authorities. Although in life the Prince's passage through the colony
had aroused no more than mild curiosity, in death both the Army and
settler society were determined to 'receive [him] with all due respect and
sorrow'.[19]

The Prince's servant, Uhlmann, who had remained in Durban during
Louis' time at the front, was sent to meet the cortege in Pietermaritzburg.
General Clifford, taking no chances with etiquette, asked Commodore
Richards, commanding the warships anchored off Durban, to provide
'one large French and one large English flag'.[20] It was expected that a
large civilian crowd would gather in Pietermaritzburg when the body
passed through the capital, and Major Chamberlain, 24th Regiment,
commanding the garrison at Fort Napier above the town, made meticulous arrangements to escort it through the streets. The cortege was to be
met on the outskirts of town by the leading military and civil authorities
– Clifford himself and Sir Henry Bulwer, the Lieutenant-Governor of
Natal – and the principal mourners. Here it was to be transferred from
the mule wagon to a gun carriage. The arrival of the cortege was to be
heralded by a twenty-one gun salute from Fort Napier, and the route
through the streets was to be lined with both Imperial and Colonial
troops. The pall-bearers were carefully picked, and a Guard of Honour,
one hundred strong, was to march on either side of the carriage The
body was to be taken first to the Roman Catholic school in town, where
it was to be formally identified, then placed in the Catholic church overnight, before passing on to Durban the following day.

The ambulance wagon arrived as scheduled at 2 pm on Sunday, 8
June. It was a perfectly choreographed event, and the impact on those
who witnessed it was electric:

Never has there been a greater sensation in this city than was caused … by the arrival of the funeral cortege of the late lamented Prince. People of all classes came forward to show their respect, and flocked in large masses to the various places through which the cortege was to pass, while numbers went out to meet it, and to join the procession. Many citizens had taken steps to indicate that the city was in mourning, [shops and] Hotels were draped, while the tri-colour flew half-mast high at the Town Hall, and on several houses in Church Street. At 1.15 p.m. a gun was fired from Fort Napier announcing that the body had arrived within two miles of the city, and by two o'clock a number which must have exceeded 3000 had assembled at the place of rendezvous on the Commercial Street. Here the procession was formed, the military headed by Major-General the Hon. H. H. Clifford, Inspector General on one side; and the civilians, headed by His Excellency Sir Henry Bulwer, the Lieutenant-Governor of the Colony, on the other …

… The arrangements being completed, amid the solemn booming of the minute guns, and the tolling of the church bells, the gun-carriage bearing the coffin was seen slowly coming down the hill, accompanied by the escort of regulars and mounted police, which had come with it. As it approached the military fell into their places, and there was a hush which spoke more eloquently than any words, the feelings of the vast concourse of people as the body of the late Prince approached. As the cortege passed, every hat was raised in respect, and the military presented arms. The coffin was wrapped in a large tri-colour, and upon it was a helmet and sword, together with wreaths of roses and camelias, and a beautiful cross of violets; while the grey charger, draped with a black pall, with the letter 'N' on the corners, and with boots reversed, according to military tradition, followed …

… It marched slowly up Commercial Road to the corner of Church Street, up which it turned and then wheeled along Chapel Street into Longmarket Street, arriving at the Roman Catholic School at about ten minutes to four. Here the coffin was taken from the gun-carriage by the pall-bearers, and conveyed into the Chapel followed by as many of the procession as the building would hold …

… The silence and decorum which were observed was marked, and showed that the vast concourse of people had been brought out not by mere curiosity, but by heart-felt sympathy. At the windows of the various shops were a large number of ladies all dressed in mourning, and many were seen to be much touched by the impressive ceremony, some indeed being moved to tears.[22]

At the Catholic school, the coffin which the Engineers had improvised at the Thelezeni camp was opened, and Clifford, Deleage and Uhlmann steeled themselves to look again upon Louis' face. Despite the crude methods available to him, Surgeon Scott's attempts at embalment had been largely successful:

> ... the body did not show any great marks of disfigurement. The injury to the eye ... was not visible, the lid being closed over it, while the wounds on the other parts of the body had been so carefully dealt with that they were hardly visible. The face wore a peaceful expression, and it is satisfactory to know that in no way had the remains been disfigured.[23]

Clifford had arranged for a Mr Ford to make a new coffin of lead, lined with tin,[24] and after the surgeons had treated the body with 'carbolic and arsenical preparations, to guard against too quick a decay',[25] it was placed inside. The witnesses all signed three copies of a note formally identifying the corpse, and one copy was placed inside the coffin before it was sealed.

The body lay in state overnight at St Mary's, the Catholic church in Pietermaritzburg, and on the following morning, after a brief funeral mass, Louis began the last leg of his journey on South African soil. Major William Butler, who was responsible for organising the ceremonies in Durban, took the precaution of issuing a Special Order to remind the troops:

> *First*; That [Louis] was the last inheritor of a mighty name, and of a great military renown.
> *Second*; That he was the son of England's firm ally in dangerous days.
> *Third*; That he was the sole child of a widowed Empress, who is now left throneless and childless, in exile, on English shores.
> Deepening the profound sorrow, and the solemn reverence that attaches to these memories, the Troops will also remember that the PRINCE IMPERIAL of FRANCE fell fighting as a British soldier.[26]

If Butler was afraid of an outbreak of latent anti-French feeling in the army, however, he need not have worried; the display of public grief which greeted the cortege in Durban on 11 June was, if anything, more intense than it had been in Pietermaritzburg. The procession reached the outskirts of town late on Tuesday afternoon, and as it descended the Berea ridge the Mayor, Richard Vause, and a crowd of dignitaries assembled to meet it at the Toll Gate. Some 600 men of the 24th, 58th and 80th Regiments, together with detachments of the Army Service Corps, Ordnance Department and Army Hospital Corps, formed up beside the road. Preceded by an advanced guard and a military band playing the *Dead March*, the cortege passed through the town, en route to the Catholic church in West Street:

> Numbers of flags were flying at half mast, and the whole of the stores along the line of route were closed. On either side of the Berea Road there were Indian infantry, who looked remarkably well, and did the duty they were charged with very creditably. The Native police, with their assegais and sticks, also behaved in a most becoming mariner ...[27]

One figure, in particular, seemed to personify the collective sense of grief and shame:

> An elderly man riding a grey horse, and leading a small bay, came slowly up the road, and the fact that he was weeping bitterly caused many to make enquiries as to who he was. It was ascertained that he was an old groom whom the Prince had brought with him from Chislehurst, and the grey horse he was riding was the one which his master was using on the day he met his tragic end.[28]

The body remained in state in the church overnight, and early the following morning, 11 June, a large crowd had gathered outside:

> It had been arranged that there should be a high mass at half past eight, and a limited number of tickets were issued, but long before that time the building was crowded, and precisely at the half-hour the doors were closed. An immense crowd of persons however remained outside reverentially awaiting the moving of the remains of the deceased Prince to the gun carriage ...
>
> ...The principal object of interest outside was the grey horse belonging to the late Prince, which strange to say he had purchased from a Durban gentleman ...[29]

It was all too much for the faithful Uhlmann, who had been broken by the news of Louis' death. When asked by a bystander how long he had been with the Prince, he replied mournfully, 'for twenty-three years'. During the service,

... he succumbed to the long and intense strain, and fainted away; nor did he revive until an hour's assiduous tendance on the part of friendly hands brought him back, alas! to the recollection of his woe. On the final day of embarkation he succeeded in passing through the great popular demonstration, but the sadness of his appearance and expression was beyond description; 'What shall I say to the Empress, when she asks me for her son', was the remark constantly on his lips ...[30]

At 9.45 the church doors opened, and the coffin was carried from the church to the gun carriage.[31] Again the band struck up the *Dead March*, and to the sound of the tolling bells and a distant minute gun, a large crowd followed the procession through the streets towards the landing stage at the Point. As the cortege drew near the harbour,

... most of those who had not joined the procession made a rush to the Point taking short cuts, so as to get a good position to witness the marching of the cortege onto the wharf, which had been kept clear for the occasion.[32]

At the Point, the senior Naval officers in southern Africa, Commodore Richards and Captain Bradshaw, were on parade with their men to take official charge of the body. The coffin was loaded onto the SS *Adonis*, which had been chosen to carry it across the bar to the deep-sea anchorage, where HMS *Boadicea* was waiting. The *Adonis* had been painted a suitably drab shade of grey for the occasion, and as the coffin was taken aboard a private yacht fired a 21-gun salute.[33] All the boats in the harbour were flying flags at half-mast. At about noon the *Adonis* steamed away from the wharf, and the crowd began to disperse. The sea was choppy due to a stiff westerly breeze, and several of the dignitaries who accompanied the coffin 'suffered martyrdom, in mild form, accordingly'[34] in the rough passage across the bar. Indeed, the sea was responsible for one last bloody postscript to Louis' fated adventures; a sudden roll of the waves ground the *Adonis* against *Boadicea*'s side, and a seaman who had the misfortune to trap his hand between the anchor point of the *Boadicea* and the bulwark rail of the *Adonis* had two fingers sliced off.

And on that unromantic note, the body of Eugene Louis Jean Joseph Bonaparte, Prince Imperial and Child of France, last direct heir to the Second Empire, took leave of the country to which he had come to earn his reputation, in a fight against strangers with whom he had no quarrel. Many times he had remarked that the honour and glory of his name were more important to him than life itself, and in the end, and in ways he could hardly have imagined, he had fulfilled that vision of his destiny.

On the same day that the body left Durban, General Order no. 113, issued at the camp on the Ntinini river in Zululand, removed Lieutenant Carey from his position on the Headquarters Staff, in preparation for his trial by court martial.[35] For Carey, the struggle for his professional life was about to begin.

The court convened at 9 am on the morning of 12 June. Colonel Glyn, the nominal commander of the old Centre Column, was appointed president, and while Carey was given a defending counsel, he chose to conduct his own defence. The prosecuting counsel, in yet another bizarre twist of fate, was Captain Brander of the 24th, Carey's colleague during the wreck of the *Clyde*.[36] The charge against Carey was that,

> In having misbehaved before the enemy on 1st June 1879 when in command of an escort in attendance on His Imperial Highness Prince Napoleon, who was making a reconnaissance in Zululand, in having, when the said Prince and escort were attacked by the enemy, galloped away, and in not having attempted to rally the said escort, and otherwise defend the said Prince.[37]

From the very beginning, there was much in the trial which might have amused Kafka. Privately, several of the senior officers sympathised with Carey, but they realised, too, that the real object of the trial was the honour of the officer class of the British Army. The bald facts of the incident were clear enough, and neither Carey nor the prosecutor chose to contest them in anything other than minor detail. Everything, in effect, hung on the circumstances, and whether they could be taken to excuse Carey's behaviour. As a result, Carey chose to address two issues in the charge – whether indeed he was in command of the escort, as specified, and whether anything could in any case have been done to save Louis. This approach was nothing if not realistic, but it trod on dangerous ground. Any argument that Carey was not actually in command was essentially a technicality, since it begged the question of his moral responsibility to support men serving with him, whatever the circumstances. Moreover, such a defence implicitly shifted the burden of blame for the day's misjudgements back onto Louis. Since Louis was no longer able to defend himself, and while alive had been a guest of the British Army, this argument was liable to create a bad impression among the court, and might again rebound on the defendant. If convicted, Carey would be held as a coward; if acquitted, he ran the risk of seeming a cad. It was hardly a position of strength from which to begin his case.

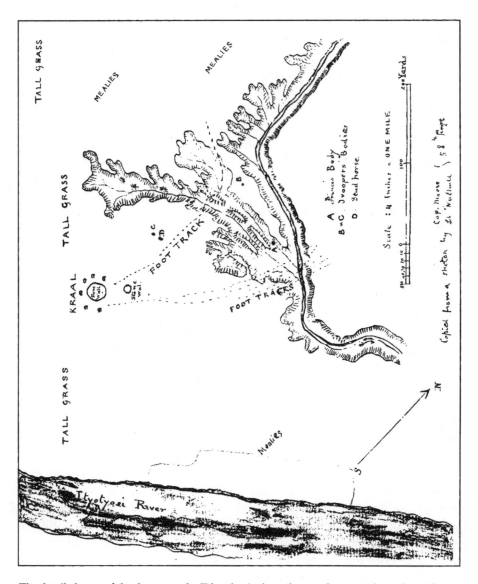

The detailed map of the donga on the Tshotshosi where the attack occurred, produced for Carey's Court Martial. (Reproduced by Gracious Permission of H.M. the Queen. Royal Archives, Windsor).

The prosecution opened the proceedings. The first two witnesses were Captain Morris and Lieutenant Nuthall, both of the 58th Regiment, who had produced a map of the site of the skirmish, which the court used as a reference. Morris confirmed that he had sketched the site on 4 June, three days after the incident, and that the bodies had by that time been removed. While he was reasonably confident of the position where Louis' body was found, he was less certain about those of Abel and Rogers – the first hint that, during the entire proceedings, no very great concern would be taken to establish the truth of the deaths of the troopers. The court went to some pains to establish the physical nature of the obstacle posed by the donga, but the results were hardly revealing; the gulley was between four and six feet deep, steep in some places, but less so in others. Morris agreed that men trying to cross it in a hurry would have their visibility impaired as a result.

The next witness was Captain Molyneux, Chelmsford's ADC, who was questioned regarding the Prince's exact position on the Staff. The point was important, because it was crucial to Carey's case that the Prince had exercised a legitimate authority in the field. Molyneux's replies merely exposed the ambiguity of Louis' position. He confirmed that 'he was one of the personal staff of Lord Chelmsford, without being gazetted in orders to any particular appointment', but when Carey cross-questioned him a asked 'when the Prince was performing duties in the Q. M. Genl. Depart., what relative position did you consider I held to him?', Molyneux could only reply 'I don't know'.[38]

Next, the four survivors of the escort were called in turn, and each taken through the events of the day. Inevitably, the cross-examination returned each time to the same issues – who was in command? What preparations for the defence of the party were made? Did Carey exercise any control during the retreat, and could anything have been done to save Louis?

The evidence of Corporal Grubb, the first of the four, generally supported Carey's case, although when asked 'who led the party during the flight?', he replied immediately 'Lieutenant Carey'. However, asked if he had overheard any conversations between Carey and Louis earlier in the day, when the patrol first halted on the ridge below Thelezeni he answered 'Yes. The Prince gave the order to off-saddle'. Questioned about the command structure on the day, he remained evasive:

> Q: Who was in command of the escort that day, and what was its strength?
> A: There were 6 of Bettington's Horse, the Prince, Lieut. Carey – and a Native guide. I do not know who was in command of the escort.

Q: Who gave the words of command during the day?

A: The Prince did.

Q: Did you hear during the day any words, as Halt, Move on, Walk, Gallop – or did the escort move without them?

A: I cannot recollect whether they were given or not.[39]

Cross-examined by Carey as to whether he heard any instructions or commands after they had crossed the donga, Grubb hedged his bets. 'No, I did not', he replied, 'but you might have said it without my hearing owing to the firing.' Asked if there had been any warning of the attack, he replied 'I cannot answer for the others, but certainly I was taken by surprise'. When Carey turned to the question of whether the Prince might have been saved, however, Grubb was adamant – 'if a man fell from his horse,' he said, 'he had no chance at all, as they were close on him'.

The evidence of the next witness, Trooper Le Tocq, was no less ambiguous. Le Tocq emerges from the trial as a man cool under fire, and with a realistic appreciation of the circumstances of the attack. He too, confirmed the impression that it had been Louis who had taken all the command decisions during the day. Asked whether, during the attack, Louis 'had not ... if he was on horseback a better chance of escaping than any of us on account of the quality of his horse', he remarked pointedly, 'I don't know about any of us, but he was riding a better horse than Lieut. Carey'. On the question of Carey's role under fire, however, he was less helpful. Like Grubb, he claimed not to have heard any words of command, and when asked what might have been done to save Louis, he was unnervingly forthright:

Q: Would you have expected any of your comrades to render any assistance had you been in the Prince's place?

A: I would have expected somebody to have tried to come and assist me.

Q: What might have been done towards assisting you?

A: They might have assisted me by firing and keeping the enemy in check.[40]

The third witness, however, took a more pragmatic view. Trooper Cochrane was particularly useful to Carey's case because he was an old soldier, and his evidence would therefore carry more weight with the court. In his opinion, the position had been hopeless from the first:

Q: How many of the Zulus had firearms?

A: All that I saw.

Q: How many was that?

A: About 12 or 14.

Q: How near to the donga do you think the party might have rallied?

A: They could not have raffled much nearer than a mile – as there were only three carbines, Corporal Grubb having lost his.

Q: Supposing you had been in command of the party, how far do you think you would have gone before you would have got your men together and fronted the enemy?

A: I should not have rallied at all as I had not enough men. I knew the Prince was killed as I saw the Kaffirs close to him ...[41]

When Carey asked him 'could we do anything else than gallop away from the kraal?', Cochrane replied 'no, we could do nothing else'. 'Had any of us remained in the kraal and fired', persisted Carey,

... what do you think would have been the result?

A: In my opinion, we would all have been killed ...

Q: Do you think if a man once fell from his horse between the kraal and the donga, he had any chance of escaping?

A: None.

Q: Could any help, in your opinion, have been rendered by us to the Prince?

A: None.[42]

Sergeant Willis was the last of the survivors called to give evidence. As the senior NCO, he was clearly vulnerable to a similar degree of criticism as Carey, and while his account of the attack was detailed enough, he was evasive on a number of important issues. 'I could not say', he told the court, 'who was in command, the Prince or Lieut. Carey.' When pressed as to who issued orders throughout the patrol, he hedged. 'I cannot be sure', he said, 'but I think it was the Prince.' On one issue, however, he was unequivocal, and flatly contradicted Cochrane:

Q: Do you think it would have been possible for mounted men to have rallied on the far side of the donga, and yet make good their escape?

A: Yes, I think so. About 250 yards [beyond].[43]

The next witness was Lieutenant Colonel Harrison, whose evidence was no less ambivalent. Keen to determine whether Harrison had established a clear chain of command, the prosecutor, Captain Brander, asked, 'did you, on the morning of the 1st June, give Lieut. Carey, 98th Regt., his orders as officer proceeding in command of the proposed escort for the Prince?' With refreshing honesty, Harrison replied, 'I gave him no clear order about the command of the escort'. When he was pressed on this point, the exchange took a particularly semantic turn:

Q: Who was in command of the whole party?
A: The senior combatant officer – it must be so by the Queen's Regulations.
Q: Did you give Lieut. Carey any official order as senior combatant officer, relative to his conduct towards the Prince?
A: I did not know who was the senior combatant officer – not having seen the escort before it started, and therefore not knowing whether any officer would accompany it, but when Lieut. Carey volunteered to go, to the best of my belief I said, 'I was glad he had volunteered because then he could look after the Prince'. If he had not gone I should have requested another officer of the Staff to go for that purpose.[44]

In cross-examination, Carey sought to suggest that since he and Louis were on different duties – he verifying a sketch of the road, and Louis confirming the location of the camp – it was not practical to have expected him to protect the Prince at all times:

Q: Is it usual for an officer who is performing reconnaissance duties to be sent in command of an escort over another officer who is similarly employed?
A: I cannot say – but I have never stated that Lieut. Carey was in command of the escort. What I said was that the senior combatant officer must command troops on any duty by the Queen's Regulations.[45]

Surgeon Scott was then called to testify to the nature of Louis' injuries. Despite the presence of two wounds in Louis' back, Scott reassured the court that the Prince had been killed while facing his enemies, and by so doing he effectively placed Louis' conduct beyond reproach. The contrast with Carey's situation was no more than implicit, but it was obvious enough, and the evidence of the remaining witnesses – called to establish the previous good conduct of both Carey and Bettington's men – could do nothing to displace it in the minds of the court officials.

It took several days for the court to gather and consider the evidence, to the discomfort of several of those presiding. Colonel Harness

considered it 'a most unfortunate business'[46], while Major Anstruther
admitted in a private letter that,

> I am very sorry for poor Carey – and hope the papers won't criticise
> him too severely. I expect that whatever way the verdict goes we
> shall be called rogues or fools, as the case may be ... I certainly think
> they ought to have gone back when they discovered the Prince
> was missing though certainly they would have done no good, they
> would only have found him dead ...[47]

On the 14th Carey submitted his summation of his defence, and he chose
to confront the contradictions of his position directly:

> ... I do not propose myself to deal in any legal quibbles or techni-
> calities of any kind. I therefore candidly admit and wish to press
> upon your notice the scope of that somewhat ill defined word
> 'misbehaved' which is the essence of the charge. To my mind the
> interpretation thereof is cowardice ... and I confidently hope to
> prove to you that I am innocent of such an accusation and to spare
> you the necessity of placing upon me a punishment which, if falling
> short of death itself, can, however much my conscience may acquit
> me, lead to lifelong remorse ...
>
> No matter how deplorable is the death of the Prince, and it
> is impossible that anyone can more deeply deplore it than I do,
> nevertheless I shall venture to assume that if I am guilty, I should
> have been equally guilty if my conduct had led to the death of the
> humblest soldier in this force.
>
> Now as regards the escort, it is said to be under my command;
> of whether this was the case or not, you will have to judge the
> evidence, but I wish to state that such a charge was not in any way
> placed upon me by the Asst. Qr. Mr. General, either in camp or when
> I met him and rode with him on the Itelezi ridge, and imagined
> throughout that it was I who was accompanying the Prince Imperial
> as a brother officer of junior rank[48] preparing similar duties.
>
> However this might affect the previous occurrences of the day,
> and remove from me the stigma of having been remiss in my care
> of H. I. Highness, as regards the present charge, I do not consider
> the matter to be of any importance, in so much as whether senior or
> junior to the Prince, at the moment of the attack, it was unquestion-
> ably my duty to do all in my power to rescue the Prince from the
> perilous position in which he was placed. I trust to show the court
> that this was done.

I am charged with galloping away ... that I did this, I admit, and in making the admission I affirm that in my opinion no other reasonable course was open to me. I would now ask the members of the court to place themselves in my position, and each to ask of himself what course he would have pursued ...

... the vastly superior numbers rendered it as a matter of impossibility for any joint action to have taken place, and at the time I maintain I was justified in thinking that the Prince was mounted ... My position, however, was this – a heavy fire, the shouts of the enemy, a rush of horses and in that rush I was carried away by my horse with the others ...

It may be said, why did I not rally at the kraal and charge the enemy? If such a course was possible, with 6 men, unloaded carbines, no swords, horses bolting, long grass for yards in our front, as well as unknown country, may I not, under the existing circumstances, point to the fact that the greater part of the escort was saved, although unhappily the Prince was killed. I think I may now infer our only course was to gallop from the kraal, a course adopted on the spur of the moment ...

I may be next charged with not having rallied beyond the donga. Until I had crossed it, I was under the impression that all had got across, and then turned round to see where everyone was. At that moment [I could] see nothing but Zulus on the left running to try and cut us off, Zulus in and about the donga, and a riderless grey horse five or six hundred yards to my right ...

I would ask the court to remember that everything took place in a moment, that there was no time to weigh the reports made to me, and that I acted on the spot for the best, and as I thought, for the safety of my party. I deeply regretted the loss of the young Prince and would willingly have changed places with him, but I did not believe, and I do not now believe, that any effort of mine could have saved him.[49]

It was as eloquent an appeal to the realities of the fog of war as could have been made, and the officers of the court were clearly moved by it. They retired for the night to consider, but on the following day Captain Brander summed up the case for the prosecution. His argument was predictable enough – that Harrison had placed Carey in charge, and that Carey had run away – but on one point he was devastating:

I have carefully read through the whole 'Defence' and I fail to see that *anything* was done. The evidence is reviewed at great length: but no word of any witness goes to show that the slightest attempt was made either to rally or defend the Prince, whereas all agreed that they galloped away ...

I must remind the court that all these witnesses are to some extent defending their own character and are therefore more likely to exaggerate their difficulties and the numbers of the enemy than the reverse – excepting perhaps Le Tocq, who together with Rogers who was killed comes well out of the affair ...[50]

Whatever their private sympathies, the officers of the court knew that Brander's argument was unassailable; Carey was indeed guilty of everything specified in the charge. The best that Colonel Glyn could do, when he passed on his report of the proceedings to Lord Chelmsford on 17 June, was attach a lengthy plea of extenuating circumstances:

1. That the Prisoner was out for the second time only with the Prince Imperial and for the first time as senior officer and did not appear to realise that he was in that position.

2. That the Prisoner was employed on duty independent of that of taking charge of the Prince.

3. The weakness of the escort, that it was composed of men not under the same discipline as soldiers and that they were not under one of their own officers.

4. That the Prisoner was evidently under the impression that the Prince Imperial held some military status and was the senior officer.

5. The Prisoner's length of service and the high character he bears as testified by several superior officers.[51]

The court did not offer any view on the appropriate punishment – indeed, it pondered whether Carey's dismissal from the Staff was in itself sufficient punishment, but decided that they were unable to judge, as they 'cannot find a book of references on Courts Martial in camp'.[52] Neither did Chelmsford, who merely appended a recommendation of his own, and sent the findings home to England for confirmation. He, too, clearly had sympathy for Carey:

The suddenness and unexpected nature of the attack seems to have caused him entirely to have overlooked the duty which had devolved upon him as commander of the escort, or to rally as many of them as he could as soon as possible – I have no reason to believe however that Lieut. Carey is wanting in courage – but think that he lost his head, and consequently failed to take the action which the circumstances demanded.[53]

Since the findings of the court needed to be confirmed by the Queen's representatives, they were neither revealed to Carey, nor made public in Zululand. Nevertheless, the end of the trial spelt humiliation for Carey, and on 19 June a General Order was published which directed that he be sent home, and 'to remain under arrest until arrival in England and until the decision of H. M. The Queen consequent on his trial by General Court Martial has been notified'.[54] He was to be escorted down the line of communication in the custody of a Captain Evans RA. In accordance with the ancient ritual which stripped him of his military authority – and of which Louis would no doubt have approved – he was forbidden to wear his sword in camp or quarters, 'but may have it with him for Defence on line of route if he desires it'.[55] His passage through Natal caused remarkably little interest in the press, and he embarked at Durban on HMS *Euphrates*. At Cape Town he transferred to the troopship *Jumna*, which was returning to England.

Behind him, the war soon moved on. For ten days the advance had been delayed on the Nondweni river, while Wood's Flying Column had been employed in transferring supplies from the border to Fort Newdigate. During that time, while Carey was being tried, the British had made demonstrations against the Zulus assembled in the hills around eZungeni, and at last they had dispersed them. By the 18th, the columns were reunited and ready to advance.

The move was spurred on by the news that Lord Chelmsford was to be replaced as Commander-in-Chief in southern Africa. The Disraeli administration had remained largely loyal to him throughout the Isandlwana crisis, even though the war had begun without its express sanction. The Cabinet had become increasingly exasperated, however, with the length and escalating cost of the campaign, and by a steady deterioration in the relationship between the military authorities and the civil administration in Natal. Chelmsford's unrelenting bad luck, the defeats at Ntombe and Hlobane and the death of the Prince, were not officially a consideration, but they can hardly have helped. Moreover, the choice of replacement must have been particularly galling for Chelmsford, who was very much part of the conservative military establishment; his successor was to be General Sir Garnet Wolseley, a radical and a reformer who enjoyed a dashing reputation among press and public alike. The contrast between Chelmsford's plodding manner and the brisk and brash Sir Garnet could hardly have been more obvious – or more damaging to Chelmsford's reputation.

News of his impending replacement reached Chelmsford on the Nondweni on 17 June, just as he was poised to resume his advance.

There was one last chance left to him; it would be weeks before Wolseley could arrive at the front, and if Chelmsford could reach the Zulu capital at oNdini in that time, he might yet defeat the Zulu army. The stain of Isandlwana would be eradicated, and all that would remain of the war would be the inevitable mopping-up operations, and dreary peace negotiations. Wolseley was welcome to them.

The renewed advance was carried on in the face of increasingly desperate attempts by King Cetshwayo to resolve the conflict by diplomatic means. Since the battles of March and April, Cetshwayo had tried to establish channels of communication with the British, and he had sent emissaries to each of the British columns. For the most part, however, the British regarded the Zulu envoys with suspicion, and if Chelmsford had not been willing to negotiate in the dark days after Isandlwana, he was even less so now, with the war turning in his favour, and his replacement looking over his shoulder. The Zulu were met with a blank refusal to discuss the British demands, which remained unaltered from the days of the ultimatum, six months before; the king must give up his authority, and disband the regimental system. To this, of course, the king and his counsellors could not agree. Moreover, if the king realised that his army was unlikely to win another major confrontation in the field, his young warriors were not yet ready to accept the inevitability of defeat, and clung to the illusion that they might yet overcome the British if only they could catch them once again in the open, as they had at Isandlwana.

Throughout June Zulu envoys trudged between oNdini and the various British columns in pursuit of a mission which even they realised was increasingly hopeless. Many British officers treated them simply as spies. Aware that his diplomatic offensive was being rebuffed, the king reluctantly called up his army.

Thus was the stage set for the final, conclusive tragedy of the war.

The peace movement at least provided one curious postscript to Louis' misadventures. Several times the king had sent gifts of cattle and ivory to the British as proof of his good intentions. On 30 June, as the 2nd Division and Flying Column descended the steep Mthonjaneni heights towards the White Mfolozi river and oNdini, Grenfell,

> ... riding ahead with the cavalry, met some Zulus with a white flag. They were sent by the King to say that, hearing the officer killed at the Ityotyozi Camp was a great Prince, he returned his sword in order that he might be despatched to his relatives – a noble act on the part of Cetewayo.[56]

Chelmsford kept the sword, and in due course returned it to Eugénie,[57] but his answer to the envoys remained the same – there could be no peace without a full capitulation to British authority. It was perhaps a decisive moment; when the senior envoy, Mfunzi, returned to the king to report, the great chiefs of the royal council refused to allow him into Cetshwayo's presence. They, too, had seen the charade for what it was, and wished to prolong it no further.

By the beginning of July Chelmsford had reached the banks of the White Mfolozi. On the far bank a line of bluffs hid the Mahlabathini plain, and the great cluster of royal homesteads, including oNdini, which constituted the Zulu capital. Time was running out for Lord Chelmsford, too; Wolseley had arrived in Natal, and had despatched a stream of telegrams instructing Chelmsford to halt operations until he arrived. But for once Chelmsford was lucky; he simply pretended Wolseley's messages had not reached him, and when Wolseley attempted to reach the front by a short cut – up the Zululand coast – bad weather defeated him.

On 4 July, with his preparations quite complete, and the ground ahead of him thoroughly scouted, Chelmsford crossed the river to destroy what remained of the Zulu army.

This time he was taking no chances. The combined 2nd Division and Flying Column totalled 4,166 white and 958 black troops, supported by twelve artillery pieces and two hand-cranked Gatling machine-guns. They marched out into the plain and took up a position on top of a low rise, facing oNdini, formed up in a large hollow rectangle with the infantry four deep on each side. Curiously, this was the most open part of the field, the very spot upon which the Zulu had hoped to attack them, and at about 8.30 the first Zulu regiments began to emerge from the surrounding amakhanda[58] or descend from the surrounding heights. The Zulu deployed in their traditional encircling formation, but to their surprise they found that the square offered no undefended areas, vulnerable to attack. The British artillery began to shell them as they came within range, and the infantry followed with a crash of volley-fire which rippled round the square, and stunned the senses. Here and there the Zulu mounted determined assaults, but for the most part they were shot down before they could come close enough to charge. One particularly fierce attack almost reached the corner on the right rear of the square, and Chelmsford had to move his reserves to block it. The Zulu withered away under a storm of fire, and after the battle the nearest corpse was found just nine paces from the British lines.

Several of those who had played a part in Louis' story were present at the final battle. The irregulars, some of Bettington's men among them, had provoked the Zulu to attack in the opening stages, and had then sheltered inside the square until the fury of the attacks subsided. The guns of 11/7 Battery held the front right corner of the square, with Frederick Slade beside them; Jocelyn Wodeshouse was present with N/6 Battery, which defended the rear corners. Most of the staff – Harrison, Grenfell, Molyneux – were by Lord Chelmsford's side as he rode round the crowded interior of the square, directing the fight. 'Through the smoke we could hear the hoarse voices of the Indunas urging on their men,' recalled Grenfell,

> and could see the dark forms of the Zulu warriors brandishing their spears. Had any panic occurred, we should have been lost, but the men stood well up to their rifles, and their well-sustained fire, supported by the guns and gatlings, soon told ...[59]

Just before 9.30 Lord Chelmsford decided that the Zulu attack had stalled, and gave the order for his cavalry to ride out from the square and chase them from the field. At last the 17th Lancers had the chance to prove their worth, and this time they did not waste it. Pausing for a few moments to form in line, they broke into a charge which struck the right wing of the Zulu army, and scattered it back across the plain. The irregulars, riding behind them, shot down any Zulu who attempted to hide in the grass or take refuge in dongas, and soon the Zulu army broke into open flight. To the British, who had lived so long in the shadow of Isandlwana, it was a glorious sight, and the lines of infantry broke into wild cheers. The pursuit was particularly ruthless, and the NNC were sent out to kill any wounded Zulu lying close to the square.

By 10 o'clock the battle was over, and Chelmsford ordered his cavalry to set fire to the surrounding *amakhanda*. The officers rushed to be among the first into oNdini, to search for treasure or curios. To their disappointment, they found nothing of any great value, and had to content themselves with the wealth of Zulu artefacts to be found in the huts. Harrison 'got from there two wooden milk pails and some assegais and shields'.[60] The British then set fire to the huts of the king's great place, and in the early afternoon they retired back across the White Mfolozi.

That evening a great pall of smoke hung over the Mahlabathini plain. The bodies of over a thousand warriors lay in a great circle around the site of the square; over the next few days, friends and relatives returned to seek out and cover over some of the remains. Nevertheless, when Wolseley returned to the site in August, the ground was still scattered with hundreds of skeletons.

Among the dead was Xabanga of the uMbonambi regiment, the man whom the Zulu had acknowledged as first to stab the Prince Imperial. The Mbonambi had been in the thick of the attack, and had tried to rush the right front of the British square; perhaps Xabanga had been killed by Frederick Slade's guns. His body was later found and buried by his brother, Mboza – who had also been among the attacking party on 1 June.[61]

For Chelmsford the war was over. His columns retired back onto the Mthonjaneni ridge, and within days of the battle he had resigned his command.

In England, meanwhile, the news of Louis' death had broken. Lord Chelmsford himself had sent an official despatch as soon as Carey had reported to him on the evening of 1 June, and as it passed through Cape Town Lady Frere had added telegrams addressed to Sir Henry Ponsonby – the Queen's private secretary – and Lord Sydney, the Lord Lieutenant of Kent. All three messages arrived on 19 June – by which time Louis' body had long since been at sea. Queen Victoria was at Balmoral when,

> At twenty minutes to eleven, Brown knocked and came in, and said there was bad news; and when I, in alarm, asked what, he replied 'The young French Prince is killed'; and when I could not take it in, and asked several times what it meant, Beatrice, who then came in with the telegram in her hand, said, 'Oh! The Prince Imperial is killed!' I feel a sort of horror now while I write the words.
>
> I put my hands on my head and cried out, 'No, no! it cannot be true! It can't be!' And then dear Beatrice, who was crying very much, as I did too, gave me the ... telegram from Lady Frere ...
>
> To die in such an awful, horrible way! Poor, poor dear Empress! Her only, only child – her all gone! And such a real misfortune! I was quite beside myself; and both of us have hardly had another thought since.
>
> We sent for Jane Ely, who was in the house when he was born, and was so devoted to him; and he was so good! Oh! It is too, too awful! The more one thinks of it, the worse it is! I was in the greatest distress. Brown so distressed; everyone quite stunned. Got to bed very late; it was dawning! And little sleep did I get.[62]

That afternoon, Disraeli, the Prime Minister, was at the opening of an exhibition at the Grosvenor Gallery in London when word reached him. 'This is terrible news', he said, and one of his companions remarked, 'I am afraid that the French will accuse our people of having deserted him and left him to his fate'. 'I am not so sure they will be wrong', Disraeli replied,

> Well! My conscience is clear. I did all that I could to stop his going. But what can you do when you have to deal with two obstinate women![63]

There was worse to follow at Camden Place. Lord Sydney went at once to Chislehurst, but according to Filon:

> The age and rank of the Duc de Bassano entitled him to the cruel distinction of conveying this dreadful message to his sovereign, and the poor man remembered the morning of June 21 to his dying day. The moment that he entered the Empress' room she read tragedy in the agitated face of the old Duke.
> 'Is my son ill?' cried the Empress.
> There was no reply.
> 'Is he wounded? ... I will leave for Africa at once.'
> Still there was silence. Thereupon the Empress rose from where she was sitting and walked up to the unhappy Duke. She looked straight into his eyes, but he could not meet her gaze. Then she understood, and, uttering one heartbroken cry, she fell fainting into the arms of her old Chamberlain. The Empress remained in this miserable condition, shattered and broken, one fainting fit succeeding the other, all that fatal day. Those around her feared for her life, and it was only at the end of several days that she regained strength to face her overwhelming sorrow and to fulfil the duties which circumstances demanded of her. Her first thought was to let both the French and English know that she wished no one to suffer in his person or in his position on account of the events of June 1 ...[64]

That first night, the Queen 'had a bad, restless night, haunted by this awful event, seeing those horrid Zulus constantly before me'.[65] The Court went into official mourning.

When the story broke in the press over the next few days, it created a furore which far exceeded news of the disaster at Isandlwana. *The Illustrated London News* devoted a special supplement entirely to Melton Prior's sketches of the incident. In an editorial it pondered ominously:

> How he came to accompany the small reconnoitering party which encountered the attack in which he was killed, to whom the

PUMPING PUBLIC OPINION.—THE COLD WATER CURE.

John Bull :—" YOU'D BETTER TAKE IT QUIETLY, MY MEN; YOU GOT YOURSELVES INTO HOT WATER AND REQUIRE COOLING."

John Bull pours the cold water of common sense over bickering army officers in this view of the Carey controversy by the satirical magazine Fun.

mismanagement is attributed owing to which he lost his life, and what explanation can be given of his being left behind by his comrades as soon as danger declared itself, we have yet to learn, and the information will be awaited with general anxiety.[66]

It was, perhaps, the logical conclusion to a life lived out before the European media. The press had reported exhaustively on Louis' birth, on his childhood, on his fall from grace in 1870, and on his departure for Zululand; now it was saturated with his death. The sense of shock and outrage experienced by the literate classes in Britain in 1879 might perhaps be likened to that unleashed in more recent times by the death of Princess Diana.

'Paris', recalled Filon,

learned the news after London and was moved by it as it had not been since the terrible year. It recalled that child it had loved, to whom it had presented his cradle, after whom it flocked in crowds, whom it had familiarly called 'The Little Prince'. Was it really he who had been killed out there? And who was responsible? Whose fault was it? Imagination ran riot. Already ridiculous stories flew about, which many repeated without knowing their source, only because they flattered the people's taste for the astonishing and especially its incurable leaning to believe in treachery. The English, the International, the Republican Government, were all the subjects of accusation. Others, stupefied, still doubted. Men struggled for the fugitive sheets, the special editions the paper-sellers carried from street to street shouting, 'Death of the Prince Imperial!'[67]

Louis' mortal remains, meanwhile, made the long journey back to England. At Cape Town on 15 June they had been transferred from the *Boadicea* to the troopship *Orontes*, which arrived off Plymouth on 9 July. She was directed to Spithead, where she was intercepted by the Admiralty yacht *Enchantress*, carrying a delegation from both the Royal and Imperial families, and the coffin was transferred to their care. Louis' friend Arthur Bigge and the servants, Uhlmann, Deleage, Lomas and Brown, accompanied it; the only representatives from the field to follow the body to its final resting place.

It had been arranged that the coffin should be taken up the Channel and into the Thames, and from there landed at Woolwich. Here, accompanied by a crowd of mourners, it would make the journey to Chislehurst, down the road which Louis had travelled so many times in life. Queen Victoria had intended to stage a full state funeral for Louis, but Disraeli had flatly refused, sticking by his old argument that the Prince was not only a foreign national, but a head of state in exile. A full British state funeral would be both inappropriate and politically insensitive. The Queen reluctantly backed down, but gave her support instead to a private funeral, which in the event could hardly have been more lavish had it been for one of her own sons. From the moment the *Enchantress* arrived at Woolwich on 11 July, it was clear that no pomp and majesty would be spared to honour Louis' memory:

> That vessel arrived at Woolwich in Friday afternoon about two o'clock, and lay at the T Pier of the Royal Arsenal. A distinguished company, both French and English, was there assembled to receive the Prince's body, for which elaborate preparations had been made. On the part of the members and friends of the Bonaparte family and of the late French Imperial Government, there were Prince Lucien Bonaparte, Prince Charles Bonaparte, the Duc de Bassano, General Count Fleury, M. Rouher, formerly Minister of State, M. Paul de Cassagnac, and many others. Their Royal Highnesses the Prince of Wales, the Duke of Edinburgh, and the Duke of Connaught were present to show their kindly regard for the late Prince Imperial and for the Empress, but did not mix with the phalanx of Bonapartist courtiers and partisans. The Duke of Cambridge arrived soon afterwards. A number of British officers of rank, including Sir John Adye, General Sir Lintorn Simmons, Major-General Turner, holding special authority at Woolwich, were there in full uniform. The coffin was borne ashore by sailors of the admiralty yacht, while M. Rouher, General Fleury, and another French General, with Major-General Turner, walked beside it, and the Roman Catholic clergy intoned their Latin prayers. It was followed by several hundred persons to a small domed building in the Arsenal, which had been fitted up as a temporary mortuary. Here the bier was visited by the principal personages of the company; after which the medical men, Baron Clary, Baron Courvisart, and Mr T. Evans, dentist, had the coffin opened and inspected the body, for the purpose of identification. The corpse was then placed in a new shell, a leaden, and an oaken coffin, which was put on one of the guns of the Royal Horse Artillery, covered with the British flag. It was escorted from Woolwich to Chislehurst, by way of the common, Shooter's Hill, and Eltham, by a troop of the Royal Artillery and Horse Artillery, and by a procession on foot, which reached Camden Place, the residence of the Empress, about nine o'clock in the evening.[68]

'We dare not attempt to inquire,' wrote *The Illustrated London News*, with a thrill of restrained horror,

> ... how it was received by the widowed mother. All that night, with but slight intermission, the Empress passed beside the body of her son. Very early in the morning, at about four or five, when the tall candles burning beneath the silver cross in the little chapel had not long paled in the light of the dawn, the Empress heard mass. It was said before her there, and before the dead, by Monsignor Goddard, who had kept the vigil with Monsignor La Casas, Bishop of Constantine, and two of the aides-de-camp of the Prince. Afterwards, the Empress retired to her room, which she did not leave during the day ...[69]

While Eugénie grieved in private, Louis' remains were carried on a gun carriage from Camden Place to St Mary's Roman Catholic Church, and on Saturday 12 July 1879 were laid to rest. An extraordinary crowd, estimated at between 35,000 and 40,000, had gathered from both sides of the Channel to pay their respects. Queen Victoria herself had travelled on the Royal train to Camden, while the Prince and Princess of Wales led the mourners. Indeed, the list of dignitaries in attendance filled the best part of a column in *The Illustrated London News*, which, for all the sombre mood, could still detect the unmistakable whiff of glamour:

> ... now the Prince of Wales wore an artillery uniform with spiked busby (the uniform of the Prince of Wales' Own Norfolk Artillery, of which his Royal Highness is hon. Colonel) and the Grand Cross of the Legion of Honour, with the French military order founded by the late Emperor, and other orders on his breast. Similar uniforms and decorations were worn by the other Princes, the Duke of Edinburgh, the Duke of Connaught, and the Duke of Teck. Prince Leopold wore the Windsor dress. The Duke of Cambridge and Prince Edward of Saxe-Weimar were in scarlet, against which the bars of crape on the arm which, like all the officers, they wore, showed more distinctly. The Crown Prince of Sweden was conspicuous in his handsome light buff cavalry dress; Prince Leningen was in naval uniform. There were also in the train Prince Christian, the Hereditary Grand Duke of Baden, Prince Louis of Battenberg, and Count Gleichen.

The Queen herself laid a wreath of golden laurel-leaves on the coffin – according to Filon, bystanders heard her say 'He deserved it!'[70]

– and the Prince and Princess of Wales wrote a tribute to Louis' 'most spotless of lives, [who] died a soldier's death fighting for our cause in Zululand'.[71] Many of the surviving Bonapartes attended – Plon-Plon was there with his sons, Prince Victor and Prince Louis, and so were 'Prince Lucien Bonaparte, Prince Joachim Murat, Prince Napoleon Charles Bonaparte, and Prince Louis Murat',[72] together with dozens of Counts and Ducs. Indeed, as Filon recalled with more than a touch of wistful pride, 'the whole of the Second Empire, at least all that remained of it, was present',[73] while dozens of representatives from the principal towns in France had come to pay their respects.

At Camden Place the path was lined with two hundred cadets from Woolwich, who presented arms as the coffin passed. The gun carriage was drawn by six dark-brown horses, and behind one of Louis' favourite English chargers, Stag, 'caparisoned in white and silver starred trappings of Imperial state',[74] was led by his grooms, Lomas and Brown, and by the faithful Uhlmann. A battery of artillery beyond the grounds fired a mourning salute, while drums beat the slow march with muffled sound. The Royal Artillery band played the *Dead March*, and as the cortege drew near the church, the bells began to toll. 'It was in this wise,' wrote Filon,

> that the son of Napoleon III left for the last time that house where he had known joy and sorrow, where I had left him so happy, the home which only a few months before he had animated with his vivid life, illumined with his hopes and gaiety.[75]

After the ceremony in the chapel – which struck the Duke of Cambridge as 'a long one, full High Mass'[76] – the coffin was placed in the ante-sacristy, to await the construction of a tomb beside that of Napoleon III, and the crowd dispersed. Before she returned to Windsor, Victoria paid her respects to Eugénie. 'This interview,' remarked Filon, 'which lasted only a minute, can have been no more than a silent and mournful embrace'.[77]

Disraeli, however, was unimpressed:

> I have just got a telegram from the Queen who has returned to Windsor and who seems highly pleased at all that occurred at Chislehurst this morning. I hope the French Government will be as joyful. In my mind, nothing could be more injudicious than the whole affair.[78]

Five weeks after Louis' funeral at Chislehurst, Carey arrived back in England.

The *Jumna* had passed Madeira on 4 August, and made a good passage home. She arrived off Plymouth Sound on the 20th, but while a detachment of Royal Marines, also returning from South Africa, were allowed to disembark, Carey was not. Journalists were allowed on board to interview him, however, and they brought with them two surprises.

Firstly, Carey had been promoted. His previous good conduct had earned him the rank of Captain, which had been approved before the affair on the Tshotshosi, and announced in *The London Gazette* on 6 June – five days after it. The news had not reached Zululand before his departure, and this was the first he had heard of it, though the British press had been referring to him as Captain Carey for some weeks.

Secondly, he had become a celebrity. Once the first shock of Louis' death had worn off, the press had fallen to debating the inevitable question of blame. While some jumped to the obvious conclusion that 'Captain Carey was guilty of conduct so cowardly as to have ruined the character of the British Officer in the eyes of the whole Continent of Europe'[79], others felt that there were wider issues to be considered. *The Times* articulated the general sense of public unease:

> The conclusion, we apprehend, which the public will be apt to draw from ... these facts will be by no means that which the chief military authority in this country seem to suggest when the sad news first arrived. That which is of importance to observe at the moment is that the disaster arose essentially out of the fact of the Prince being present in South Africa in a false position, which exposed both himself and all around him to constant difficulties and temptations. It would have been wonderful if no error had been committed in dealing with such exceptional circumstances, and any error might be fatal.[80]

The sense that Carey was being made a scapegoat for the folly of his superiors led to vigorous debate in a wide range of publications. Surprisingly, military opinion remained largely divided.[81] For some, it was indisputable that, as a high-ranking guest of the British army, Louis' status overrode any technicalities of command, and should have compelled Carey to make his safety his first priority. Others cited current military theory to argue that the first duty of any reconnaissance party was to return to the commander with information, rather than become involved in combat, and that flight under such circumstances was perfectly justified. Would Louis, they wondered, have been facing such criticism had he survived, and had it been Carey who was killed in the rout?

For the most part, criticism was levelled at everyone involved in the incident except the one who perhaps most deserved it. The Reverend H.R. Haweis, when preaching a sermon at St James, Marylebone, was an exception. Carey, he suggested,

> ... may have believed, and believed rightly, as we have since been assured by military authorities, that the first duty of a reconnoitring party is to reconnoitre and report – not to save the lives of the men; but Lieutenant Carey did all three. He reconnoitered, he reported, and he saved the lives of most of his men. He might have thought that to subject himself and his men to a general massacre, for an impossible object, i.e. the saving of one life already taken, would be to fail in the first duty of the expedition, and to render impossible the second. And depend upon it, continued the preacher, when this fever of excitement over the untimely death of the poor Prince Imperial has subsided, Lieutenant Carey's side of the question will make itself felt. Sad as was the Prince's fate, it was no one's fault but his own, and had he survived, he would, with his manly common sense, have been the first to admit this, and to acquit Lieutenant Carey. The Prince represented the Imperial interests of France; he went out in opposition to – his mother, to his political advisers, to his personal friends. When there he used the prestige of his high social rank to override the judgement of experienced officers. He went where he had no business to go, without a sufficient escort, alighted at the wrong place, and having gone out to shoot the Zulus, who had never done France or the Imperial cause any injury, the Zulus shot him, and then we are told that he died in his 'Master's Service'. It could not have been the master who said, 'The Son of Man is not come to destroy men's lives, but to save them.' It must have been some other master ...[82]

Such a view was unlikely to be widely accepted, however, for the implications were obvious and embarrassing, as one modern historian has observed:

> ... few members of the public, least of all the Queen and Empress, could really acknowledge the reality of what happened that day ... there could hardly be public recognition that the Prince himself was as equally engaged as the others in fleeing from the kraal; that

he had taken no steps of his own to assist those who were in the greatest danger of losing their lives before his was even threatened. Despite his known prowess with pistol and sword, could there be public acknowledgement of the fact that the Prince had failed to kill, let alone wound any of his attackers – that all his pistol shots had gone wide of their target?[83]

Carey first learned of the controversy which surrounded his name when, on board the *Jumna*, he was presented with letters announcing petitions of support from his native Devon. His reply reveals a distinct hint of relief, as well as the first hint of a self-righteous tone which was to become more marked in his manner over the following months. 'You can well imagine', he told his supporters,

> that I have gone through a period of great trial, and that I look forward with a great longing to the moment when I shall be out of suspense. It would not do in my present position for me to comment on the events of June 1, but I may be allowed to assure you that what I desire is justice – not mercy. Had not the justice of my cause, and trust in God and my fellow-countrymen upheld me, I could never have supported the time of suspense ...[84]

Indeed, that suspense, which had lasted since the conclusion of the court martial proceedings two months previously, was about to come to an end. After two days anchored off Plymouth, the *Jumna* was ordered to Spithead, and Carey was escorted ashore, to be interviewed by Prince Edward of Saxe-Weimar, the General Commanding the Southern District. The Prince had powerful news; the Queen had decided not to confirm the findings of the court martial, and Carey was free to return to his regiment without a stain on his character.

Under the circumstances, this was perhaps an astonishing decision – and it had more to do with legal technicalities than any true acceptance of Carey's innocence. The findings of the court had been passed to Judge James O'Dowd, the deputy judge advocate general, who had undertaken a lengthy and detailed review of the proceedings, and found a number of faults with the way the case had been handled. In one particular respect, the inexperience of the court's officers in matters of procedure had rendered the findings illegal, although O'Dowd had other doubts, too, about the conclusions they had drawn:

> Upon the face of the proceedings it would appear that the members of the Court were not sworn. For this reason, and having regard

to all precedent, it would be illegal to give confirmation (in their present shape) to proceedings which are wanting an essential element of validity.

It is possible that this defect arose simply from an omission to record the fact of the swearing of, and that the members were duly sworn. If this were so it would be competent for the confirming Authority to have the record amended with the fact.

Apart from this apparently fatal omission, I have however deemed it my duty carefully to peruse and weigh the evidence in order to see to what extent, if any, it would legally justify the conviction, had the proceedings been regularly conducted and recorded.

To justify a conviction upon the charge it was necessary that evidence should be given that (1) in galloping away, or (2) in not attempting to rally the escort or otherwise defend the Prince, Lieutenant Carey from an undue regard for his personal safety, or from an unjustified want of professional efficiency, failed in respect of some distinct and feasible act of duty imposed upon him either by a specific order or by the well understood rules and customs of the service as applicable to the position in which he then stood.

The evidence proves that on being surprised by a body of from 40 to 50 Zulus the party of which Lieutenant Carey was one, endeavoured to effect their escape as quickly as they could. It also proved that Lieutenant Carey did not attempt to rally the escort or otherwise rescue the Prince.

The specific allegations in the charge are thus established. The question for consideration is therefore whether there is any evidence to show that this conduct constituted the kind of misbehaviour described above as being essential to warrant a conviction.

Regarding the second allegation (the omission to rally the escort) the matter is free from doubt. There is no evidence to prove, while there is a unanimous concurrence of evidence to disprove the assumption, that it was feasible to rally the escort with any advantage to life or to the performance of military duty. The evidence shows that an attempt to rally would have been not only useless to those who had fallen, but attended with unjustifiable sacrifice of life.

The sole question for consideration is, where any evidence has been adduced to show that in galloping away in the first instance, Lieutenant Carey failed in a distinct and feasible duty in a manner constituting the military crime of misbehaviour?

I cannot say upon this, as upon the second allegation, that there is a complete and absolute want of evidence. To my mind there is no direct evidence, but certain circumstances are disposed to which admit of an inference at variance with the theory that Lieutenant Carey's conduct in precipitately retreating was free from the taint of military misbehaviour as charged. But I do not think this inference is that which the evidence reasonably and probably justifies.

In convicting the prisoner the court might have been to some extent influenced by the statement in the charge that he was in command of the escort and therefore primarily and specially responsible for what occurred. To my mind, however, the evidence fails to show that Lieutenant Carey was in command in the sense that would throw this responsibility upon him. It is indeed shown that he was the senior combatant officer, and that he therefore by the rules of the service ought to have been in command. But the evidence distinctly shows that the command was exercised by another up to the last moment, and the court in its recommendation to mercy find that Lieutenant Carey was under the impression that he was not in command. Whatever military accusation would apply to Lieutenant Carey in respect of his being in the position of command would be disposed of by the fact that he was ignorant and had reasonable ground for being ignorant, that the position of command belonged to him.

It does not properly speaking fall within my functions to weigh conflicting evidence. So long as there is some legal evidence to go to a court, its value is a matter for the opinion of the court itself. There being, as I have stated, in this case, some evidence, however slight, to sustain the charge, the course which strictly speaking I should take would be to advise the reassembly of the court for a revision of the finding, affording them at the same time a full explanation of the law applicable to evidence.

I should have had no hesitation in recommending this course in ordinary circumstances, where there existed no obstacle in point of time or distance or of a legal nature.

But in this case there are several obvious objections to a reassembly of the court, one of them being the possibility that upon reassembly it might be found that the whole of the proceedings were null and void and that the court had no power whatever by reason of the members not having been duly sworn.

I feel therefore that in all the circumstances I am bound to go somewhat beyond the lines of my duty as that duty is usually discharged. In this sense and having given my most careful consideration to the evidence I cannot but conclude that as regards the charge of misbehaviour in respect of the first allegation, while there is on the one hand some evidence, although of the slightest and most indirect kind, to sustain it, the great preponderance of the evidence lies in the opposite direction and is inconsistent with the guilt of the prisoner, and that as regards the second allegation the evidence wholly fails. Therefore I consider that looking to the law and substantial justice of the case, it is my duty to advise that the proceedings should not be confirmed.[85]

O'Dowd's summary was as clear headed as any view then expressed on the case, but in the event neither the Army establishment, nor Carey himself, could let the matter rest. After all the furore, it seemed impossible that Carey could simply be acquitted, and returned to duty without further comment. On 16 August General C.H. Ellice, the Adjutant-General, responded in a despatch from the Horse Guards[86] with the views of the Duke of Cambridge. While accepting that the charge against Carey was 'not sustained', and that he was to be 'relieved of all the consequences of his trial', the Duke still offered a stiff rebuke to those involved:

His Royal Highness desires it to be known that he entirely approves of Lord Chelmsford's arrangements for the reception and occupation of the Prince; and that he considers the orders issued for his protection were marked with judgement and adapted to the occasion.

The reconnaissance which the Prince was allowed by Lieutenant-Colonel Harrison, the Assistant Quartermaster-General, to make on the 1st June extended to a considerable distance from the camp. Lord Chelmsford's permission had not been sought or obtained; all the arrangements were made under Lieutenant-Colonel Harrison's orders; and the Lieutenant-General commanding had reason to believe that throughout the day the Prince was in the company of Lieutenant-Colonel Harrison, who was occupied in guiding a column in its change of camp.

Lieutenant-Colonel Harrison doubtless believed that in his arrangements for the expedition he had sufficiently complied with Lord Chelmsford's instructions to himself. In the opinion of the Field-Marshal Commanding-in-Chief he was mistaken. His orders to Lieutenant Carey were not sufficiently explicit, and he failed to impress upon the Prince the duty of deferring to the military orders of the officer who accompanied him, and the necessity of guiding himself by his advice and experience.

If Lieutenant-Colonel Harrison had displayed more firmness and forethought in his instructions to Lieutenant Carey and to the Prince, His Royal Highness cannot but think that the train of events would have been averted, which resulted in bringing a handful of men, in the middle of the enemy's country, into a position so well calculated to invite surprise and to court disaster.

Lieutenant Carey from the first formed a wrong conception of his position. He was sent, not only to perform the duties of his staff office, but to provide the military experience which his younger companion had not acquired. If his instructions were defective his professional knowledge might have prompted him as to his duty.

He imagined, but without the slightest foundation for the mistake, that the Prince held a military rank superior to his own, and acting throughout on this strange misconception, he omitted to take for the safety of the party those measures of precaution which his experience had taught him to be essential.

At the moment of the attack, defence was impossible, and retreat imperative. What might have been done, and what ought to have been done when the moment of surprise had passed, can only be judged by an eye-witness; but His Royal Highness will say, and he feels that he speaks with the voice of the army, it will ever remain to him a source of regret that, whether or not an attempt at rescue was possible, the survivors of the fatal expedition withdrew from the scene of the disaster without the full assurance that all efforts on their part were not abandoned until the fate of their comrades had been sealed.[87]

This despatch was a masterpiece of political manoeuvre, deftly absolving Chelmsford – who retained the Duke's support – from any responsibility, while grudgingly acknowledging the public concern that Carey had been made a scapegoat for the failings of his superiors. Instead, Horse Guards had found someone new to blame – Harrison. This came as something of a surprise to Harrison himself, since the despatch only reached South Africa much later. By that time the Anglo-Zulu War was over, and Harrison had been appointed Commander of British troops in the Transvaal. He at once replied justifying his own behaviour, but 'the answer to my protest was to the effect that the matter should now be allowed to rest'.[88] And so it was; it did not affect Harrison's career at all, and he ended his service as a General.

When the news broke that his conviction had not been sustained, Carey blossomed briefly in the full sunlight of an approving press. For the best part of a month, he continued to issue press statements, and the self-righteousness evident in his early communiqués became more pronounced. Encouraged by the collapse of the legal proceedings, he clearly hoped for a full public rehabilitation. Indeed, he seems to have gone further; perhaps he saw the chance in his fifteen minutes of fame to profit from the damage done earlier to his reputation. 'I hope,' he declared, playing to the gallery,

> ... that as I have done nothing to be ashamed of, and I desire nothing more than ample publicity and inquiry into all the facts of the case, a full and complete account of these proceedings may yet be given forth ...
>
> ... these opinions now having been ratified by the voice of my fellow countrymen I feel that my honour and character as a soldier, and as an English gentleman, have been vindicated. Therefore it is, gentlemen, that I am doubly grateful to you for having been the first to announce to me, and to proclaim to the world at large, that such was your verdict and opinion.[89]

In a letter to a religious journal, *The Christian*, Carey ascribed his acquittal to the Divine, seeing a reward for the injustices he had suffered in the way 'He in His good time brought me to the haven where I would be'.[90] By the end of August, even the *Army and Navy Gazette*, which had supported him vigorously throughout, was moved to recommend the hope that 'Captain Carey himself will observe a discreet silence concerning the wrongs he has undoubtedly suffered'.[91]

In one area Carey's behaviour was particularly ill judged. He wrote to Eugénie, asking to be granted an audience, on the pretext of offering his condolences and of giving an account of Louis' last days. Under the circumstances, such an approach was at best tasteless, and at worst a shameless attempt to secure a public vindication. Perhaps Carey had been misled by the extensive public support he enjoyed into thinking that he had the sympathy of the establishment, too; in fact, the opposite was the case.

Once she had recovered from her initial shock, Eugénie had made a magnanimous gesture of public forgiveness:

> My only source of earthly consolation I derive from the thought that my beloved son fell like a soldier, obeying orders in a duty assigned to him, and that those who gave him these orders did so because they believed him competent and useful. Enough of recrimination; may the remembrance of his death join in a common regret all who

loved him, and may no one suffer either in reputation or material interests – I who can desire nothing more in this world make this last request.

Eugénie

Speak in this sense to all, English or French.[92]

But if Eugénie had been prepared to issue such a statement in the spirit of martyred motherhood, and to prevent Louis' name being sullied by an unseemly wrangle, she still held Carey personally responsible for the tragedy, and the idea of meeting him appalled her. Similar views prevailed among the Royal Family; the Queen herself expressed the view that Carey was simply 'a coward!!!'[93] Among senior military circles, who could never afford to admit that an officer was, under any circumstances, justified in running away, there was a surprising degree of unanimity. Sir Garnet Wolseley – who seldom agreed with the Duke of Cambridge on anything – was nonetheless dismissive of Carey:

Carey had published a semi-religious, semi-blasphemous letter he addressed to some Christian association which is such a palpable bid for the sympathy and assistance of the religious set in England that he has injured his already bad cause by doing so. My own feelings are these, I would not shake hands or associate with such a man ...[94]

Nor, of course, would Eugénie. As Filon put it, 'to have been received by the Empress would have been the best of acquittals. The audience was denied him.'[95]

In Zululand, meanwhile, the end of the British military occupation had produced a further curious post-script to Louis' story. After the battle at oNdini, Lord Chelmsford had withdrawn his troops towards the coast, but his successor, Wolseley, considered this a mistake. The old columns were re-organised once again, and Wolseley had re-occupied oNdini. From here he sent punitive columns into the more remote parts of the country, to suppress the last flickers of resistance, and put pressure on the regional chiefs to surrender. The capture of King Cetshwayo by a patrol of Dragoons at the end of August undermined whatever remained of the will to fight among the Zulu, and perhaps marks the real end of the war. In Britain, a change of government from Conservative to Liberal meant that there was no longer the political will to annex Zululand; instead, Wolseley imposed a deliberately divisive peace settlement, which paved the way for a decade of suffering and conflict which broke up the old Zulu kingdom far more effectively than the British invasion had done.

One of Wolseley's last acts before he withdrew from Zululand was to instruct Lieutenant Colonel the Hon. George Villiers, Grenadier Guards, to 'make a private search'[96] for Louis' uniform, which had been stripped from his body. Villiers, who had been heavily involved in suppressing resistance in northern Zululand, took up the task when his column was disbanded on 12 September. Two days later, he set off for the Tshotshosi valley with an African named Clas, and a small herd of cattle to offer as bribes. Here he instructed Clas

> To go into the district where the Prince Imperial was killed, and pretend that he was only on a visit to some friends who lived in the neighbourhood – he was gradually to learn all he could about the uniform etc; and if he could gain any certain information to endeavour to exchange the cattle he took with him for the things. I impressed on him not to use threats or attempt violence of any kind as I knew if he did that all chance would be lost of regaining the uniform. In order to give weight to my words, I kept his wife and children as hostage.[97]

Clas' task was not a particularly easy one. The Prince's uniform had been distributed among the attacking party – who had long since scattered – and only his sword had since been recovered. After the Battle of Ulundi, Mboza had hidden the items taken by Xabanga amongst some rocks, for fear of British retribution.[98] Nevertheless, 'Clas soon persuaded the Zulus that it was in their interest to give up the things',[99] and on 6 October he returned to Villiers with a collection of clothes and uniform items. They were still covered in blood and appeared in poor condition, having been hidden for several months, but Villiers carefully brushed them out, and 'whenever there was a ray of sunshine as we journeyed through Zululand, I had the uniform out to air'.[100] The Zulus, of course, had taken many uniforms from the British dead at Isandlwana, Hlobane and Ntombe, and it was important to establish that these particular items had belonged to the Prince. Fortunately, Louis' uniform had been distinctive in a number of minor respects; Captain Alleyne RA confirmed that he had seen Louis wearing an obsolete Artillery officers' pattern patrol jacket in camp two days before his death. The recovered jacket proved to be of this type, while a chamois leather waistcoat and shirt were of the same size, and had spear holes which corresponded with those in the jacket. Clas had also managed to recover Louis' helmet

– which had an unusual blue stopper on the top – trousers, and revolver, although the latter was 'covered in rust, and the spring broken in the centre'.[101] Villiers was particularly keen to find Louis' watch, but despite sending Clas on a second expedition, he could only learn that the watch had been broken up by the Zulus, in the mistaken belief that it was a snuff container.[102]

Villiers himself brought the recovered items to England and presented them to the Queen in January 1880. Two of Louis' servants travelled from Chislehurst to Windsor to identify them, and a few days later Villiers formally gave them into the care of Eugénie's secretary.

Legend has it that when the Empress first saw them, still covered with Louis' blood and the mud of the donga, she fainted.

And so the story of Louis' involvement in Zululand was almost done. Little that he brought with him remained to tell of the incredible story of his death; his body, his possessions, even his clothes had been returned to the people for whom he fought. Through the intense interest of the British, after the war was done, the Zulus had come to learn of his importance, but it is unlikely that the men who killed him ever really understood who he was, or what he was doing there. More than a century later, one can only sympathise with their confusion.

All that was left to mark his impact on Zulu history was a monument on the spot where he fell.

When Lord Chelmsford's columns had first passed by, within days of his death, the 21st Regiment had placed a wooden marker on the slope above the spot where his body had been found. A small pile of stones was placed in the donga itself, and by the end of the war this had been replaced by a more impressive cairn built by a patrol of the 1st Dragoon Guards. Behind it, in a hollow, lay the graves of Abel and Rogers, marked by wooden crosses.

When Eugénie first expressed an interest in visiting the spot, Queen Victoria determined to mark the site properly. She acted not in an official capacity – hoping to avoid any revival of the political wrangles about Louis' death – but privately asked Sir Bartle Frere and Wolseley to arrange for a memorial to be constructed at her expense, to be erected before Eugénie's visit.

In March 1880 Wolseley accordingly instructed Major Henry Stabb, 32nd Regiment – who had fought at Ulundi – to organise an expedition to the spot. Stabb's party consisted of five British soldiers and his friend, Colonel Bowker, a prominent colonist who had recently been commander of the Frontier Armed and Mounted Police, and who was keen to go 'in pursuit of his studies as a naturalist'.[103] A photographer named George Ferneyhough went along to take pictures. In their charge was a large stone cross, made by Mr Jesse Smith, a stonemason of Pietermaritzburg, at the cost of £35 12s 5d, whose bill had been settled by the Queen. Stabb's interpreter was another veteran of the fighting, Jabez Molife, who had fought with the Native Horse and had survived Isandlwana.

Despite bad weather, which made the roads almost impassable in places, Stabb's party entered Zululand by the Rorke's Drift route on 16 March. They reached the Tshotshosi two days later. Along the way, Stabb recruited twenty-five Zulus as labourers, and found them 'willing and zealous fellows but unaccustomed to work'.[104] Stabb noted that a number of them had lived at Sobhuza's original homestead; if he thought to ask whether any of them had been in the attacking party, however, he did not record the fact. He found the site largely unchanged since the end of the war; the Zulus had not touched the monuments, but the cairn where Louis fell was overgrown, and the graves of Abel and Rogers had sunk in.

Stabb's intention was to leave the calm in place, and to erect the cross at its head. Since the graves of Abel and Rogers were nearby, he decided to enclose them all within a stone wall. Most of the stones were taken from the remains of the original cattle pen, which still stood on the site of the attack. Louis' body had been found at the bottom of a hollow, and this afforded Stabb some problems; he was worried that the summer rains, funnelling through the donga, might undermine the memorial's foundations. He addressed the challenge with gusto; he blew up part of the donga with dynamite to divert the flow, and dammed part of the channel. Once he had erected the cross and built the surrounding wall, he planted within the enclosure 'a few hardy trees, obtained from Pietermaritzburg Botanical Gardens'.[105]

When the work was complete,

I called together the headman and people of the neighbouring kraals to the spot ... I then explained to them, through my interpreter, Jabez M'Lifa, the reason of the cross being erected, viz., that Queen Victoria had sent it out to mark the spot where a great Chief, a brave soldier, and one who was also her friend, had been killed; that it was customary among our countrymen to mark such spots. That the English now felt no enmity towards the Zulus, they looked upon them as friends, and, as such, I called upon them to respect and preserve the memorial.[106]

When Stabb had finished his address, Ferneyhough took a picture of the assembled party standing by their handiwork. In the photograph,

Stabb stands on one side of the cross, and Bowker on the other, framed behind by obviously improvised copies of the Union Flag and Tricolour. Sobhuza, the headman, stands between them, his arm raised self-consciously in the traditional Zulu royal salute, while in the background, in similar pose, stand the Zulu labourers. The expressions on the faces of the British party are fixed; most of the Zulus look bemused.

As well they might.

NOTES

1. Capt. W.E. Montague, *Campaigning in South Africa; Reminiscences of an Officer in 1879*, Edinburgh and London, 1880.
2. Letter from anonymous correspondent, 'Camp, somewhere in Zululand' 4 June 1879. Published in the *Natal Mercury*, 11 June 1879.
3. Guy Dawnay, *Campaigns; Zulu 1879, Egypt 1882, Suakim 1885*, London, c. 1886.
4. Montague, *Campaigning*.
5. Tomasson, *With the Irregulars*.
6. Montague, *Campaigning*. Dawnay, *Campaigns*.
7. Diary of W.H. Fairlie, National Army Museum, London.
8. Lieutenant F.S. Slade to Mrs Marcus Slade, 2 June 1879. Slade letters, National Army Museum.
9. Major Anstruther, letter, 13 June 1879. Published in Paul Butterfield (ed.), *War and Peace in South Africa 1879–1881*, Melville, 1987.
10. Arthur Harness, letter dated Ntinini river, 10 June 1879. Brenthurst Collection; reproduced in Sonia Clarke, *Invasion of Zululand 1879*, Johannesburg, 1979.
11. J.N. Crealock to H.H. Crealock, 2 June 1879, reproduced in Clarke, *Zululand at War*.
12. Arthur Harness, letter dated 'Camp near Tombokala and Ityotyosi Rivers, Zululand, 4th June 1879'. Clarke, *Invasion of Zululand*. Dawnay, *Campaigns*, confirms that the court met on the 4th.
13. Findings published in *The Illustrated London News*, 12 July 1879.
14. Carey's presence is confirmed in a letter from his mother to the Queen's Private Secretary, General Ponsonby, Royal Archives, VIC/R7/102. *The Army and Navy Gazette* of 5 August 1879 also mentions Carey's presence, but inaccurately suggests he 'was by Lord Chelmsford's side'. Chelmsford did not take part in the action.
15. Dawnay, *Campaigns*.

16. Prior, *Campaigns*.
17. Anstruther, letter of 9 June 1879, Butterfield, *War and Peace*.
18. Commandant, Ladysmith, to Major General Clifford, 5 June 1879. C.2374, no. 37.
19. Major General H.H. Clifford, Special Order, HQ Pietermaritzburg, 4 June 1879. C.2374, no. 37.
20. Clifford to Commodore Richards, 4 June 1879. C.2374, no. 37.
21. The selected pall bearers were Colonel Steward, RE, Colonel Reilly, RA, Colonel East, 57th, Major Russell, 12th Lancers, Captain Fox, RA, Captain Willoughby, 21st Regt., Lieutenant Cameron, RE, and Lieutenant Bayly, 27th Regt. C.2374, no. 37.
22. *Times of Natal*, 9 June 1879.
23. *Natal Witness*, quoted in *Natal Mercury*, 11 June 1879.
24. Chelmsford to Clifford, 4 June 1879. C.2374, no. 37.
25. *Natal Mercury*, 11 June 1879.
26. Special Order, 10 June 1879.
27. *Natal Mercury*, 11 June 1879.
28. Ibid.
29. Ibid.
30. Ibid.
31. The pall-bearers in Durban were Captain Hayes (staff paymaster), Captain Granville (Commissariat), Captain Young (Commissariat), Captain Brunker (26th Regt.) Commissary Marsh (Ordnance) and Surgeon-Major Leslie. *Natal Mercury*, ibid.
32. Ibid.
33. The yacht was the *Lancashire Witch*, belonging to Sir Thomas Hesketh. Ibid.
34. Ibid.
35. At the trial Carey argued that this dismissal was prejudicial to his case, since it could only be interpreted as a punishment for misdeeds of which he had not yet been convicted.
36. The other members of the court were Lieutenant Colonel R.C. Whitehead, 58th Regt., Captain J. Plydell-Bouverie, 17th Lancers, Captain D.C. Courtney, RE, Major P.R. Anstruther, 94th Regt (judge advocate), Capt. H.H. Crookenden, RA (defending counsel).
37. Court Martial papers, WO 71/343.
38. Court Martial records, WO 71/343.
39. WO 71/343.
40. Ibid.
41. Ibid.
42. Ibid.
43. Ibid.

44. Ibid.
45. Ibid.
46. Colonel Harness, letter of 14 June 1879, 'Camp Upoko River'. Brenthurst collection; reproduced in Clarke, *Invasion of Zululand*.
47. Major Anstruther, letter of 13 June 1879, NAM; published in Butterfield, *War and Peace in South Africa*.
48. The original manuscript has 'senior' amended to 'junior'.
49. WO 71/343.
50. Ibid.
51. Ibid.
52. Submission by Major Anstruther, Judge Advocate, 'Camp, Upoko River', 16 June 1879. WO 71/343.
53. Lord Chelmsford, Fort Marshall, 19 June 1879. WO 71/343.
54. Extract from General Order, 19 June, 1879, signed by Colonel W. Bellairs, DAG. Davies Papers; Ron Sheeley Collection.
55. Memo to Colonel Collingwood, commanding Forts Marshall and Newdigate, signed by Captain C.W. Robinson, AAG., 19 June 1879. Davies Papers; Ron Sheeley Collection.
56. Grenfell, *Memoirs*. The Zulu envoys were Mfunzi and Nkisimana, two of Cetshwayo's most trusted messengers. See Laband, *Rope of Sand*.
57. Chelmsford and Buller visited Eugénie in late August 1880, to pay their respects; they returned Louis' sword to her on that occasion. Letter from Lord Chelmsford to Sir Frederick Ponsonby, 30 August 1879. Royal Archives, RA 035/123. My thanks to Colonel Digby Hague-Holmes for alerting me to this reference.
58. Royal homesteads, known to the British as 'military kraals'.
59. Grenfell, *Memoirs*.
60. Harrison, *Recollections*.
61. Information gathered in interviews at the Tshotshosi on 26 May 1880, Wood Papers, Natal Archives.
62. Queen Victoria, Highland Journal, 19 June 1879.
63. Quoted in Weintraub, *Disraeli*.
64. Filon, *Recollections of the Empress Eugénie*.
65. Queen Victoria, Highland Journal, 20 June 1879.
66. *The Illustrated London News*, 28 June 1879.
67. Filon, *Memoirs of the Prince Imperial*.
68. *The Illustrated London News*, 16 July 1879.
69. *The Illustrated London News*, 19 July 1879.
70. Filon, *Memoirs of the Prince Imperial*.
71. *The Illustrated London News*, 19 July 1879.
72. Ibid.

73. Filon, *Memoirs of the Prince Imperial*.
74. *The Illustrated London News*, 19 July 1879.
75. Filon, *Memoirs*.
76. Diary in Sheppard, (ed.), *George, Duke of Cambridge*.
77. Filon, *Memoirs*.
78. Disraeli to Anne Chesterfield, quoted in Weintraub, *Disraeli*.
79. Unnamed 'Cavalry Officer' quoted in *The Army and Navy Gazette*, 16 August 1879.
80. *The Times*, 1 July 1879.
81. For a summary of the debates, see Donald Featherstone, *Captain Carey's Blunder*, London, 1973.
82. Reported in the *Torquay Times*, 16 August 1879.
83. Digby Hague-Holmes, 'Who Was Responsible for the death of the Prince Imperial?', *Soldiers of the Queen*, Issue 90, September 1997.
84. Carey, statement issued on board HMS *Jumna*, Plymouth, 21 August 1879.
85. Reproduced in Sonia Clarke, *Zululand at War*.
86. The office of the Commander-in-Chief.
87. General C.H. Ellice, Adjutant-General, despatch of 16 August 1879. Reproduced in C.L. Norris-Newman, *In Zululand with the British*, London, 1880.
88. Harrison, *Recollections*.
89. Carey, statement of 28 August 1879, published in *The Morning Post* on 29 August 1879.
90. *The Christian*, Southsea, 25 August 1879.
91. *Army and Navy Gazette*, 30 August 1879.
92. Filon, *Memoirs of the Prince Imperial*.
93. From a conversation with Lord William Beresford, Osborne House, 26 August 1879. RA VIC/R 8/56.
94. Wolseley, journal entry for 30 September 1879. Preston (ed.), *Sir Garnet Wolseley's South African Journal*.
95. Filon, *Memoirs of the Prince Imperial*.
96. George Villiers, *Memorandum Regarding the discovery of the Late Prince Imperial's uniform and other effects*, 29 January 1880.
97. Ibid.
98. Statement of Mboza, Tshotshosi river, 28 May 1880, Wood Papers.
99. Ibid.
100. Ibid.
101. Ibid.
102. Curiously, Durban Local History Museums have a watch which was handed to a prominent Zululand missionary in the 1880s by a Zulu who claimed to have been in the attacking party. It bears

an elegant Empire-period portrait of Napoleon I, and is largely undamaged. Both the glass front and the case unhinge, however, and it is possible that the Zulus thought they had broken the watch when in fact they had merely opened it.

103. Major Stabb, report on expedition dated Pietermaritzburg, 10 April 1880. The soldiers were Sappers H. Romains, S. Pincheu and H. Brown RE, Gunner J. Ashton RA, and Private W. Ving 32nd Regiment.
104. Ibid.
105. Ibid.
106. Ibid.

EPILOGUE

'For the cause of Imperialism ...'

Eugénie's party left the monument at the Tshotshosi with a sense of relief on the morning of 3 June 1880.

Her reaction to the experience had been mixed. If she had found a sense of release in the pilgrimage, the knowledge she had gained about the events of the year before left her bitterness towards Carey unabated. She could not bring herself to speak directly to the Zulu veterans of the attack, and she was deeply disappointed that they could not confirm her romantic illusion that Louis had died the heroic death he had so often contemplated, sword in hand. Of one aspect of the Zulu accounts, however, she did take note:

> They all confirm the flight of Captain Carey, and they showed us the place where he crossed the donga, eighty paces above the point where the Prince stopped. We have crossed the donga on horseback, with the Empress, exactly at the same place, and we have verified that it is impossible not to have seen from it the whole of the hollow now occupied by the cairn and the cross; one of the Zulus even told us that, if the fugitives had turned round, they would have stopped the pursuit ...[1]

This evidence was so overwhelming that Eugénie regretted her previous public expression of sympathy for Carey, and wanted Wood's findings published. Wood, however, was uncomfortable at the thought of stirring up fresh controversy, and in England the Queen's private secretary, Sir Henry Ponsonby, agreed with him:

> The Empress (most naturally) longs for the statements being made known – but although these prove no doubt that Carey's conduct was worse even than was supposed ... At present he is dropping out of notice, and public feeling is increasingly against him. Sir

Henry Ponsonby humbly thinks that Sir Evelyn is right in asking
that this evidence should not be published now.[2]

At least Eugénie was consoled by the description, carefully coaxed from
the Zulus by Wood, that in his last moments Louis had 'fought like a
lion'.[3] As well she might; in the whole sorry saga, one thing which had
never been in doubt was Louis' personal courage.

The threat of an intrusion by the mysterious Lady Avonmore remained
throughout the stay, but she wisely kept her distance. When the party
was ready to leave, Eugénie asked that two of the police escort might
be left behind, to guard against any attempt to remove wreaths or other
souvenirs. In fact, however, even the indefatigable Theresa Longworth
finally recognised that she had been out-manoeuvred; for a day or two
the guard saw nothing of her, then she appeared at a distance to make a
sketch of the cross, before riding off across country towards Landman's
Drift, and the road to Natal.

From the Tshotshosi valley the Imperial party headed south, exploring
the Nquthu range, and the sites of Louis' adventures of May 1879. They
spent the night of the 3rd camped in the Batshe valley, and the following morning travelled south to the battlefield of Isandlwana. More than
a year on, the old camp site was still scattered with debris of the fight.
Among the rotting impedimenta of camp life – broken wooden boxes,
leather strapping of all kinds, scraps of canvas tenting, discarded boots
and brushes – which neither victorious Zulus nor the British burial parties had thought worth removing, lay human remains, buried in haste
and now exposed by the passage of another rainy season. Eugénie was
drawn to this further manifestation of human misery in Zululand, and

> ... started off on foot as soon as she arrived here and spent about
> two hours on the battlefield immensely interested in learning the
> different positions occupied by our troops, the lines of advance
> of the different Zulu corps, at the same time picking up relics and
> articles of interest with which the camp still abounds.[4]

Bigge and Wood rode down the line of retreat, marvelling at the
terrible terrain and the evidence of slaughter still hidden among the
boulders and dongas. Two Zulu veterans – one of whom had fought
on the British side, with the NNC – told them the story of the battle,
and Bigge noted with some surprise that 'the two accounts did not
materially differ'.[5] Then, on 7 June the party turned towards Rorke's
Drift, and away from Zululand, with all its sorry tale of slaughter and
sorrow.

On the way back through Natal, the Empress seemed drained of the spirit which had sustained her over the previous months. Her mood became 'very low and desponding', and she hardly ate.[6] By the 19th the entire party was back in Pietermaritzburg; three days later, Wood drove Eugénie to Botha's Hill, and the start of the railway line to Durban. Here there was one last adventure, and in Wood's flippant reaction, an unconscious, ironic echo of recent events:

> The road was engineered down the side of the mountain, and the Empress liking to travel fast, I let the horses canter most of the way down. I was always nervous when driving Her Majesty, and when I handed my wife into the train, I said 'Now my personal responsibility is over I shall not mind if the train goes off the line.' We had indeed a narrow escape; when I had assisted the ladies out of the carriage I handed the reins to a Sergeant of the Army Service Corps, who was waiting to take the team back. He had gone only half a mile at a steady trot when the connecting rod which fastens the fore-carriage to the after part of the 'Spider' snapped in two. If this had happened half an hour earlier, when we were cantering down the mountain road, the Empress and Lady Wood would have had a severe accident.[7]

The following day Eugénie and her entourage left Durban on the *Asiatic*, and at Algoa Bay, off the eastern Cape, she transferred to the Union Steamship Company's vessel, *Trojan*. The return journey to England held one last item of interest, for on 12 July the ship called in at St Helena. Louis, of course, had been bitterly disappointed that he had not been able to pay homage to this, one of the greatest of all Bonapartist shrines, and Eugénie was only too aware of the irony of her visit now. She strolled wistfully about Longwood House, drinking in the lingering atmosphere of greatness which seeped from the corridors and rooms where the founder of the dynasty had lived his last years, and died.[8] All her life she had lived in the shadow of Napoleon's legacy, and in the end she had seen her son sacrificed to it; now, the descendants of the nation who had imprisoned him were her courteous and respectful hosts. She was the first Bonaparte to have visited the island since Napoleon's death, yet in a curious way, her visit completed the circle.

The *Trojan* arrived at Plymouth on 27 July 1880, and Eugénie retired to Chislehurst.[9] The expedition had been cathartic; she was exhausted by the ordeal, but the process of healing had begun and, as she later wrote to Evelyn Wood, 'it was some consolation in my everlasting sorrow'.[10]

There were, however, new torments to be endured. She arrived back to find that Louis' reputation in the land of her hosts was as controversial as ever:

Almost immediately upon the Prince's death a subscription was opened at the suggestion of Mr. Bothwick, afterwards Lord Glenesk, the proprietor of the Morning Post, to erect to the Prince's memory a monument worthy of the great nation that mourned him. The first idea of the subscribers was that Westminster Abbey should receive this monument and add it to all the precious national relics the Abbey holds. The English government of the day, over which Mr. Gladstone presided, would not or dared not agree to this. May I be permitted to say, after so many years have passed, that this refusal added one more to all the differences that estranged Queen Victoria from her Minister. She gave one of the chapels of her church of Saint George at Windsor, the burying place of the Princes of the present dynasty, for the monument of national gratitude ...[11]

It was a monument which encapsulated so much of the mythical romance of war by which Louis had lived. It represented him in effigy, lying on his back with his hands at prayer, in the classic pose of the dead medieval knight, but wearing his Royal Artillery uniform. As usual, the satirical magazine Punch took an arch view of the whole affair:

PROPOSED INSCRIPTION FOR A PROPOSED MONUMENT.
(Found blowing about Dean's Yard)
In Memory Of
PRINCE EUGENE LOUIS NAPOLEON
Son of the Hero of Sedan,
Grand-Nephew of the Hero of Moscow,
And Pretender to the Throne of France,
Brave, amiable and accomplished,
Who made many friends,
And unfortunately lost his life
In a very doubtful quarrel,
Which in no way concerned him.
This monument is erected
By a small section of the British people
To exhibit to the world
Their slight respect

For the national feelings of France,
And their great regard
For the cause of Imperialism.[12]

Yet if it was true that for most in Britain Louis' death was no more than a passing sensation, a moment of pity and guilt, it undoubtedly made an impact on the communities which knew him best, and they responded accordingly. In Chislehurst an impressive stone cross was raised on the common by public subscription, while a striking bronze statue, sculpted by Count Gleichen and depicting Louis in British uniform, was erected in front of the Royal Academy at Woolwich. It still stands today in the grounds of the RMA's successor institution, Sandhurst.

Eugénie had not long returned from Zululand when she began to search for a more impressive mausoleum to house the remains of the two men who had dominated her life. She found the chapel at St Mary's too small, and at first she hoped to extend the church premises, but the neighbouring farmer – a Protestant – refused to sell the land. Instead, on the advice of General Sir Lintorn Simmons, she bought a house called Farnborough Hill, in Hampshire, from a Mr Longman, the publisher. In 1881 she finally left Camden Place, her home for a decade, and set about turning Farnborough Hill into a shrine to Bonapartism. She hired a French architect to give the house more Gallic panache, and to begin work on a private priory, which she commissioned for the grounds. She filled the house with Napoleonic memorabilia, retrieving her own collections from France, and Queen Hortense's impressive collection from Arenenburg. Most touchingly, she filled one room with all the relics of Louis' childhood, building a replica of his youthful study, the artefacts arranged as if he was waiting to return.

It took six years for work on the Priory, dedicated to St Michael, to be completed. On 9 January 1888 a Royal Horse Artillery battery carried the coffins of Napoleon III and Louis on gun-carriages from St Mary's to Farnborough, and laid them finally to rest in two granite sarcophagi on either side of the alter. Eugénie established a community of monks at the Priory, to pray for the souls of her husband and son, and in 1895 Pope Leo XIII raised St Michael's to the status of an Abbey.

Eugénie had paid her debts to the Bonapartes.

Yet her life was far from over. Unlike Queen Victoria, who had allowed her emotional life to atrophy following the death of Prince Albert, Eugénie passed into a new phase, best characterised as one of amused detachment. It was as if Louis' death had marked the end of a by-gone world, and of an incarnation of herself. Now Eugénie preferred to observe from the sidelines, often with relish, the antics of a new, more innocent generation. Her youthful belief that her own destiny was tragic had been curiously fulfilled, and it was as if she took some comfort in the fact; as she grew older, she became if anything more wilful, and cared less what impression that made. She allowed herself forthright opinions on politics, and on the royal families of Europe, and her taste for boisterous humour and the company of handsome young men re-emerged. She enjoyed sailing, and in particular relished the thrill of heavy water at sea. Eventually, the French government gave her grudging permission to buy a property in France, and she spent her winters in a villa on the Riviera. Curiously, for a few years in the 1880s, she employed a companion by the name of Agnes Carey; while there is nothing to suggest that Agnes Carey was related to J. Brenton Carey, one wonders at Eugénie's reaction, hearing that name constantly about the house.

And as Eugénie lived, so she outlasted almost everyone who had shaped the great drama of the Second Empire.

She remained close to the British Royal Family. Twice a year she spent cosy holidays with Queen Victoria, and the two enjoyed gossiping about old times, though Eugénie was careful never to forget who was host and who the guest. When Queen Victoria died in 1901, Eugénie was seventy-five, and her last great link with the old order was gone.

She remained close, too, to Princess Beatrice, whose life came to have curious parallels with her own. Whether or not Beatrice had been in love with Louis, she had married Prince Henry of Battenberg six years after Louis' death, and she bore him three sons and a daughter, called Victoria Eugénie. In 1895, when British troops were again at war in Africa, Prince Henry asked permission to join a punitive expedition against the Asante on the Gold Coast. With the memory of Louis before her, the Queen refused, but Beatrice talked her round; Henry died of fever in the jungle on 20 January 1896. When, a generation later, the First World War broke out, Beatrice's son, Prince Maurice of Battenberg, was killed at Ypres. He was twenty-three; the same age as Louis when he died.

The outbreak of the First World War came as little surprise to Eugénie, and she opened Farnborough Hill as a hospital for wounded officers. Despite her great age, she took a personal interest in their well-being, and openly flirted with them when she visited the wards, arranging for pretty young nurses to tend them, to give them back a hope of life and love. When the war ended, despite her age, she visited Paris and

Les Invalides with a fierce determination; she stood before the tomb of Napoleon, and read aloud from a newspaper the terms of the German surrender to the Allies.

She died on the morning of 11 July 1920, on a visit to Spain, and the scenes of her childhood.

Arthur Bigge, perhaps Louis' greatest friend in the British Army, survived her by scarcely a decade. His association with Louis had done him no harm; Eugénie introduced him to Queen Victoria, and he gave up his military career to become, eventually, the Queen's last Private Secretary. Under Edward VII he became Private Secretary to the Prince of Wales, later George V; in 1911 he was created Lord Stamfordham. He died in 1931. Katherine Campbell, Eugénie's companion on the pilgrimage of half a century before, also displayed a surprising longevity; she died in February 1934. She had never remarried, and had remained a widow for fifty years. Theresa Longworth, the mysterious Lady Avonmore, who had also played her part in that strange journey, had passed on long before; following the failure of her mission to intercept Eugénie, she had taken to journalism in Pietermaritzburg. She never left South Africa; she died in September 1881, from a mysterious illness contracted somewhere on her travels.

What Louis' future might have been in France remains one of the great unresolved questions of European history. There were, of course, Bonapartes after him – there still are – but whether he would ever have been called to government in his own country is open to doubt. By his will Louis had handed the mantle to Plon-Plon's son, Victor, an act which marginalised Plon-Plon still further, and provoked him to yet greater irascibility. The Bonapartes continued to scheme, and even Plon-Plon managed to get himself arrested once by the French authorities – an act which finally caused his party to disown him. He retired to scowl across the borders from villas in Switzerland and Italy. In truth, however, Bonapartism was a spent force politically by the 1880s, and with the onset of the new century, it seemed an anachronism.

Curiously, it was Louis' demise which finally made his reputation in his native land. As a youth in exile he had been known only through gossip and rumour, a figure of ridicule and fun. With his death, and the manner of it, he became both noble and tragic, a source of French patriotic pride in the face of that old enemy, English perfidy. When the memories of the bloodshed of Napoleon III's coup, and the terrible fiasco of 1870, had faded, nostalgia invested Louis' memory with a deep romantic appeal. He was a golden child of a golden age, and many a hardened political cynic would later claim that his would have been a new *belle époche*, for the Bonapartes and for France, had he only survived.

It was more than he might have hoped for in life. Archibald Forbes, whose path had crossed Louis' during the two defining years of Louis' life, had a more realistic appreciation:

I will call him happy in the opportunity of his death. Had he lived, what of artificiality, what of hollow unreality might there not have been in store for him? As it was, he had moved in the world a live ghost; better than this, surely, to be a dead hero: to end a Napoleonic serio-comedy with his young face gallantly to his assailants and his life-blood drawn by the cold steel.[13]

Once the dust settled on the scandal of his death, another journalist, Charles Norris-Newman, offered a surprisingly clear-sighted appraisal of his role in the conflict of 1879:

The death of the Prince Imperial, considered per se, can only be regarded as a minor episode of the [Anglo-Zulu] campaign, especially from the military standpoint. But various causes – his rank and misfortunes, his connection with the British army, the actual incidents of the fatality, arising out of the duties of the expedition, and lastly, the subsequent proceedings in connection with the inquiry by court-martial – combined to invest it with a special pathos and interest, almost world-wide.[14]

And what of the remaining players in that serio-comedy?

Lord Chelmsford returned to England as the hero of the Battle of Ulundi, rather than the vanquished of Isandlwana. The military establishment closed ranks around him, and he basked in the Queen's support. Eugénie, it seemed, never held him responsible for Louis' death; she presented Lady Chelmsford with an emerald and diamond bangle, 'with my warm thanks and acknowledgement for the kindness and affection bestowed on him by Lord Chelmsford'.[15] Chelmsford enjoyed a glittering array of home appointments – but he did not command an army in the field again. He died in 1905 at the age of eighty-one.

After Louis' death, the two horses Louis had bought in South Africa – the grey Tommy and the roan Fate – passed to the Remount Department, and were passed over to staff officers for the rest of the war. When the campaign ended, both horses were bought by Sir Richard Southey, a prominent member of colonial society at the Cape. Here the grey acquired a new name – Prince. He was the object of curiosity to visitors to Southey's estate, Southfield, for many years, and was renowned for his docile nature; Southey's niece, Rosamund, described his end:

During our stay at Southfield, Prince had to be destroyed, to the great grief of his owners, but his teeth had quite gone and it was impossible to feed him properly. We all went to say 'Good-bye' to the grand old fellow, and great was the gloom over the household on the day he was shot. I still have in my possession a little piece of Prince's mane that I asked the coachman to cut off for me.[16]

And Carey? Once judge advocate O'Dowd's decision was made public he took leave until interest in his case began to abate, and in late 1879 he rejoined his regiment, then stationed in Malta. If Filon is to be believed, his own end was in its way no less tragic than Louis':

When Carey, full of assurance, would have taken his place again in the Service, the greeting he received taught him what feelings were entertained towards him without any expression of those feelings in words. He knew the bitterness of that dumb ostracism which isolates its object in the middle of the most animated company, which ignores his presence, and even his very existence, does not see him when he is there, does not hear him when he speaks; the eyes that turn away, the hands that shun, the conversations that stop when he enters, and begin again when he goes; all that world of signs, and above all of silences that make of him an outsider among his comrades, an inferior among his equals, a stranger in his own house, a dead man in the midst of the living.[17]

Yet this was little more than wishful thinking on the part of a Bonaparte partisan. Certainly, Eugénie never forgave him, and the stain of the trial would never entirely leave him. But Carey had always had critics and supporters in equal measure, and he undoubtedly met many more of both in the years left to him. Perhaps his sense of self-righteousness, and his deep religious faith, helped him cope with the former; as no doubt did the continuing and enduring sympathy of the latter. Perhaps, like many a fellow veteran of the Zulu campaign, future opportunities might have given him the chance to excel, and to close the book on his earlier transgressions. Sadly, he was not given the chance. Within a few years he had lapsed into regimental obscurity, and his last entry in the Army List merely confirms his position as senior Captain of his regiment, the 98th, which was then on garrison duty in India.

Captain Jahleel Brenton Carey died of peritonitis at Karachi, India on 22 February 1883. The exact causes remain obscure; he probably suffered from a ruptured appendix.

There is no truth in the legend that he was kicked to death by a white horse.

NOTES

1. Marquis de Bassano, letter of 1 June 1880, reproduced in Filon, *Recollections of the Empress Eugénie*.
2. Letter dated 27 July 1880. Royal Archives, R10/10.
3. Statement of Langalibalele, 1 June 1880, Wood Papers.
4. Arthur Bigge, letter to Queen Victoria, Isandlwana, 7 June 1880. RA VIC/R10/32.
5. Ibid.
6. Evelyn Wood, letter to Queen Victoria, 10 June 1880, RA VIC/R10/34.
7. Wood, *From Midshipman to Field Marshal*.
8. Napoleon Bonaparte's body was returned to Paris and interred at Les Invalides in December 1840.
9. A fortnight later she was invited to Osborne House on the Isle of Wight, the summer retreat of Queen Victoria. Bizarrely and unknowingly, Bonaparte and Zulu paths crossed for a further time; Eugénie passed through Southampton on the same day – 16 August 1880 – that the body of Charles Rawden Maclean was interred in a pauper's grave in the city. More than fifty years before, as a boy, Maclean had been among the first settlers to establish contact with the Zulu kingdom. He had been a favourite of King Shaka; he is known to history under the name John Ross. *The Natal Papers of 'John Ross'*, edited by Stephen Gray, 1992.
10. Eugénie to Wood, 5 June 1881, Wood Papers.
11. Filon, *Memoirs of the Prince Imperial*.
12. *Punch*, July 1880.
13. Archibald Forbes, *Souvenirs of some Continents*.
14. Charles Norris-Newman, *In Zululand With The British*.
15. Eugénie to Lady Chelmsford, 5 November 1879. Reproduced in The Hon. Gerald French, *Lord Chelmsford and the Zulu War*, London, 1939. My thanks to Viscount Chelmsford for identifying the nature of the gift.
16. Rosamund Southey and Frances Slaughter (eds), *Storm and Sunshine in South Africa*, London, 1910.
17. Filon, *Memoirs of the Prince Imperial*.

Bibliography

For the most part, I have tried to use primary sources where possible – particularly for the Zululand sections – and these are identified in the footnotes. For a comprehensive review of the literature on the Anglo-Zulu War, see my *Brave Men's Blood* (1990); the following works were particularly useful, however, with regard to the story of the Prince Imperial.

Aronson, Theo, *The Golden Bees; The Story of the Bonapartes*, Oldbourne, London, 1965.

Aronson, Theo, *Queen Victoria and the Bonapartes*, Cassell, London, 1972.

Ashe, Major W. and Wyatt Edgell, Captain the Hon. E.V., *The Story of the Zulu Campaign*, Sampson Low, Marston, Searle & Rivington, London, 1880.

Barthez, Dr E., *The Empress Eugénie and Her Circle*, T Fisher Unwin, London, 1912.

Bengough, Sir Harcourt M., *Memories of a Soldier's Life*, Edward Arnold, London, 1913.

Butler, Sir William, *An Autobiography*, Constable, London, 1911.

Butterfield, Paul H., *War and Peace in South Africa 1879–1881*, Scripta Africana, Johannesburg, 1987.

Carey, Agnes, *The Empress Eugénie in Exile*, Century, New York, 1922.

Chadwick, G.A., and Hobson, E.G. (eds), *The Zulu War and the Colony of Natal*, Qualitas, Durban 1979.

Clarke, Sonia (ed.), *Invasion of Zululand 1879*, Brenthurst Press, Johannesburg, 1979.

Clarke, Sonia (ed.), *Zululand at War*, Brenthurst Press, Johannesburg, 1984.

Duff, David, *Eugénie and Napoleon III*, Collins, London, 1978.

Duminy, Andrew and Ballard, Charles, *The Anglo-Zulu War; New Perspectives*, University of Natal Press, Pietermaritzburg, 1981.

Emery, Frank, *The Red Soldier*, Hodder & Stoughton, London, 1977.

Emery, Frank, *Marching Over Africa*, Hodder & Stoughton, London, 1986.

Featherstone, Donald, *Captain Carey's Blunder*, Leo Cooper, London, 1973.

Forbes, Archibald, *Memories and Stories of War and Peace*, Cassell, London, 1898.

French, Major the Hon. Gerald, *Lord Chelmsford and the Zulu War*, John Lane The Bodley Head, London, 1939.

Filon, Augustin, *Memoirs of the Prince Imperial, 1856–1879*, Heinemann, London, 1913.

Filon, Augustin, *Recollections of the Empress Eugénie*, Cassell, London, 1920.

Grenfell, Lord F.W., *Memoirs*, Hodder & Stoughton, London, 1925.

Harrison, Sir Richard, *Recollections of a Life in the British Army*, Smith, Elder & Co., London, 1908.

John, Katherine, *The Prince Imperial*, Putnam, London 1939.

Kelly, Bernard, *Prince Louis Napoleon*, St Michael's Abbey Press, Farnborough, (n.d.)

Knight, Ian, *The Anatomy of the Zulu Army*, Greenhill Books, London, 1994.

Knight, Ian, *Brave Men's Blood*, Greenhill Books, London, 1990.

Knight, Ian and Castle, Ian, *The Zulu War; Then and Now*, After the Battle, London, 1992.

Knight, Ian (compiler), *By The Orders of the Great White Queen*, Greenhill Books, London, 1992.

Laband, John and Knight, Ian, *The War Correspondents; The Zulu War*, Sutton Publishing, Suffolk, 1998.

Laband, John (ed.), *Lord Chelmsford's Zululand Campaign 1878–1879*, Army Records Society / Alan Sutton, Manchester, 1994.

Laband, John, *Kingdom in Crisis*, Manchester University Press, Manchester, 1992.

Laband, John, *Rope of Sand*, Jonathan Ball, Johannesburg, 1995.

Laband, John and Thompson, Paul, *The Illustrated Guide to the Anglo-Zulu War*, University of Natal Press, Pietermaritzburg, 2000.

Laband, John, and Thompson, Paul, *Kingdom and Colony at War*, N&S Publishers, Pietermaritzburg and Cape Town, 1990.

Loliee, Frederic, *The Life of an Empress*, Eveleigh Nash, London, 1908.

Lugg, H.C., *Historic Natal and Zululand*, Shuter & Shooter, Pietermaritzburg, 1949.

Mackinnon, J.P., and Shadbolt, S. (compilers), *The South Africa Campaign 1879*, Sampson Low, Marston & Searle, London, 1882.

Mitford, Bertram, *Through The Zulu Country*, Kegan Paul, Trench & Co, London, 1883.

Molyneux, Major General W.C.F., *Campaigning in South Africa and Egypt*, Macmillan, London, 1896.

Montague, Captain W.E., *Campaigning in South Africa*, William Blackwood, London, 1880.

Moodie, D.F.C. (edited by John Laband), *Moodie's Zulu War*, N&S Publishers, Cape Town, 1988.

Morris, Donald R., *The Washing of the Spears*, Jonathan Cape, London, 1966.

Norris-Newman, Charles L., *In Zululand With the British throughout the War of 1879*, W.H. Allen, London, 1880.

Phillips, William Peter, *The Death of the Prince Imperial in Zululand 1879*, Hampshire County Council, Winchester, 1997.

Preston, Adrian (ed.), *Sir Garnet Wolseley's South African Journal 1879–80*, Balkema, Cape Town, 1973.

Prior, Melton, *Campaigns of a War Correspondent*, Edward Arnold, London, 1912.

Roberts, Brian, *Ladies in the Veld*, John Murray, London, 1965.

Rothwell, John Sutton (compiler), *Narrative of Field Operations Connected with the Zulu War of 1879*, War Office (Intelligence Branch), London, 1881.

Southey, Rosamund and Slaughter, Frances (eds), *Storm and Sunshine in South Africa*, John Murray, London, 1910.

Stoddart, Jane T., *The Life of the Empress Eugénie*, Hodder & Stoughton, London, 1906.

Thompson, Paul, *The Natal Native Contingent in the Anglo-Zulu War, 1879*, privately published, Pietermaritzburg, 1998.

Tisdall, E.E.P., *The Prince Imperial; A Study of his life Among the British*, Jarrolds, London, 1959.

Tomasson, W.H., *With the Irregulars in the Transvaal*, London, 1881.

Vijn, Cornelius (translated by Bishop J W Colenso), *Cetshwayo's Dutchman*, Longman Green, London, 1880.

Webb, C. de B., and Wright, J.B. (eds), *A Zulu King Speaks*, Killie Campbell Africana Library, Pietermaritzburg and Durban, 1978.

Weintraub, Stanley, *Disraeli; A Biography*, Hamish Hamilton, London, 1993.

Weider, Ben with Emile Guegen, *Napoleon; The Man Who Shaped Europe*, Spelimount, Staplehurst, 2000.

Whitton, F.E., *Service Trials and Tragedies*, Hutchinson, London, 1930.

Wood, Sir Evelyn, *From Midshipman to Field Marshal*, Methuen, London, 1906.

Index

I have followed the accepted practice of listing Zulu words by the root rather than the prefix. Thus, for example, abaQulusi – 'the people of the Qulusi' – appears under 'Q' rather than 'a'. Similarly, Zulu names are listed according to modern orthography, but where contemporary phonetic spellings appear in passages of direct quotation, I have added these in brackets, for ease of identification.